SANTIAGO!

SANTIAGO RAMÓN Y CAJAL—ARTIST, SCIENTIST, TROUBLEMAKER

JAY HOSLER

MARGARET FERGUSON BOOKS
HOLIDAY HOUSE · NEW YORK

Margaret Ferguson Books

HOLIDAY HOUSE is registered in the U.S. Patent and Trademark Office.

Printed and bound in September 2022 at C&C Offset, Shenzen, China.

www.holidayhouse.com

First Edition, 2022

Paperback Edition, 2023

3   5   7   9   10   8   6   4   2

Library of Congress Cataloging-in-Publication Data
Names: Hosler, Jay, author.
Title: Santiago! / Jay Hosler.
Description: First edition. | New York : Holiday House, [2022] | Includes
bibliographical references. | Audience: Ages 8 to 12 | Audience: Grades
4–6 | Summary: "A graphic novel biography of Santiago Ramón y Cajal,
the father of neuroscience"— Provided by publisher.
Identifiers: LCCN 2021028399 | ISBN 9780823450367 (hardcover)
Subjects: LCSH: Ramón y Cajal, Santiago, 1852-1934—Health.
Brain—Juvenile literature. | Neurosciences—Juvenile literature.
Classification: LCC QP376 .H757 2022 | DDC 612.8/2—dc23

LC record available at https://lccn.loc.gov/2021028399

ISBN: 978-0-8234-5036-7 (hardcover)

ISBN: 978-0-8234-54891 (paperback)

Excerpts from *Recollections of My Life* by Santiago Ramón y Cajal published by arrangement
with the American Philosophical Society, Philadelphia. Originally published as *Recuerdos de
mi vida* in Madrid, 1901–1917. First published in English as volume 8 of Memoirs of the
American Philosophical, 1937.

Photographs on pgs. 192 courtesy of Legado Cajal. Instituto Cajal (CSIC), Madrid.

For my mom and dad, Madonna and Scott,
who let me choose my own way and lit my path with their love and support

CONTENTS

CHAPTER 1: THE FIRST MISCHIEF

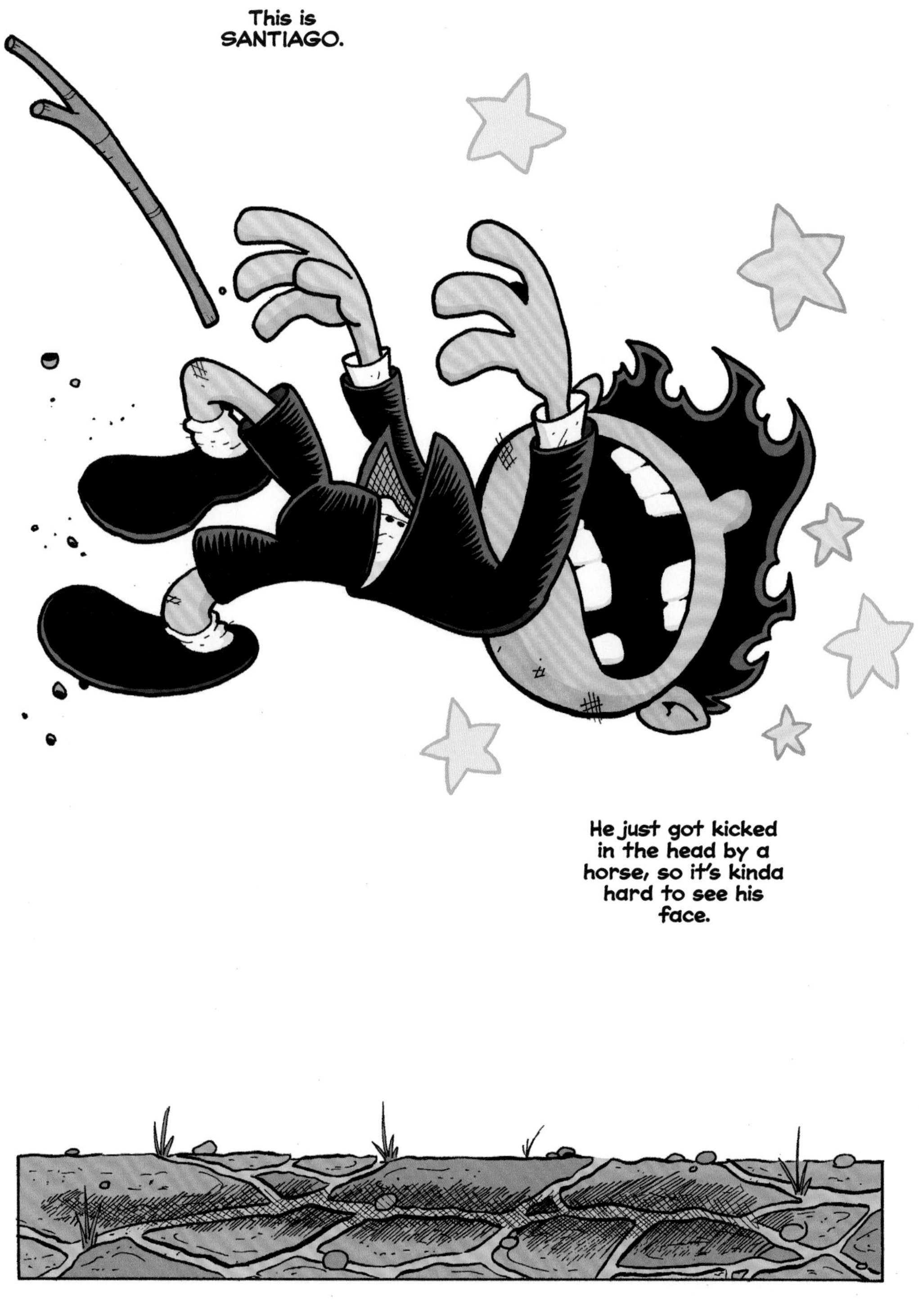
This is SANTIAGO.
He just got kicked in the head by a horse, so it's kinda hard to see his face.

Getting kicked in the head by a horse is pretty horrible, but these things happen when you try to whip an animal.

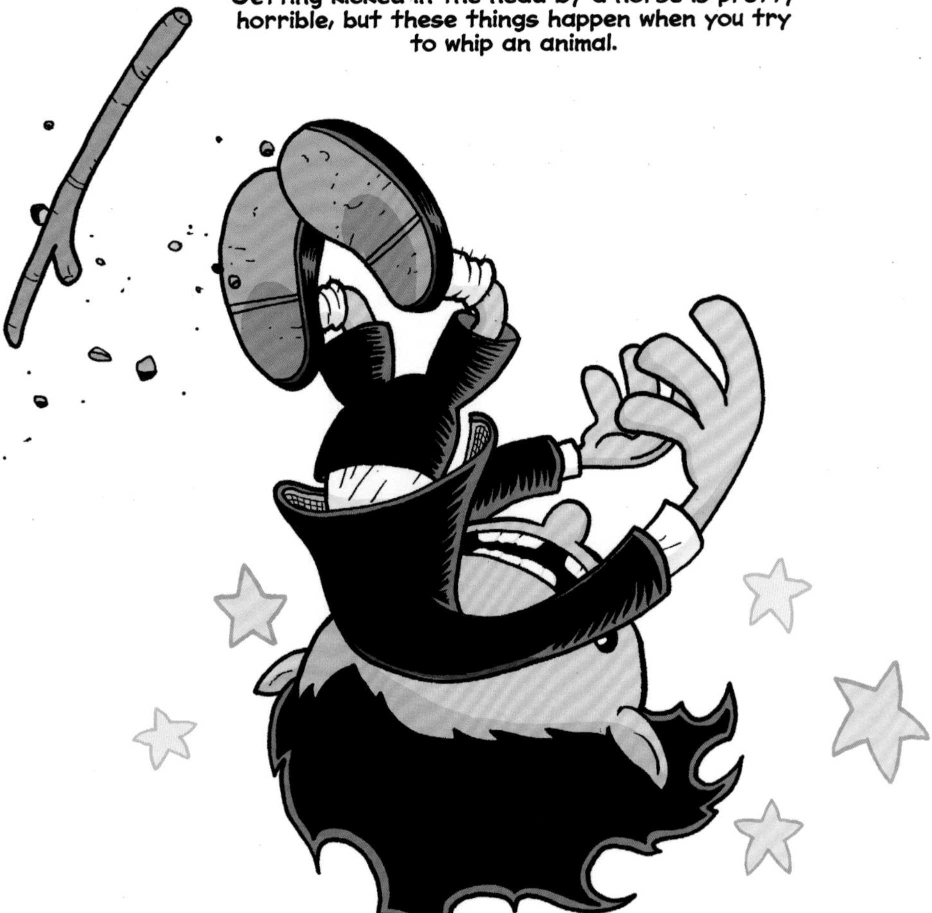

Now, most people who get kicked in the head by a horse learn some kind of lesson from it, like "Be careful" or "Don't do goofy stuff," but not Santiago.

He has many, many more years of mischief ahead of him.

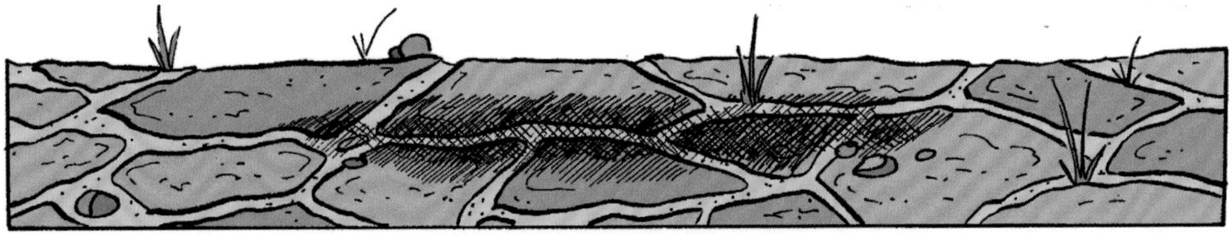

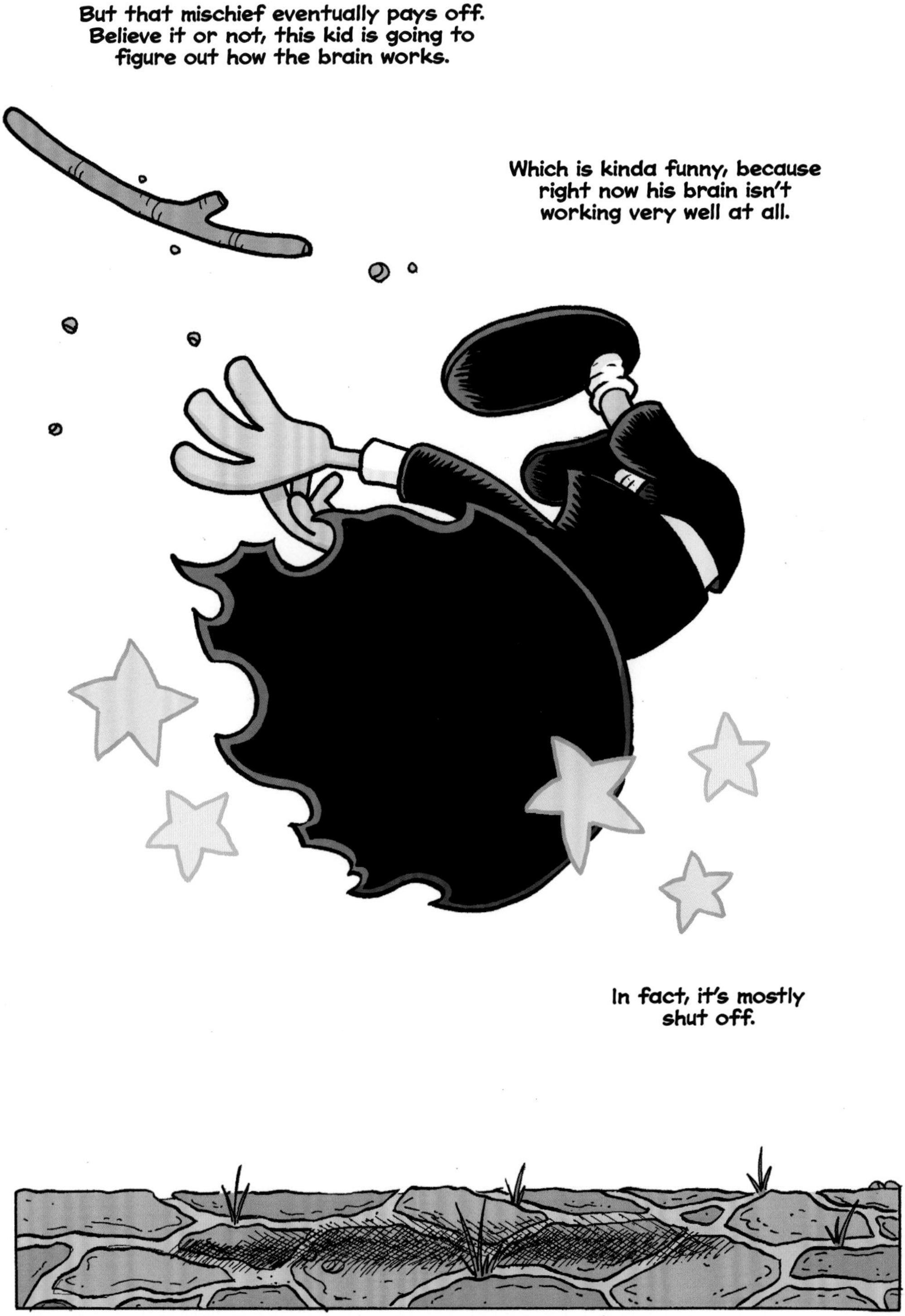
But that mischief eventually pays off. Believe it or not, this kid is going to figure out how the brain works.
Which is kinda funny, because right now his brain isn't working very well at all.
In fact, it's mostly shut off.

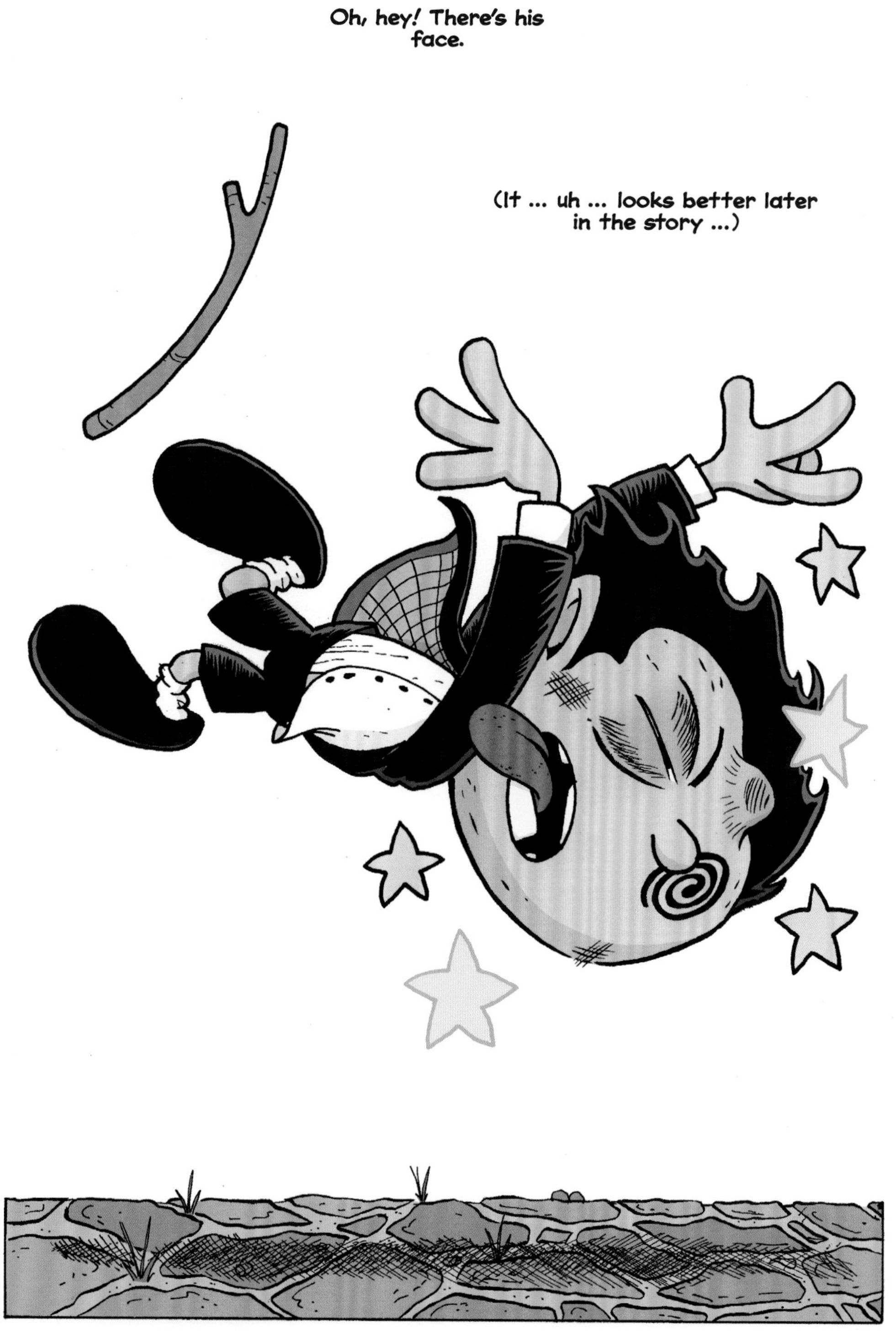
Oh, hey! There's his face.
(It ... uh ... looks better later in the story ...)

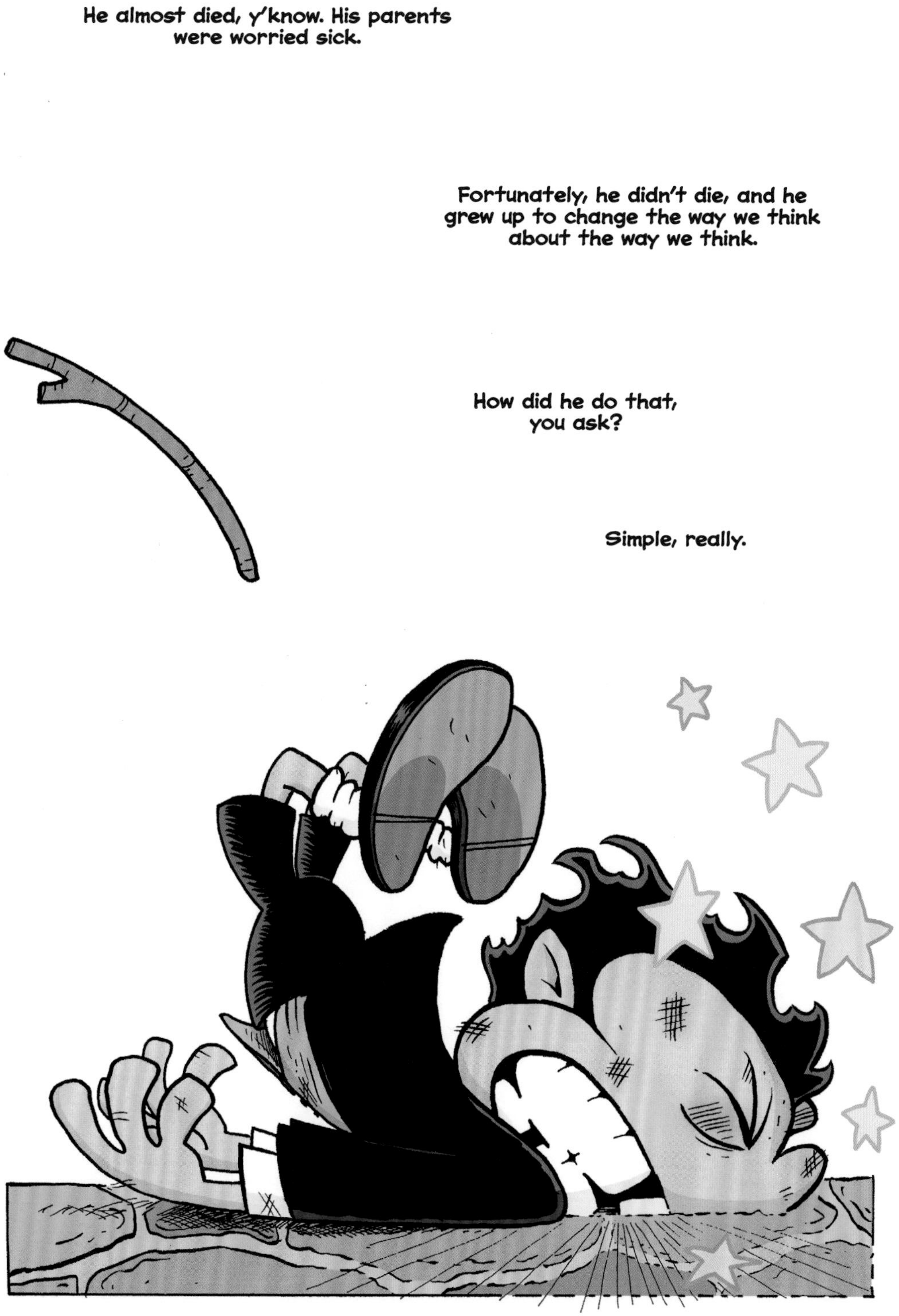
He almost died, y'know. His parents were worried sick.
Fortunately, he didn't die, and he grew up to change the way we think about the way we think.
How did he do that, you ask?
Simple, really.

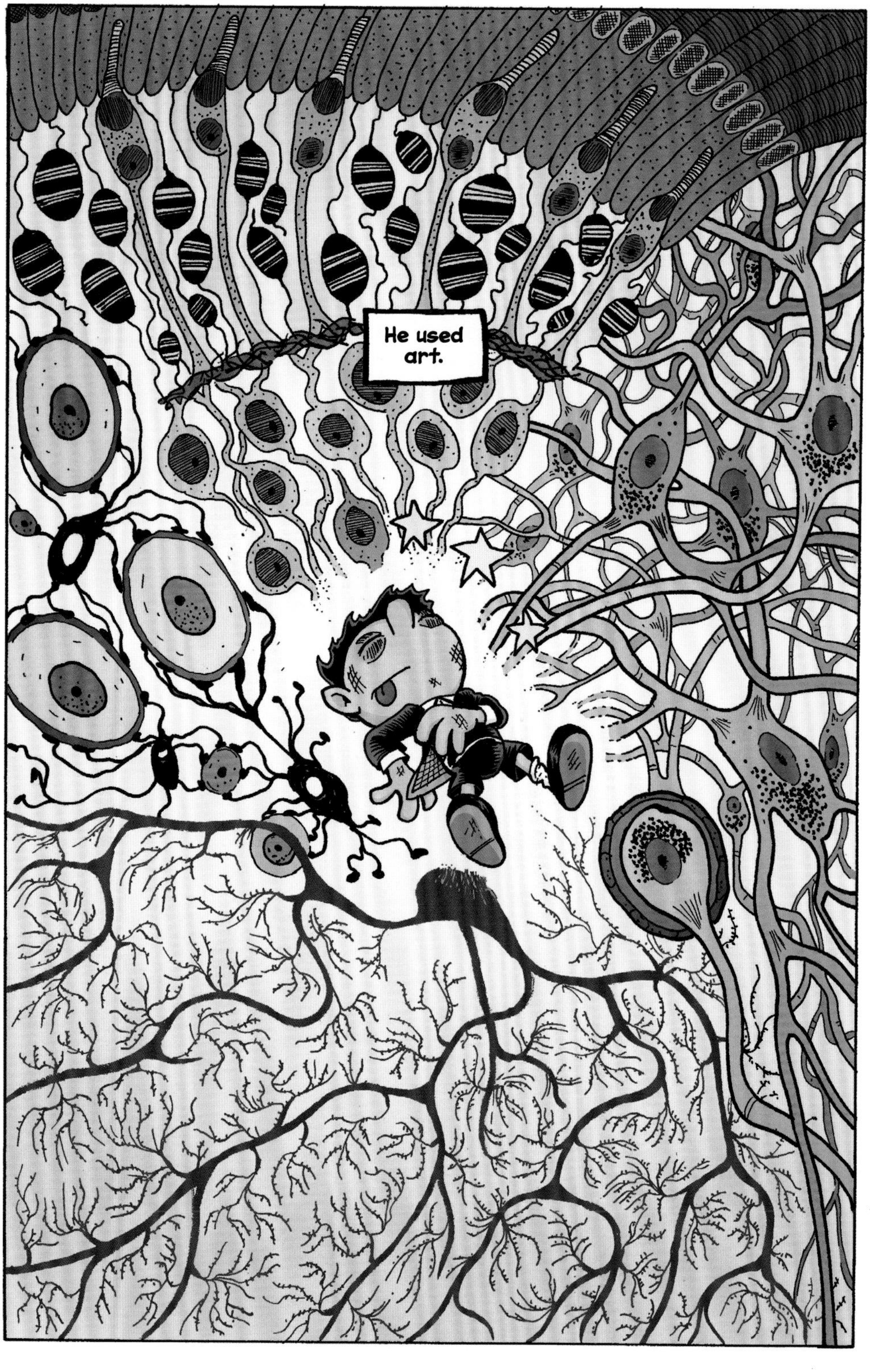
He used art.

CHAPTER 2: THE MAGIC WAND

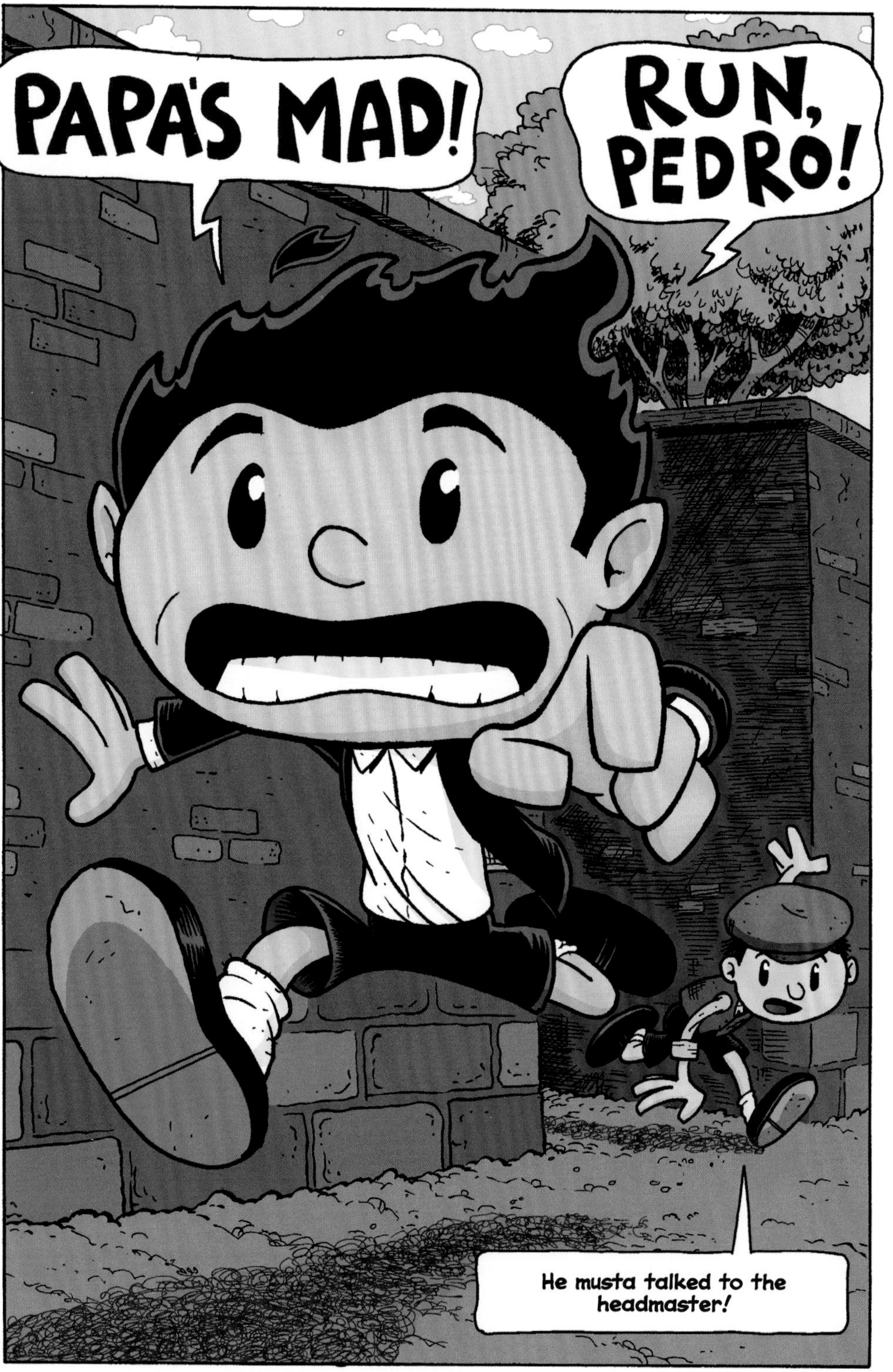
PAPA'S MAD!
RUN, PEDRO!
He musta talked to the headmaster!

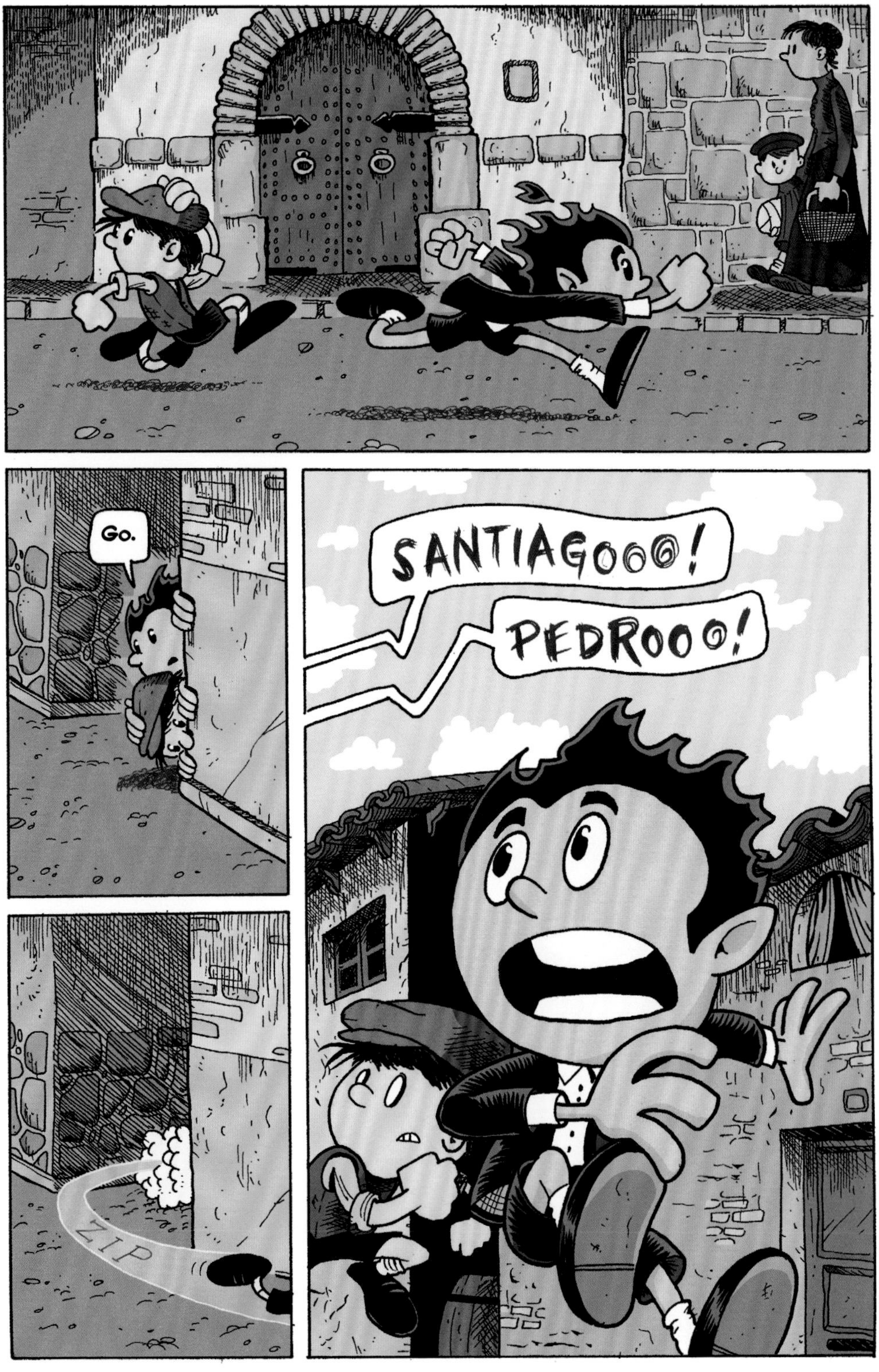
Go.
SANTIAGOOOO!
PEDROOOO!
ZIP

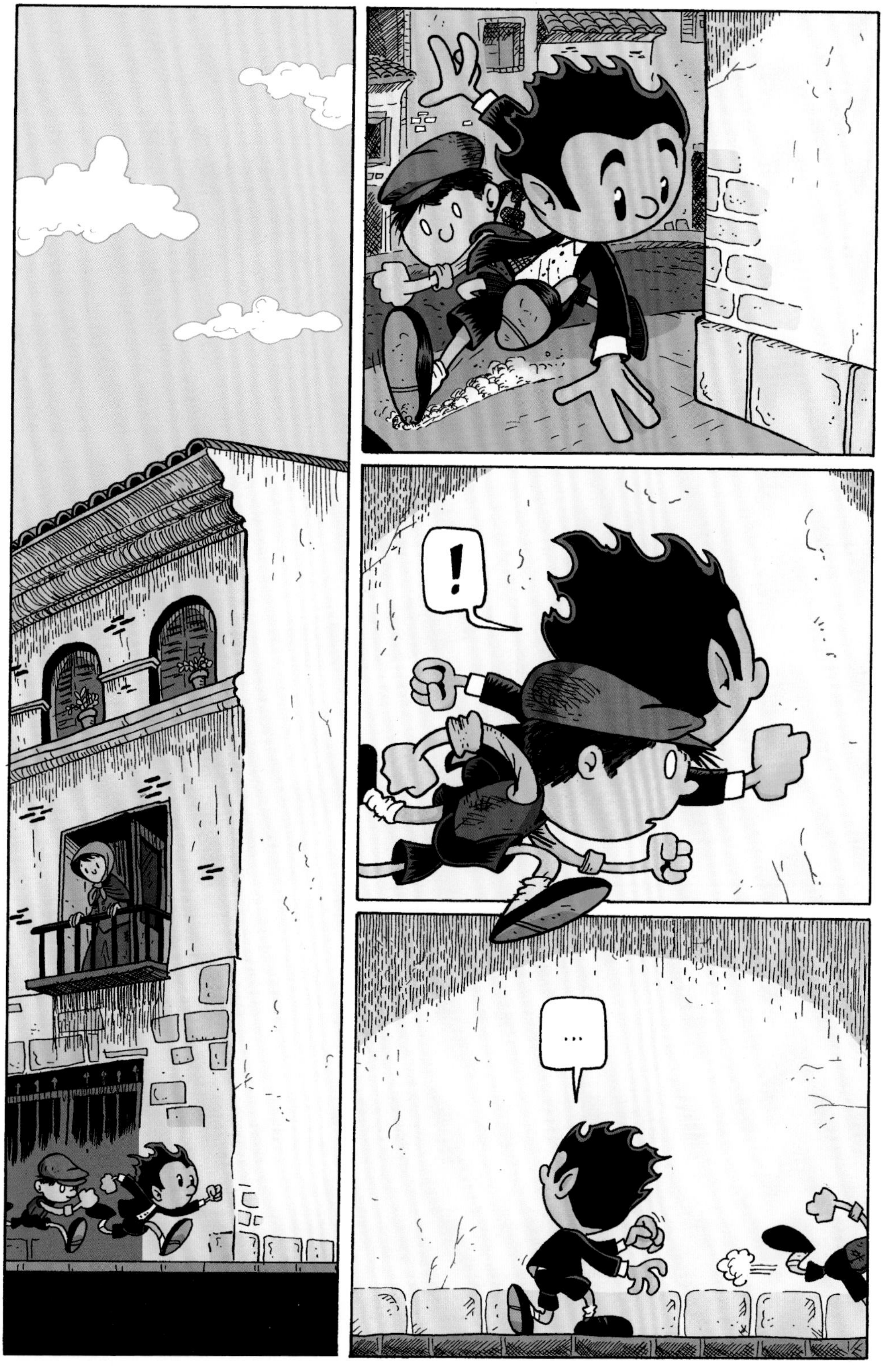
!
...

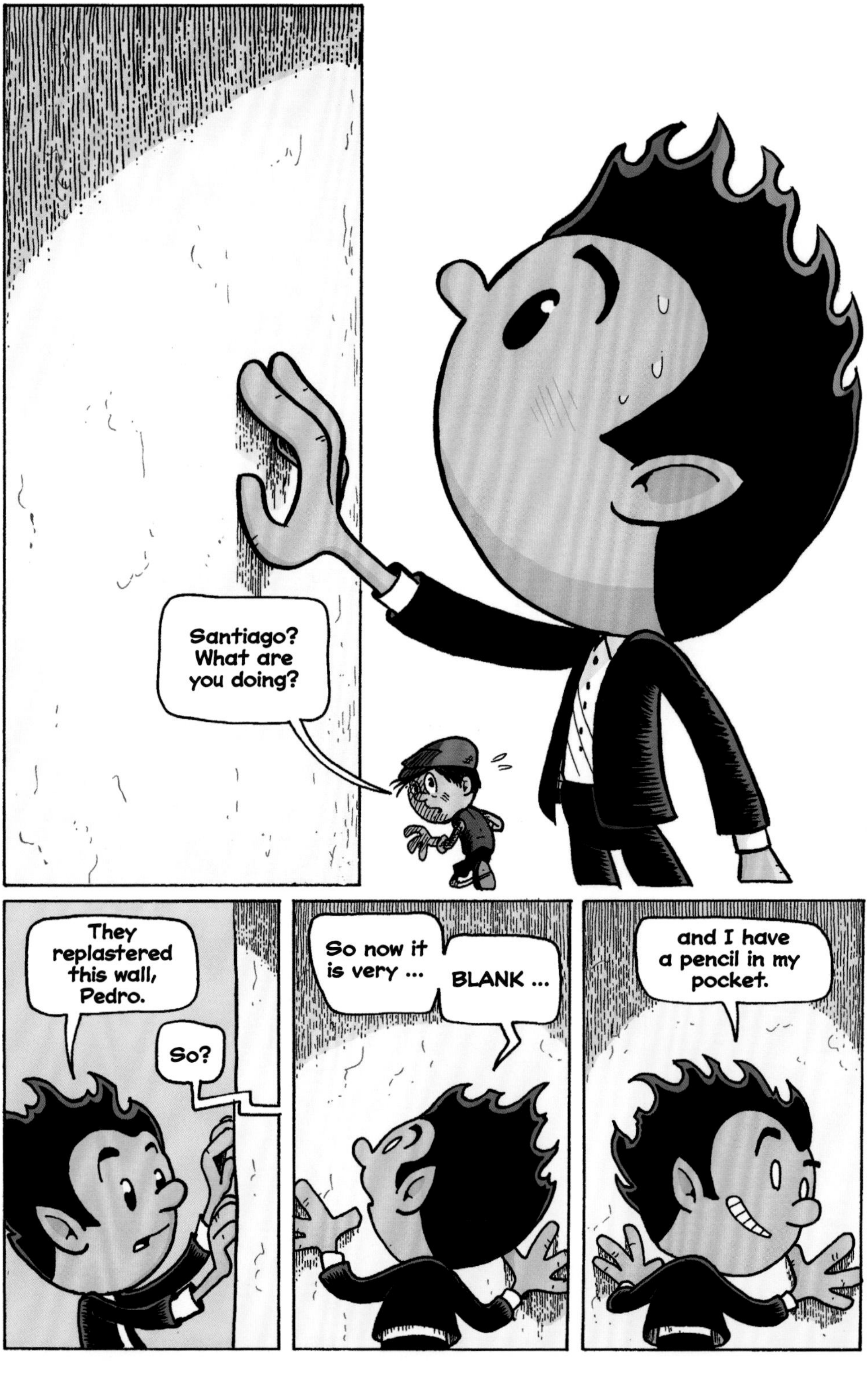
Santiago? What are you doing?
They replastered this wall, Pedro.
So?
So now it is very ...
BLANK ...
and I have a pencil in my pocket.

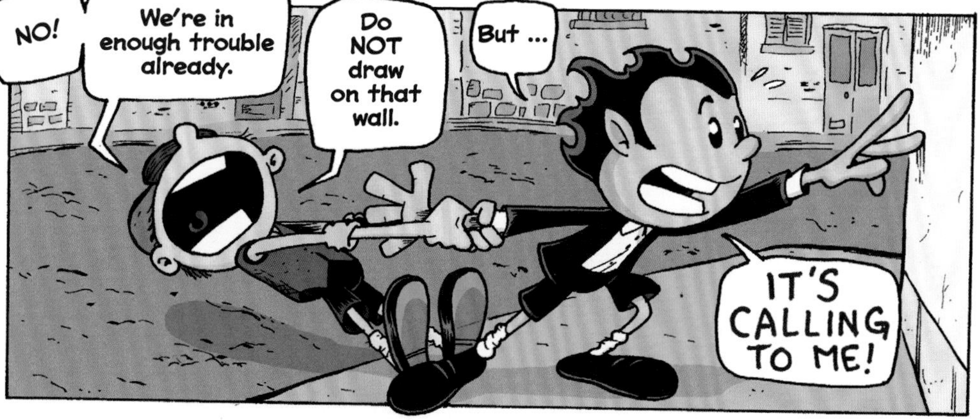
NO!
We're in enough trouble already.
Do NOT draw on that wall.
But ...
IT'S CALLING TO ME!

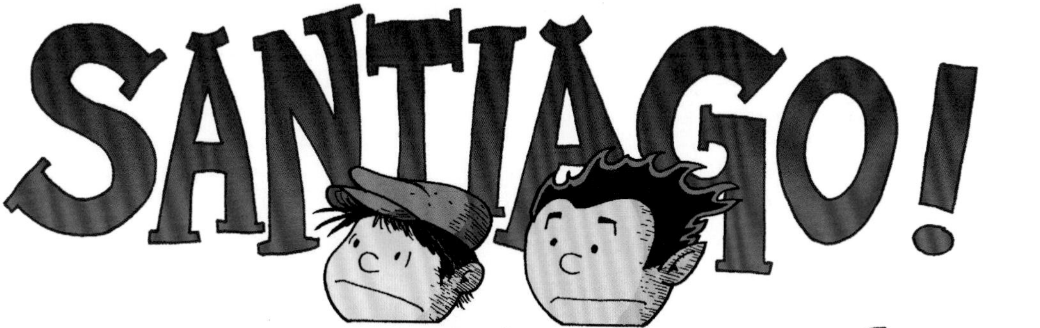
SANTIAGO!

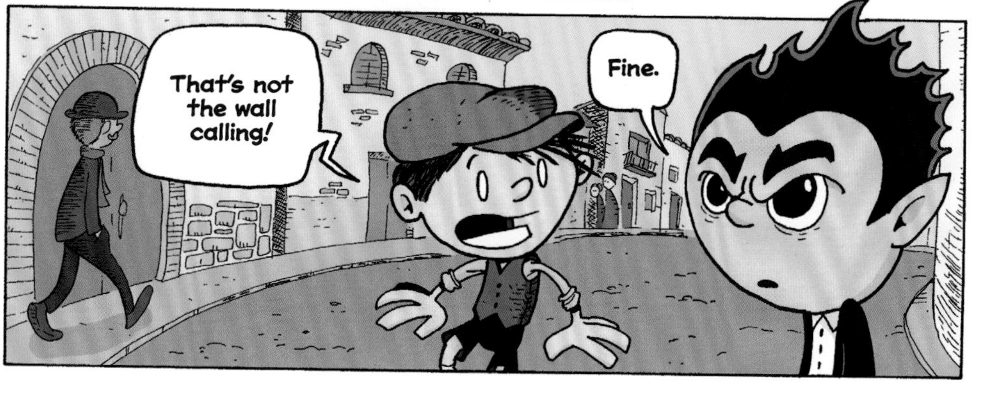
That's not the wall calling!
Fine.

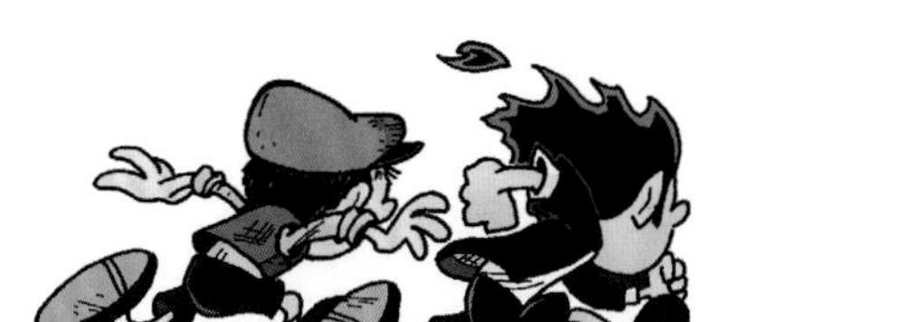

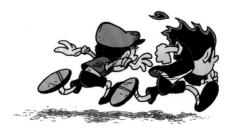

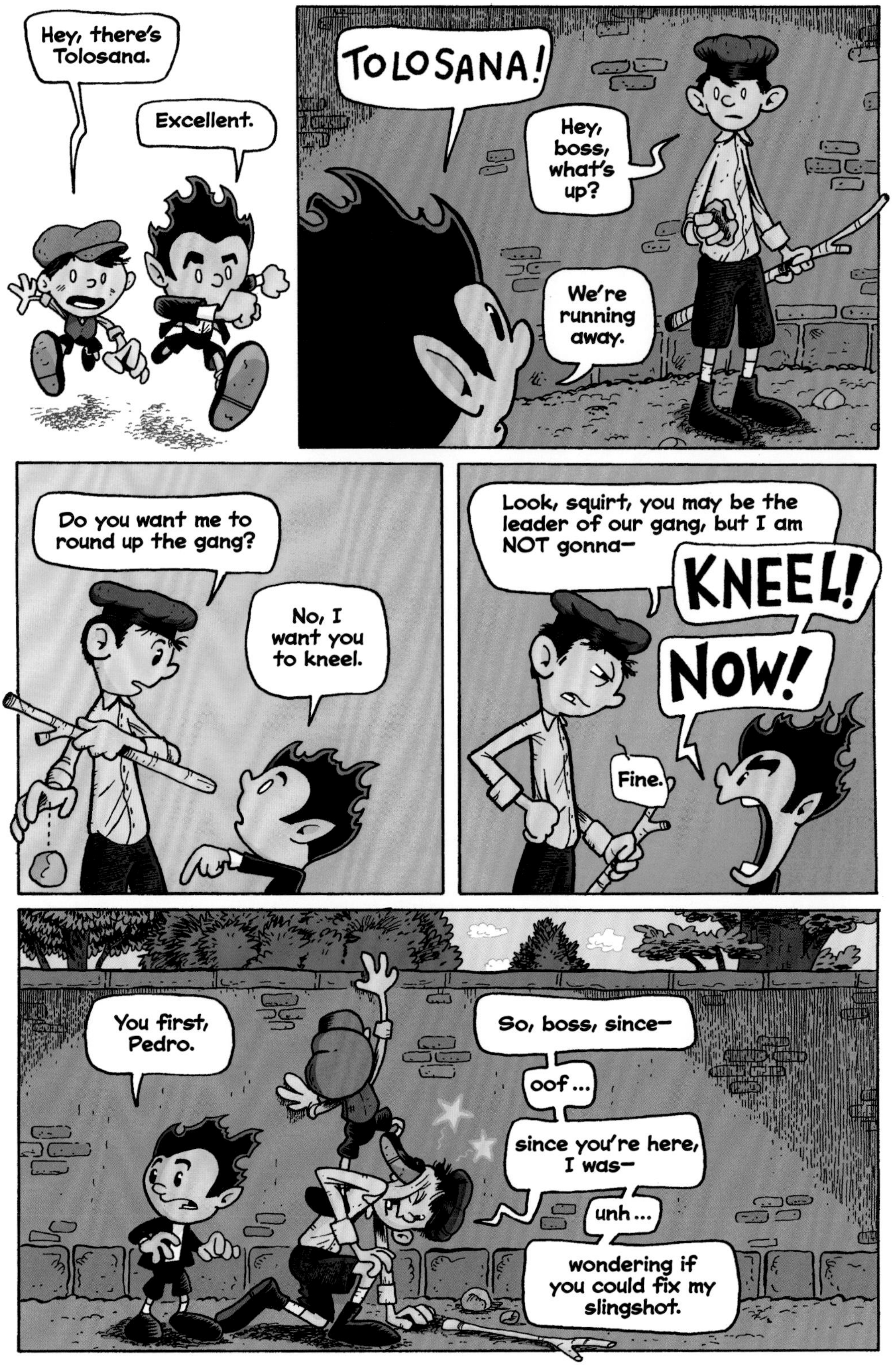
Hey, there's Tolosana.
Excellent.
TOLOSANA!
Hey, boss, what's up?
We're running away.
Do you want me to round up the gang?
No, I want you to kneel.
Look, squirt, you may be the leader of our gang, but I am NOT gonna—
KNEEL!
NOW!
Fine.
You first, Pedro.
So, boss, since—
oof...
since you're here, I was—
unh...
wondering if you could fix my slingshot.

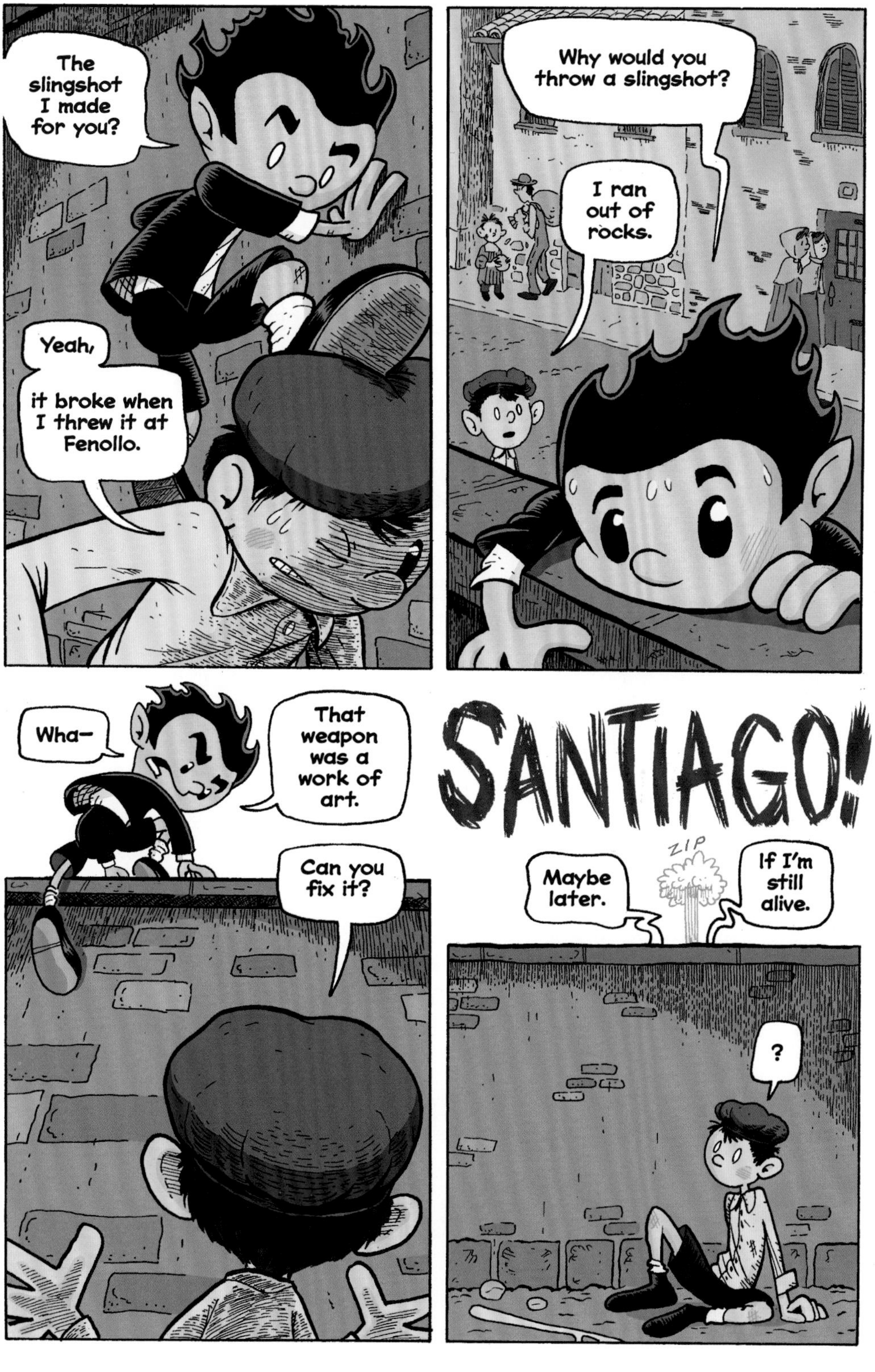
The slingshot I made for you?
Yeah,
it broke when I threw it at Fenollo.
Why would you throw a slingshot?
I ran out of rocks.
Wha–
That weapon was a work of art.
Can you fix it?
SANTIAGO!
ZIP
Maybe later.
If I'm still alive.
?

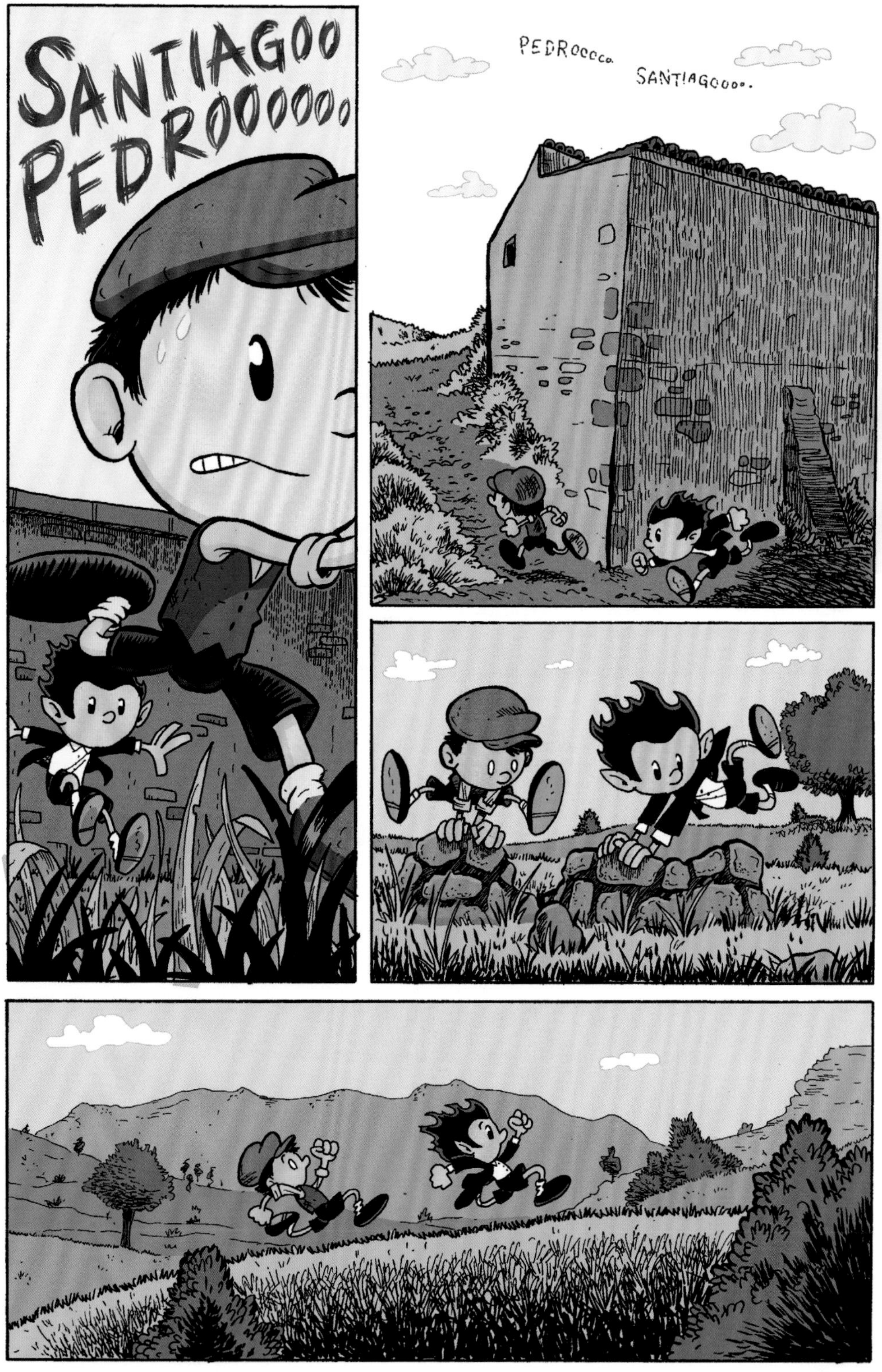
SANTIAGOO
PEDROOOOOO
PEDROcccco.
SANTIAGOooo.

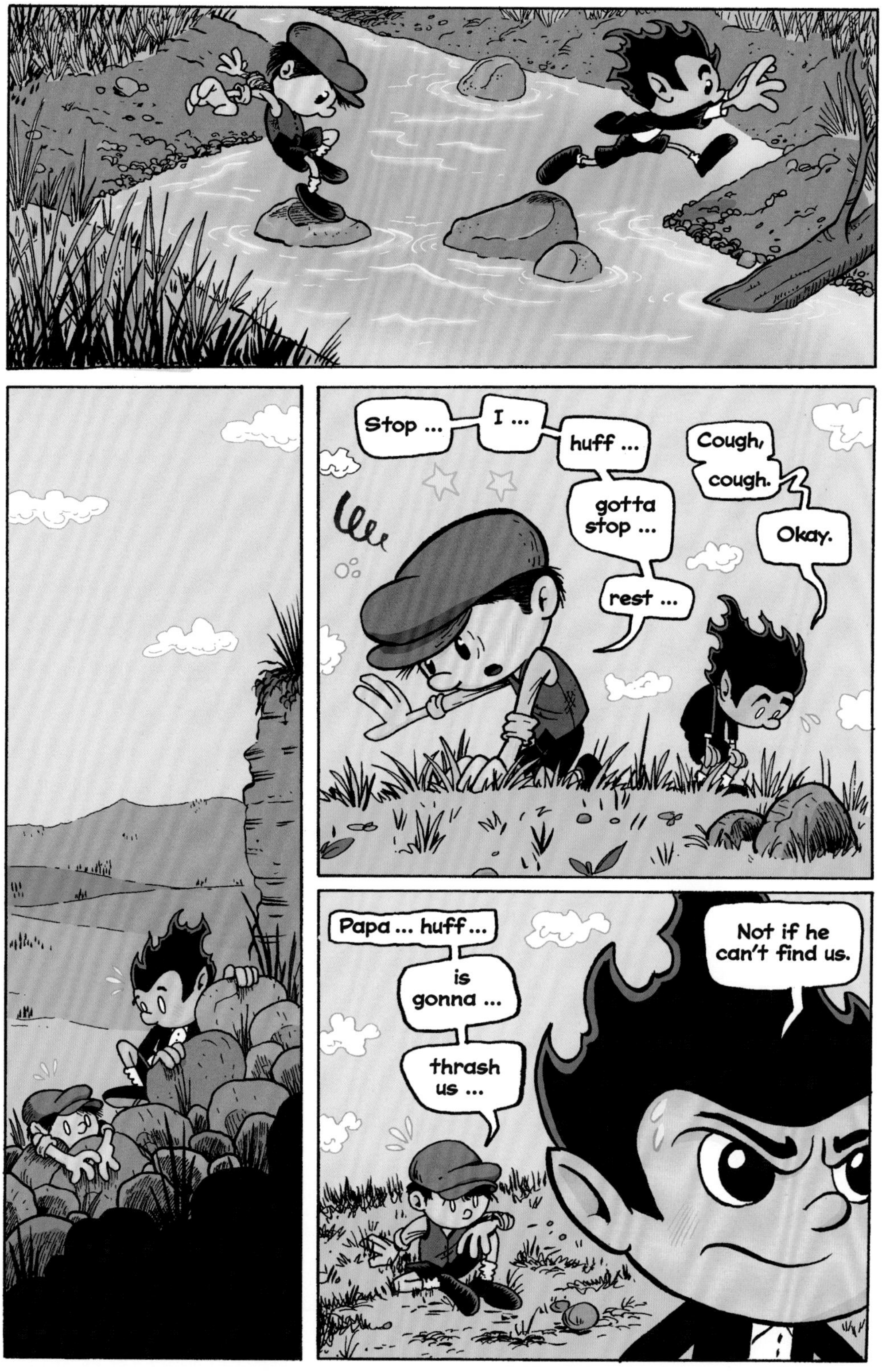
Stop ...
I ...
huff ...
gotta stop ...
rest ...
Cough, cough.
Okay.
Papa ... huff ...
is gonna ...
thrash us ...
Not if he can't find us.

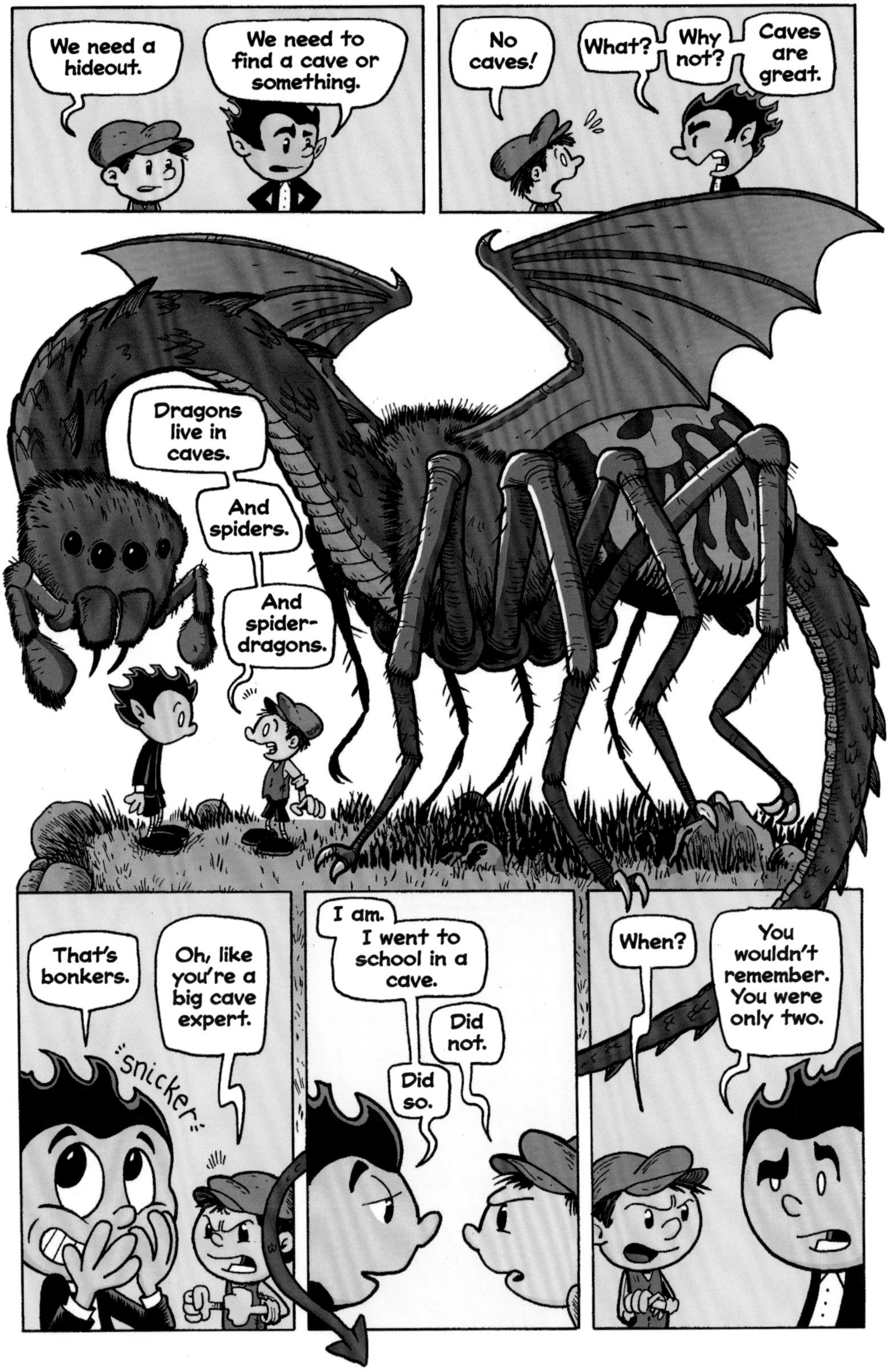
We need a hideout.
We need to find a cave or something.
No caves!
What?
Why not?
Caves are great.
Dragons live in caves.
And spiders.
And spider-dragons.
That's bonkers.
Oh, like you're a big cave expert.
snicker
I am.
I went to school in a cave.
Did not.
Did so.
When?
You wouldn't remember. You were only two.

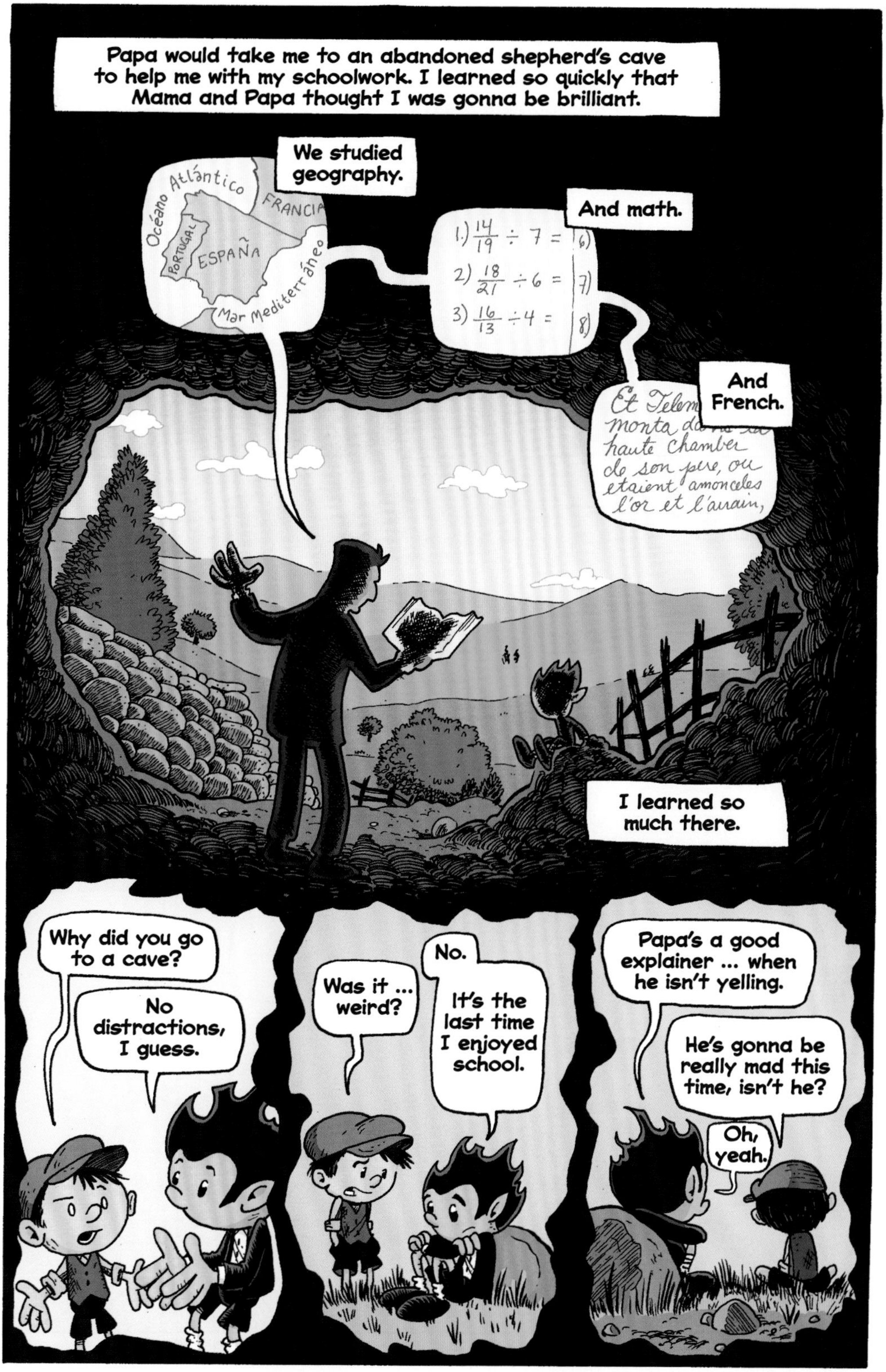

Papa would take me to an abandoned shepherd's cave to help me with my schoolwork. I learned so quickly that Mama and Papa thought I was gonna be brilliant.
We studied geography.
Océano Atlántico
FRANCIA
PORTUGAL
ESPAÑA
Mar Mediterráneo
And math.
1.) 14/19 ÷ 7 = 6)
2) 18/21 ÷ 6 = 7)
3) 16/13 ÷ 4 = 8)
And French.
Et Telem
monta
haute chamber
de son pere, ou
etaient amonceles
l'or et l'airain,
I learned so much there.
Why did you go to a cave?
No distractions, I guess.
Was it ... weird?
No.
It's the last time I enjoyed school.
Papa's a good explainer ... when he isn't yelling.
He's gonna be really mad this time, isn't he?
Oh, yeah.

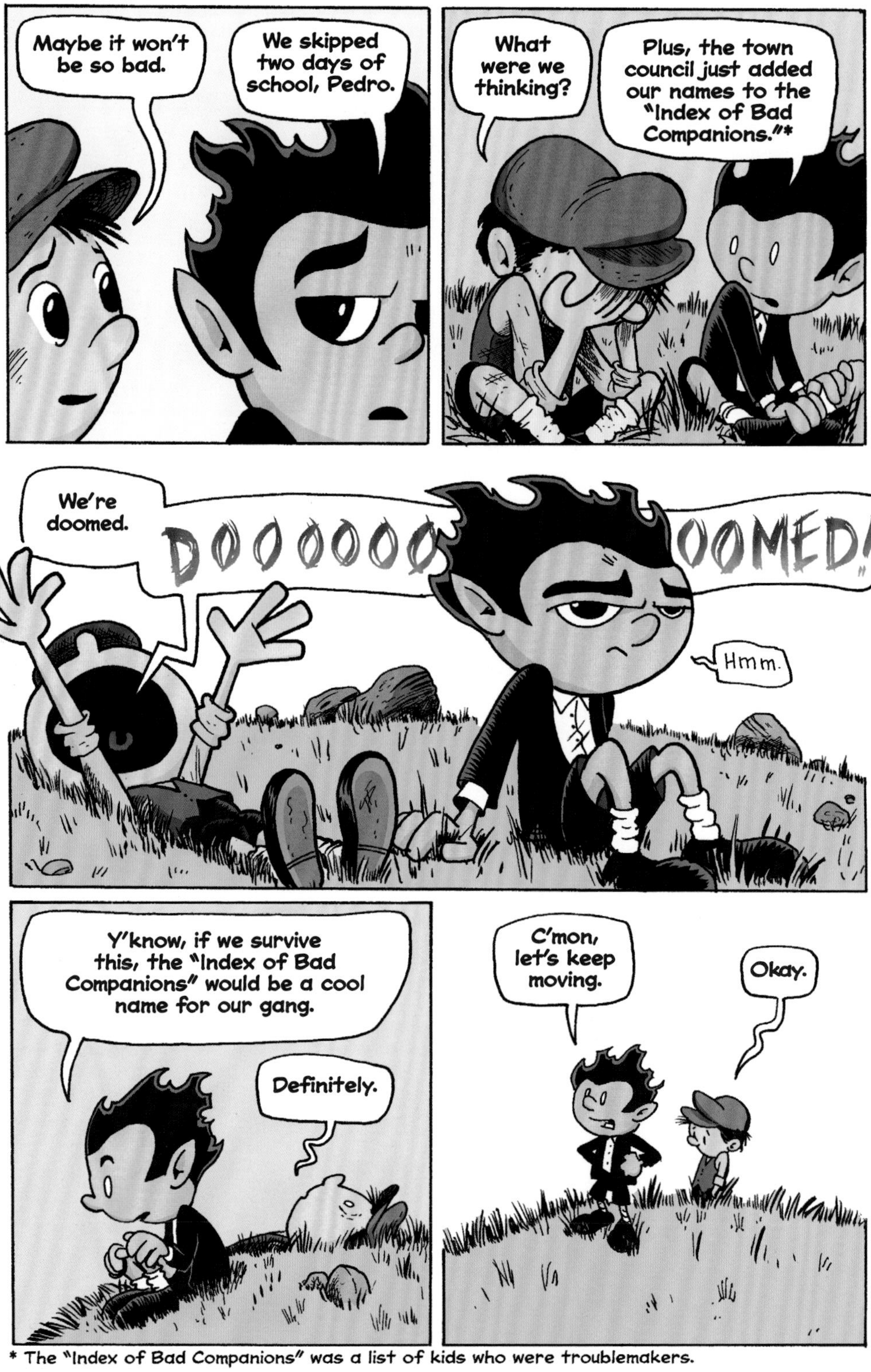
Maybe it won't be so bad.
We skipped two days of school, Pedro.
What were we thinking?
Plus, the town council just added our names to the "Index of Bad Companions."*
We're doomed.
DOOOOOOOOMED!
Hmm.
Y'know, if we survive this, the "Index of Bad Companions" would be a cool name for our gang.
Definitely.
C'mon, let's keep moving.
Okay.

* The "Index of Bad Companions" was a list of kids who were troublemakers.

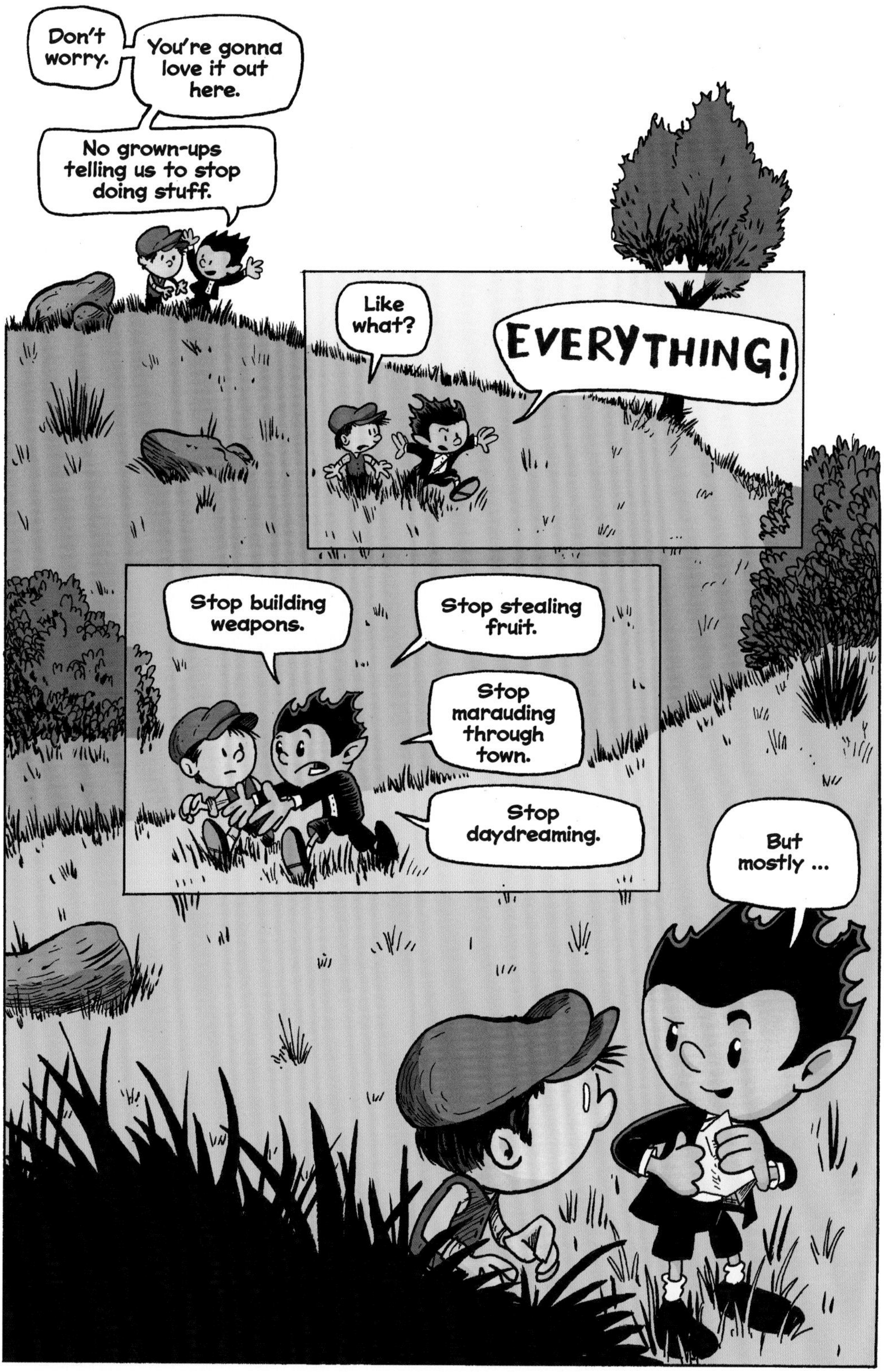
Don't worry.
You're gonna love it out here.
No grown-ups telling us to stop doing stuff.
Like what?
EVERYTHING!
Stop building weapons.
Stop stealing fruit.
Stop marauding through town.
Stop daydreaming.
But mostly ...

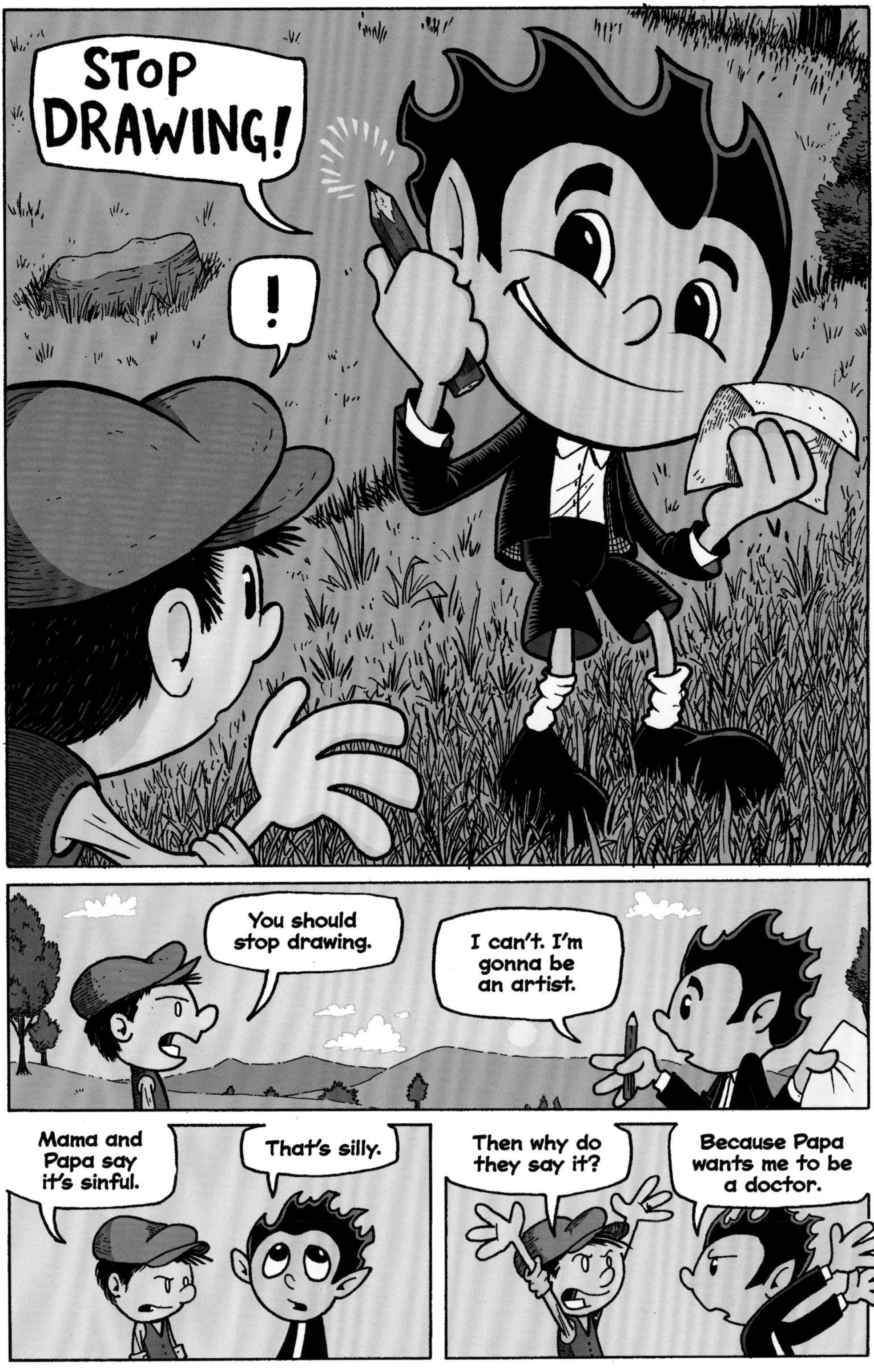
STOP DRAWING!
!
You should stop drawing.
I can't. I'm gonna be an artist.
Mama and Papa say it's sinful.
That's silly.
Then why do they say it?
Because Papa wants me to be a doctor.

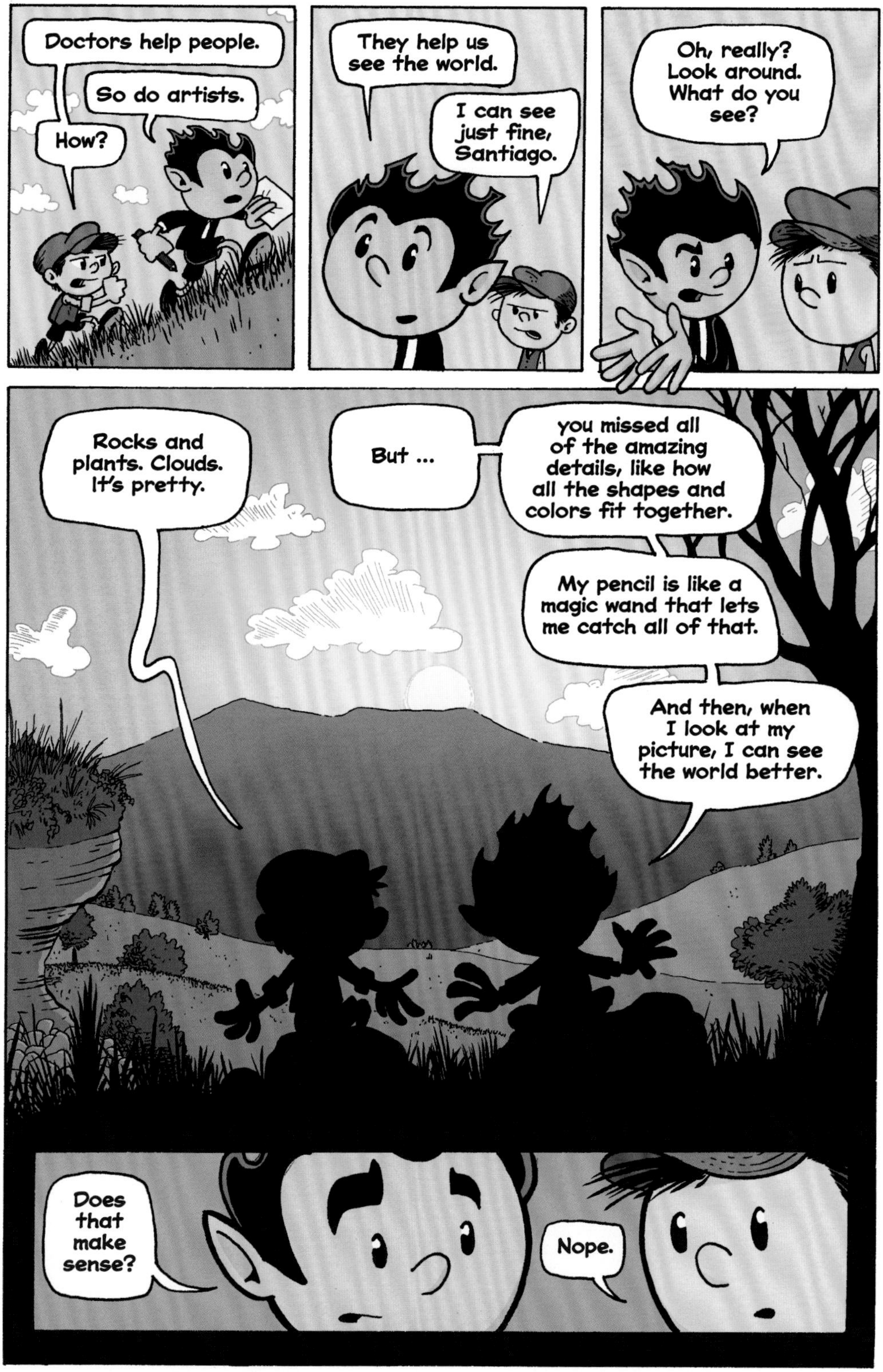
Doctors help people.
How?
So do artists.
They help us see the world.
I can see just fine, Santiago.
Oh, really? Look around. What do you see?
Rocks and plants. Clouds. It's pretty.
But ...
you missed all of the amazing details, like how all the shapes and colors fit together.
My pencil is like a magic wand that lets me catch all of that.
And then, when I look at my picture, I can see the world better.
Does that make sense?
Nope.

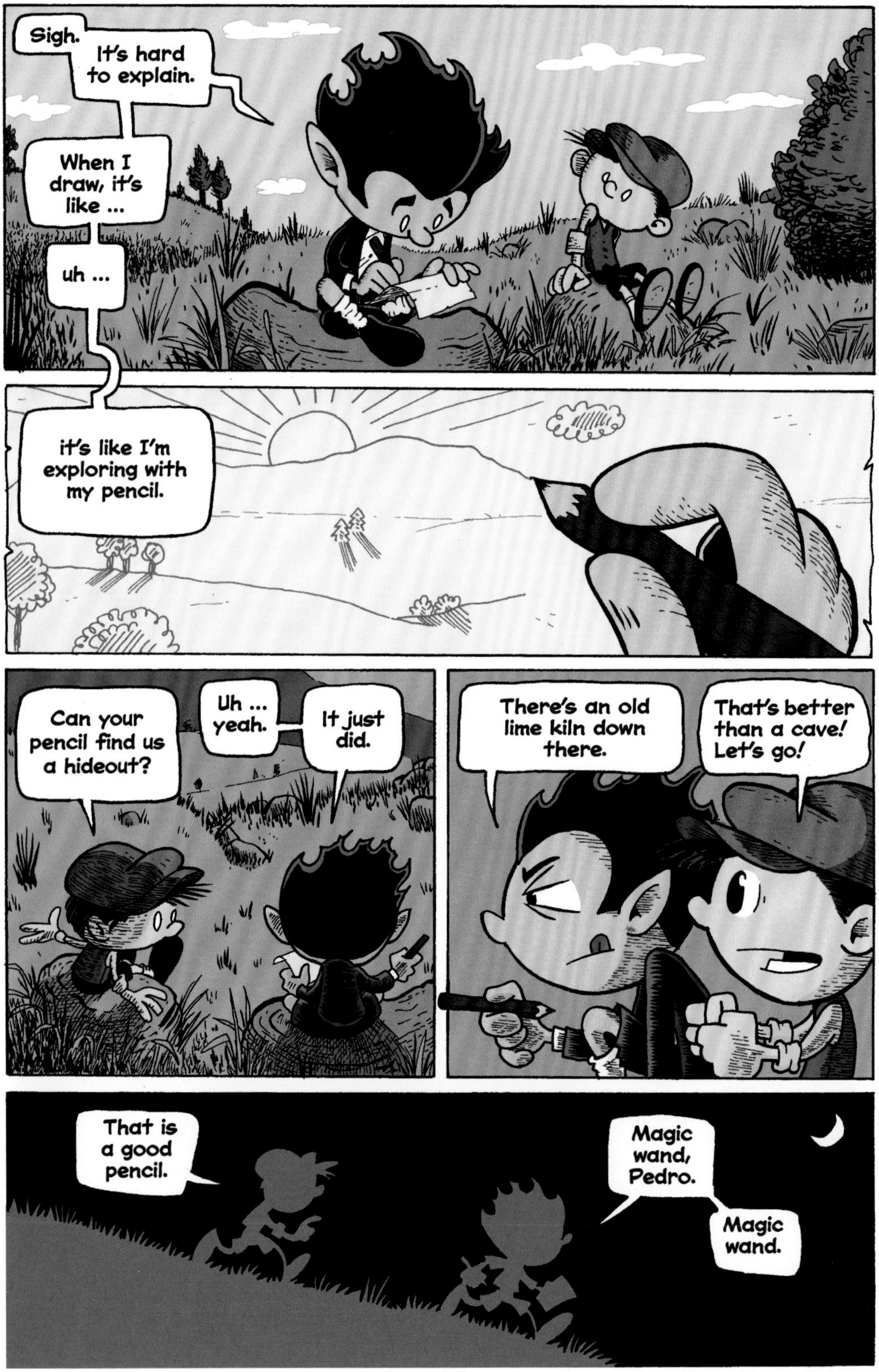
Sigh.
It's hard to explain.
When I draw, it's like ...
uh ...
it's like I'm exploring with my pencil.
Can your pencil find us a hideout?
Uh ... yeah.
It just did.
There's an old lime kiln down there.
That's better than a cave! Let's go!
That is a good pencil.
Magic wand, Pedro.
Magic wand.

CHAPTER 3: IN THE WILDERNESS

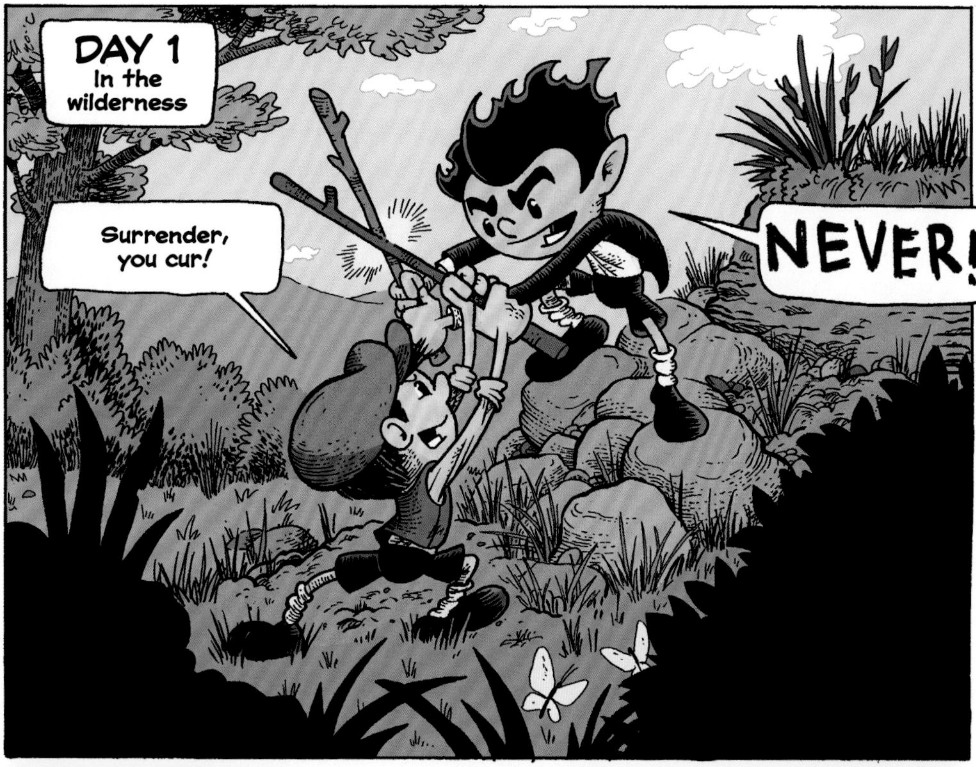
DAY 1
In the wilderness
Surrender, you cur!
NEVER!

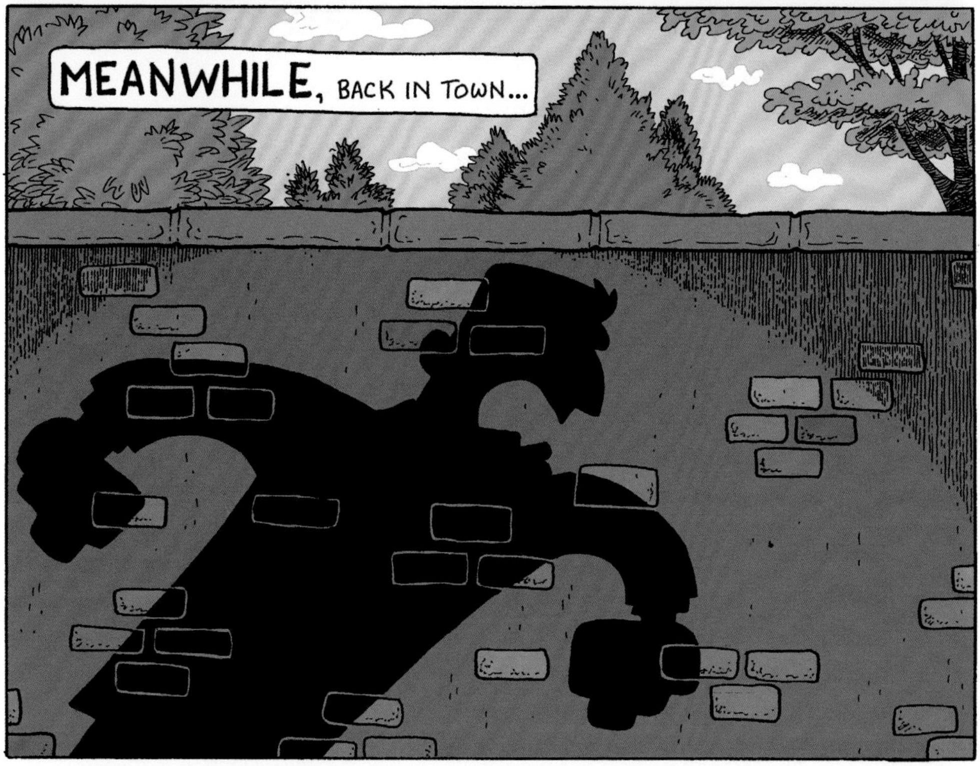
MEANWHILE, BACK IN TOWN...

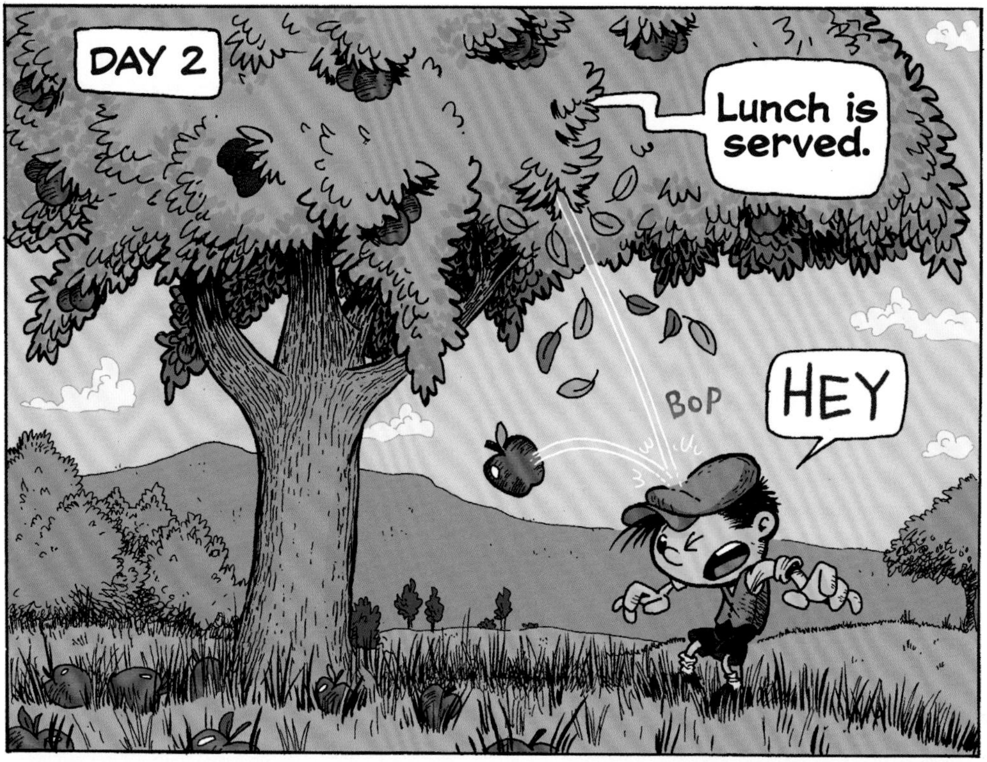
DAY 2
Lunch is served.
BoP
HEY

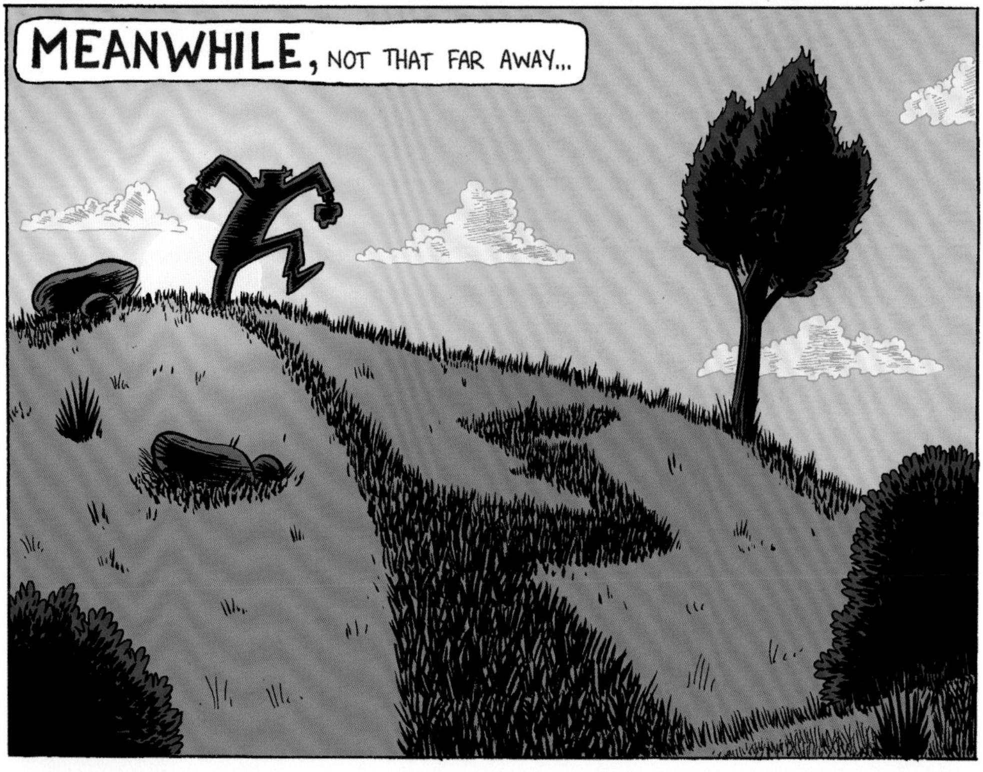
MEANWHILE, NOT THAT FAR AWAY...

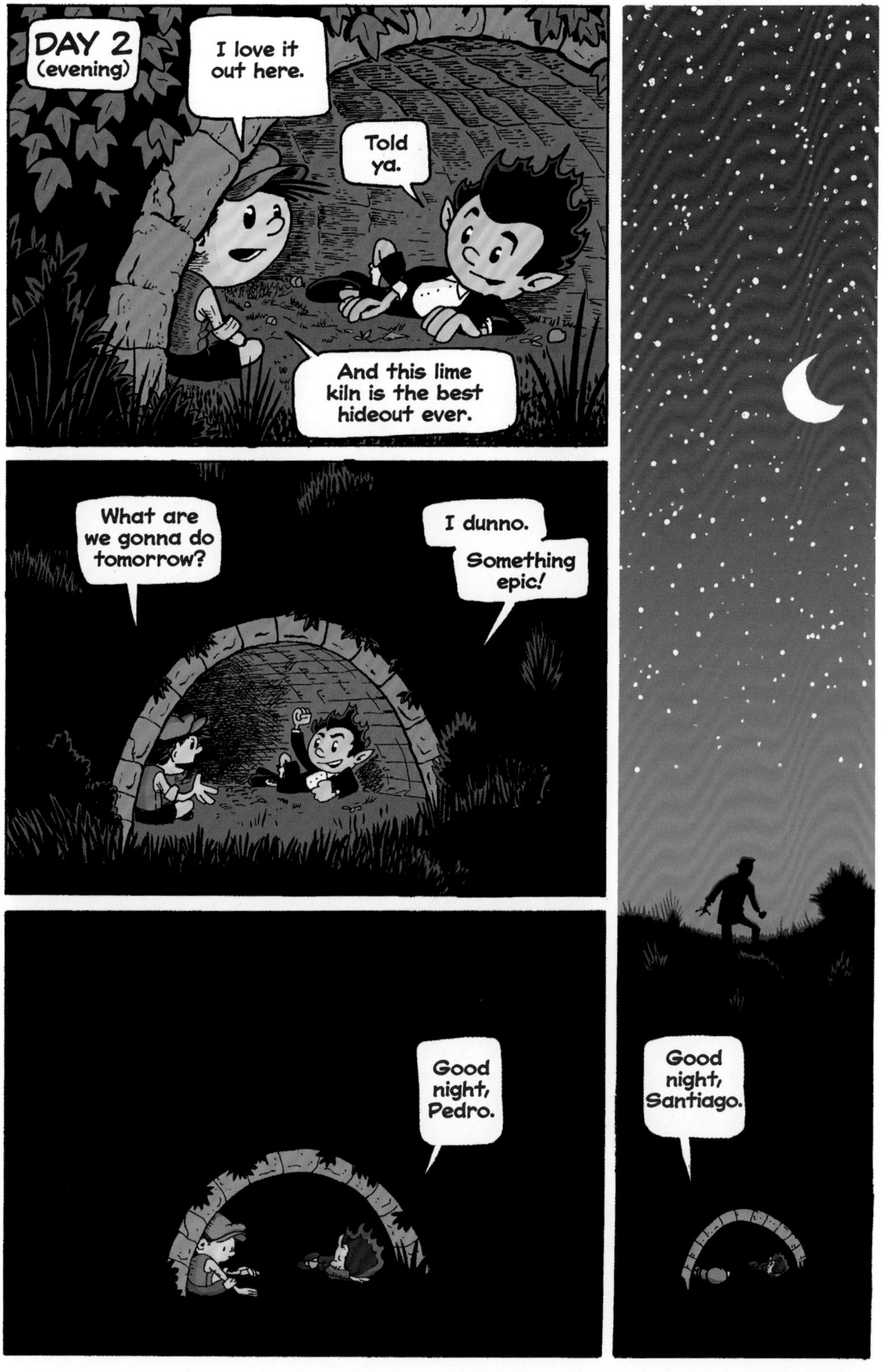
DAY 2 (evening)
I love it out here.
Told ya.
And this lime kiln is the best hideout ever.
What are we gonna do tomorrow?
I dunno.
Something epic!
Good night, Pedro.
Good night, Santiago.

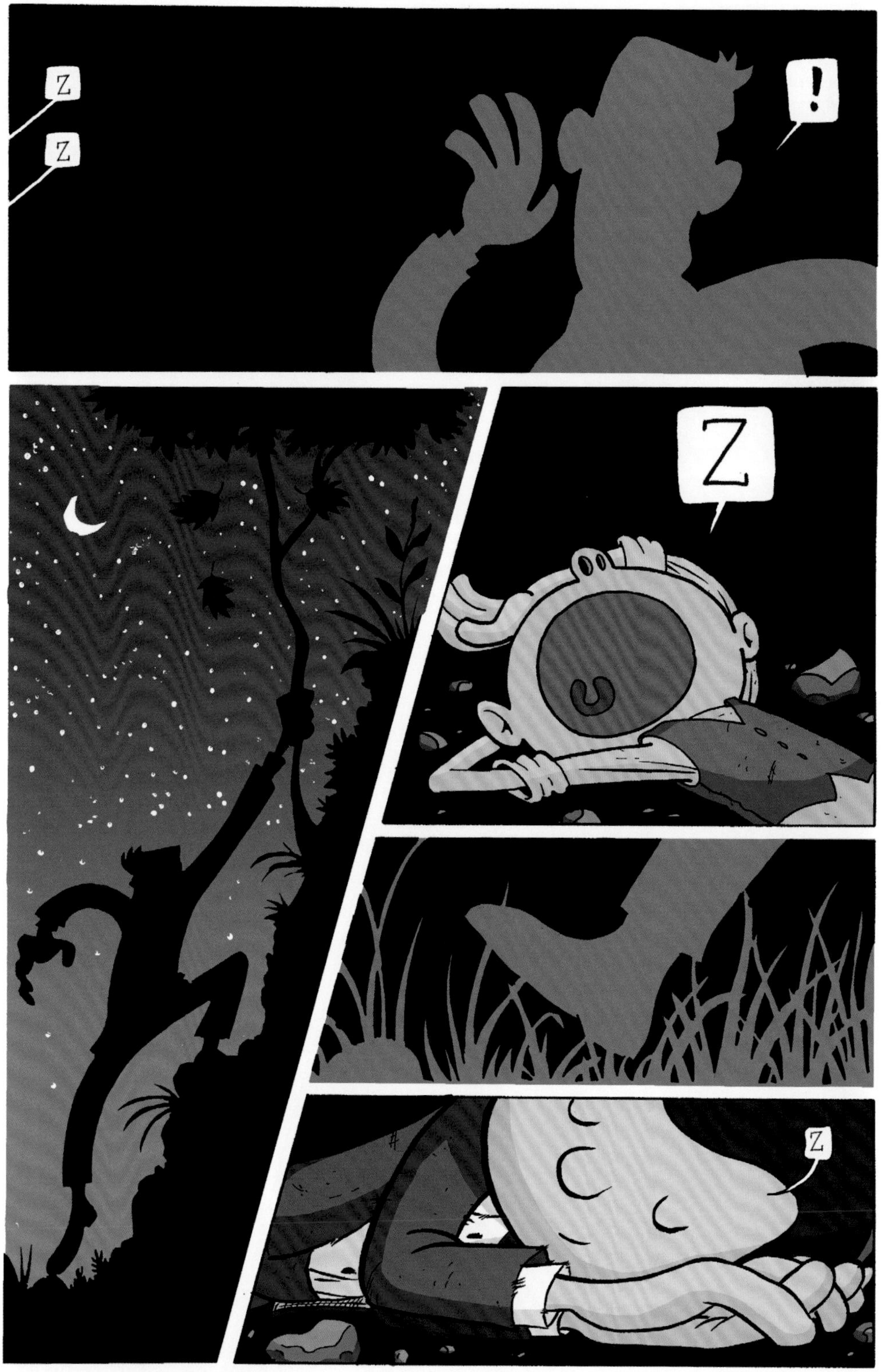
Z
Z
!
Z
Z

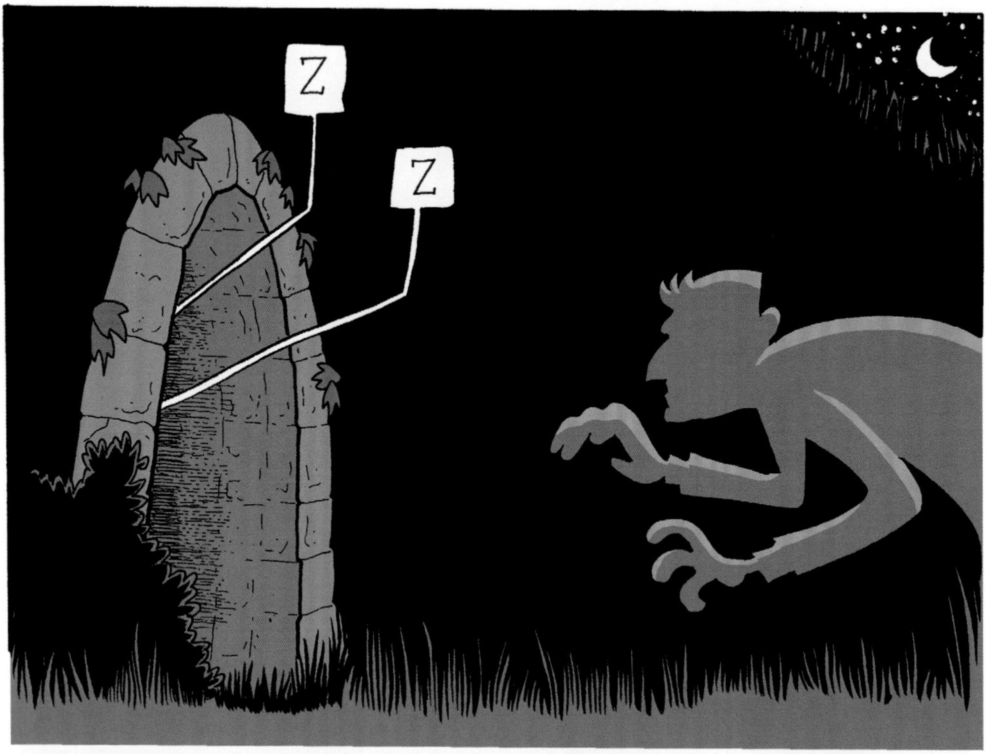
Z
Z

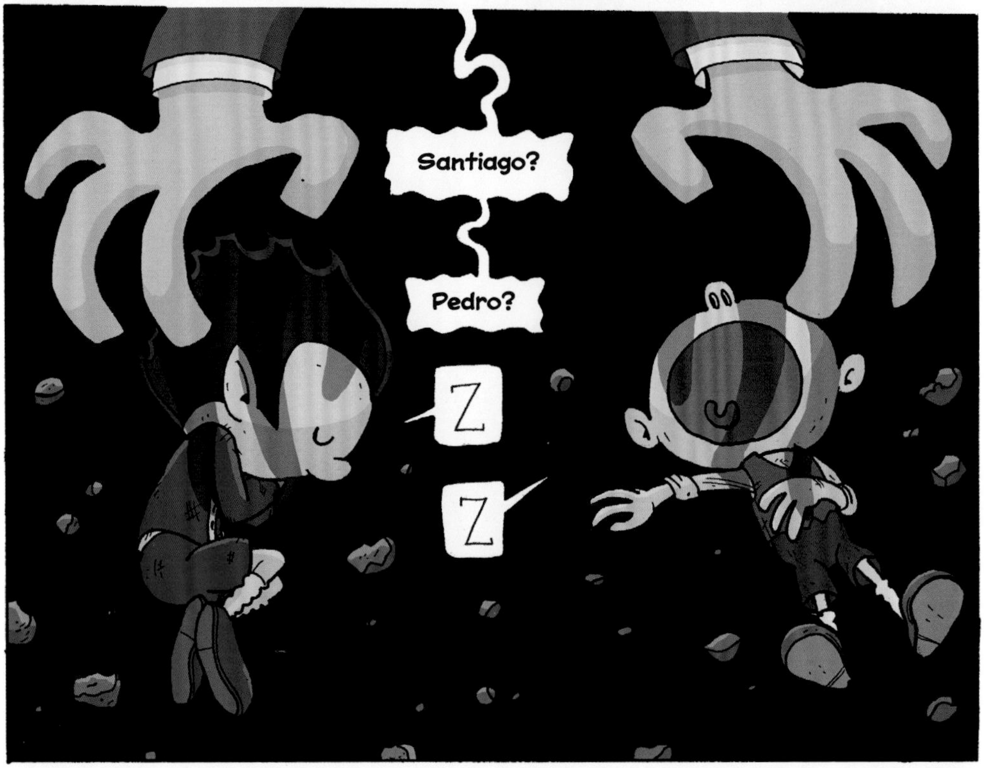
Santiago?
Pedro?
Z
Z

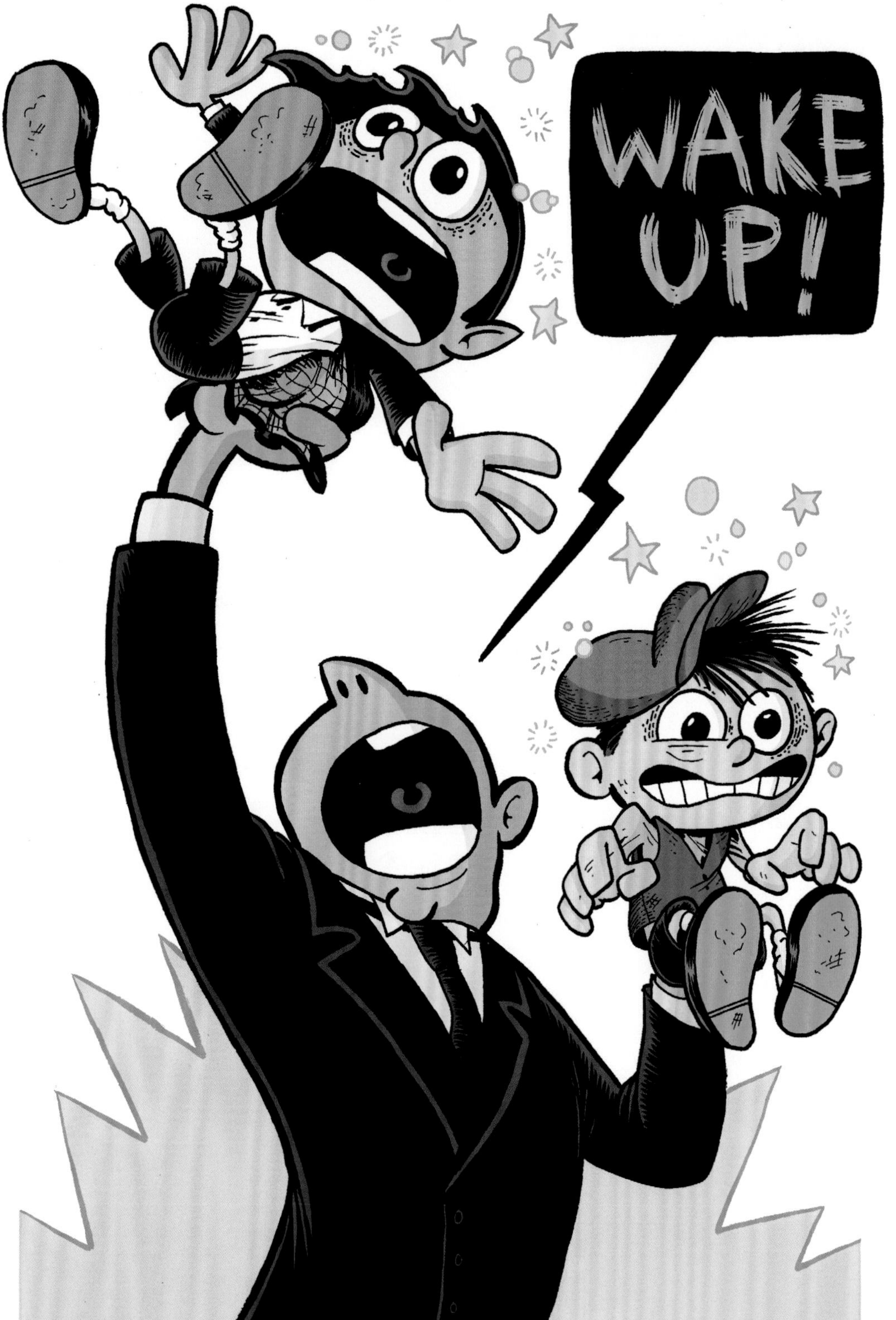
WAKE UP!

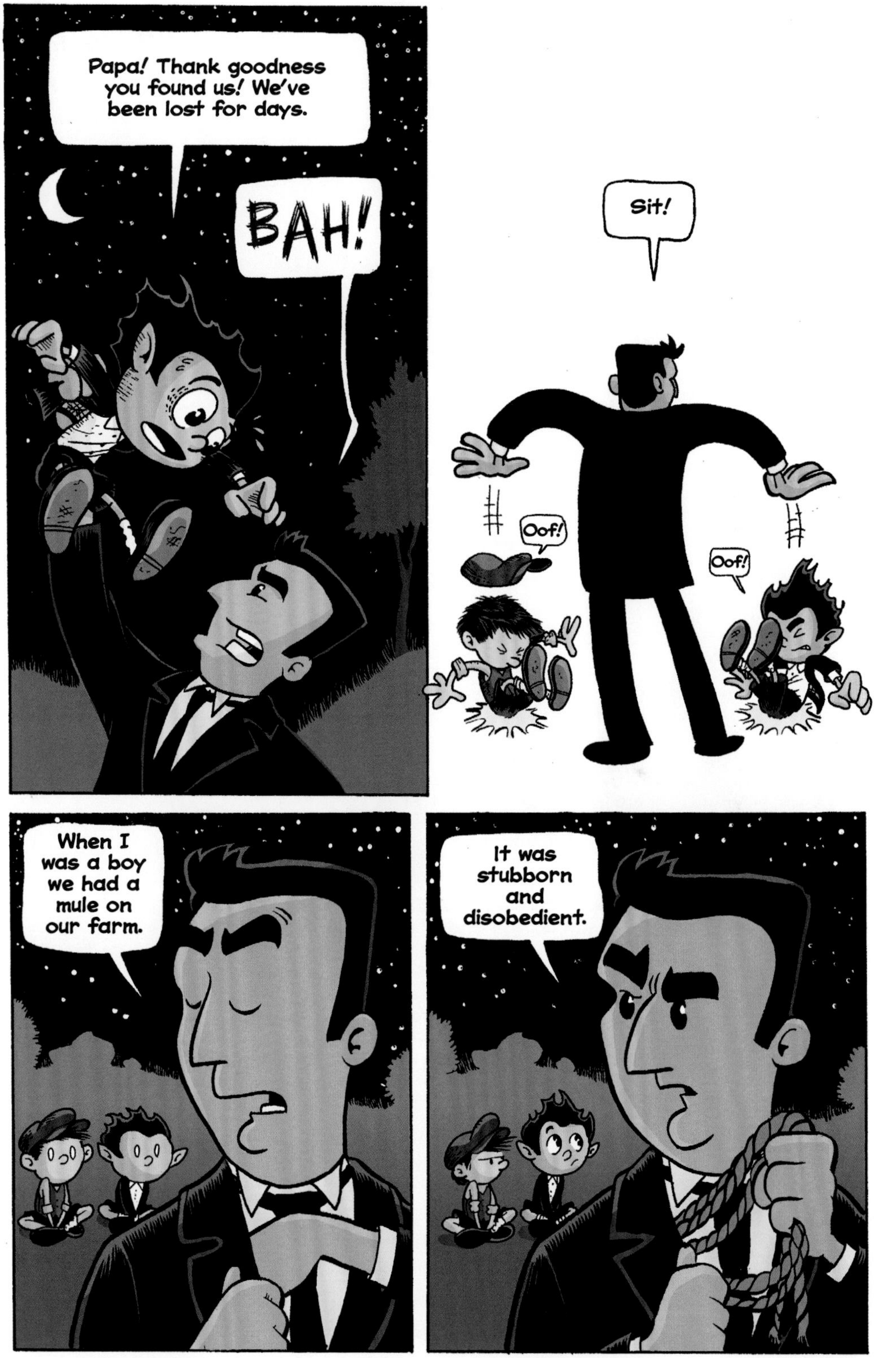

Papa! Thank goodness you found us! We've been lost for days.
BAH!
Sit!
Oof!
Oof!
When I was a boy we had a mule on our farm.
It was stubborn and disobedient.

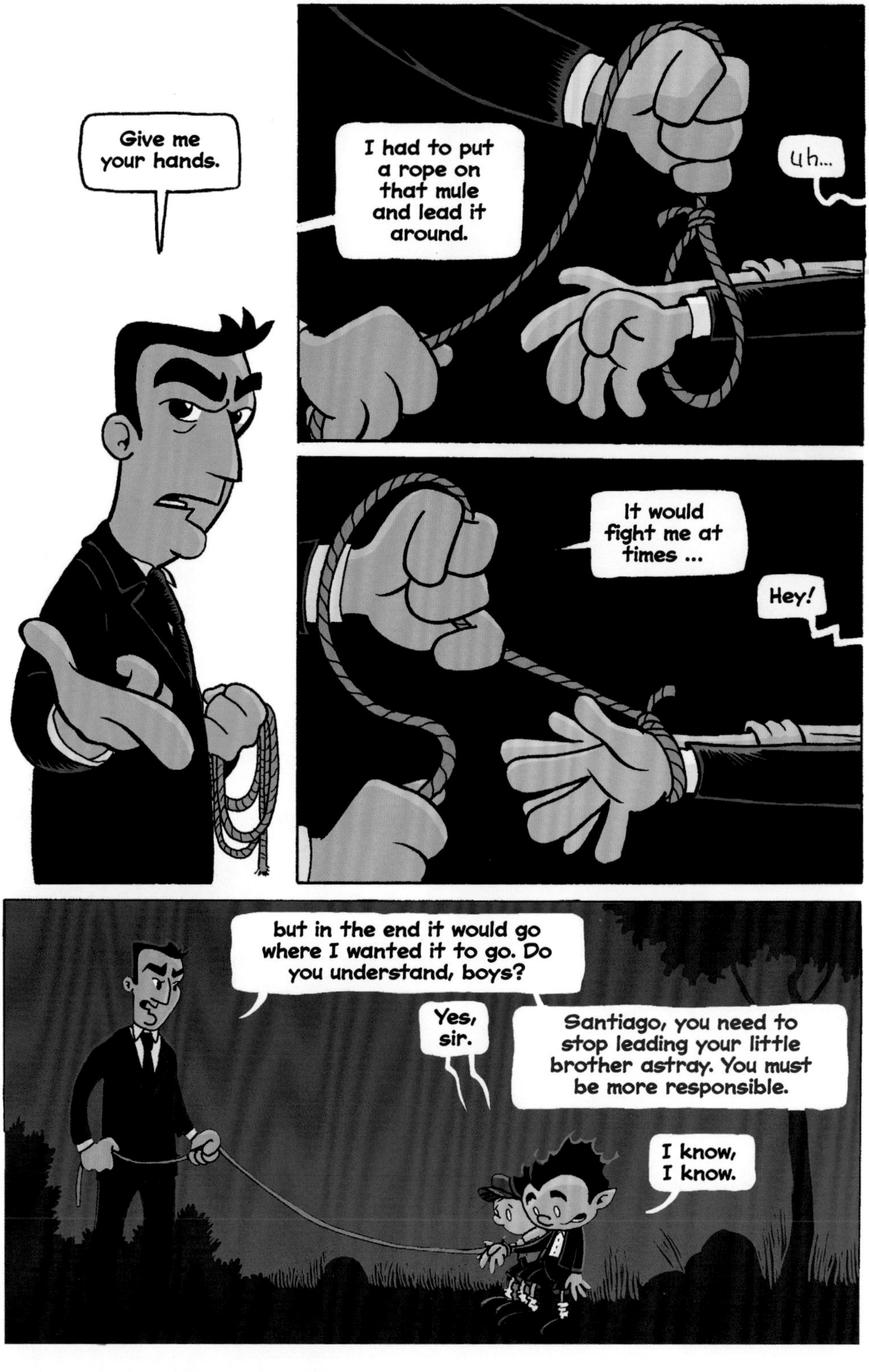
Give me your hands.
I had to put a rope on that mule and lead it around.
Uh...
It would fight me at times ...
Hey!
but in the end it would go where I wanted it to go. Do you understand, boys?
Yes, sir.
Santiago, you need to stop leading your little brother astray. You must be more responsible.
I know, I know.

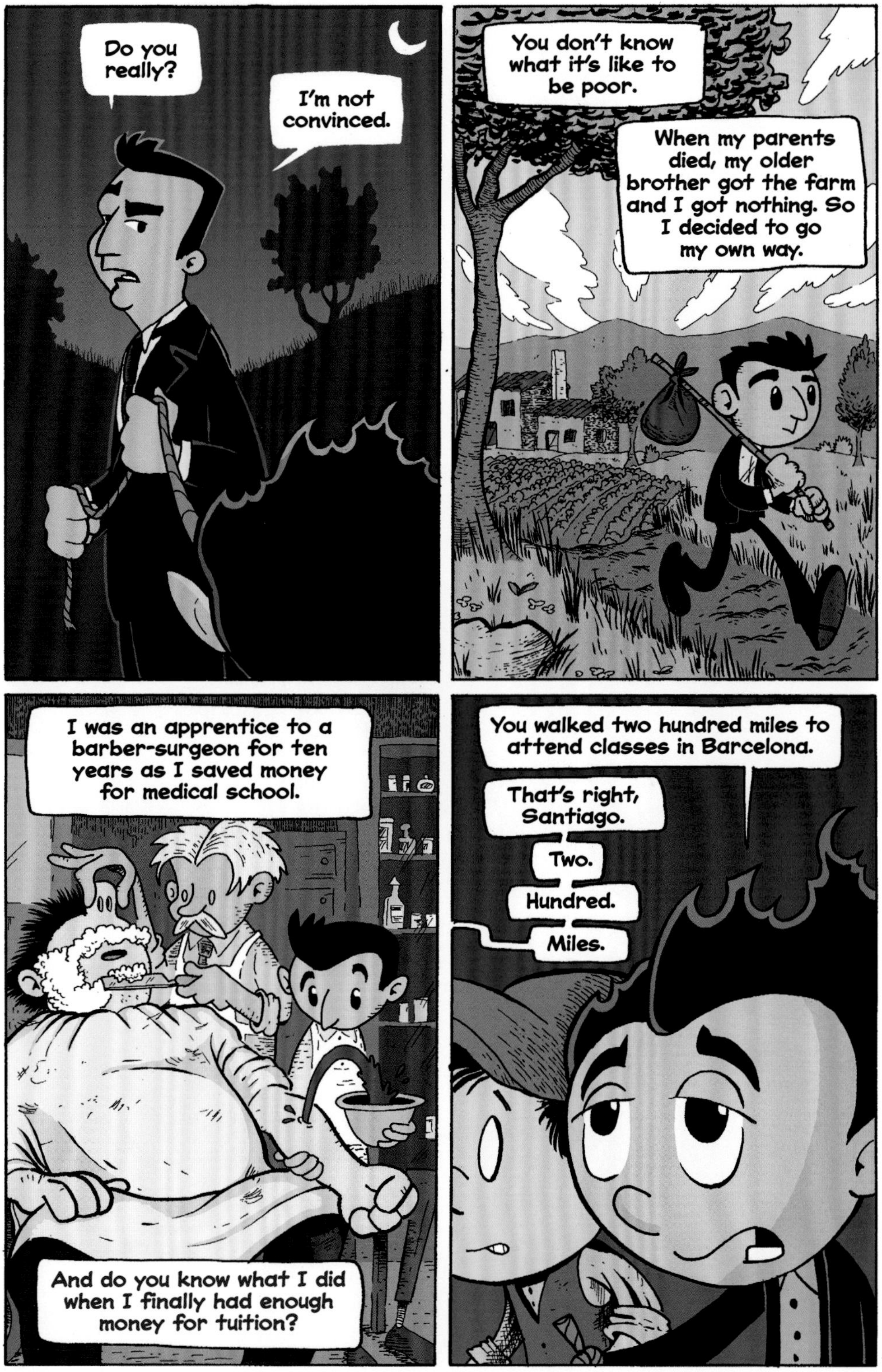
Do you really?
I'm not convinced.
You don't know what it's like to be poor.
When my parents died, my older brother got the farm and I got nothing. So I decided to go my own way.
I was an apprentice to a barber-surgeon for ten years as I saved money for medical school.
And do you know what I did when I finally had enough money for tuition?
You walked two hundred miles to attend classes in Barcelona.
That's right, Santiago.
Two.
Hundred.
Miles.

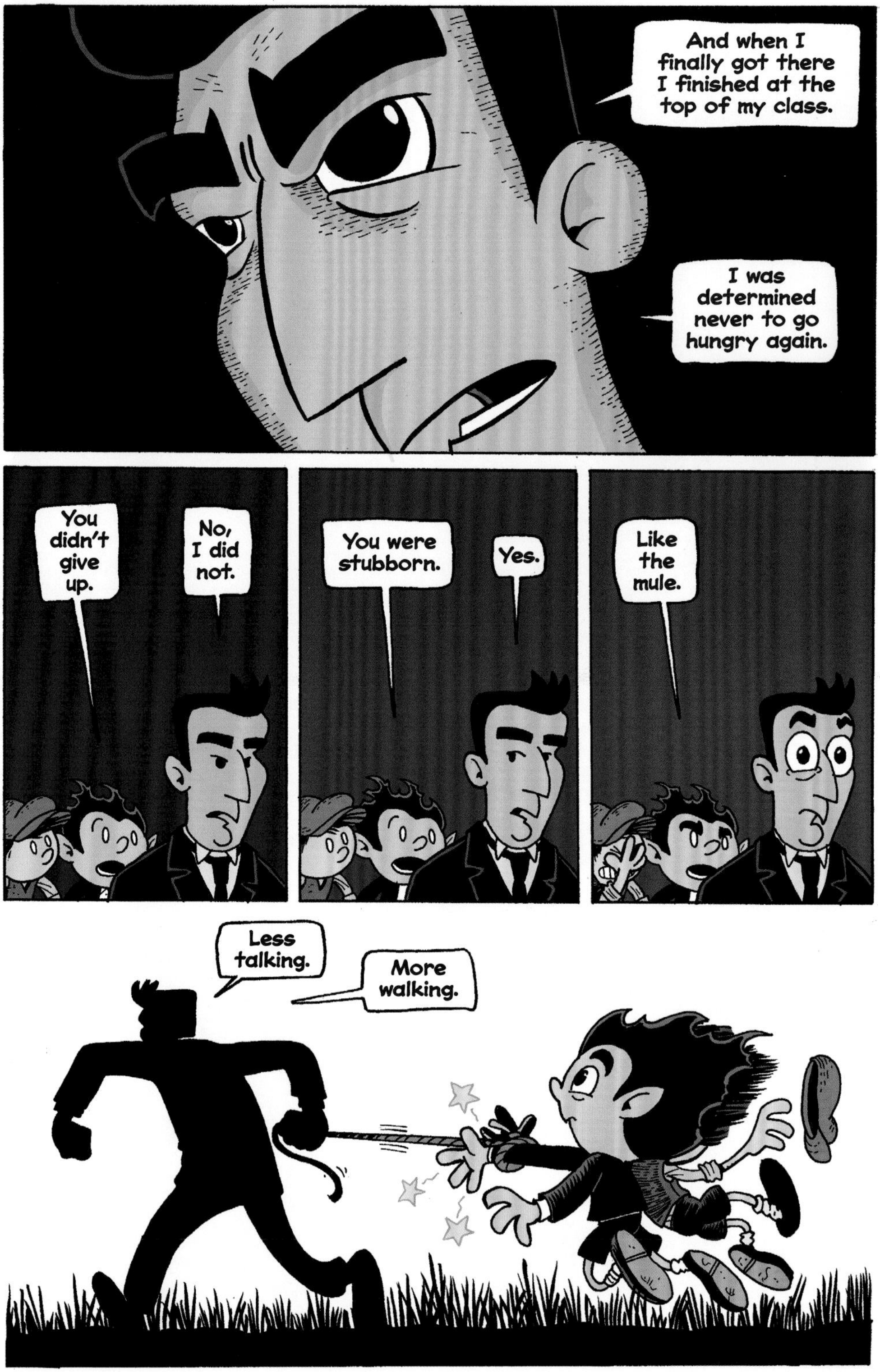

And when I finally got there I finished at the top of my class.
I was determined never to go hungry again.
You didn't give up.
No, I did not.
You were stubborn.
Yes.
Like the mule.
Less talking.
More walking.

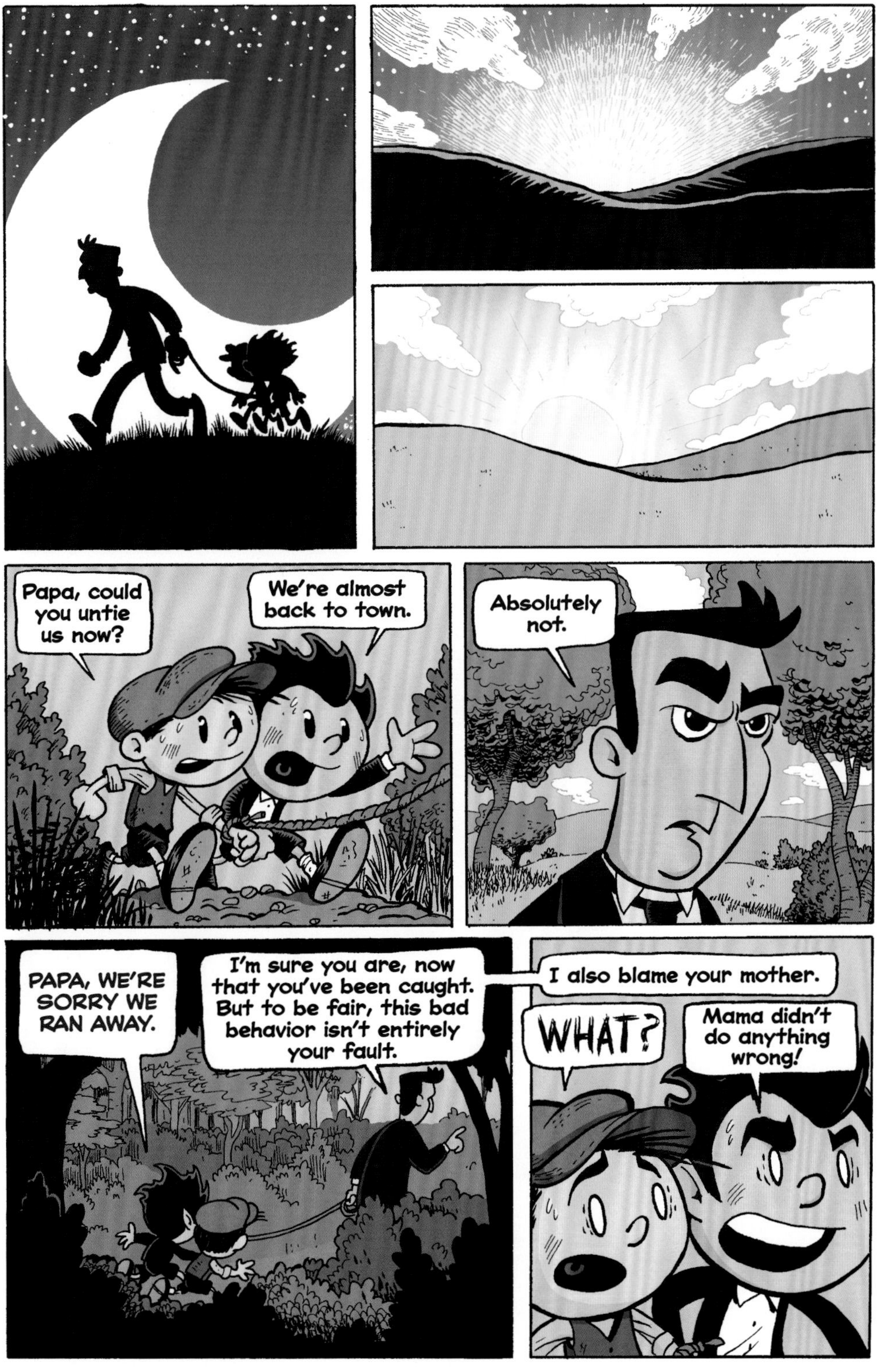
Papa, could you untie us now?
We're almost back to town.
Absolutely not.
PAPA, WE'RE SORRY WE RAN AWAY.
I'm sure you are, now that you've been caught. But to be fair, this bad behavior isn't entirely your fault.
I also blame your mother.
WHAT?
Mama didn't do anything wrong!

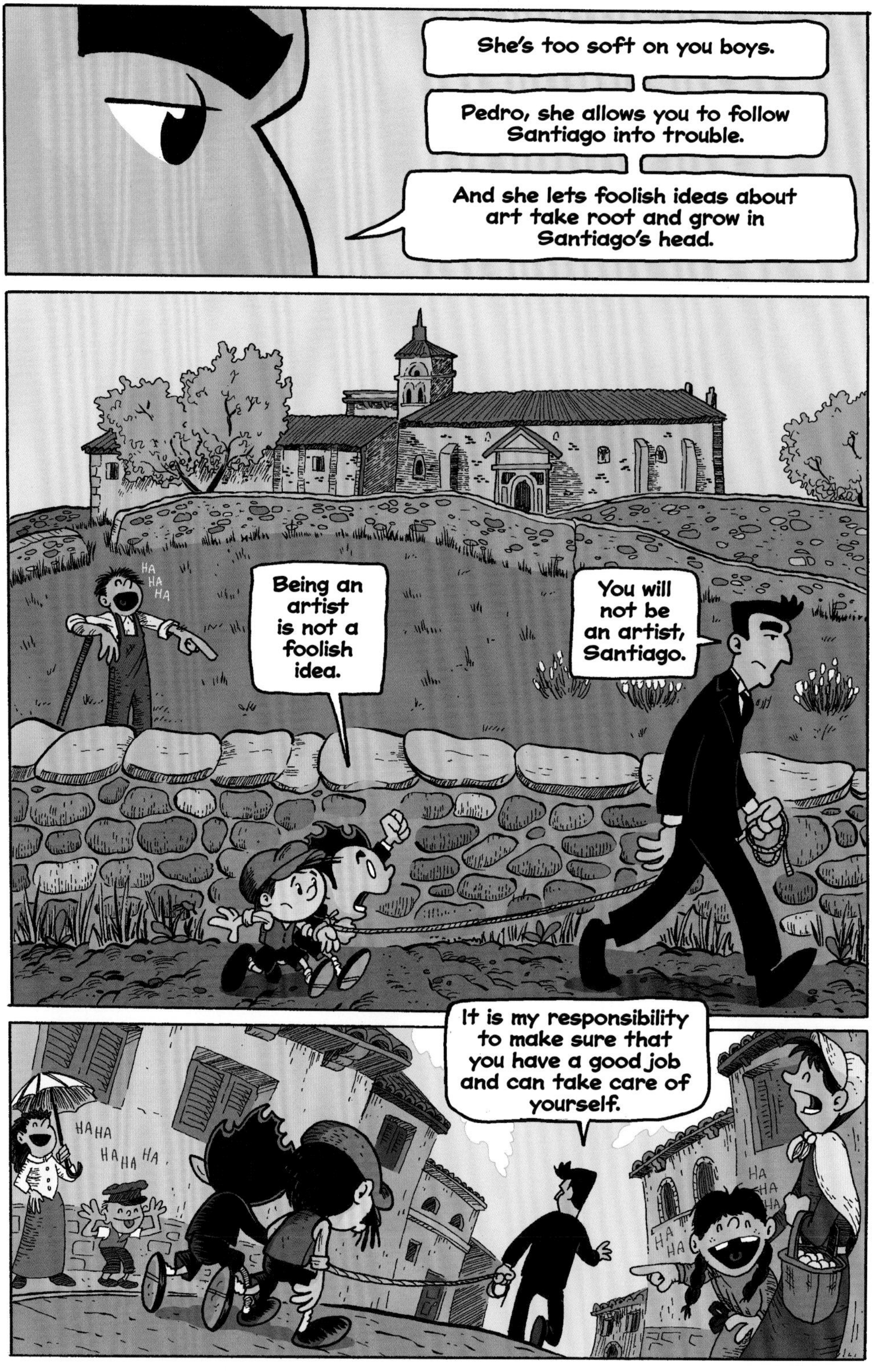
She's too soft on you boys.
Pedro, she allows you to follow Santiago into trouble.
And she lets foolish ideas about art take root and grow in Santiago's head.
HA HA HA
Being an artist is not a foolish idea.
You will not be an artist, Santiago.
HAHA HAHA HA
It is my responsibility to make sure that you have a good job and can take care of yourself.
HA HA HA
HA HA

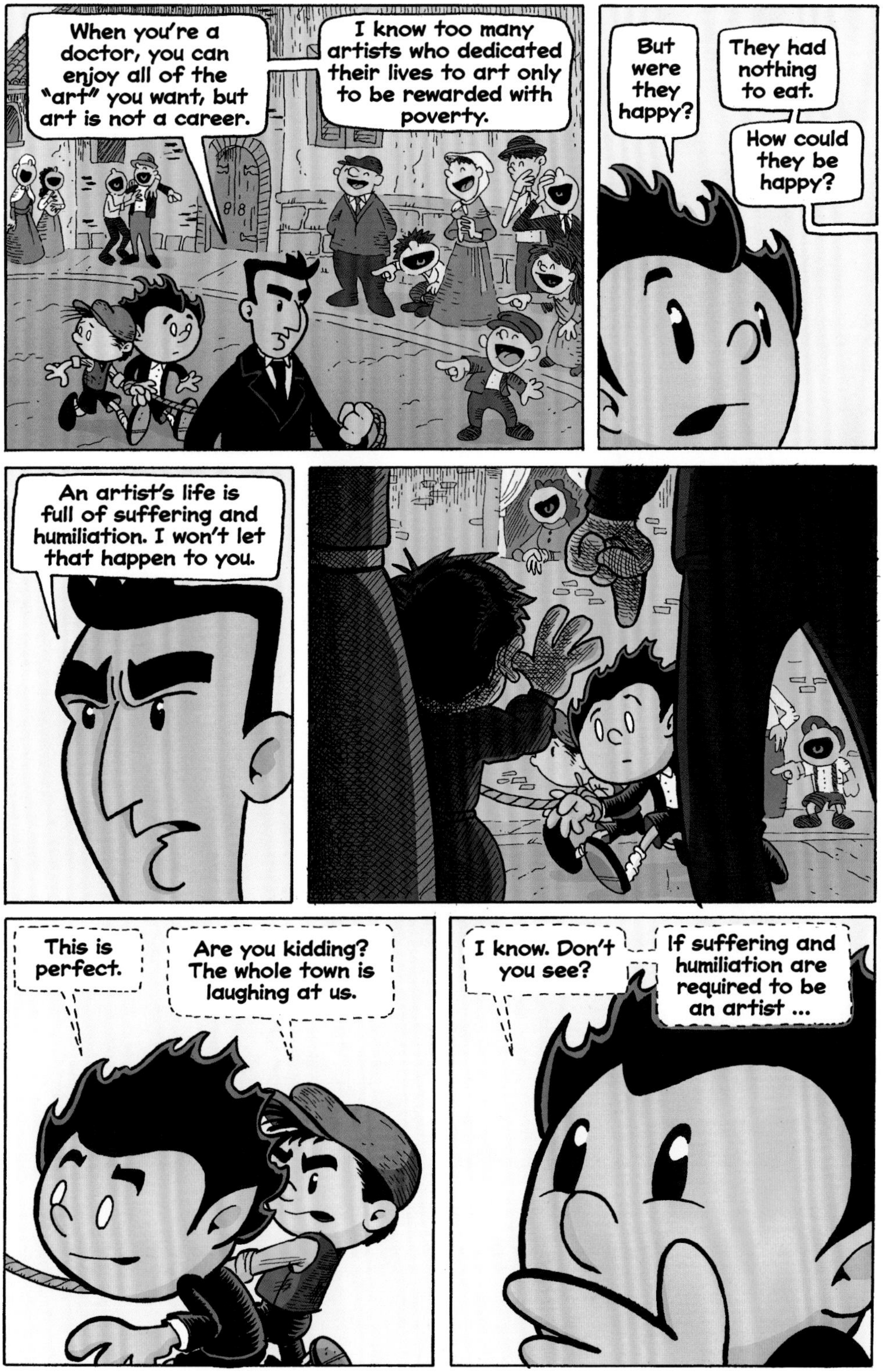
When you're a doctor, you can enjoy all of the "art" you want, but art is not a career.
I know too many artists who dedicated their lives to art only to be rewarded with poverty.
But were they happy?
They had nothing to eat.
How could they be happy?
An artist's life is full of suffering and humiliation. I won't let that happen to you.
This is perfect.
Are you kidding? The whole town is laughing at us.
I know. Don't you see?
If suffering and humiliation are required to be an artist ...

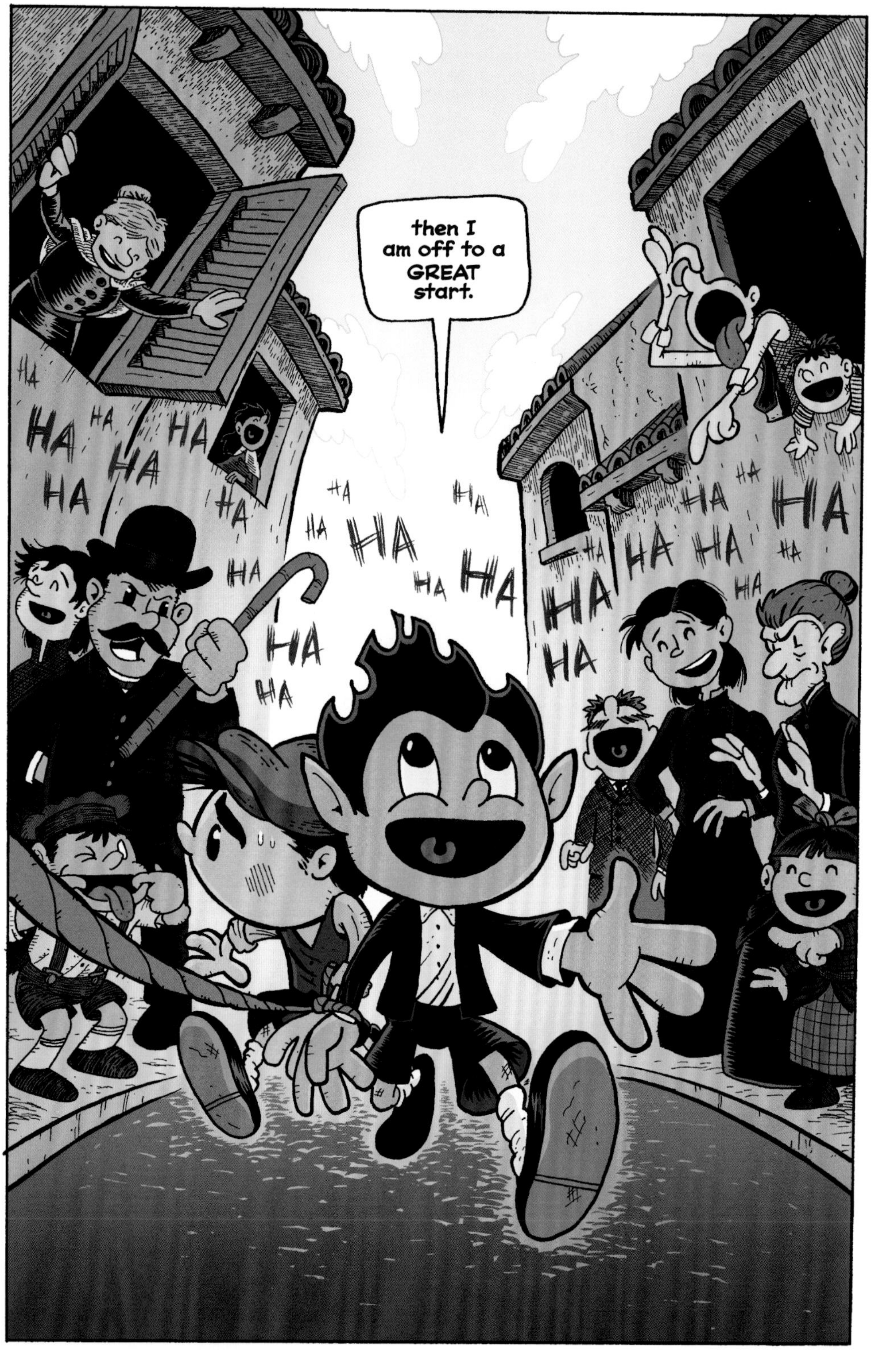
then I am off to a GREAT start.
HA HA HA HA HA HA HA
HA HA HA HA HA HA HA HA HA HA
HA HA HA HA HA HA HA HA HA HA HA HA HA

CHAPTER 4: THE PAINTER

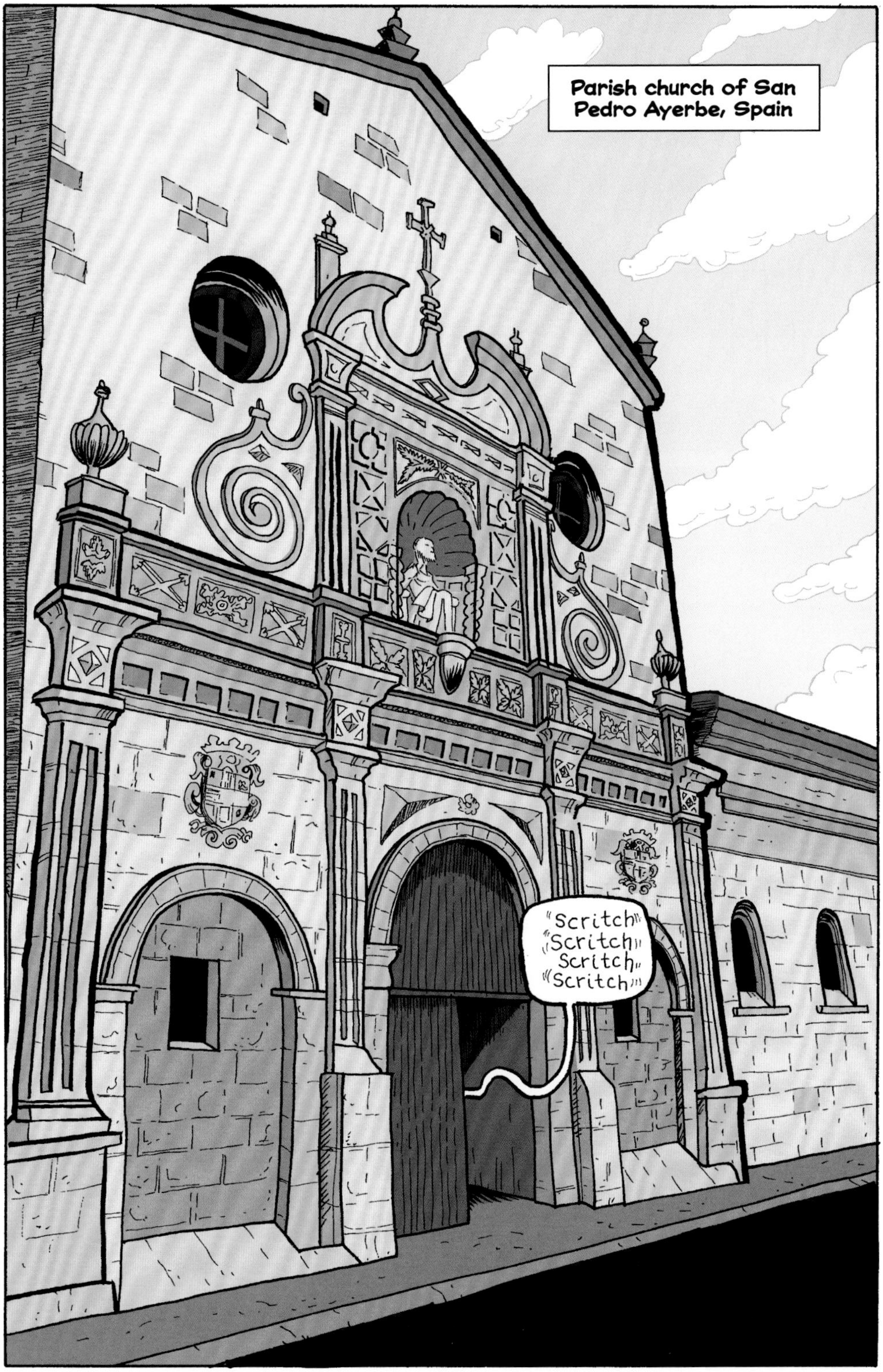
Parish church of San Pedro Ayerbe, Spain
"Scritch" "Scritch" "Scritch" "Scritch"

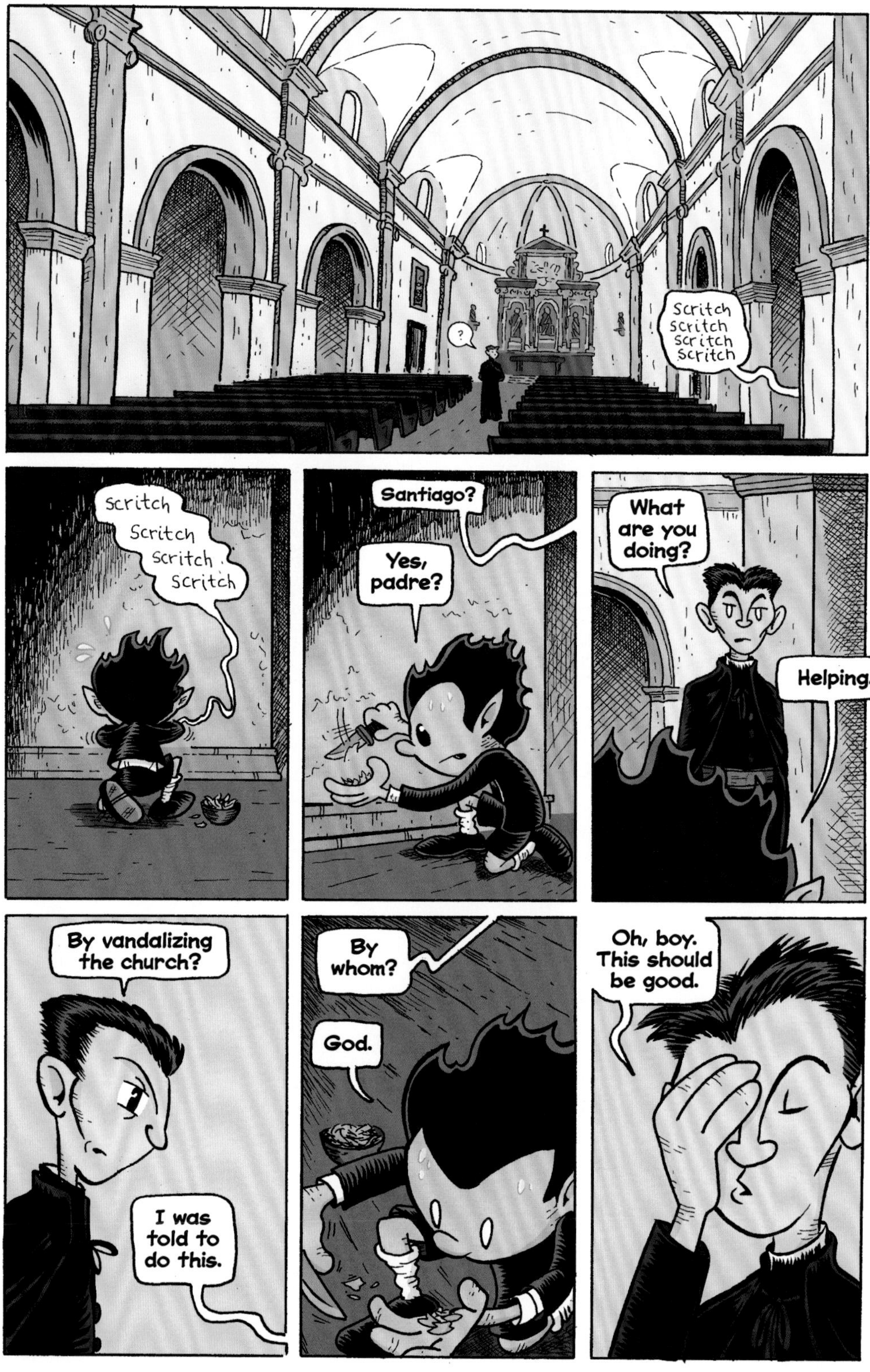
?
Scritch scritch scritch scritch
scritch scritch scritch scritch
Santiago?
Yes, padre?
What are you doing?
Helping.
By vandalizing the church?
I was told to do this.
By whom?
God.
Oh, boy. This should be good.

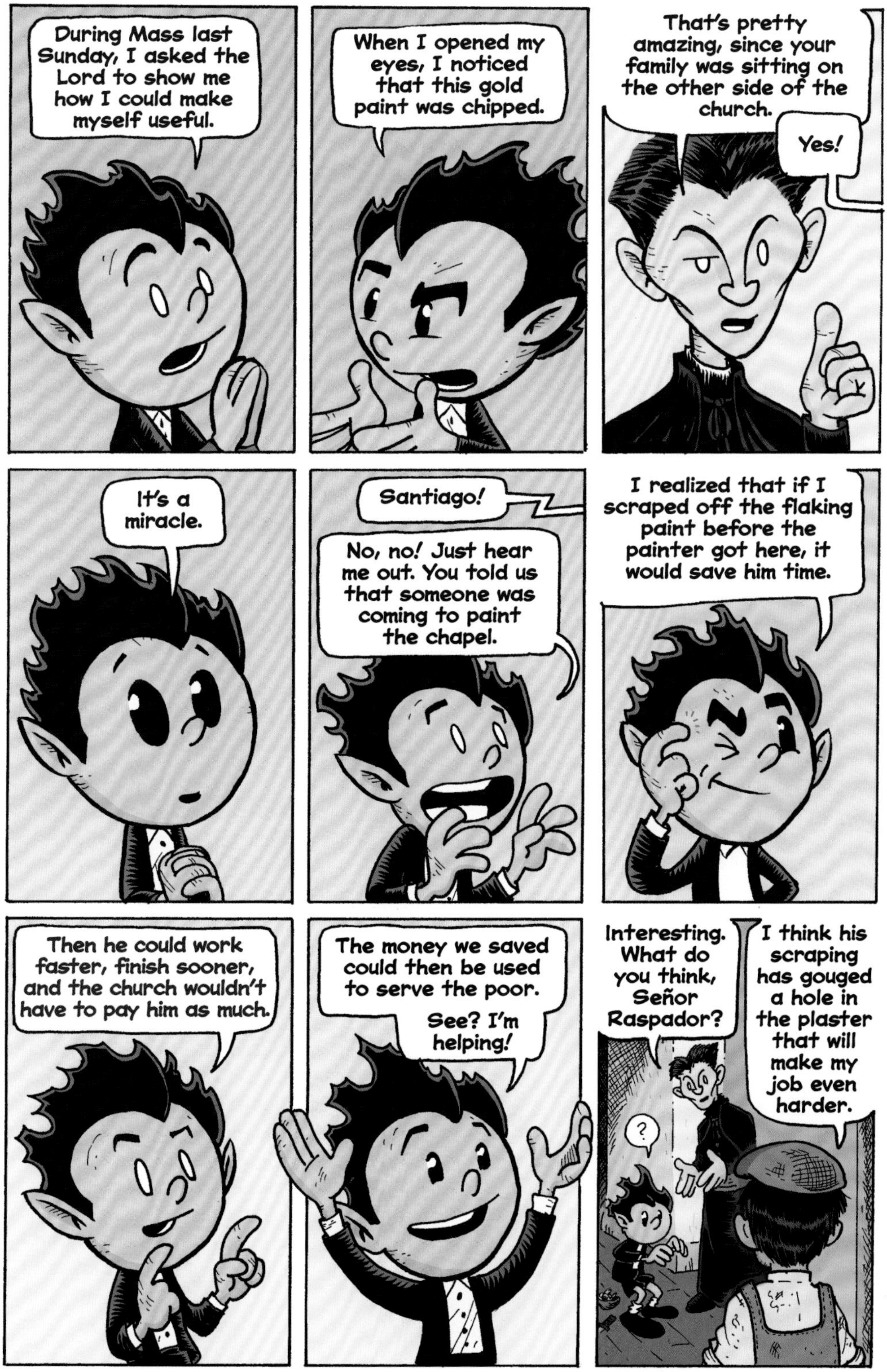
During Mass last Sunday, I asked the Lord to show me how I could make myself useful.
When I opened my eyes, I noticed that this gold paint was chipped.
That's pretty amazing, since your family was sitting on the other side of the church.
Yes!
It's a miracle.
Santiago!
No, no! Just hear me out. You told us that someone was coming to paint the chapel.
I realized that if I scraped off the flaking paint before the painter got here, it would save him time.
Then he could work faster, finish sooner, and the church wouldn't have to pay him as much.
The money we saved could then be used to serve the poor.
See? I'm helping!
Interesting. What do you think, Señor Raspador?
I think his scraping has gouged a hole in the plaster that will make my job even harder.
?

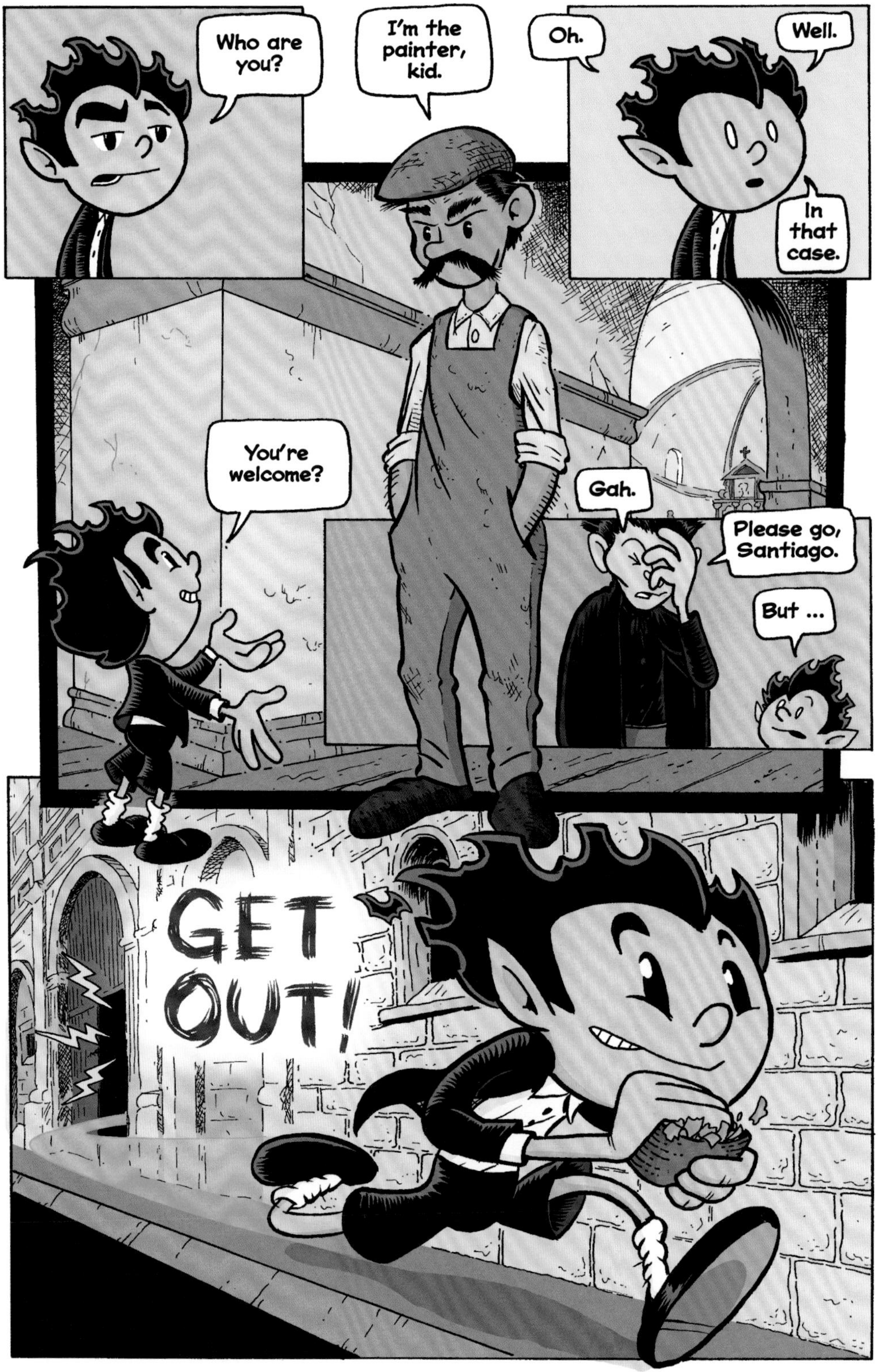
Who are you?
I'm the painter, kid.
Oh.
Well.
In that case.
You're welcome?
Gah.
Please go, Santiago.
But ...
GET OUT!

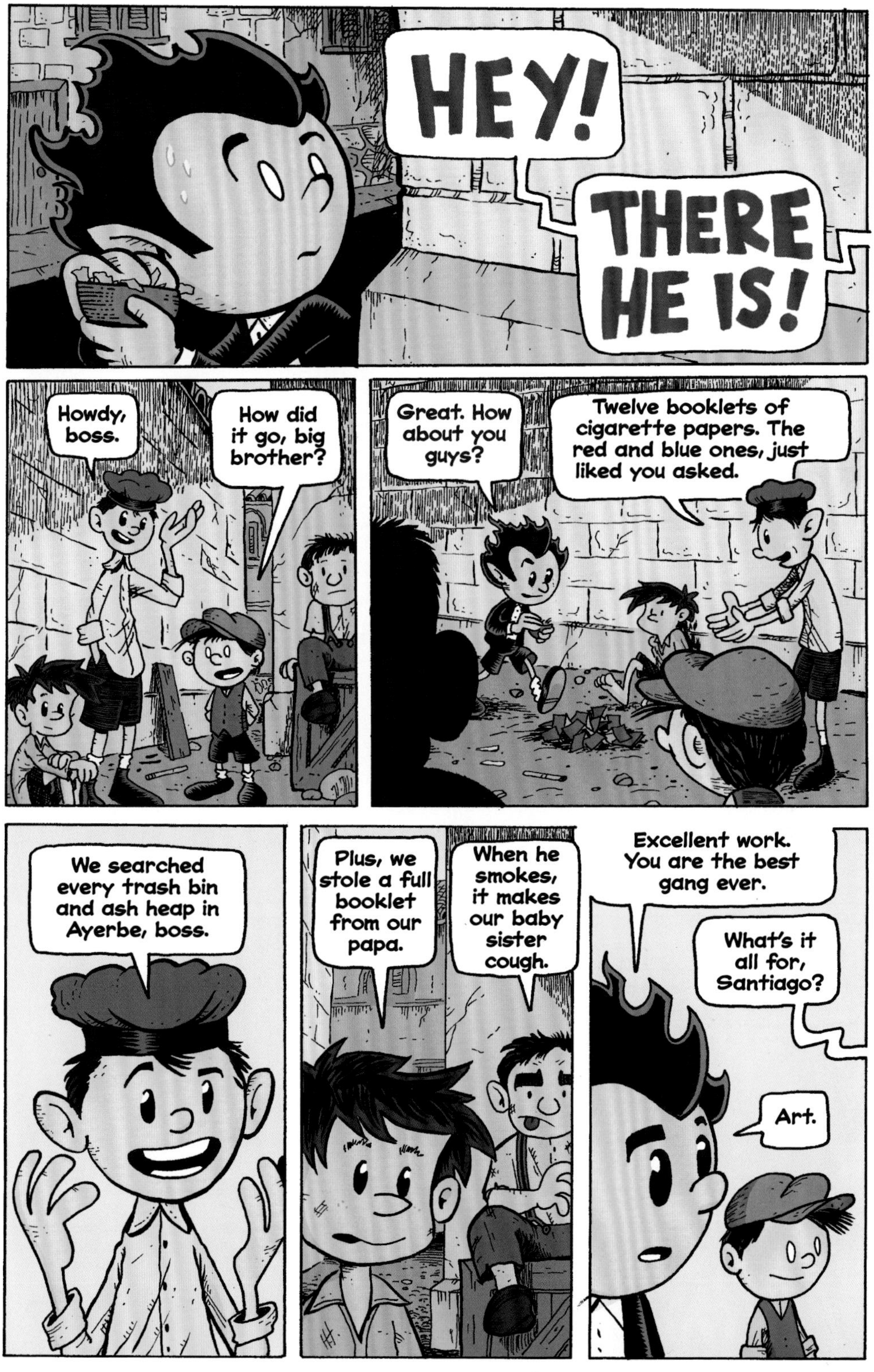
HEY!
THERE HE IS!
Howdy, boss.
How did it go, big brother?
Great. How about you guys?
Twelve booklets of cigarette papers. The red and blue ones, just liked you asked.
We searched every trash bin and ash heap in Ayerbe, boss.
Plus, we stole a full booklet from our papa.
When he smokes, it makes our baby sister cough.
Excellent work. You are the best gang ever.
What's it all for, Santiago?
Art.

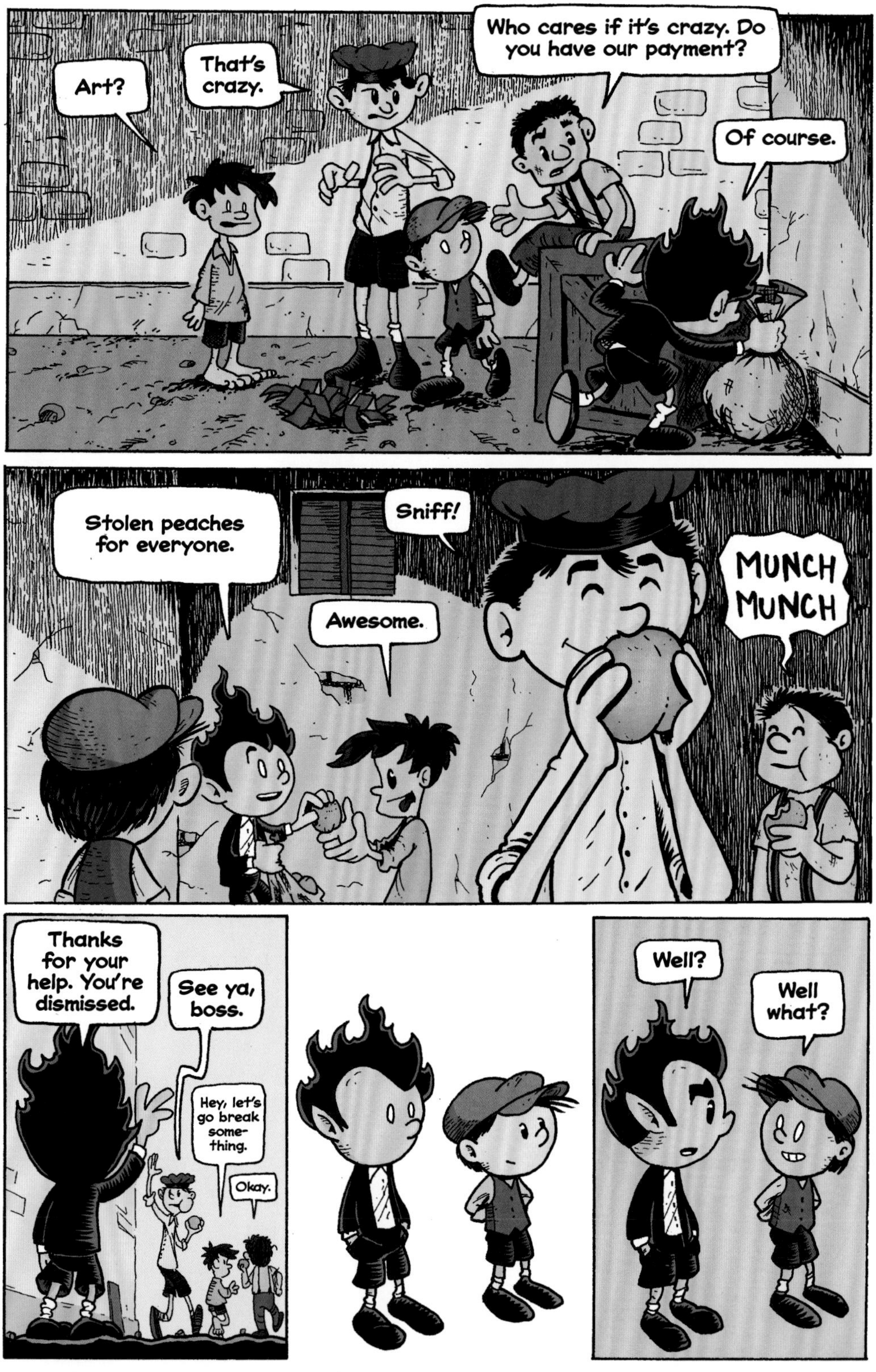
Art?
That's crazy.
Who cares if it's crazy. Do you have our payment?
Of course.
Stolen peaches for everyone.
Sniff!
Awesome.
MUNCH MUNCH
Thanks for your help. You're dismissed.
See ya, boss.
Hey, let's go break some-thing.
Okay.
Well?
Well what?

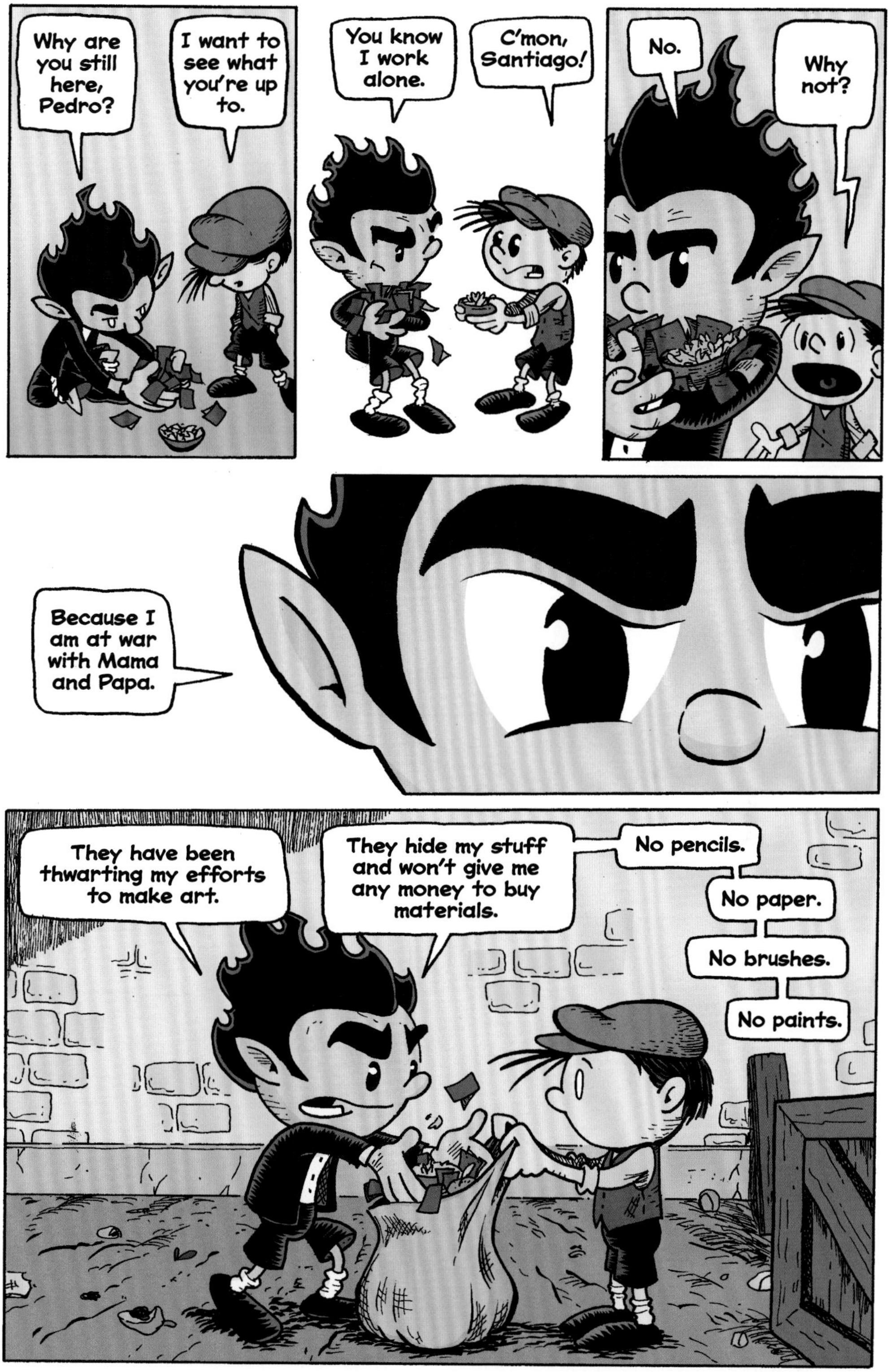
Why are you still here, Pedro?
I want to see what you're up to.
You know I work alone.
C'mon, Santiago!
No.
Why not?
Because I am at war with Mama and Papa.
They have been thwarting my efforts to make art.
They hide my stuff and won't give me any money to buy materials.
No pencils.
No paper.
No brushes.
No paints.

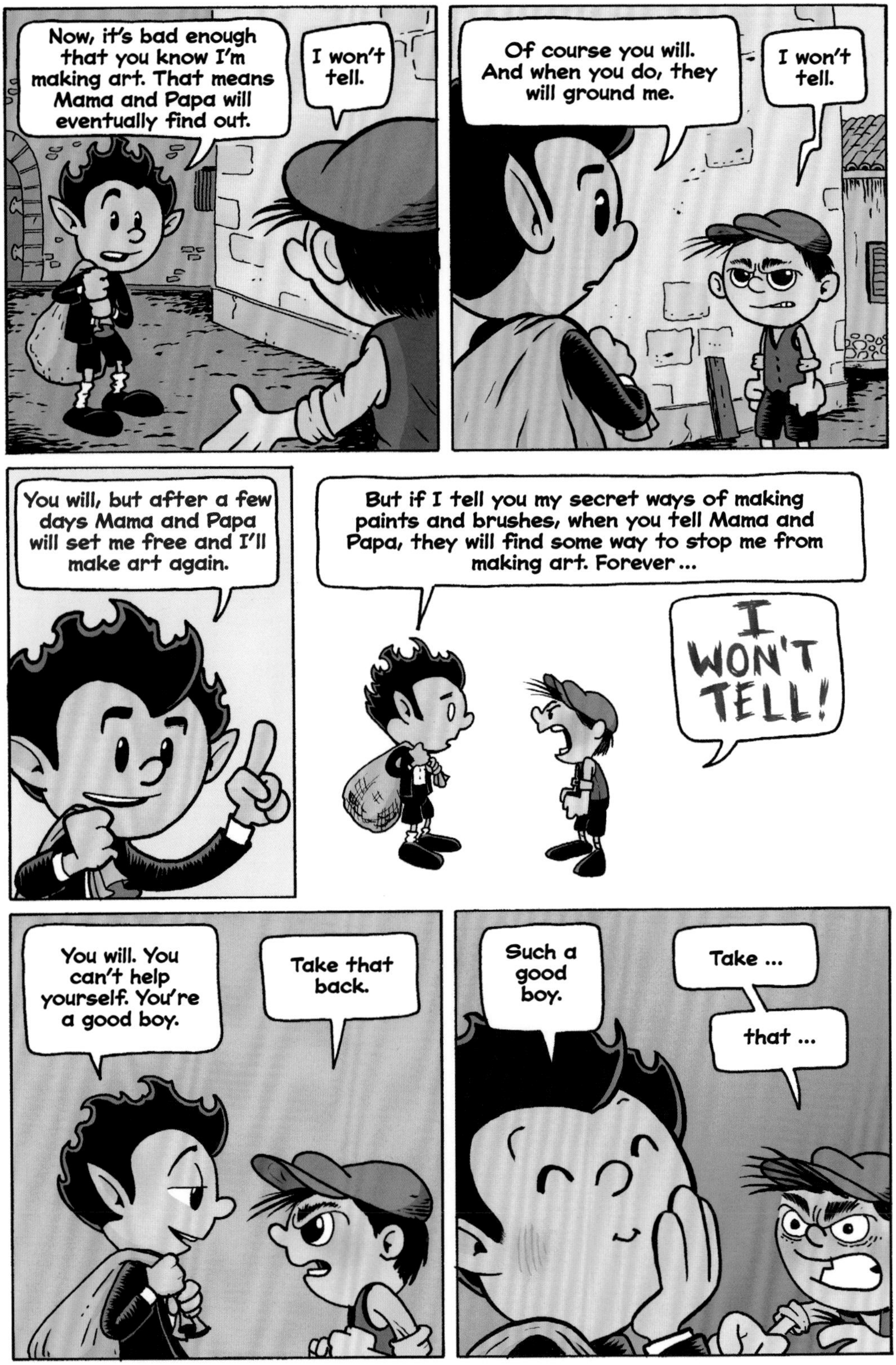
Now, it's bad enough that you know I'm making art. That means Mama and Papa will eventually find out.
I won't tell.
Of course you will. And when you do, they will ground me.
I won't tell.
You will, but after a few days Mama and Papa will set me free and I'll make art again.
But if I tell you my secret ways of making paints and brushes, when you tell Mama and Papa, they will find some way to stop me from making art. Forever …
I WON'T TELL!
You will. You can't help yourself. You're a good boy.
Take that back.
Such a good boy.
Take …
that …

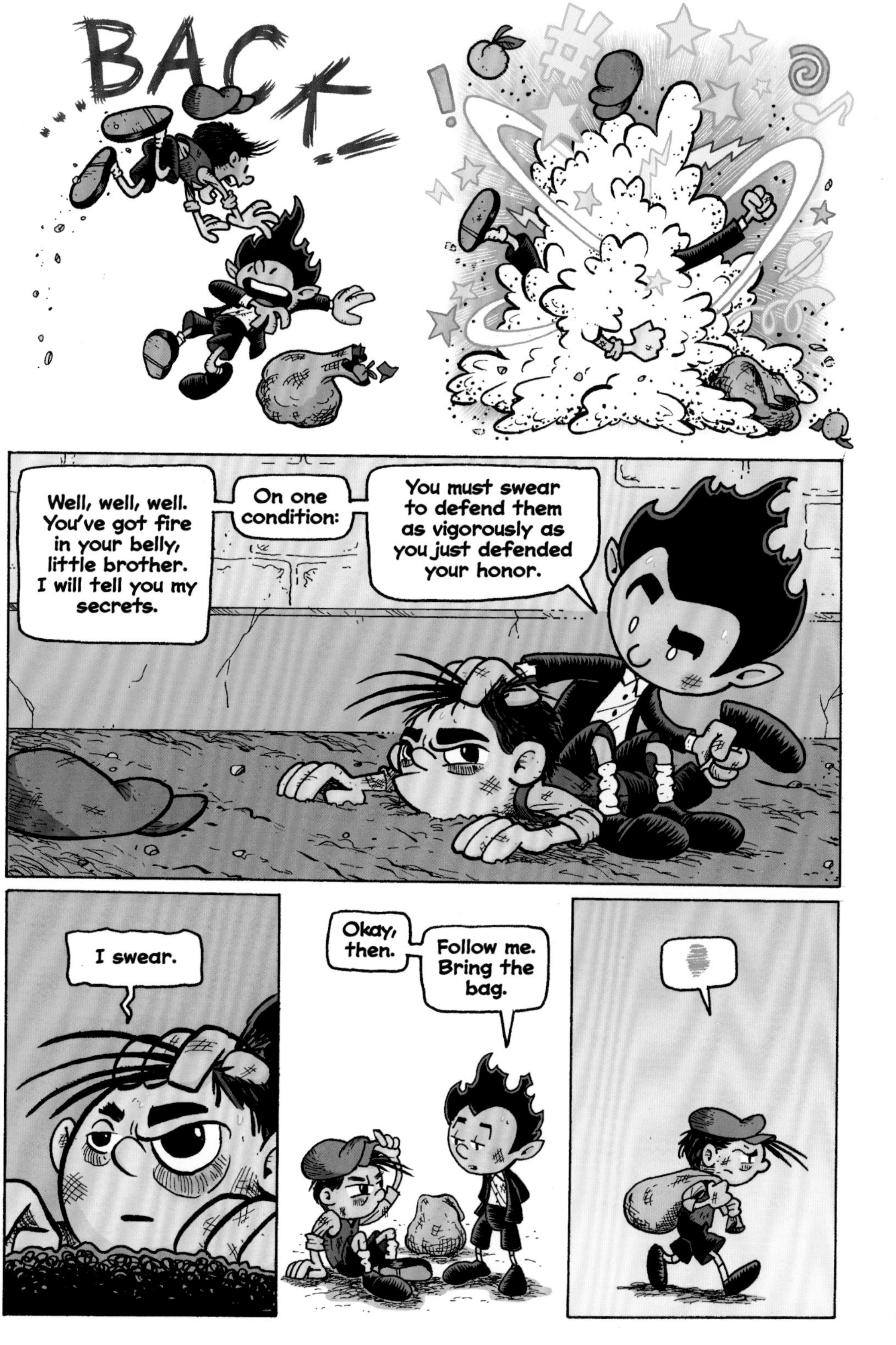
BACK
Well, well, well. You've got fire in your belly, little brother. I will tell you my secrets.
On one condition:
You must swear to defend them as vigorously as you just defended your honor.
I swear.
Okay, then.
Follow me. Bring the bag.

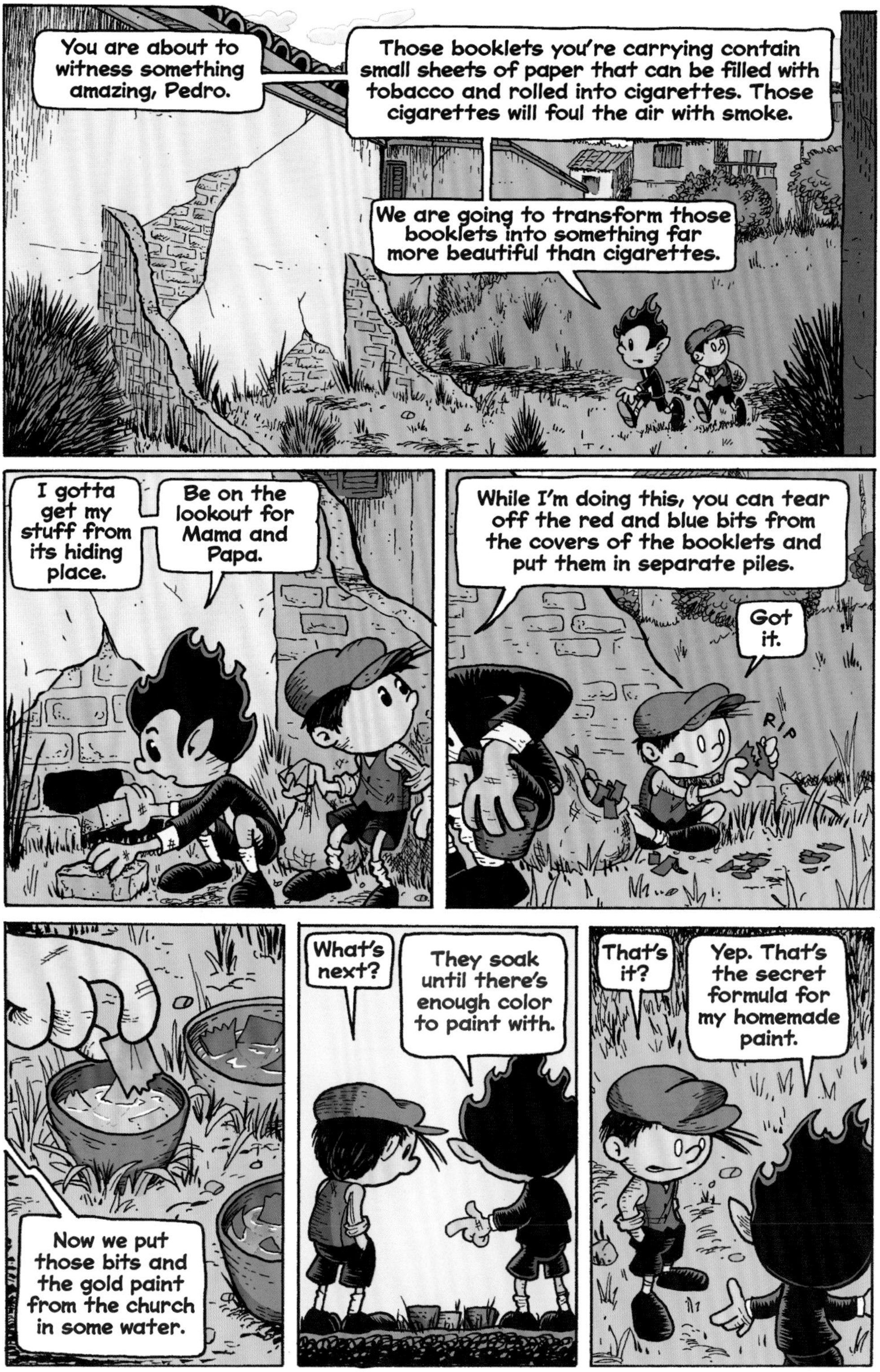
You are about to witness something amazing, Pedro.
Those booklets you're carrying contain small sheets of paper that can be filled with tobacco and rolled into cigarettes. Those cigarettes will foul the air with smoke.
We are going to transform those booklets into something far more beautiful than cigarettes.
I gotta get my stuff from its hiding place.
Be on the lookout for Mama and Papa.
While I'm doing this, you can tear off the red and blue bits from the covers of the booklets and put them in separate piles.
Got it.
RIP
Now we put those bits and the gold paint from the church in some water.
What's next?
They soak until there's enough color to paint with.
That's it?
Yep. That's the secret formula for my homemade paint.

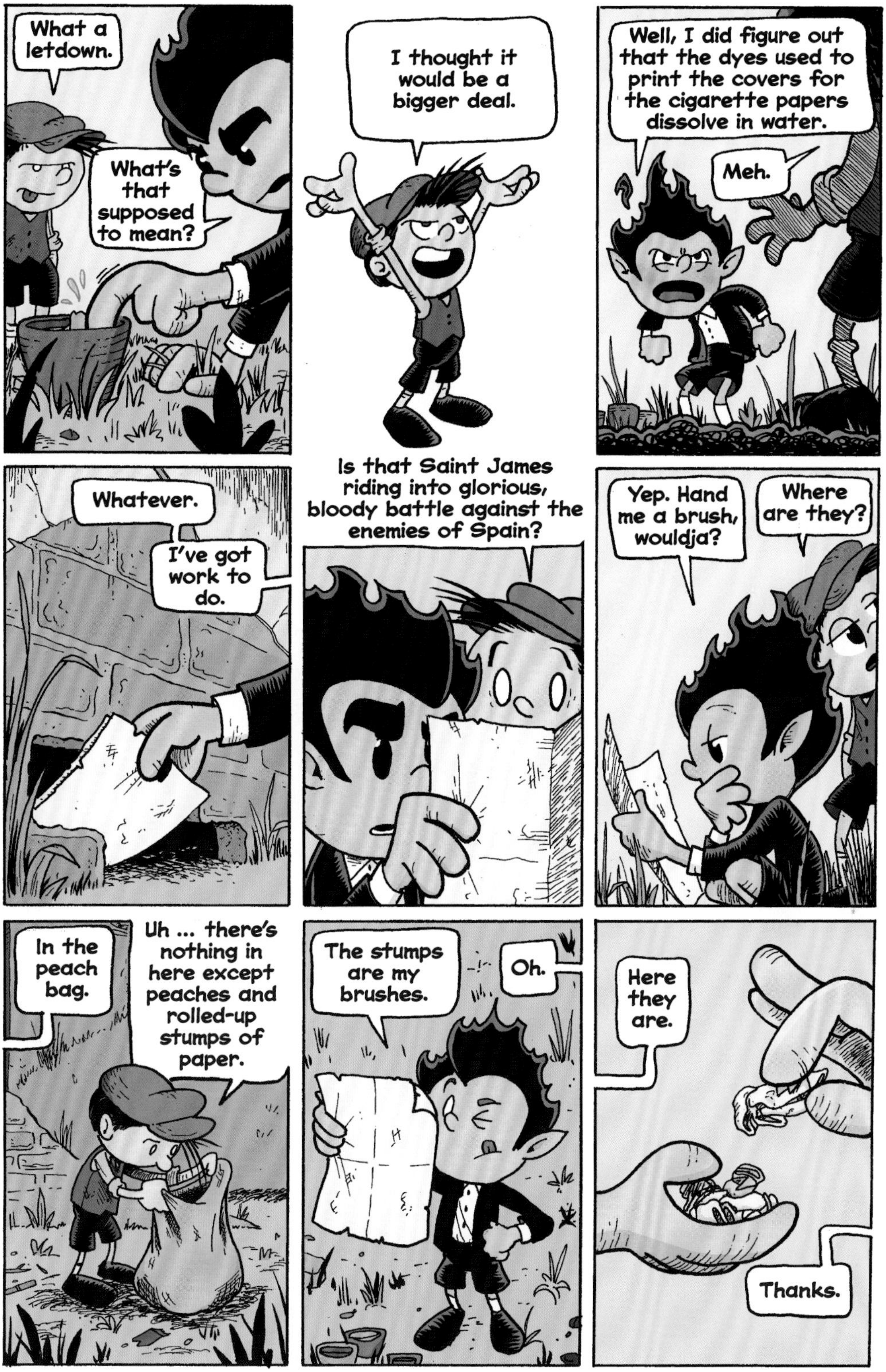
What a letdown.
What's that supposed to mean?
I thought it would be a bigger deal.
Well, I did figure out that the dyes used to print the covers for the cigarette papers dissolve in water.
Meh.
Whatever.
I've got work to do.
Is that Saint James riding into glorious, bloody battle against the enemies of Spain?
Yep. Hand me a brush, wouldja?
Where are they?
In the peach bag.
Uh ... there's nothing in here except peaches and rolled-up stumps of paper.
The stumps are my brushes.
Oh.
Here they are.
Thanks.

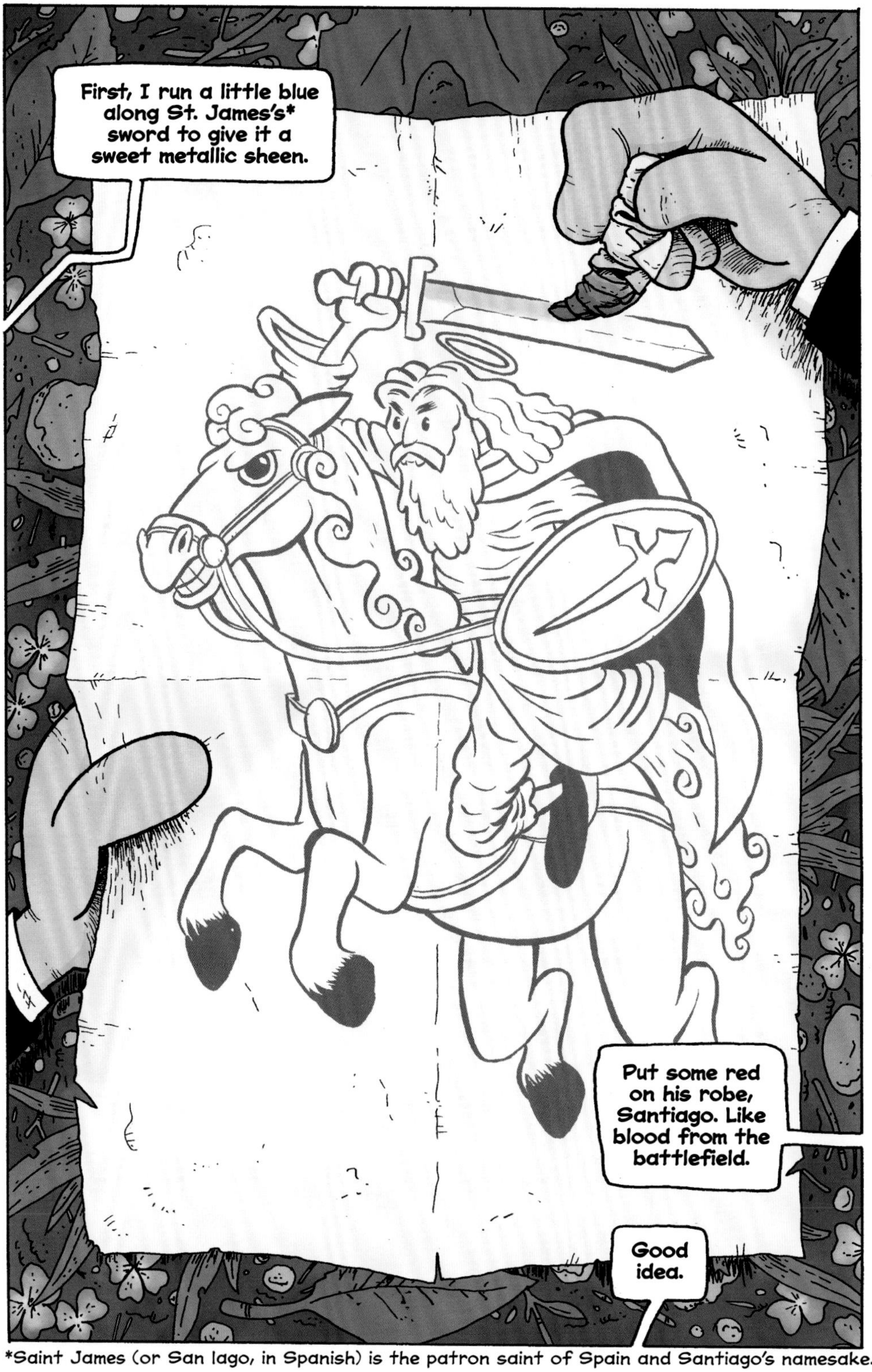
First, I run a little blue along St. James's* sword to give it a sweet metallic sheen.
Put some red on his robe, Santiago. Like blood from the battlefield.
Good idea.

*Saint James (or San Iago, in Spanish) is the patron saint of Spain and Santiago's namesake.

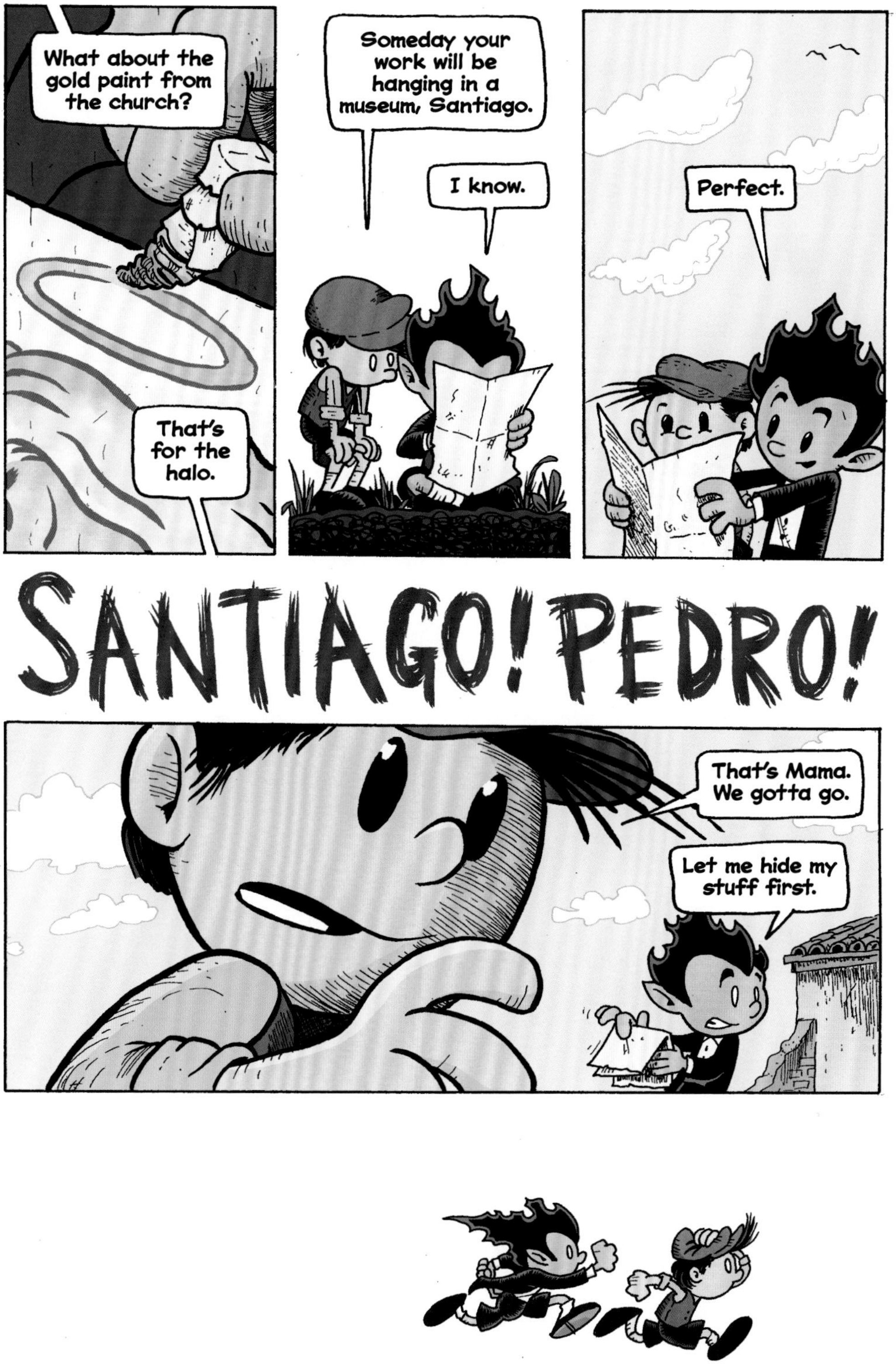
What about the gold paint from the church?
That's for the halo.
Someday your work will be hanging in a museum, Santiago.
I know.
Perfect.
SANTIAGO! PEDRO!
That's Mama. We gotta go.
Let me hide my stuff first.

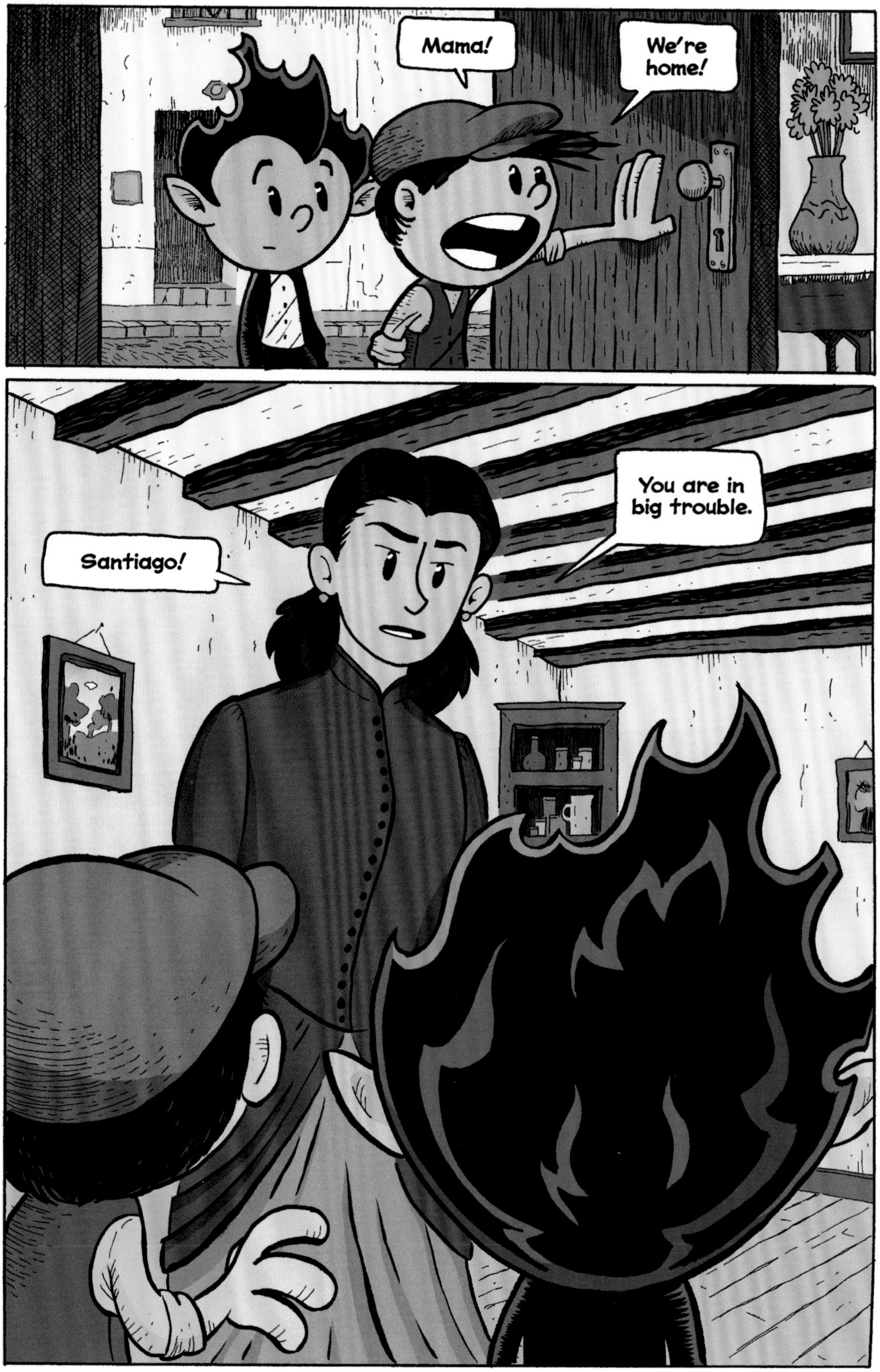
Mama!
We're home!
Santiago!
You are in big trouble.

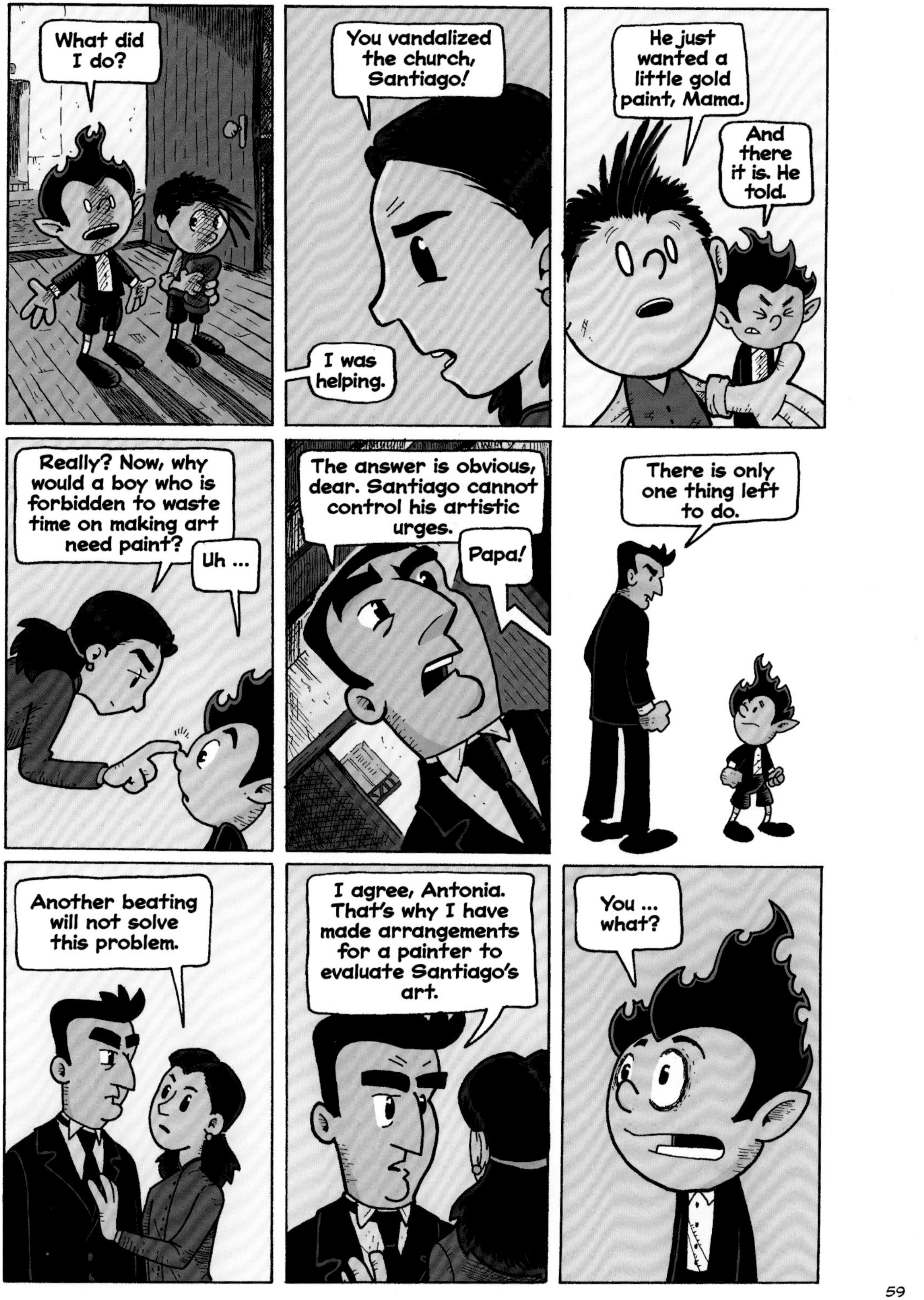
What did I do?
You vandalized the church, Santiago!
I was helping.
He just wanted a little gold paint, Mama.
And there it is. He told.
Really? Now, why would a boy who is forbidden to waste time on making art need paint?
Uh ...
The answer is obvious, dear. Santiago cannot control his artistic urges.
Papa!
There is only one thing left to do.
Another beating will not solve this problem.
I agree, Antonia. That's why I have made arrangements for a painter to evaluate Santiago's art.
You ... what?

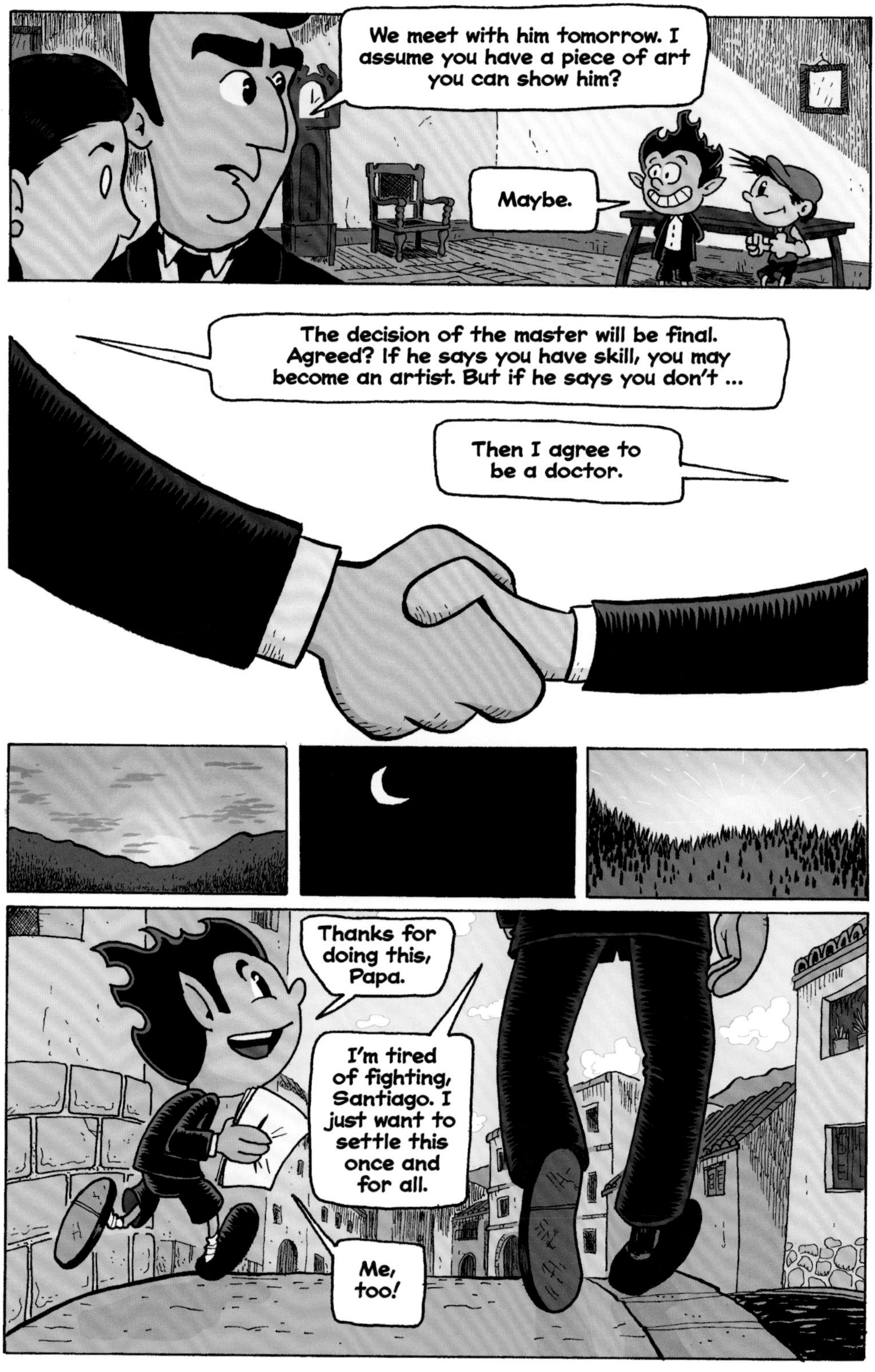
We meet with him tomorrow. I assume you have a piece of art you can show him?
Maybe.
The decision of the master will be final. Agreed? If he says you have skill, you may become an artist. But if he says you don't ...
Then I agree to be a doctor.
Thanks for doing this, Papa.
I'm tired of fighting, Santiago. I just want to settle this once and for all.
Me, too!

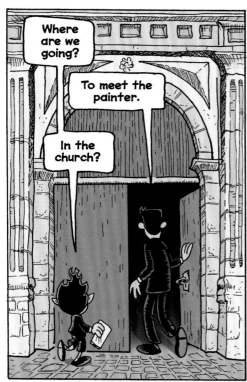

Where are we going?

To meet the painter.

In the church?

Well, well, if it isn't the scraper of walls.

Whoa, wait, Papa. This is your art expert?

Is there a problem, Santiago?

He's a house painter.

Well, even a humble painter of walls could see that you have a feeble grasp of basic anatomy.

Is this supposed to be Saint James?

WHAT A MESS!

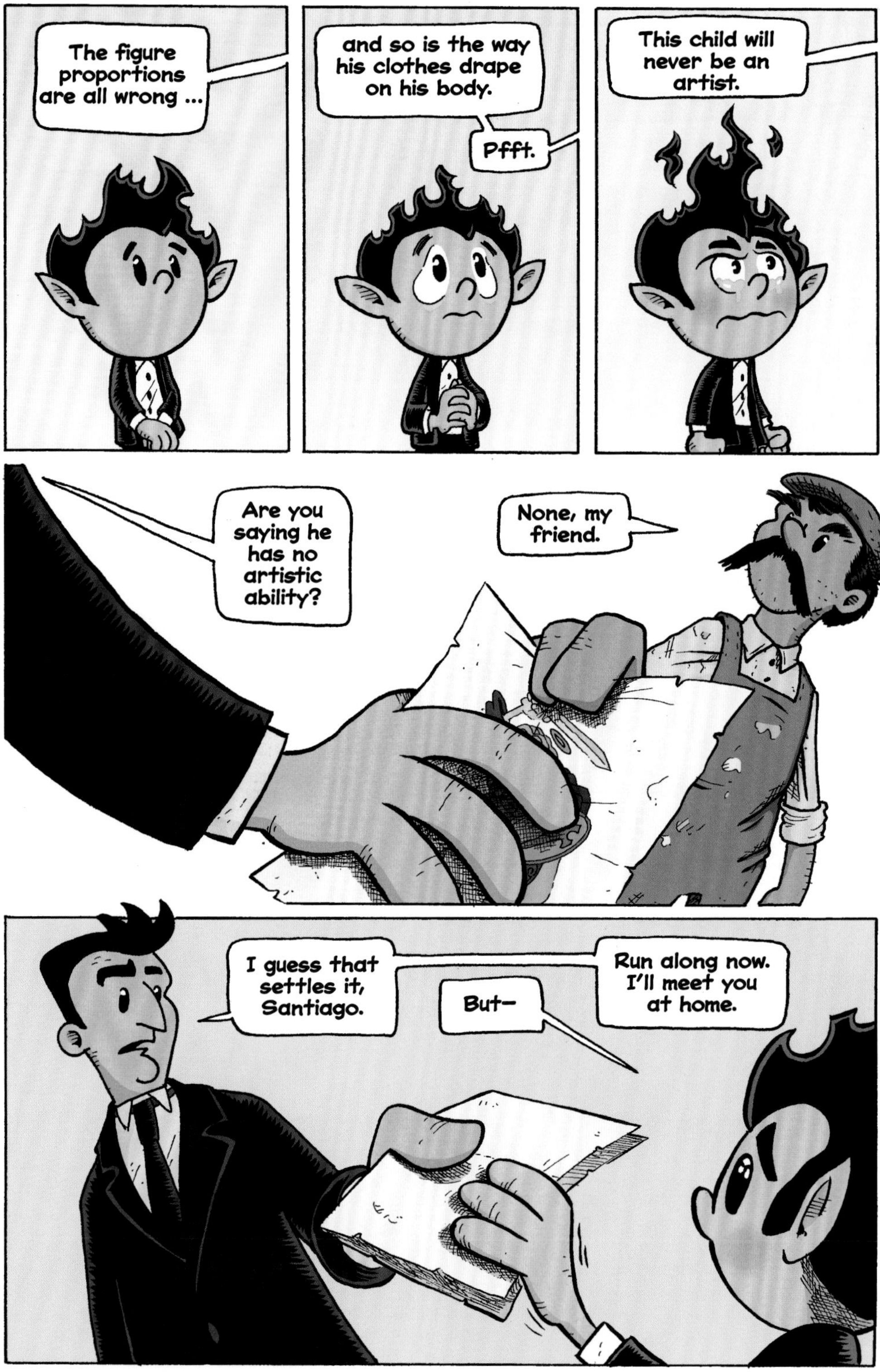
The figure proportions are all wrong ...
and so is the way his clothes drape on his body.
Pfft.
This child will never be an artist.
Are you saying he has no artistic ability?
None, my friend.
I guess that settles it, Santiago.
But—
Run along now. I'll meet you at home.

How was that?

Did I say it right?

Yes.

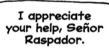

I appreciate your help, Señor Raspador.

It was my pleasure, Don Justo.

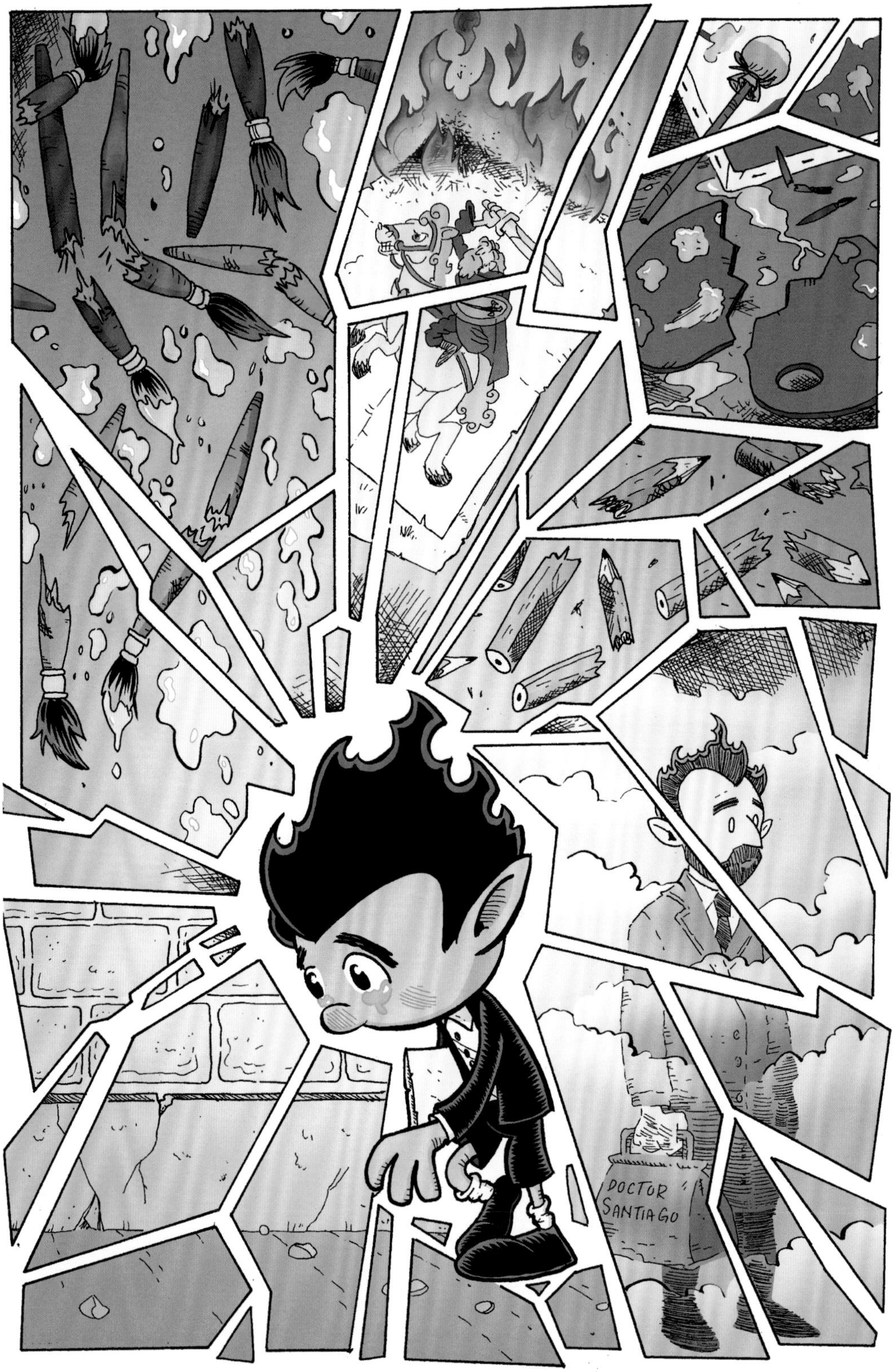
DOCTOR SANTIAGO

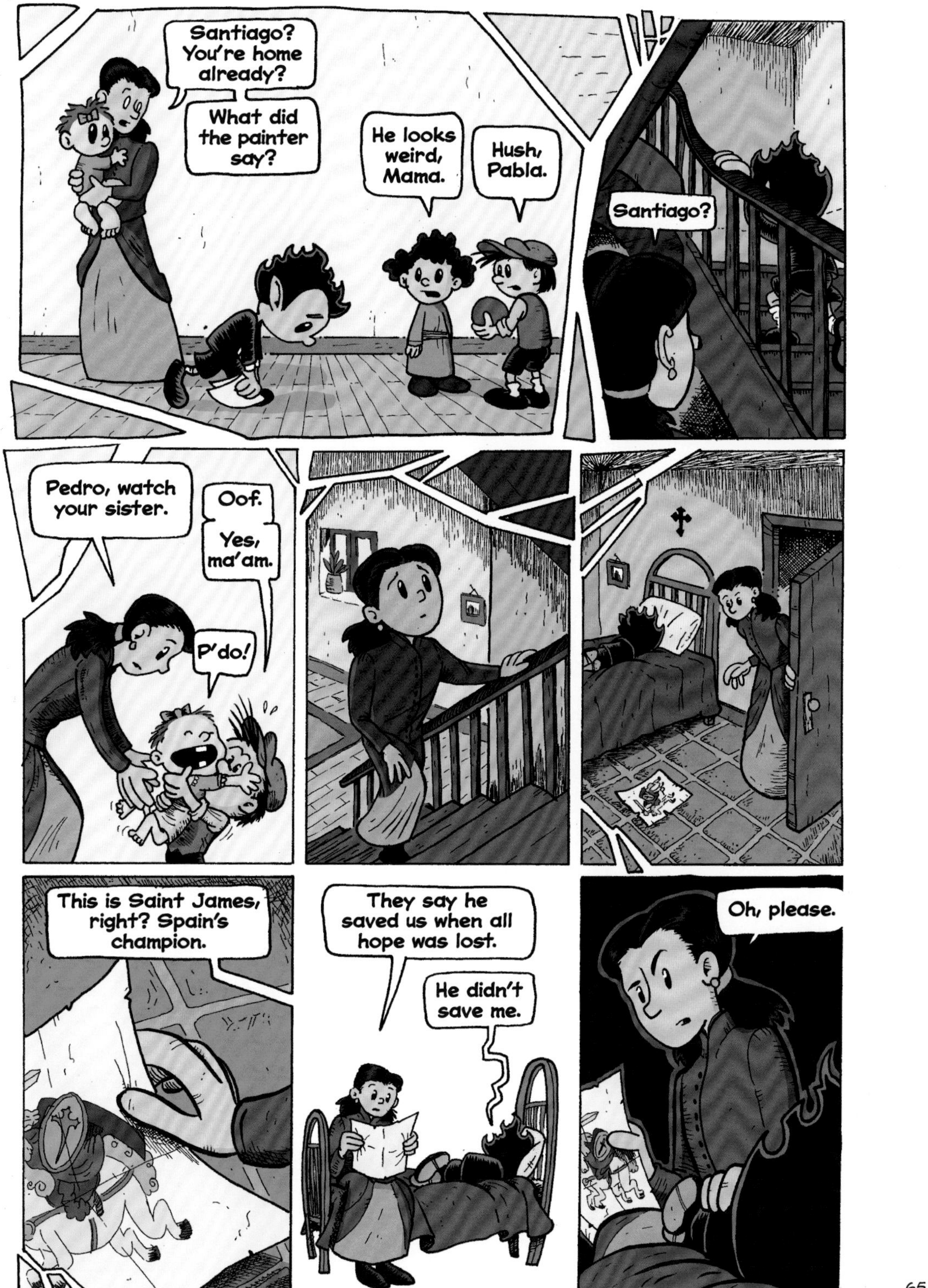

Santiago? You're home already?
What did the painter say?
He looks weird, Mama.
Hush, Pabla.
Santiago?
Pedro, watch your sister.
Oof.
Yes, ma'am.
P'do!
This is Saint James, right? Spain's champion.
They say he saved us when all hope was lost.
He didn't save me.
Oh, please.

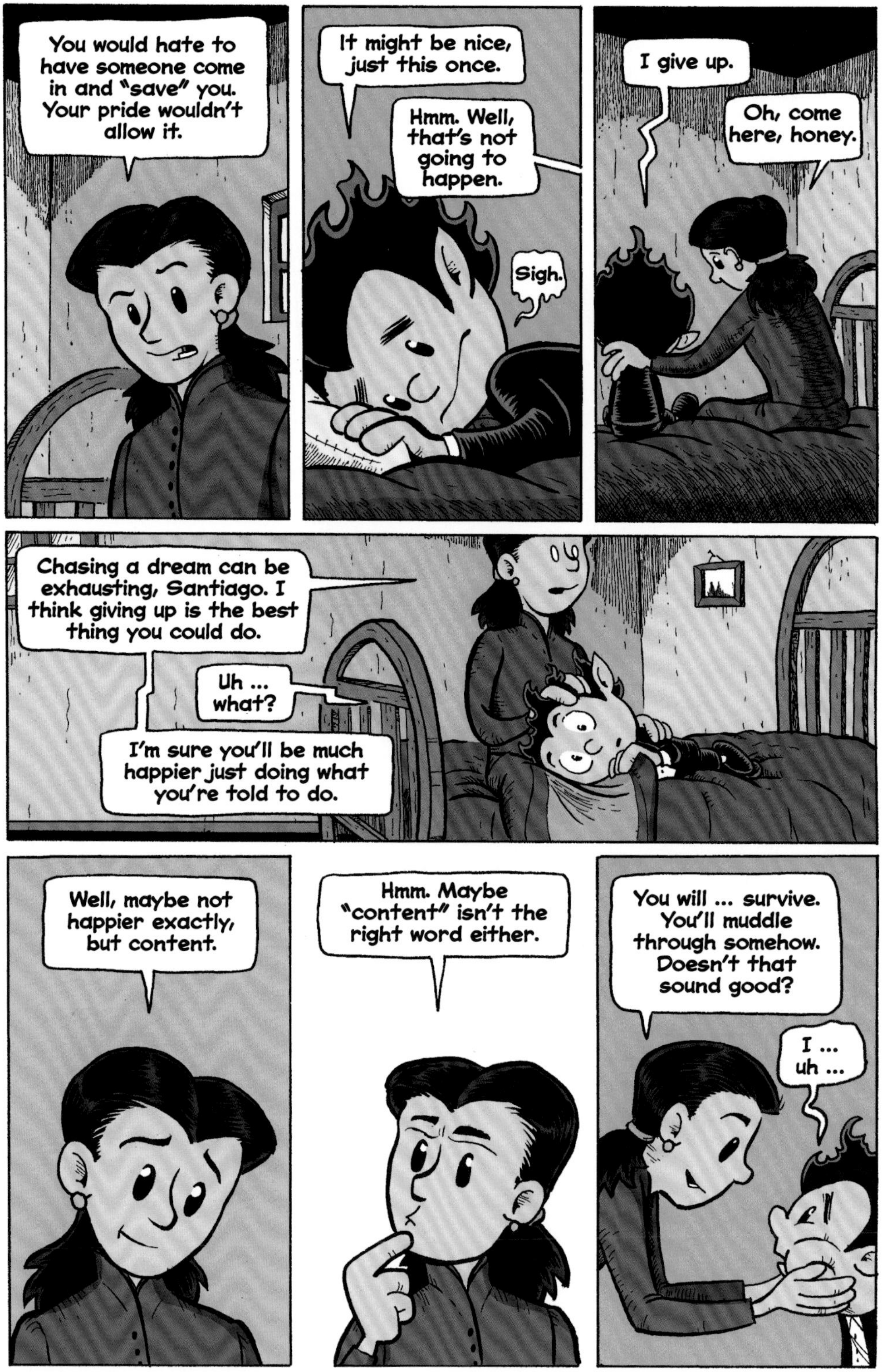

You would hate to have someone come in and "save" you. Your pride wouldn't allow it.
It might be nice, just this once.
Hmm. Well, that's not going to happen.
Sigh.
I give up.
Oh, come here, honey.
Chasing a dream can be exhausting, Santiago. I think giving up is the best thing you could do.
Uh ... what?
I'm sure you'll be much happier just doing what you're told to do.
Well, maybe not happier exactly, but content.
Hmm. Maybe "content" isn't the right word either.
You will ... survive. You'll muddle through somehow. Doesn't that sound good?
I ... uh ...

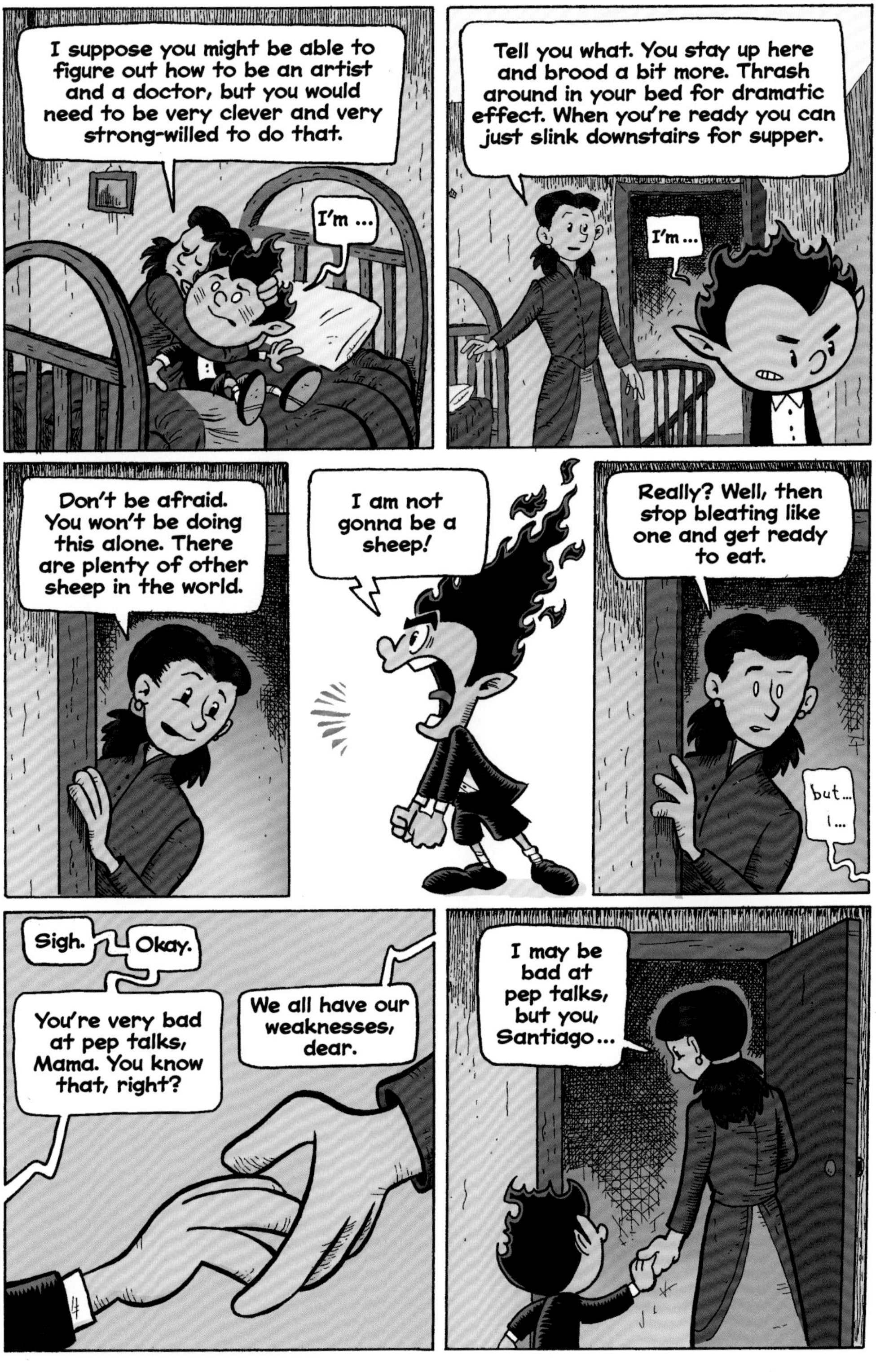
I suppose you might be able to figure out how to be an artist and a doctor, but you would need to be very clever and very strong-willed to do that.
I'm ...
Tell you what. You stay up here and brood a bit more. Thrash around in your bed for dramatic effect. When you're ready you can just slink downstairs for supper.
I'm ...
Don't be afraid. You won't be doing this alone. There are plenty of other sheep in the world.
I am not gonna be a sheep!
Really? Well, then stop bleating like one and get ready to eat.
but... I...
Sigh.
Okay.
You're very bad at pep talks, Mama. You know that, right?
We all have our weaknesses, dear.
I may be bad at pep talks, but you, Santiago...

you are very bad at giving up.

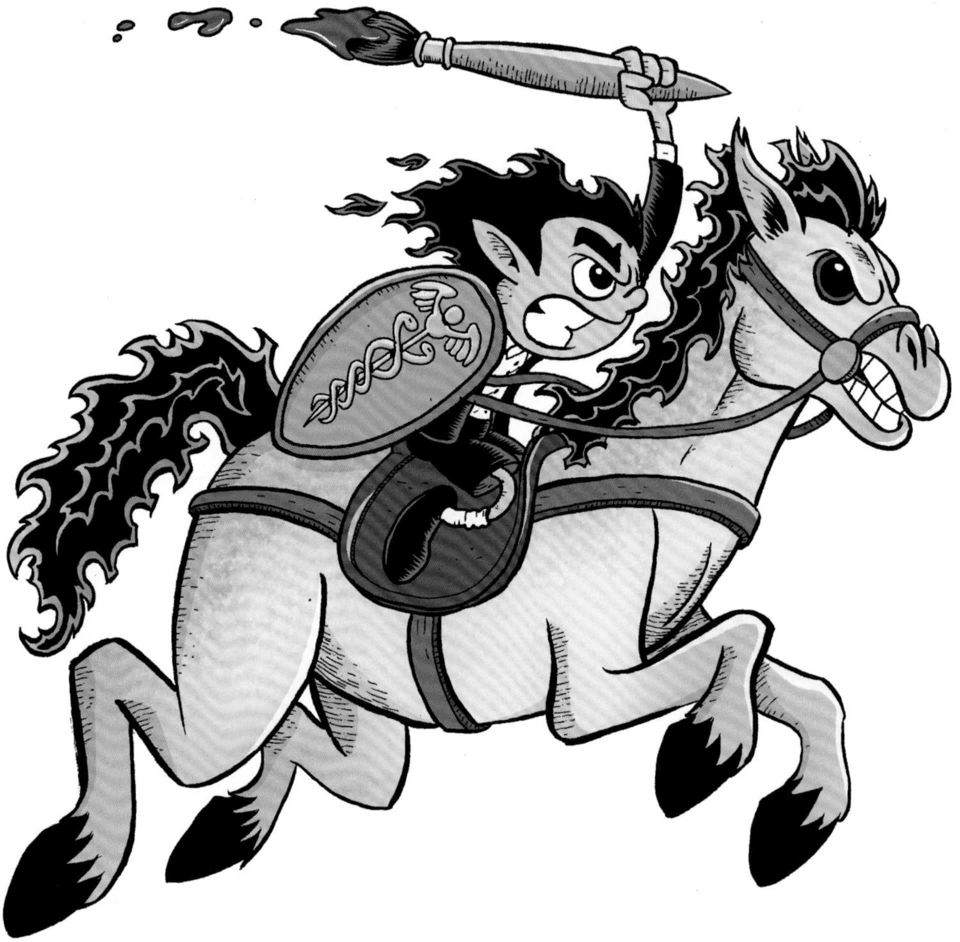

CHAPTER 5: THE KING OF ROOSTERS

To prepare him for medical school, Don Justo sent Santiago to a Catholic school run by priests of the Piarist order. The school was 40 miles away in Jaca, and Santiago was forced to leave his mama and younger siblings behind. It was not a popular decision.

While he attended school in Jaca, Santiago would live with his Uncle Juan.

The priests would teach Santiago to be a scholar and a gentleman.

Blegh!

Santiago's Latin teacher was Father Jacinto.

Good grief.

Father Jacinto specialized in breaking the spirits of rebellious boys.

We'll see about that.

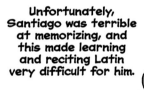

Unfortunately, Santiago was terrible at memorizing, and this made learning and reciting Latin very difficult for him.

Quisnam ... quaenam ... uh ... quiche?

WRONG!

TRY AGAIN!

Father Jacinto employed many "teaching" techniques to help Santiago.

He yelled at him.

Beat Santiago's wrists with a leather strap.

Smacked Santiago with a pointer.

And flogged Santiago with a cat-o'-nine-tails.

WRONG! WRONG! WRONG! WROOOOONG!

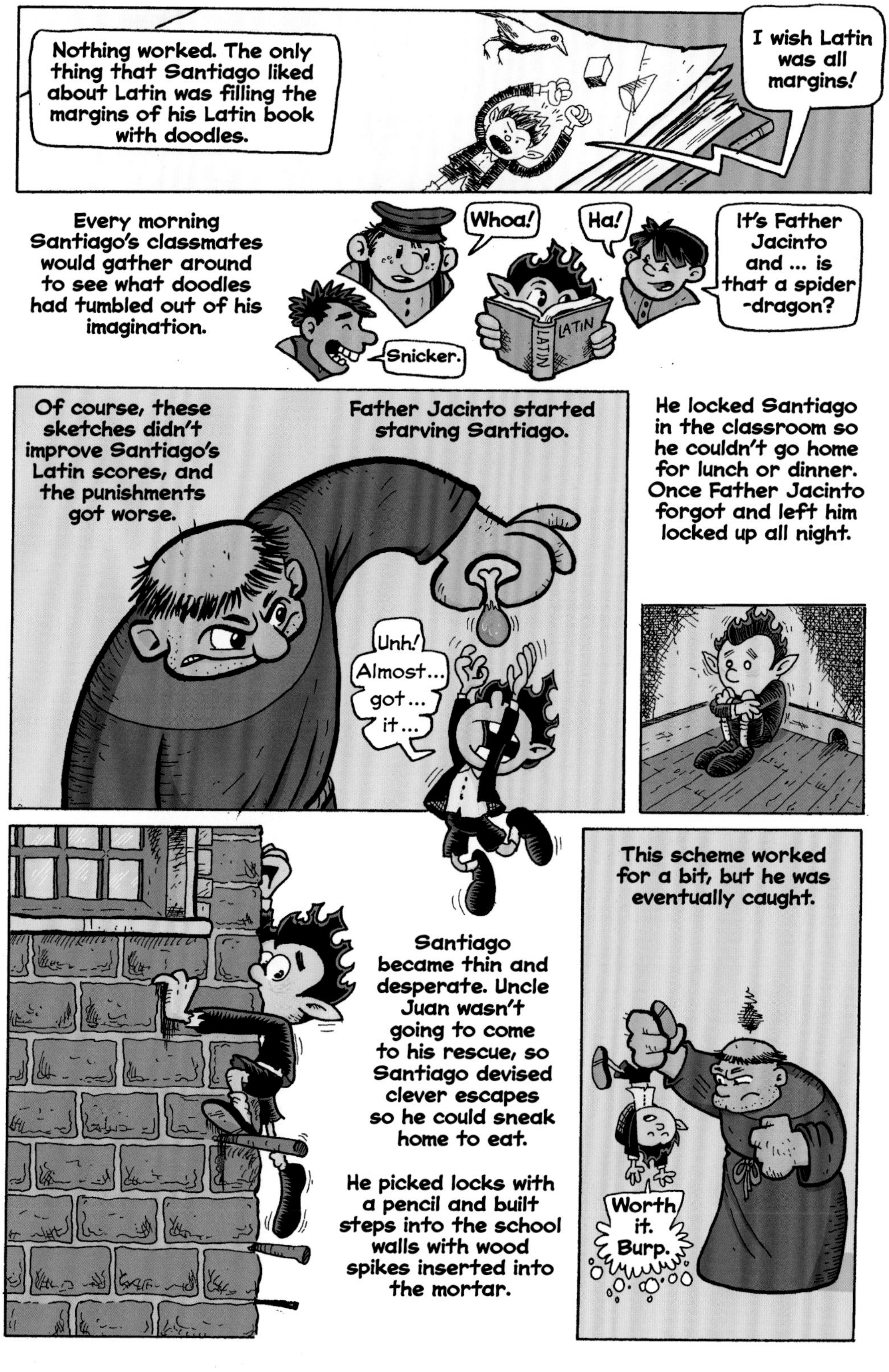
Nothing worked. The only thing that Santiago liked about Latin was filling the margins of his Latin book with doodles.
I wish Latin was all margins!
Every morning Santiago's classmates would gather around to see what doodles had tumbled out of his imagination.
Whoa!
Ha!
It's Father Jacinto and ... is that a spider-dragon?
Snicker.
LATIN
Of course, these sketches didn't improve Santiago's Latin scores, and the punishments got worse.
Father Jacinto started starving Santiago.
Unh! Almost... got... it...
He locked Santiago in the classroom so he couldn't go home for lunch or dinner. Once Father Jacinto forgot and left him locked up all night.
Santiago became thin and desperate. Uncle Juan wasn't going to come to his rescue, so Santiago devised clever escapes so he could sneak home to eat.
He picked locks with a pencil and built steps into the school walls with wood spikes inserted into the mortar.
This scheme worked for a bit, but he was eventually caught.
Worth it. Burp.

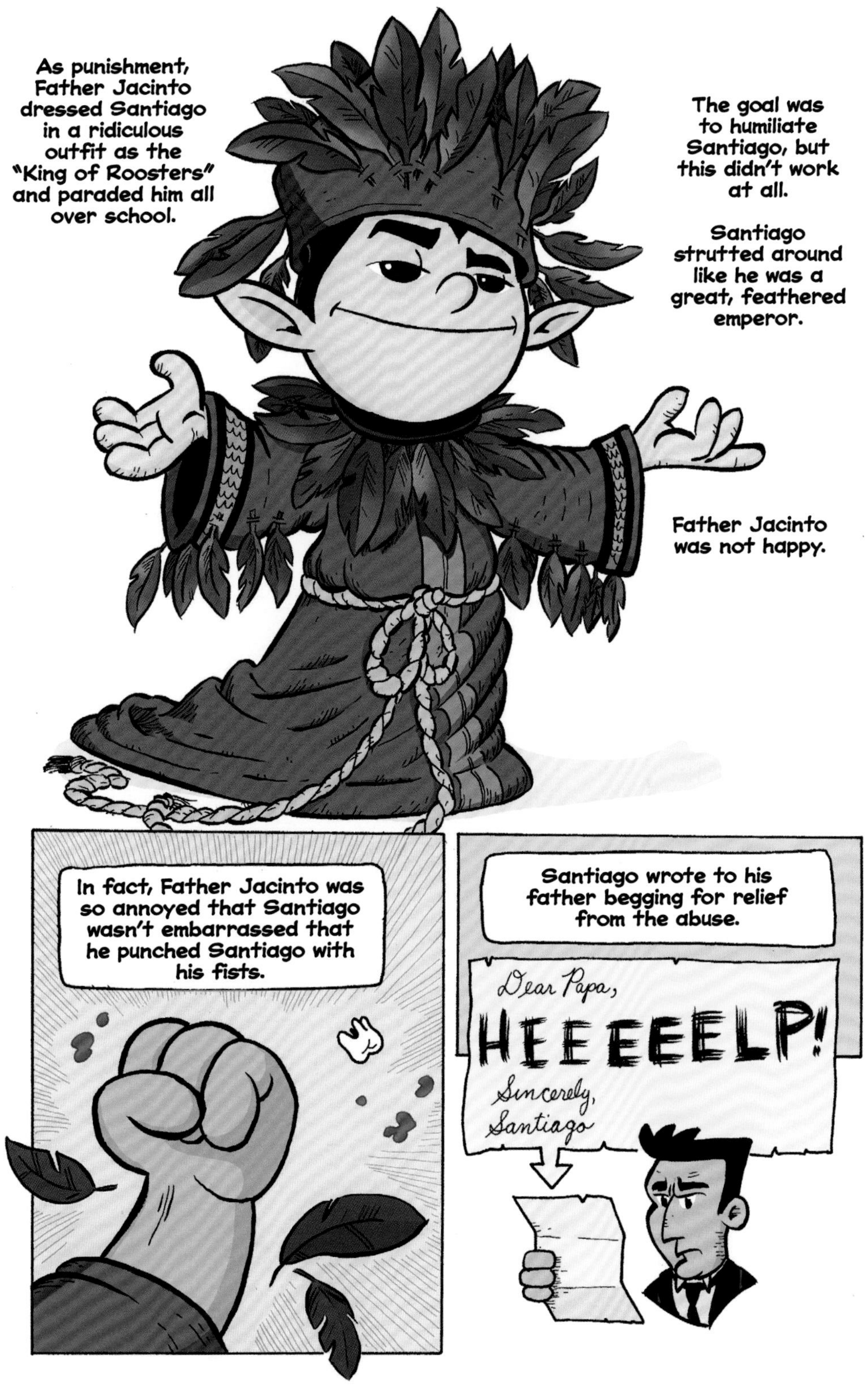
As punishment, Father Jacinto dressed Santiago in a ridiculous outfit as the "King of Roosters" and paraded him all over school.
The goal was to humiliate Santiago, but this didn't work at all.
Santiago strutted around like he was a great, feathered emperor.
Father Jacinto was not happy.
In fact, Father Jacinto was so annoyed that Santiago wasn't embarrassed that he punched Santiago with his fists.
Santiago wrote to his father begging for relief from the abuse.
Dear Papa,
HEEEEELP!
Sincerely,
Santiago

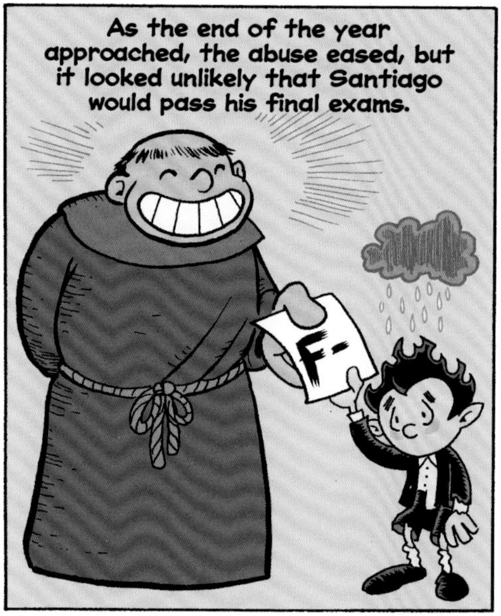
As the end of the year approached, the abuse eased, but it looked unlikely that Santiago would pass his final exams.
F-

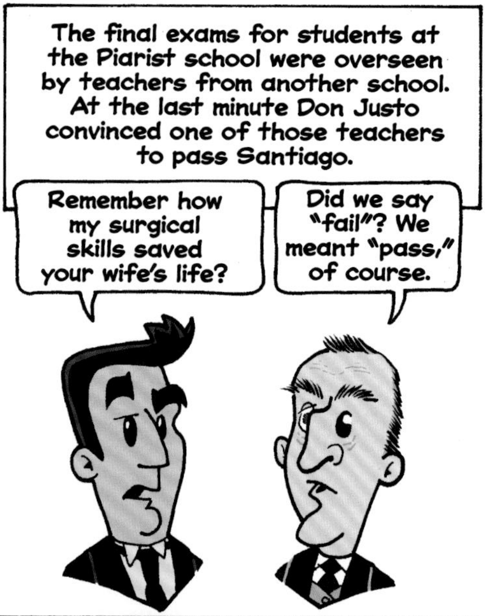
The final exams for students at the Piarist school were overseen by teachers from another school. At the last minute Don Justo convinced one of those teachers to pass Santiago.
Remember how my surgical skills saved your wife's life?
Did we say "fail"? We meant "pass," of course.

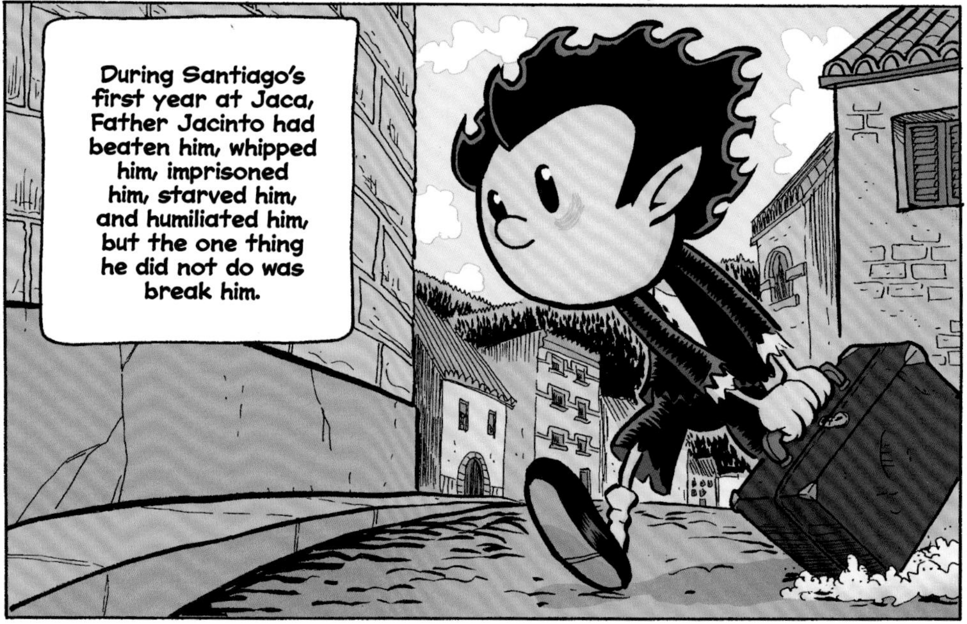
During Santiago's first year at Jaca, Father Jacinto had beaten him, whipped him, imprisoned him, starved him, and humiliated him, but the one thing he did not do was break him.

When Santiago came home for the summer, he was thin, tired ...

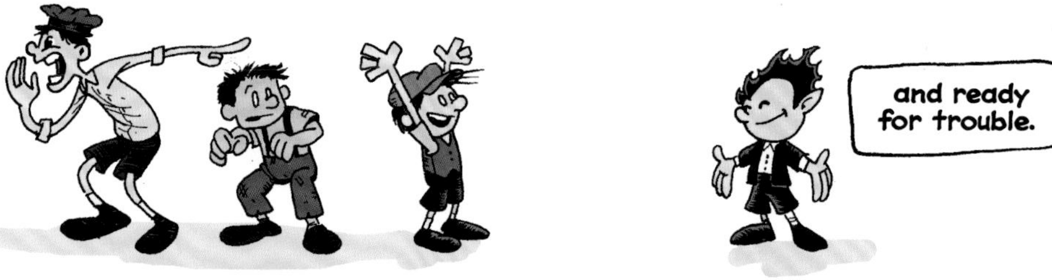
and ready for trouble.

CHAPTER 6: THE CALAMITY CANNON

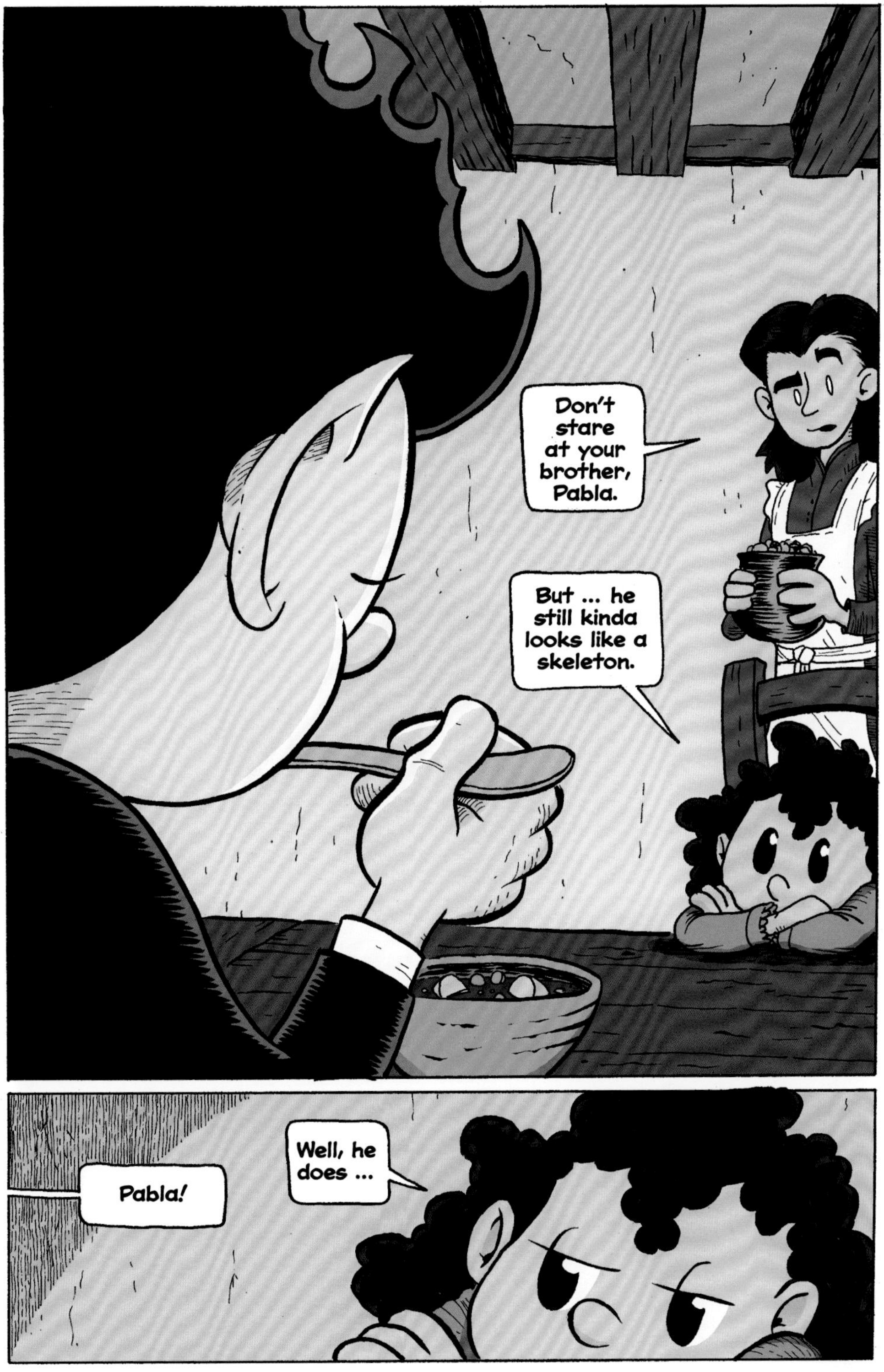
Don't stare at your brother, Pabla.
But ... he still kinda looks like a skeleton.
Well, he does ...
Pabla!

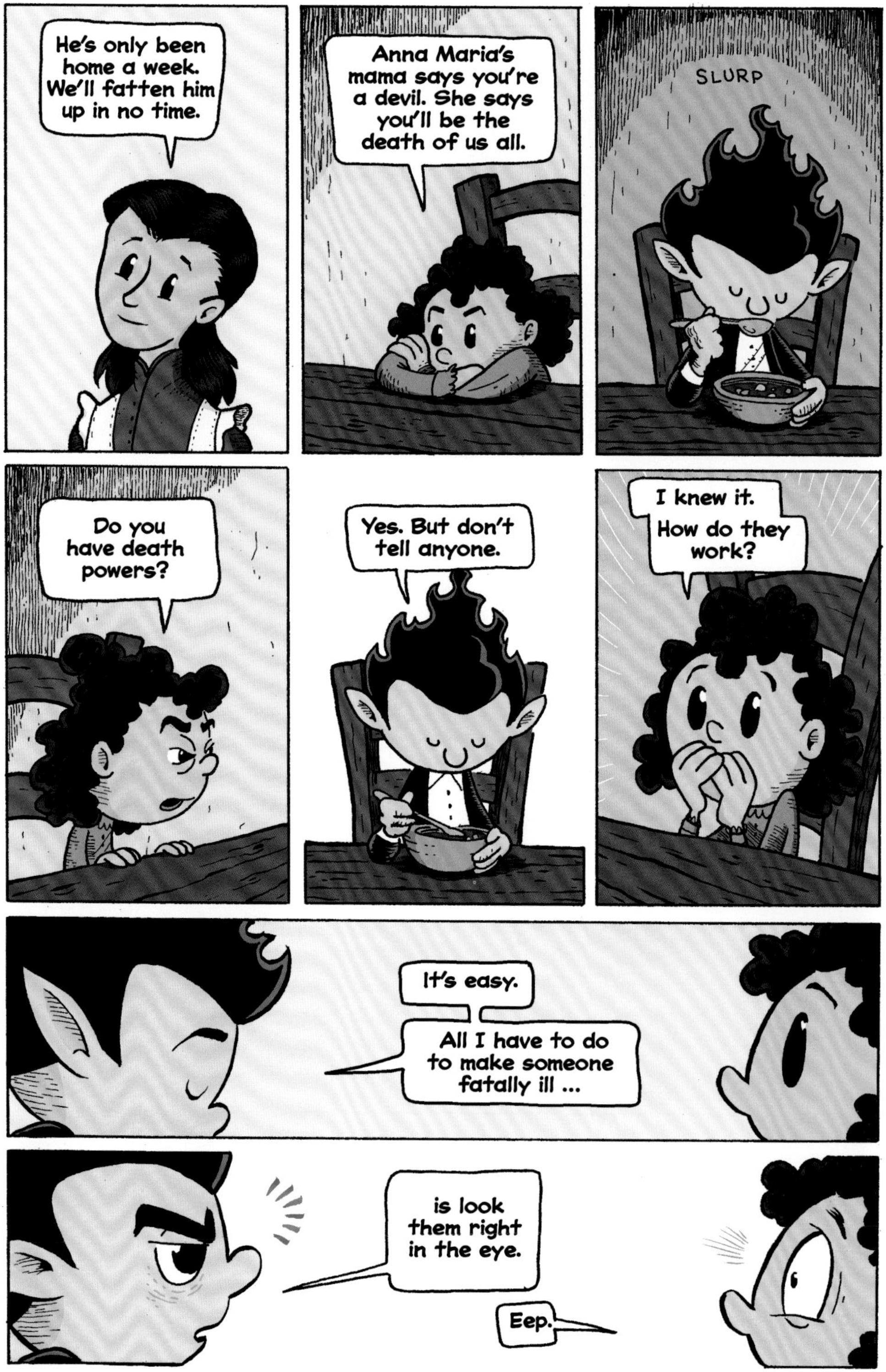
He's only been home a week. We'll fatten him up in no time.
Anna Maria's mama says you're a devil. She says you'll be the death of us all.
SLURP
Do you have death powers?
Yes. But don't tell anyone.
I knew it.
How do they work?
It's easy.
All I have to do to make someone fatally ill ...
is look them right in the eye.
Eep.

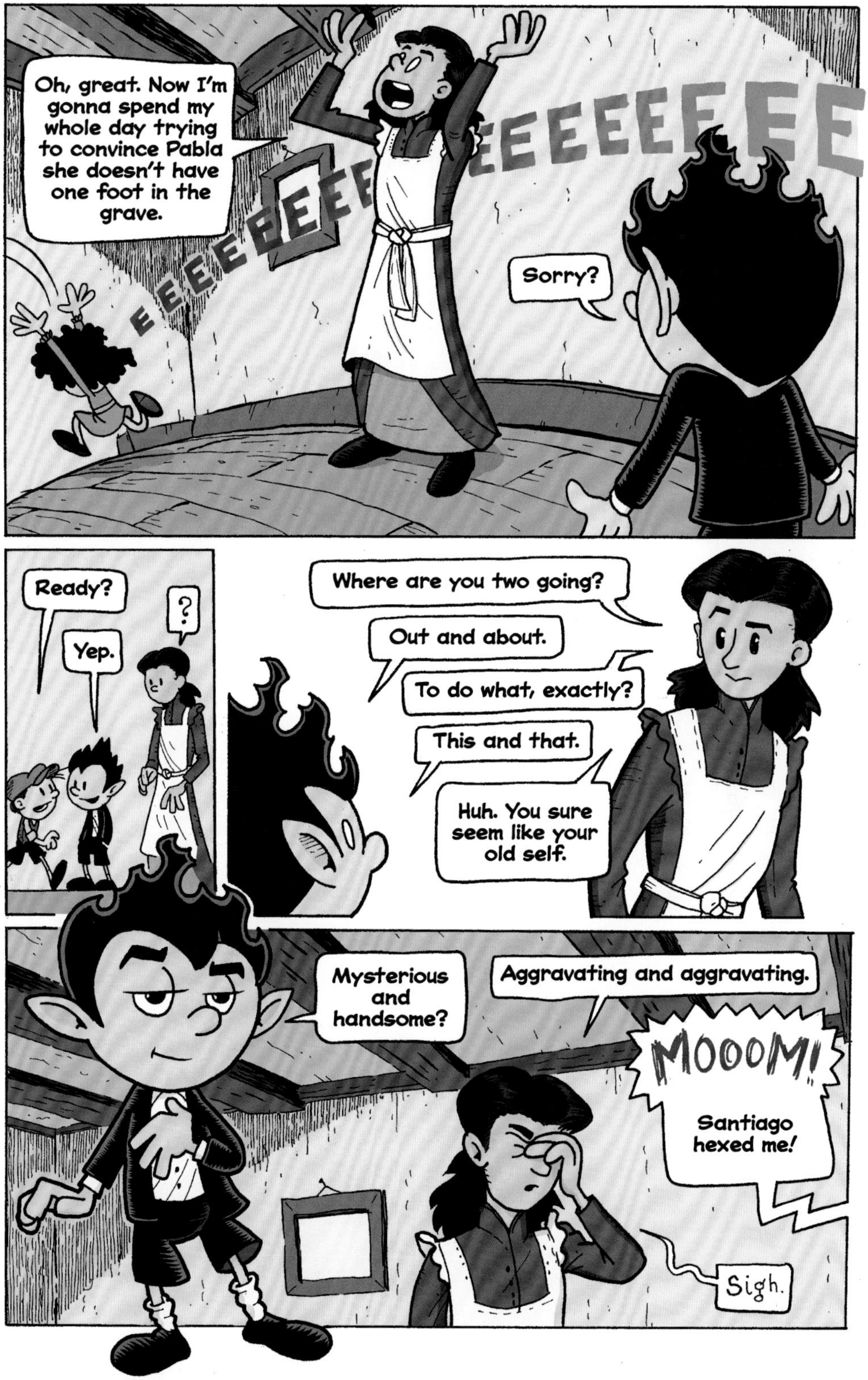
Oh, great. Now I'm gonna spend my whole day trying to convince Pabla she doesn't have one foot in the grave.
EEEEEEEEEEEEEEEEEE
Sorry?
Ready?
Yep.
?
Where are you two going?
Out and about.
To do what, exactly?
This and that.
Huh. You sure seem like your old self.
Mysterious and handsome?
Aggravating and aggravating.
MOOOM!
Santiago hexed me!
Sigh.

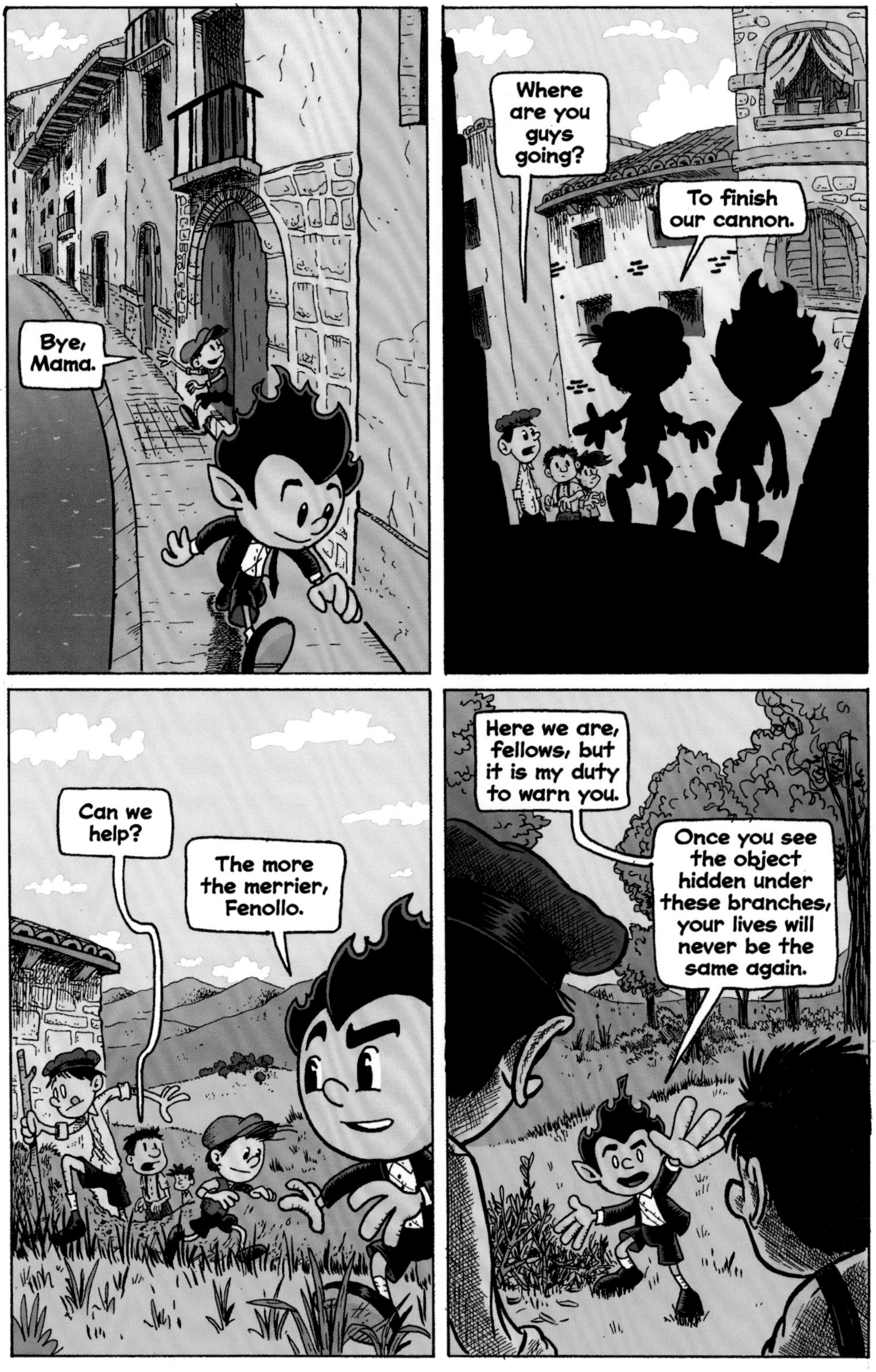
Bye, Mama.
Where are you guys going?
To finish our cannon.
Can we help?
The more the merrier, Fenollo.
Here we are, fellows, but it is my duty to warn you.
Once you see the object hidden under these branches, your lives will never be the same again.

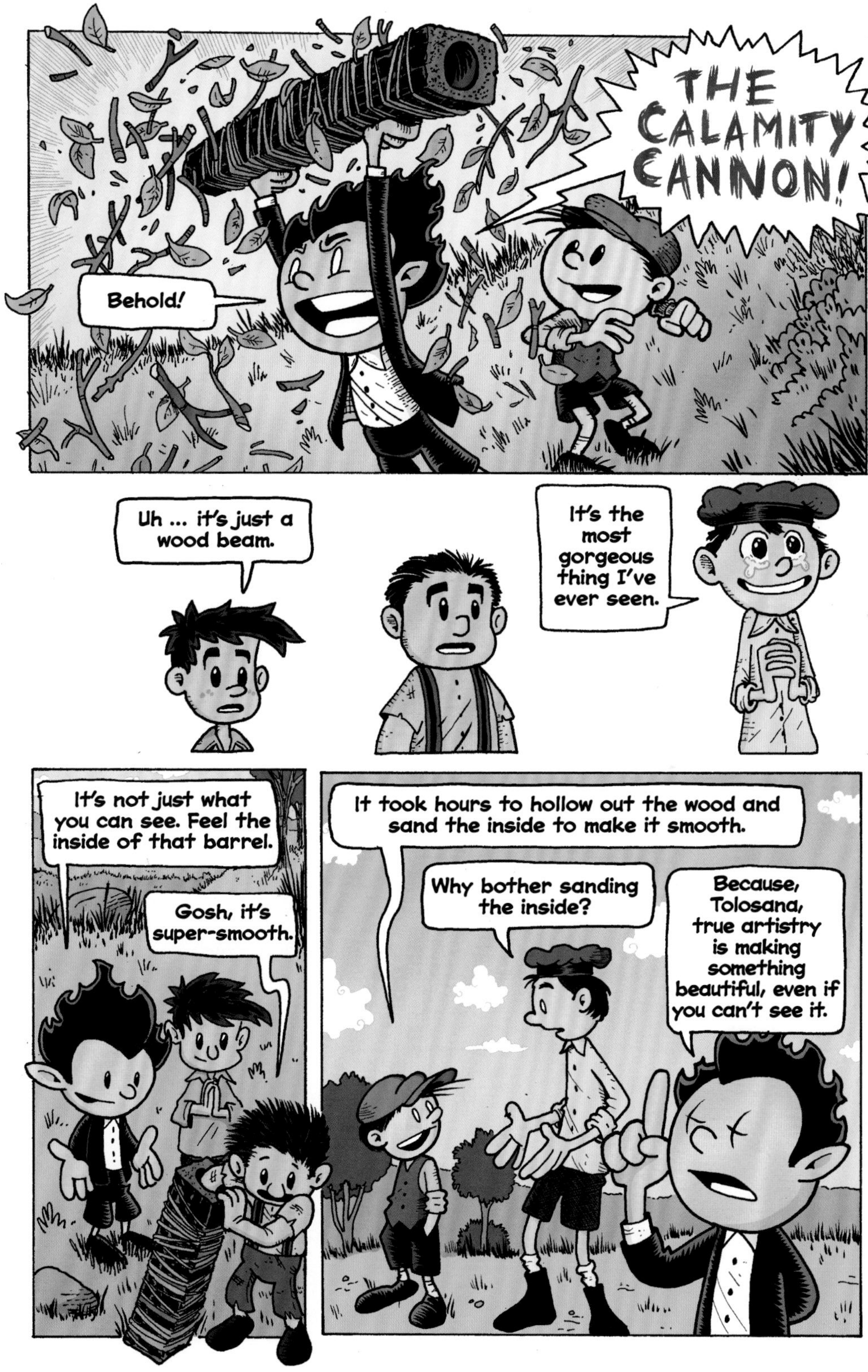
THE CALAMITY CANNON!
Behold!
Uh ... it's just a wood beam.
It's the most gorgeous thing I've ever seen.
It's not just what you can see. Feel the inside of that barrel.
Gosh, it's super-smooth.
It took hours to hollow out the wood and sand the inside to make it smooth.
Why bother sanding the inside?
Because, Tolosana, true artistry is making something beautiful, even if you can't see it.

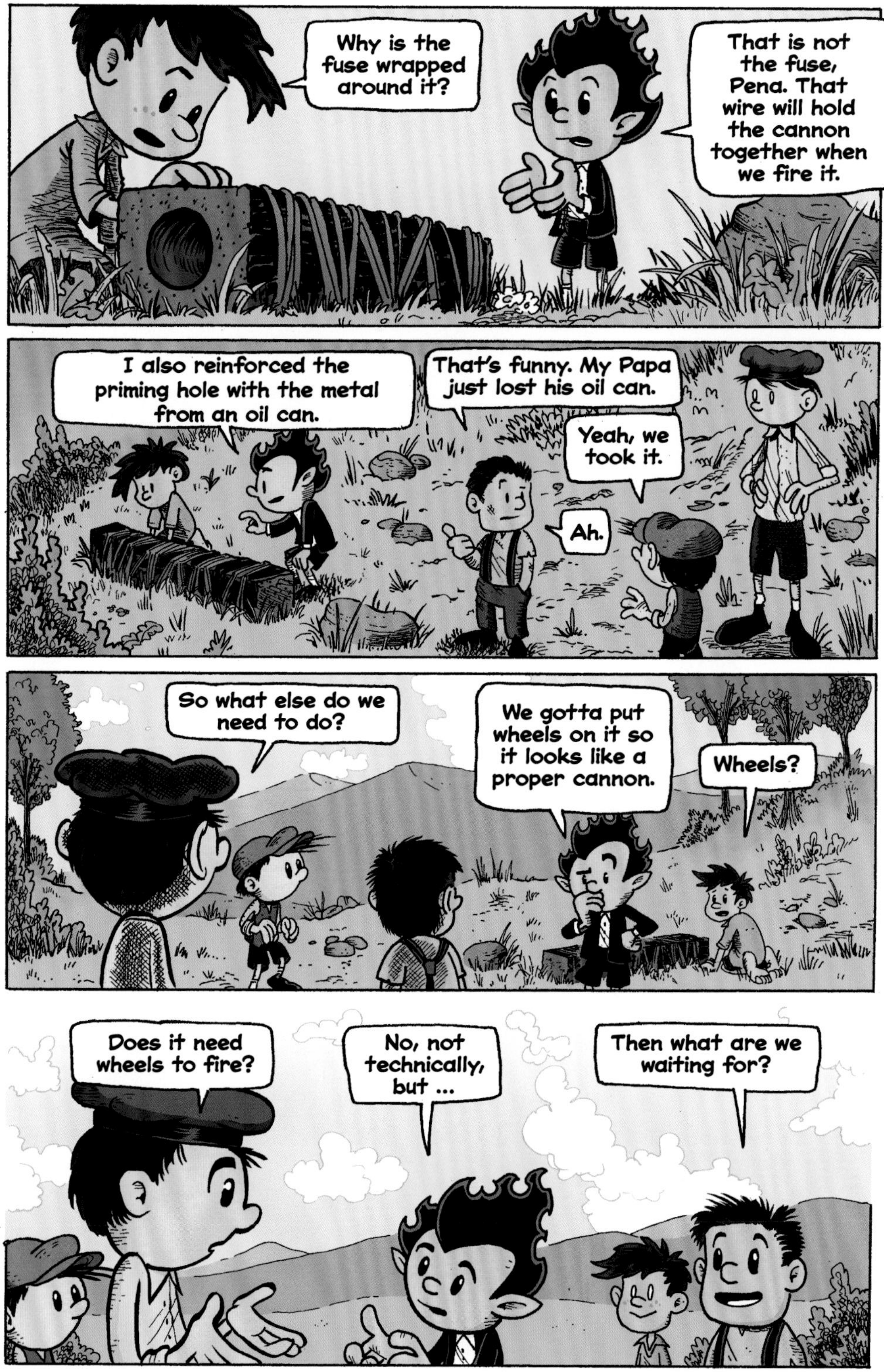
Why is the fuse wrapped around it?
That is not the fuse, Pena. That wire will hold the cannon together when we fire it.
I also reinforced the priming hole with the metal from an oil can.
That's funny. My Papa just lost his oil can.
Yeah, we took it.
Ah.
So what else do we need to do?
We gotta put wheels on it so it looks like a proper cannon.
Wheels?
Does it need wheels to fire?
No, not technically, but ...
Then what are we waiting for?

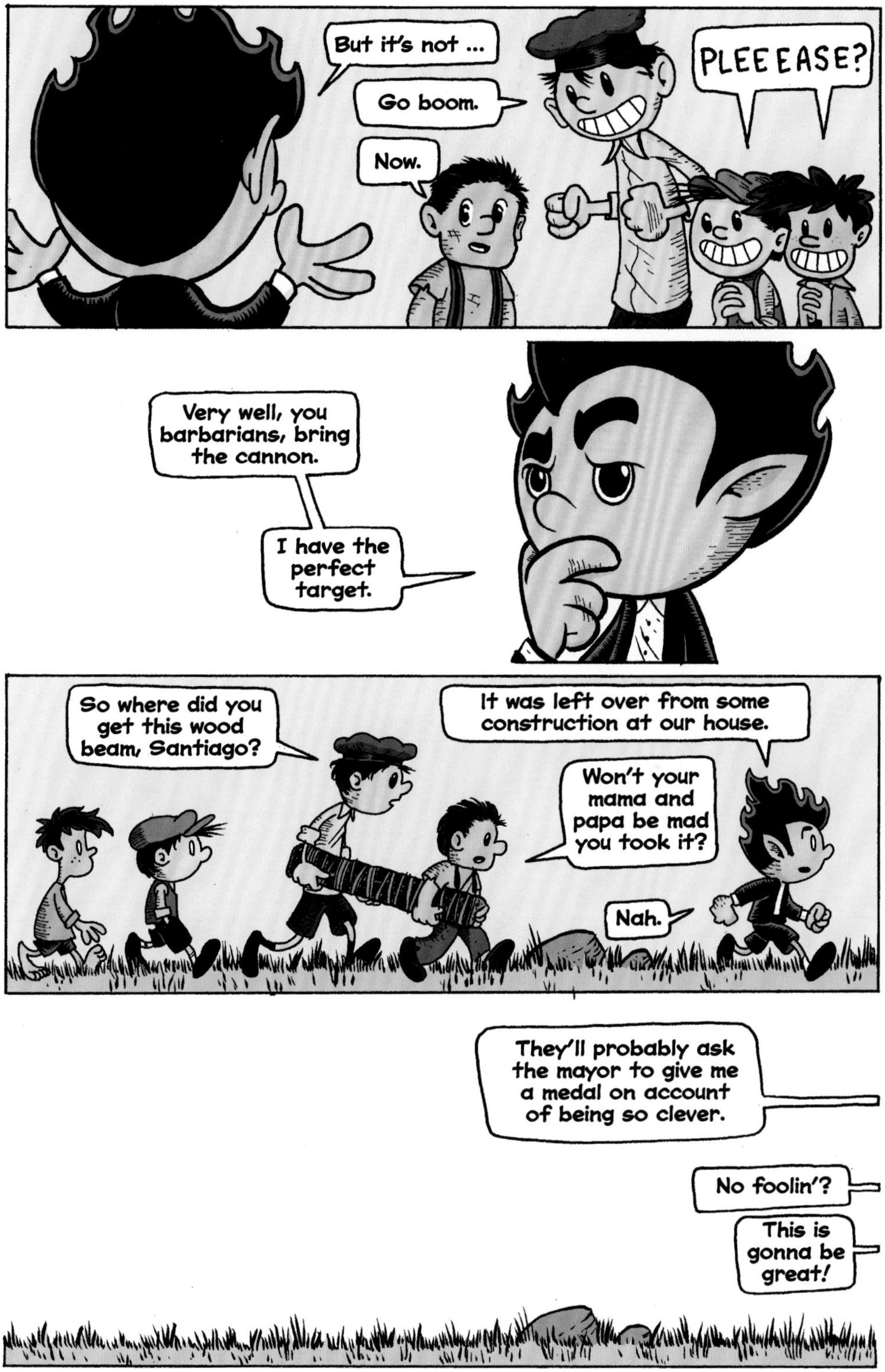

But it's not ...
Go boom.
Now.
PLEEEASE?
Very well, you barbarians, bring the cannon.
I have the perfect target.
So where did you get this wood beam, Santiago?
It was left over from some construction at our house.
Won't your mama and papa be mad you took it?
Nah.
They'll probably ask the mayor to give me a medal on account of being so clever.
No foolin'?
This is gonna be great!

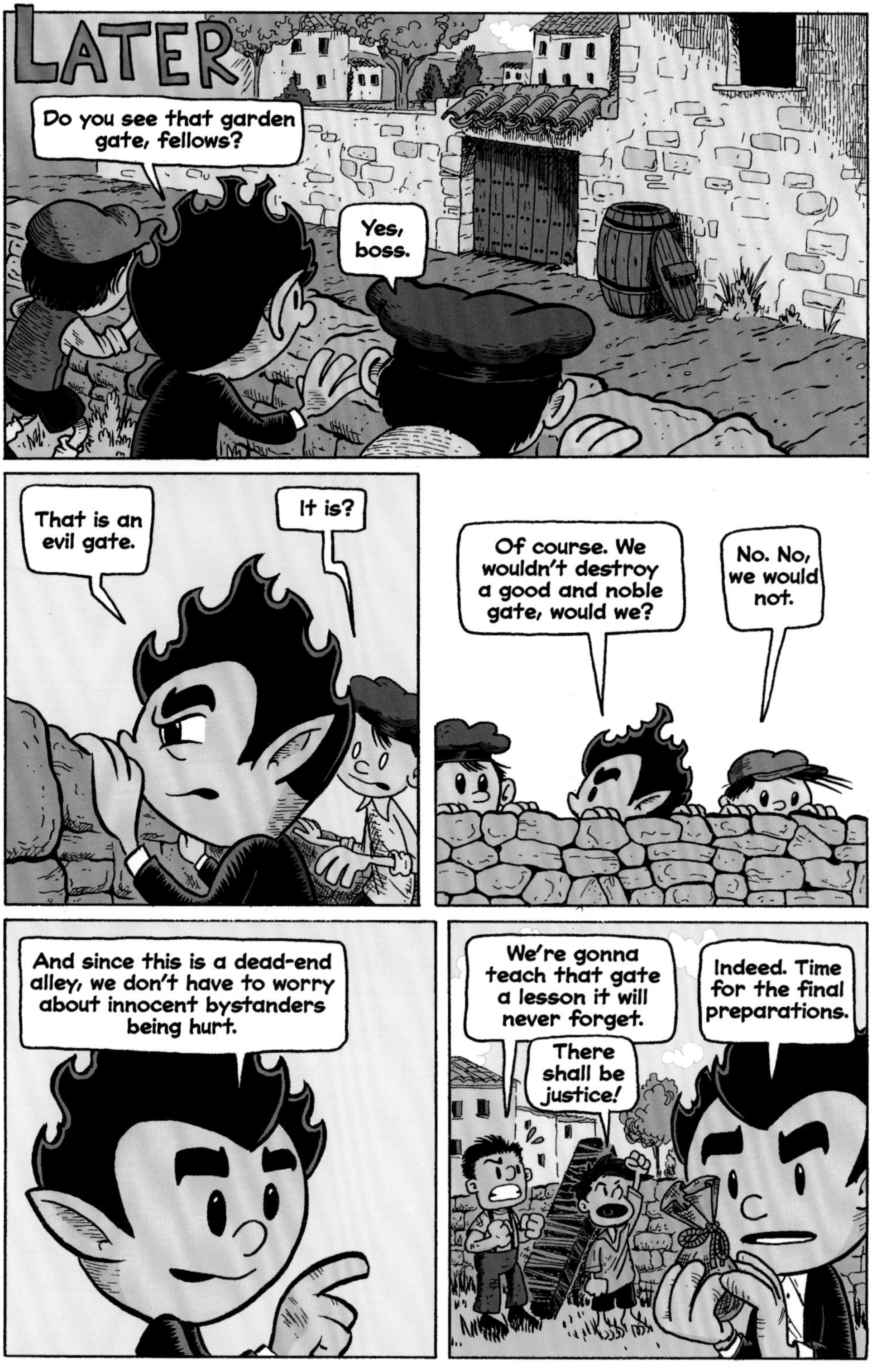
LATER
Do you see that garden gate, fellows?
Yes, boss.
That is an evil gate.
It is?
Of course. We wouldn't destroy a good and noble gate, would we?
No. No, we would not.
And since this is a dead-end alley, we don't have to worry about innocent bystanders being hurt.
We're gonna teach that gate a lesson it will never forget.
There shall be justice!
Indeed. Time for the final preparations.

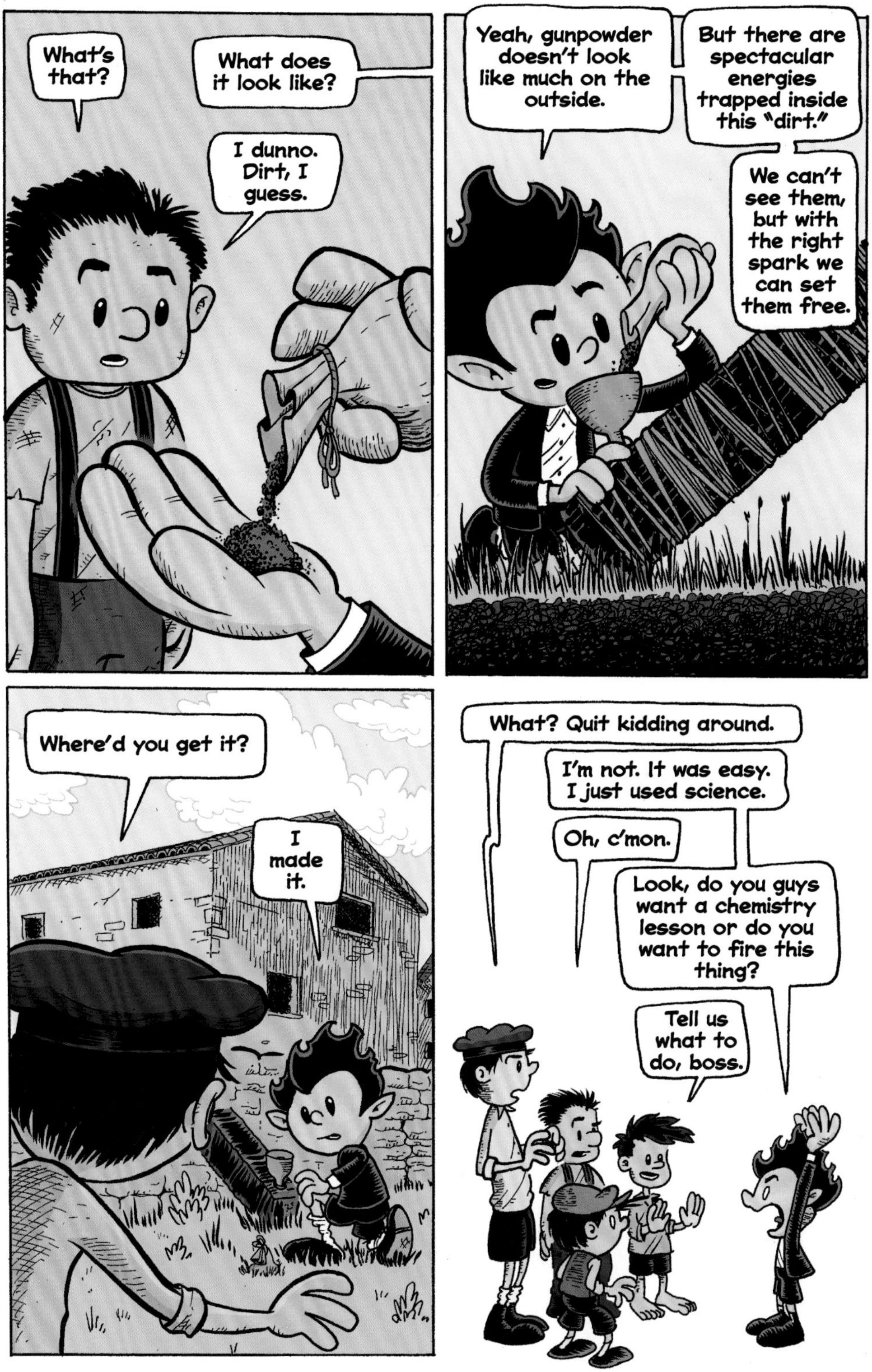
What's that?
What does it look like?
I dunno. Dirt, I guess.
Yeah, gunpowder doesn't look like much on the outside.
But there are spectacular energies trapped inside this "dirt."
We can't see them, but with the right spark we can set them free.
Where'd you get it?
I made it.
What? Quit kidding around.
I'm not. It was easy. I just used science.
Oh, c'mon.
Look, do you guys want a chemistry lesson or do you want to fire this thing?
Tell us what to do, boss.

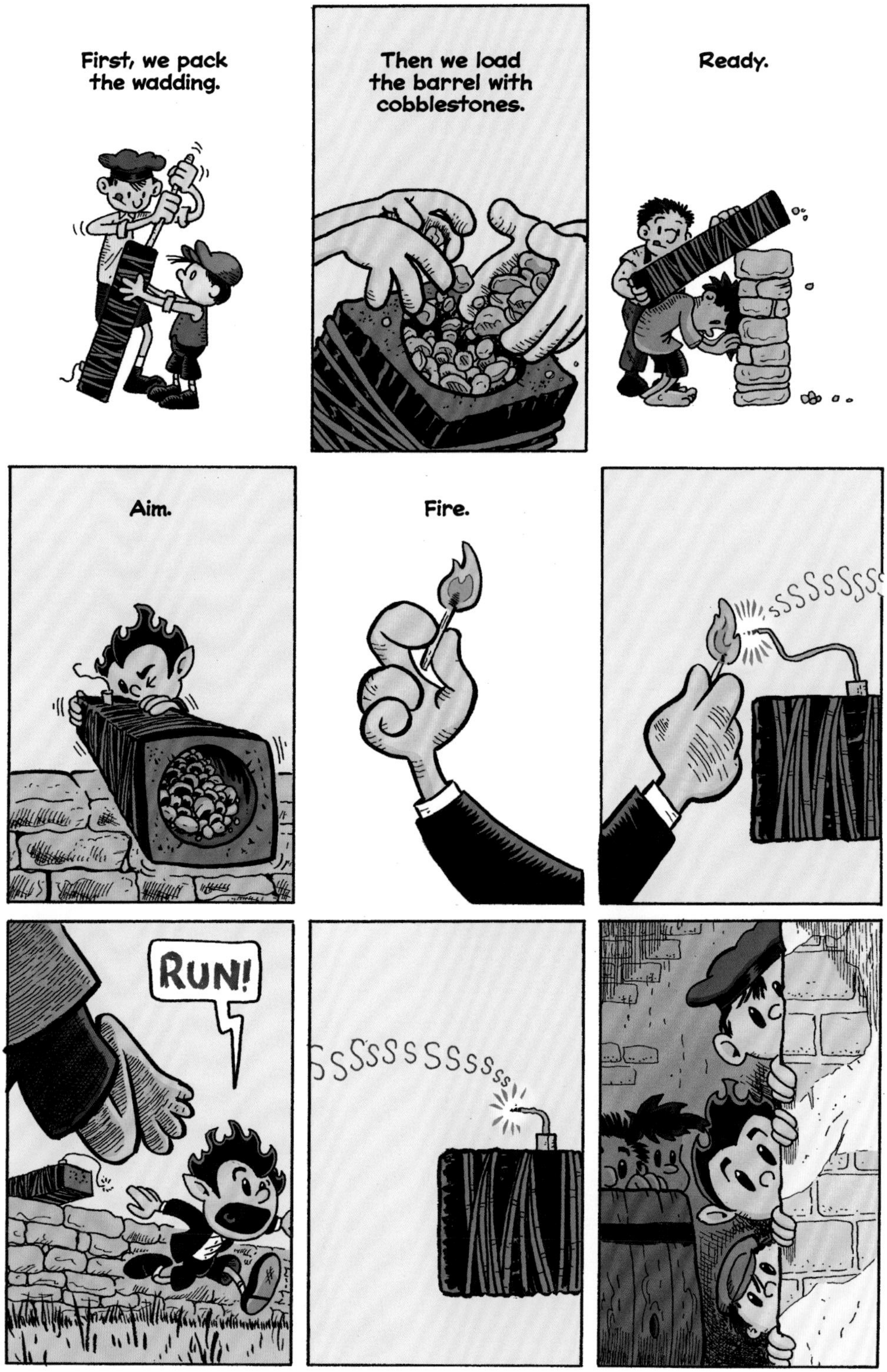
First, we pack the wadding.
Then we load the barrel with cobblestones.
Ready.
Aim.
Fire.
sSSSSSS
RUN!
SSSSSSSSSSSsss

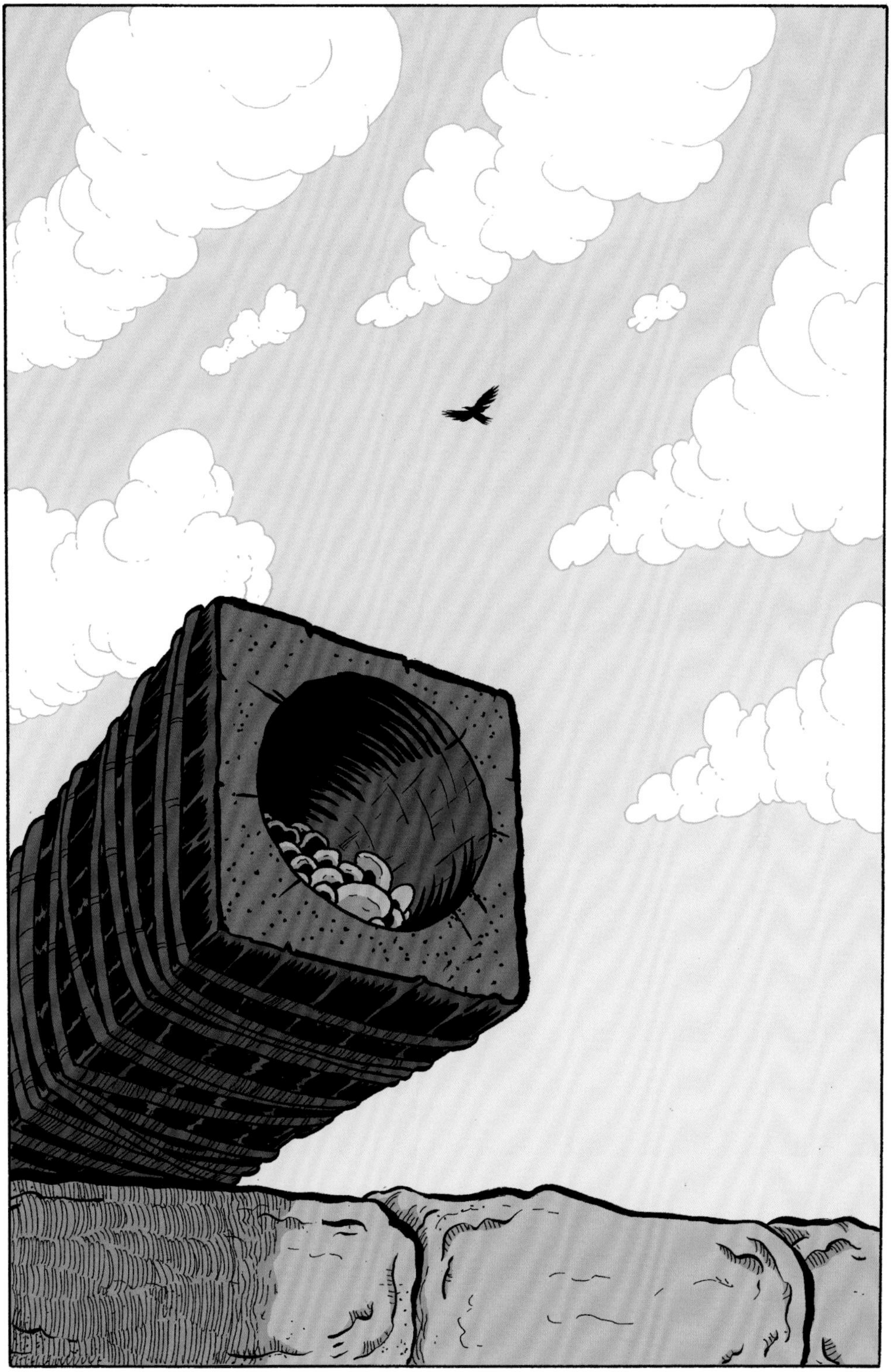

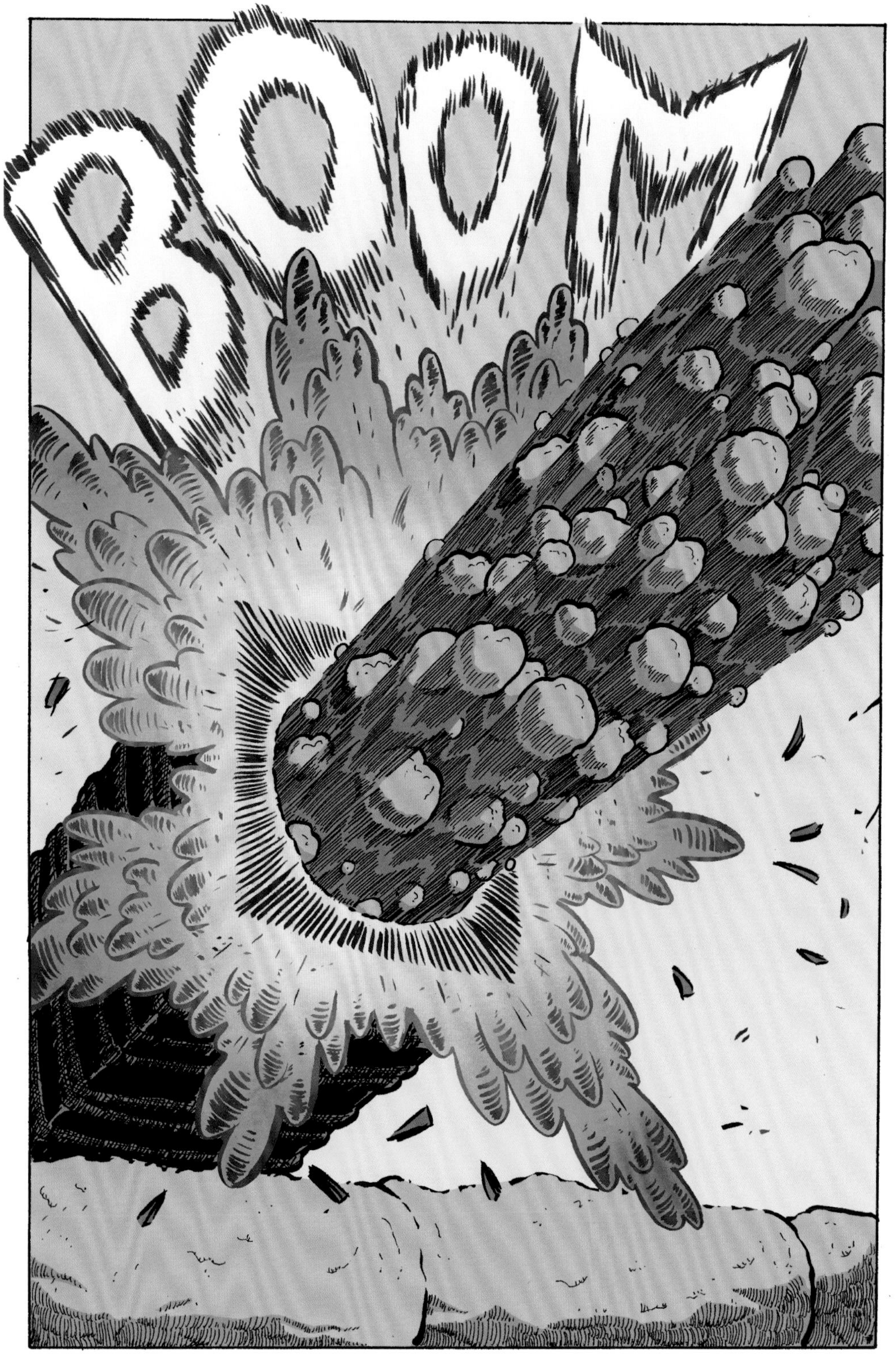
BOOM

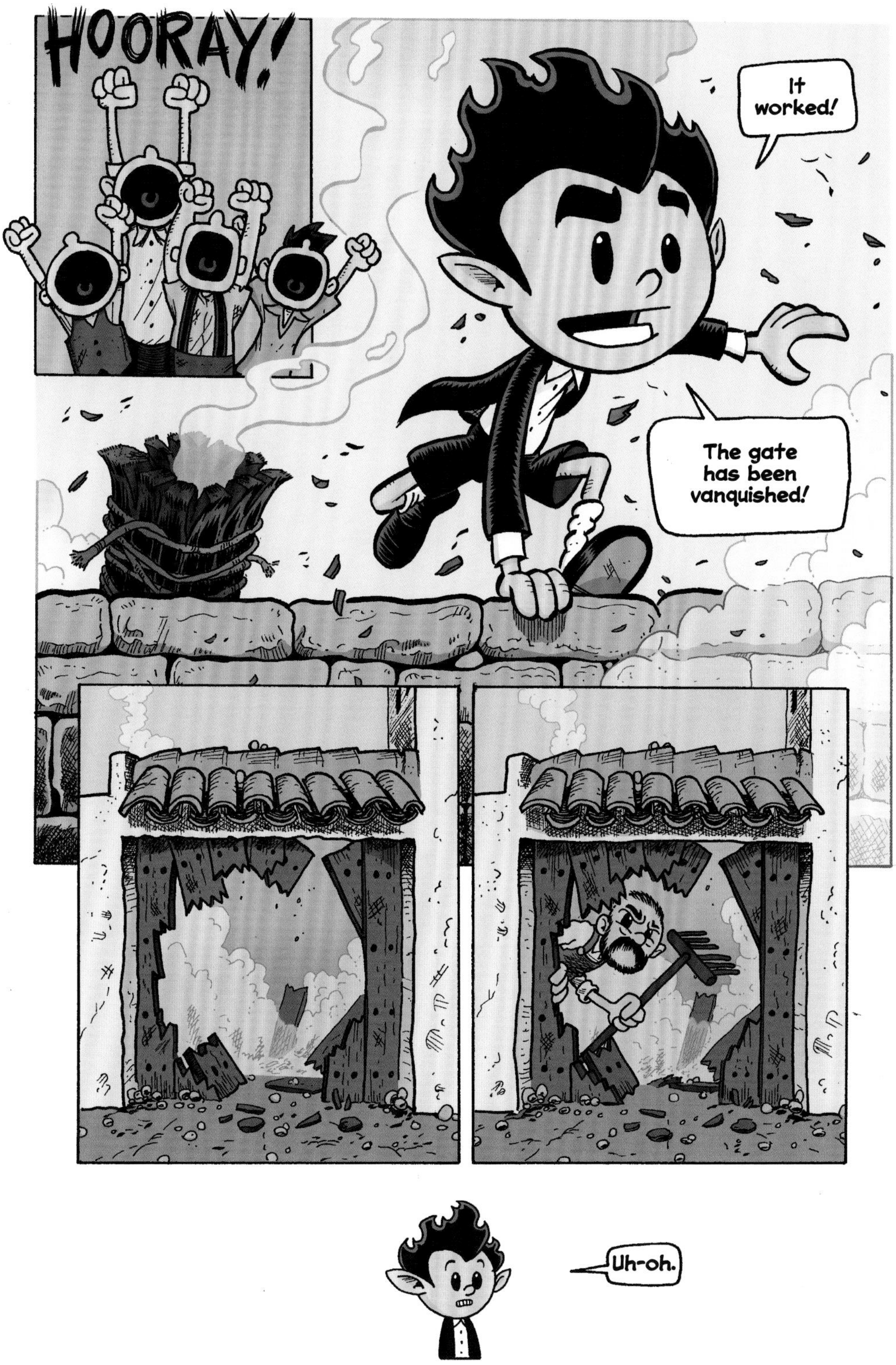
HOORAY!
It worked!
The gate has been vanquished!
Uh-oh.

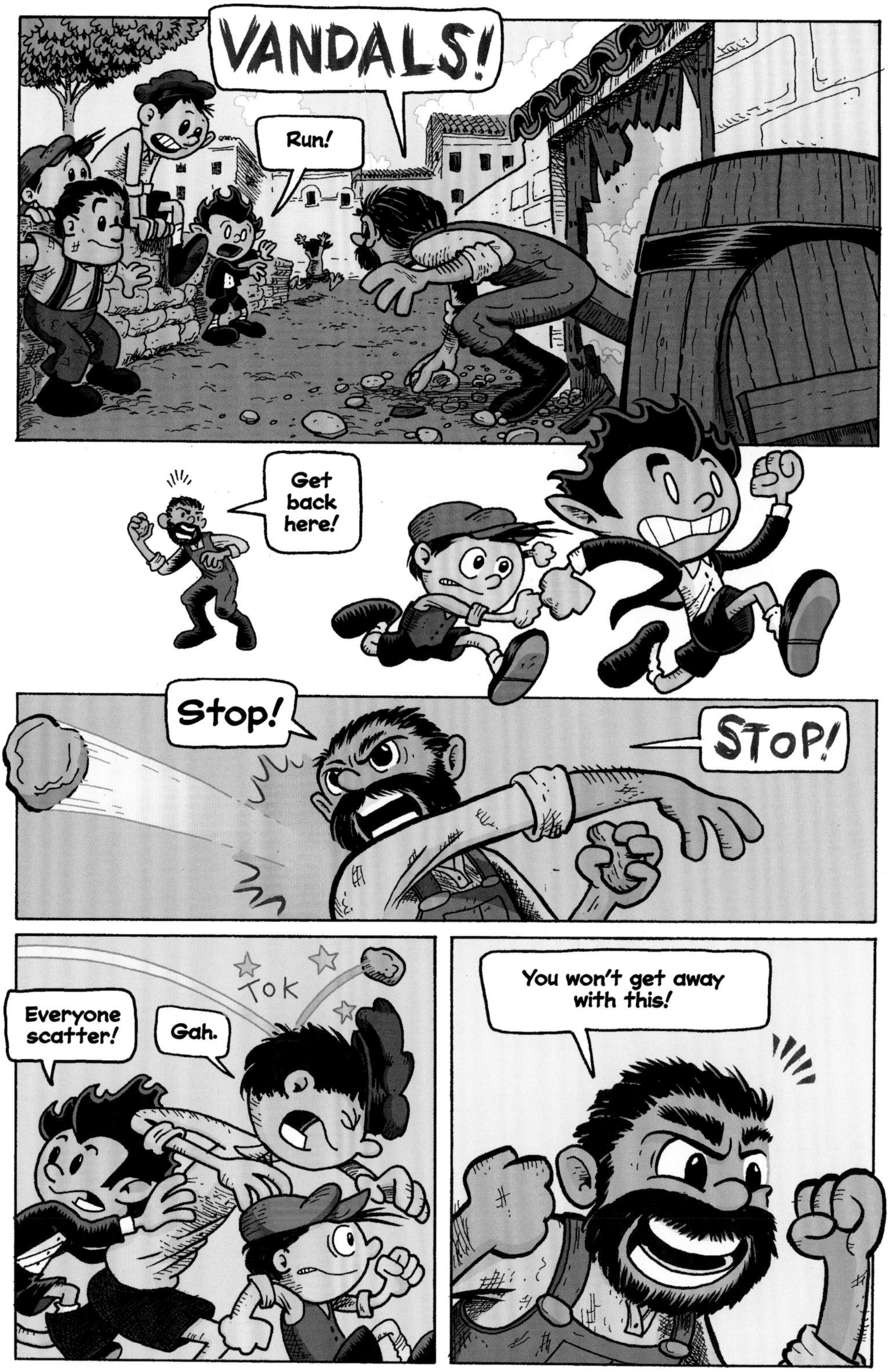
VANDALS!
Run!
Get back here!
Stop!
STOP!
Everyone scatter!
Gah.
TOK
You won't get away with this!

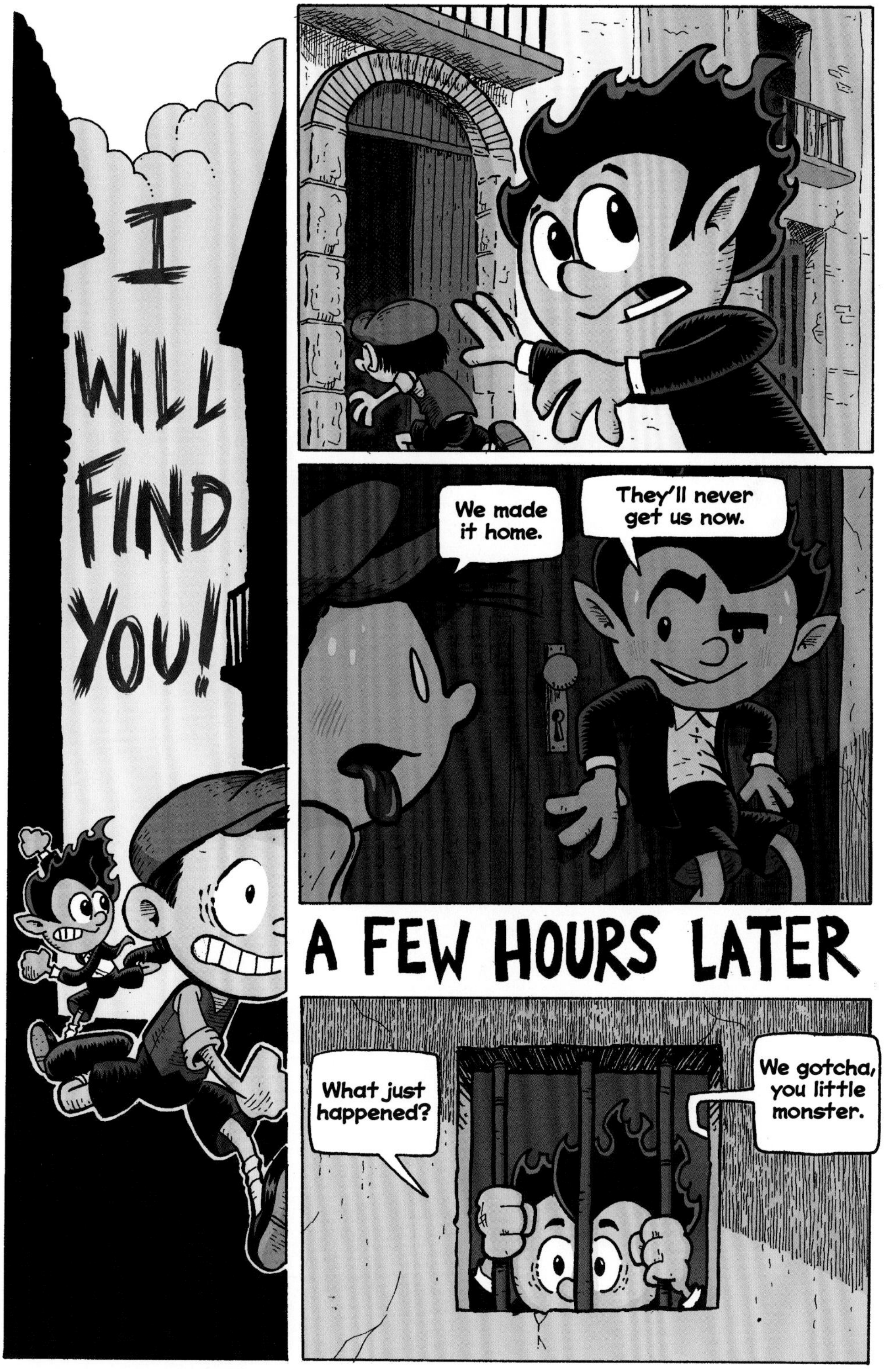
I WILL FIND YOU!
We made it home.
They'll never get us now.
A FEW HOURS LATER
What just happened?
We gotcha, you little monster.

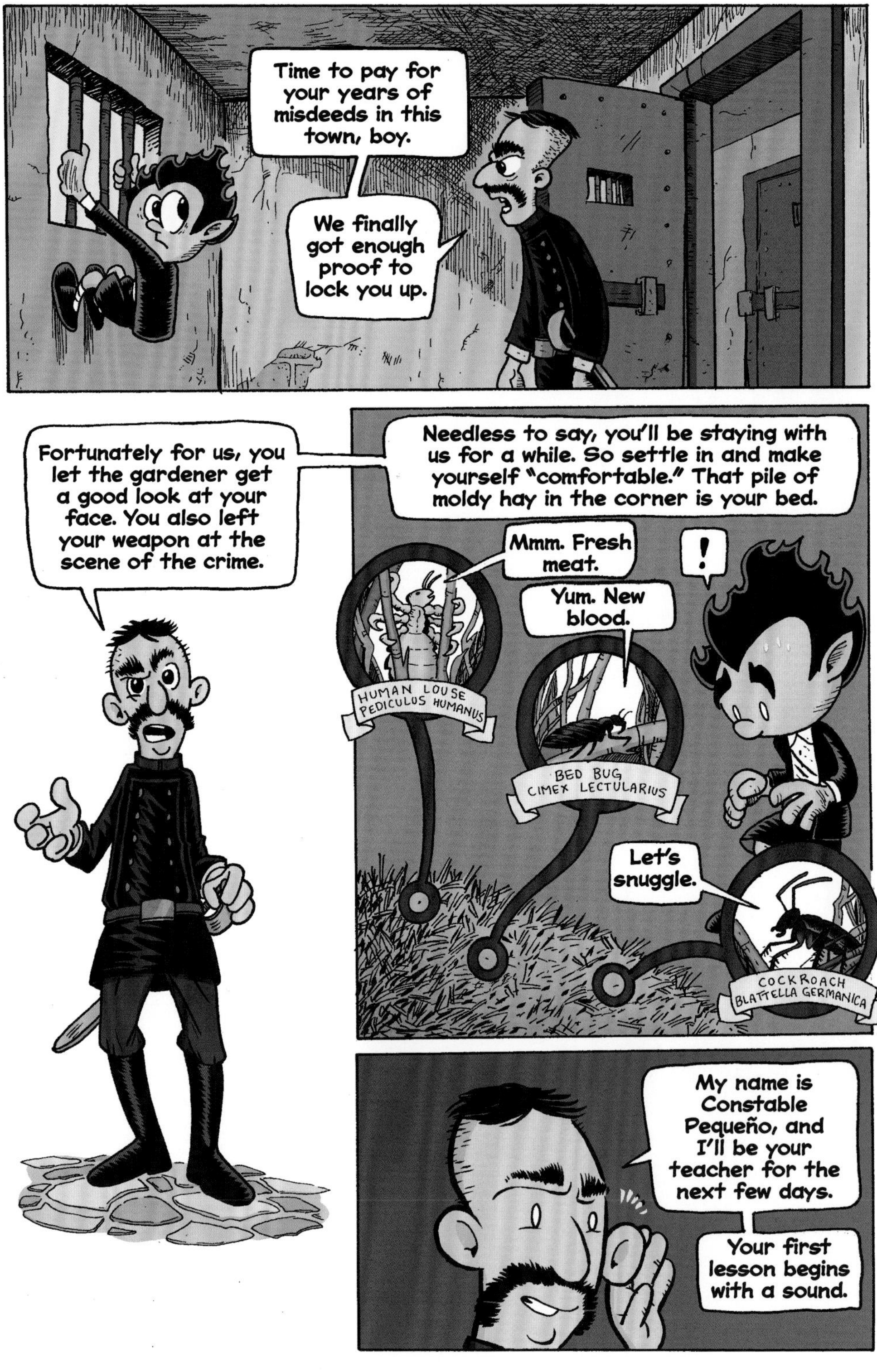

Time to pay for your years of misdeeds in this town, boy.
We finally got enough proof to lock you up.
Fortunately for us, you let the gardener get a good look at your face. You also left your weapon at the scene of the crime.
Needless to say, you'll be staying with us for a while. So settle in and make yourself "comfortable." That pile of moldy hay in the corner is your bed.
Mmm. Fresh meat.
!
Yum. New blood.
HUMAN LOUSE
PEDICULUS HUMANUS
BED BUG
CIMEX LECTULARIUS
Let's snuggle.
COCKROACH
BLATTELLA GERMANICA
My name is Constable Pequeño, and I'll be your teacher for the next few days.
Your first lesson begins with a sound.

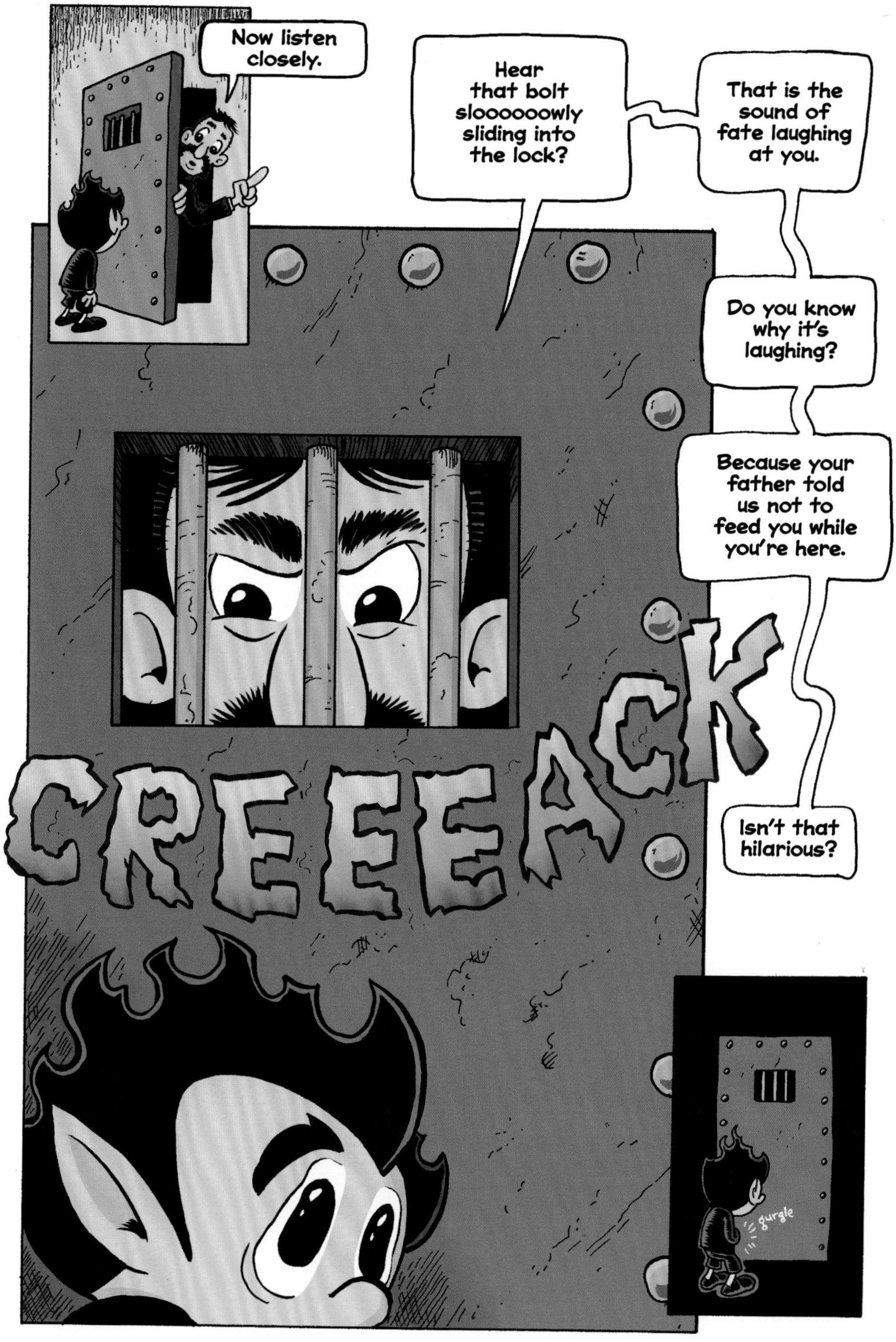

Now listen closely.
Hear that bolt slooooowly sliding into the lock?
That is the sound of fate laughing at you.
Do you know why it's laughing?
Because your father told us not to feed you while you're here.
Isn't that hilarious?
CREEEACK
gurgle

THAT NIGHT

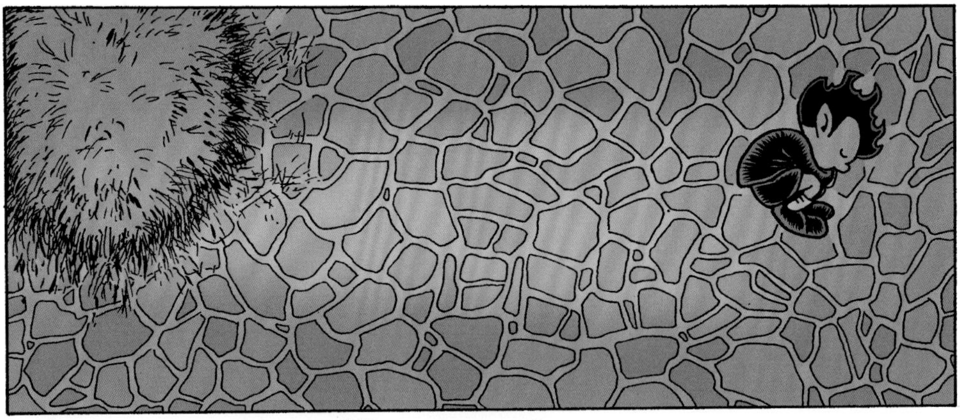

THE NEXT DAY

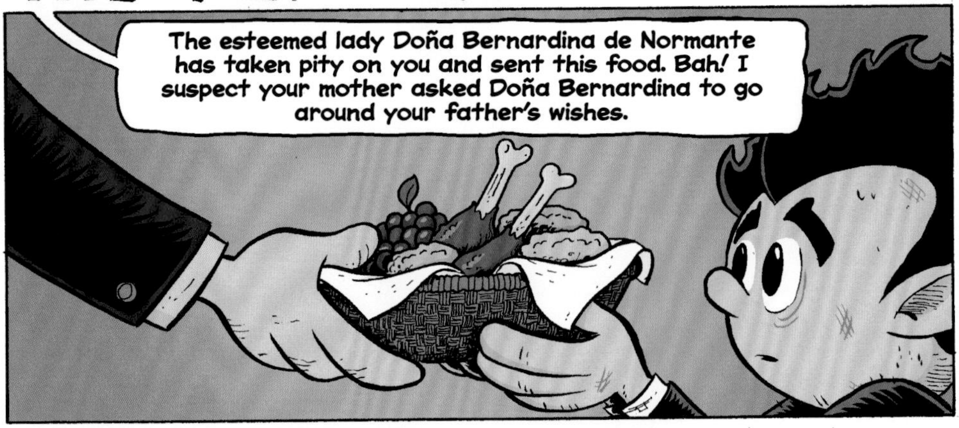
The esteemed lady Doña Bernardina de Normante has taken pity on you and sent this food. Bah! I suspect your mother asked Doña Bernardina to go around your father's wishes.

THREE DAYS LATER

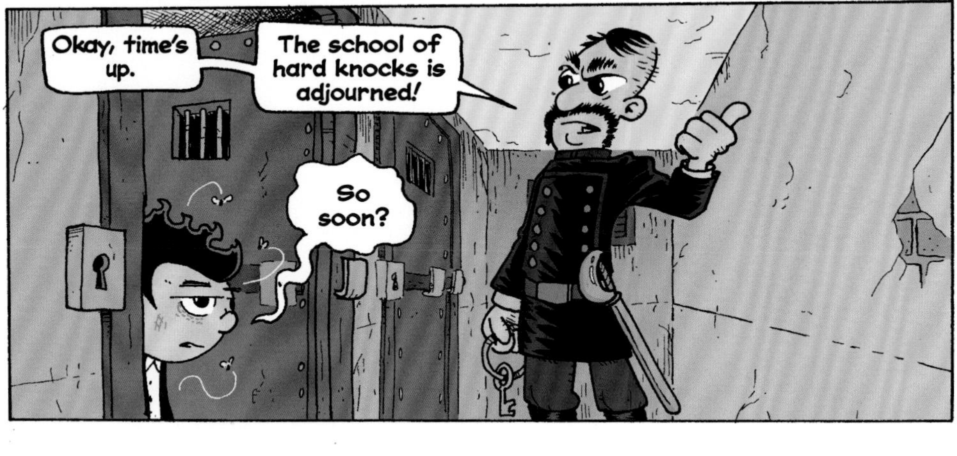
Okay, time's up.
The school of hard knocks is adjourned!
So soon?

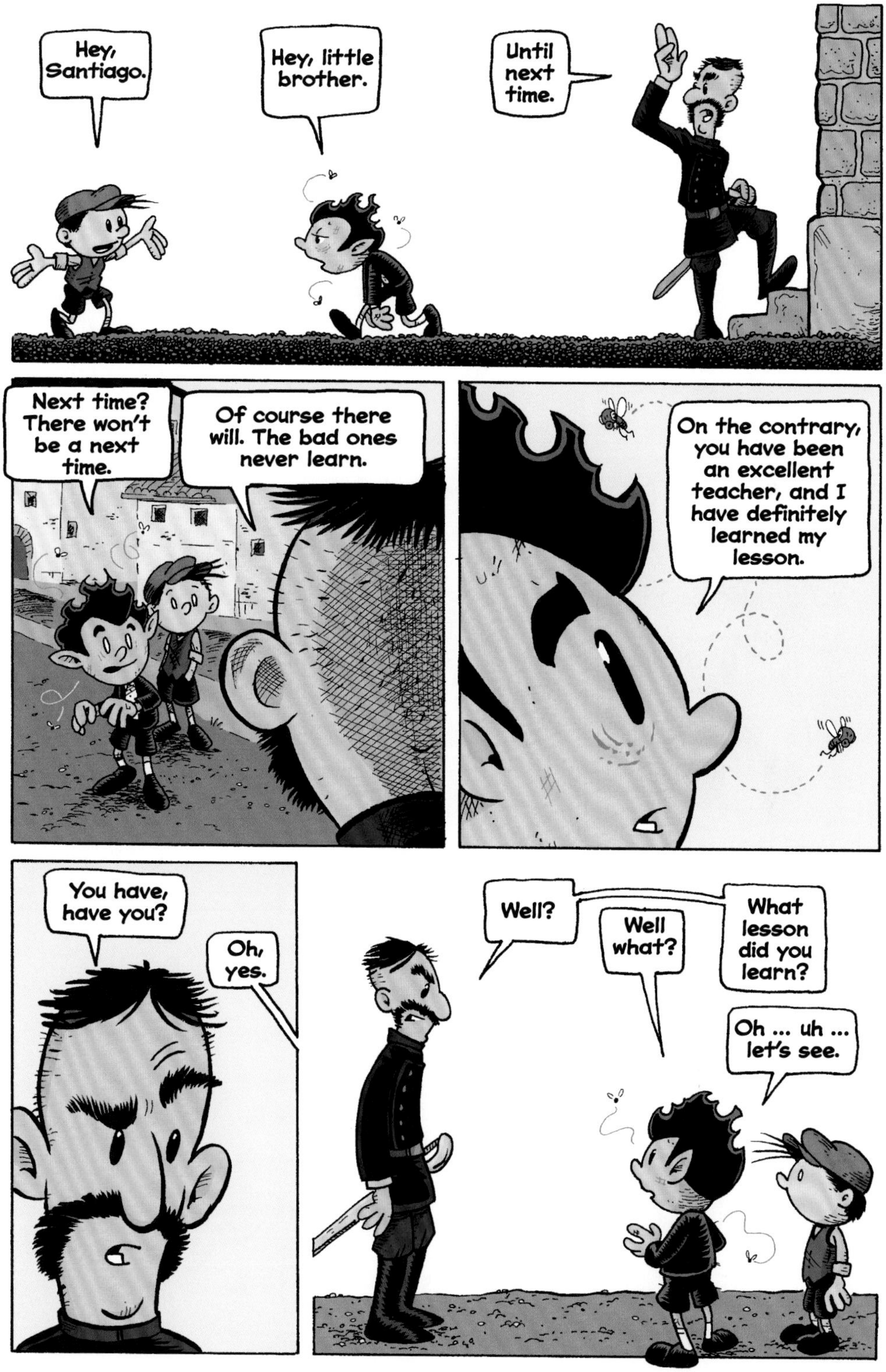
Hey, Santiago.
Hey, little brother.
Until next time.
Next time? There won't be a next time.
Of course there will. The bad ones never learn.
On the contrary, you have been an excellent teacher, and I have definitely learned my lesson.
You have, have you?
Oh, yes.
Well?
Well what?
What lesson did you learn?
Oh ... uh ... let's see.

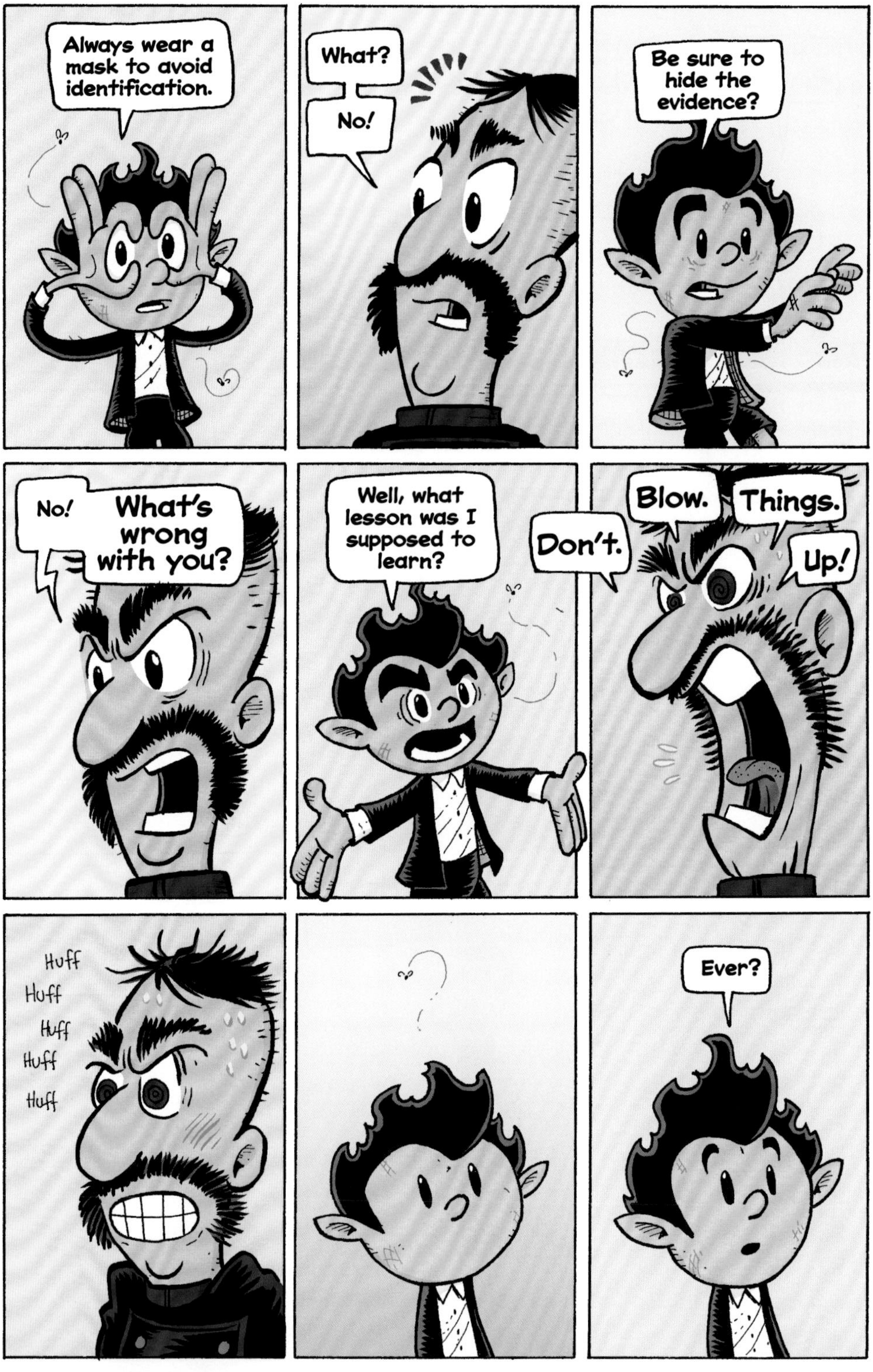

Always wear a mask to avoid identification.
What?
No!
Be sure to hide the evidence?
No!
What's wrong with you?
Well, what lesson was I supposed to learn?
Don't.
Blow.
Things.
Up!
Huff
Huff
Huff
Huff
Huff
Ever?

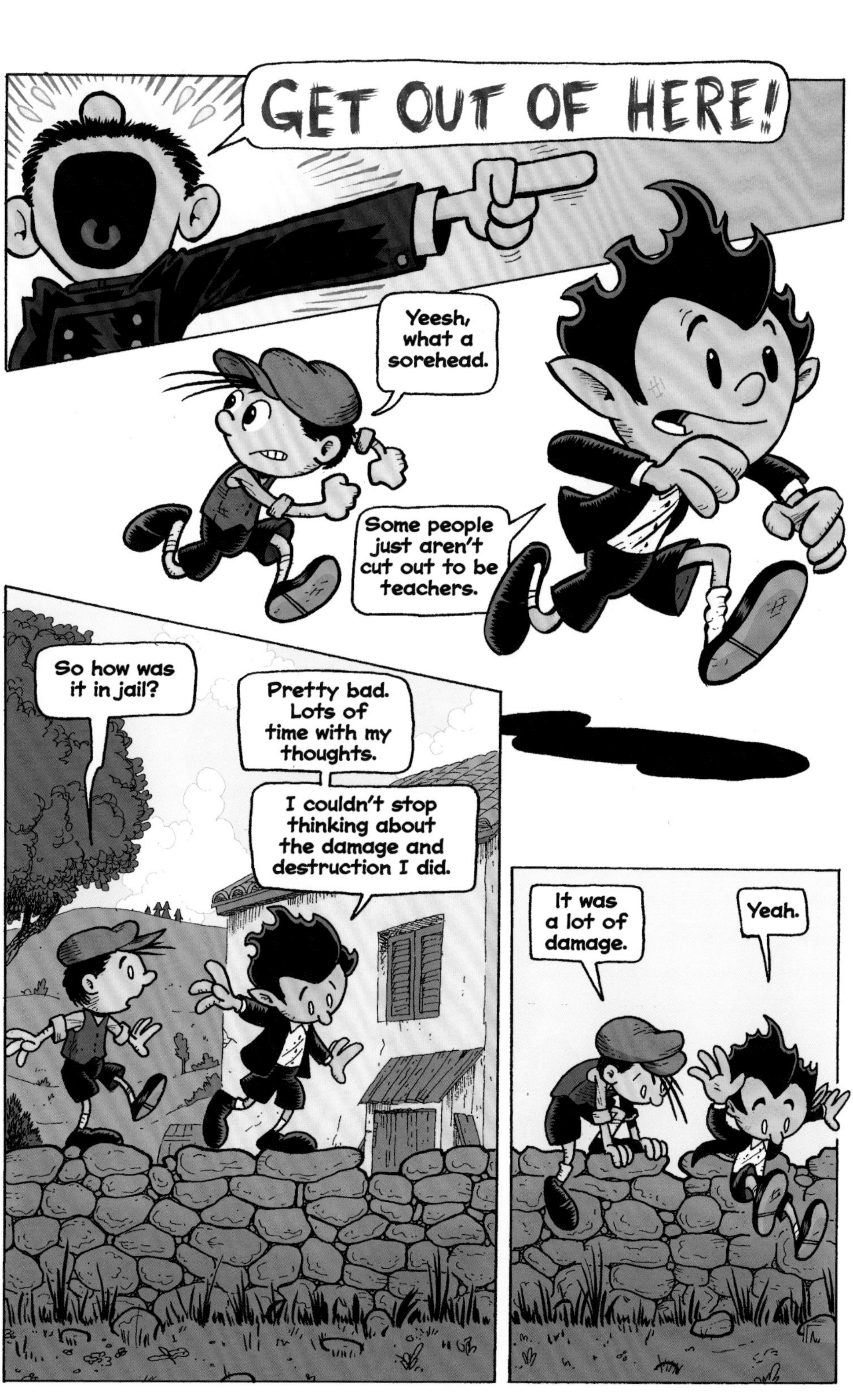
GET OUT OF HERE!
Yeesh, what a sorehead.
Some people just aren't cut out to be teachers.
So how was it in jail?
Pretty bad. Lots of time with my thoughts.
I couldn't stop thinking about the damage and destruction I did.
It was a lot of damage.
Yeah.

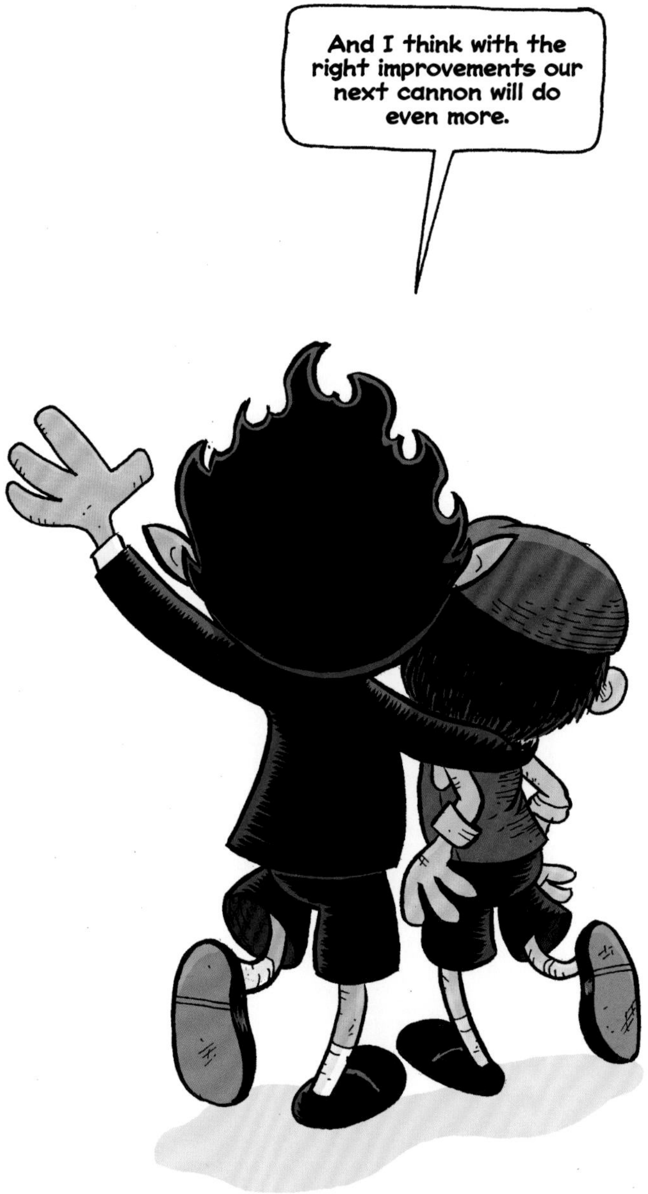
And I think with the right improvements our next cannon will do even more.

CHAPTER 7: COLOR QUEST

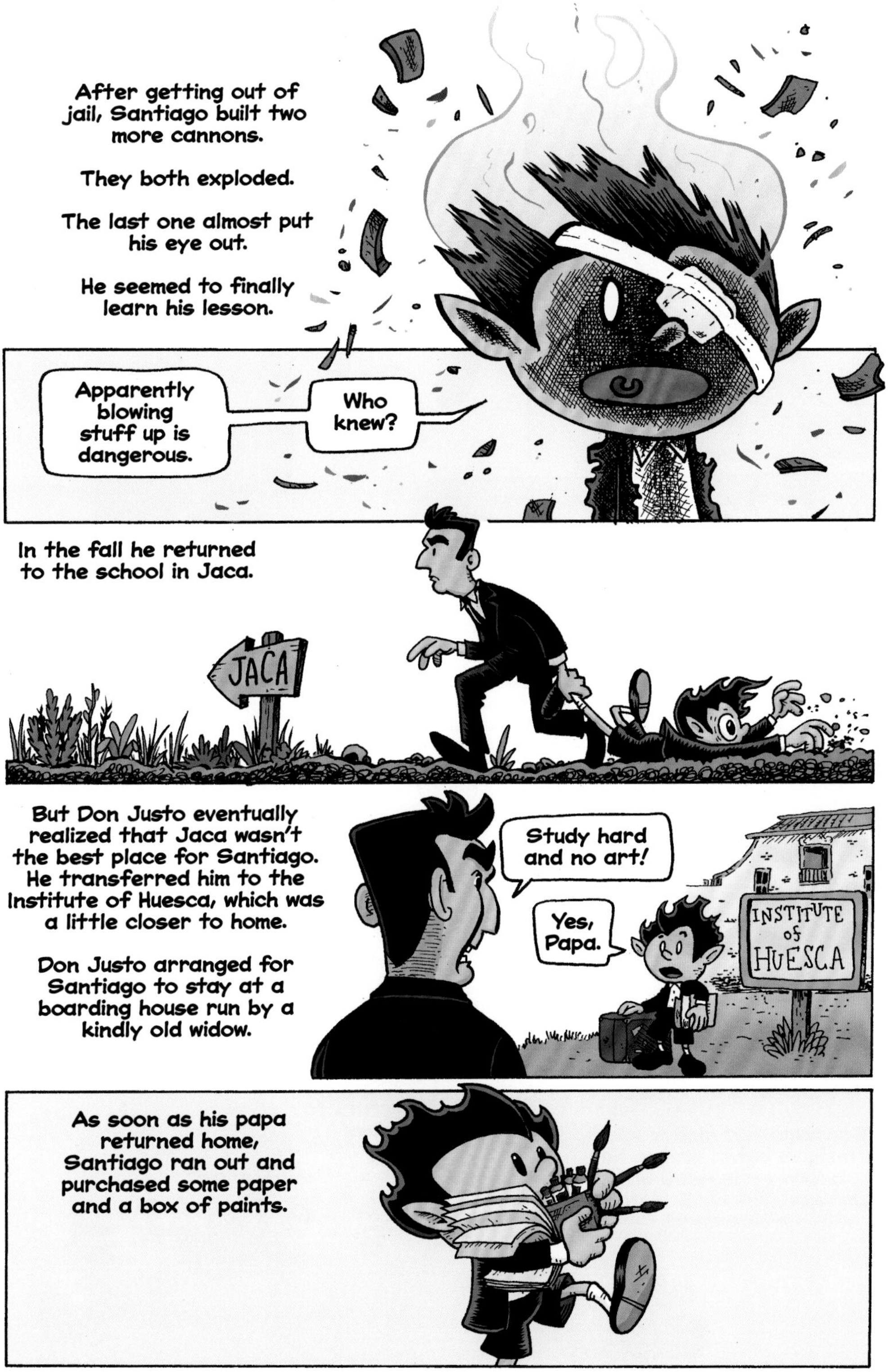
After getting out of jail, Santiago built two more cannons.
They both exploded.
The last one almost put his eye out.
He seemed to finally learn his lesson.
Apparently blowing stuff up is dangerous.
Who knew?
In the fall he returned to the school in Jaca.
JACA
But Don Justo eventually realized that Jaca wasn't the best place for Santiago. He transferred him to the Institute of Huesca, which was a little closer to home.
Don Justo arranged for Santiago to stay at a boarding house run by a kindly old widow.
Study hard and no art!
Yes, Papa.
INSTITUTE of HUESCA
As soon as his papa returned home, Santiago ran out and purchased some paper and a box of paints.

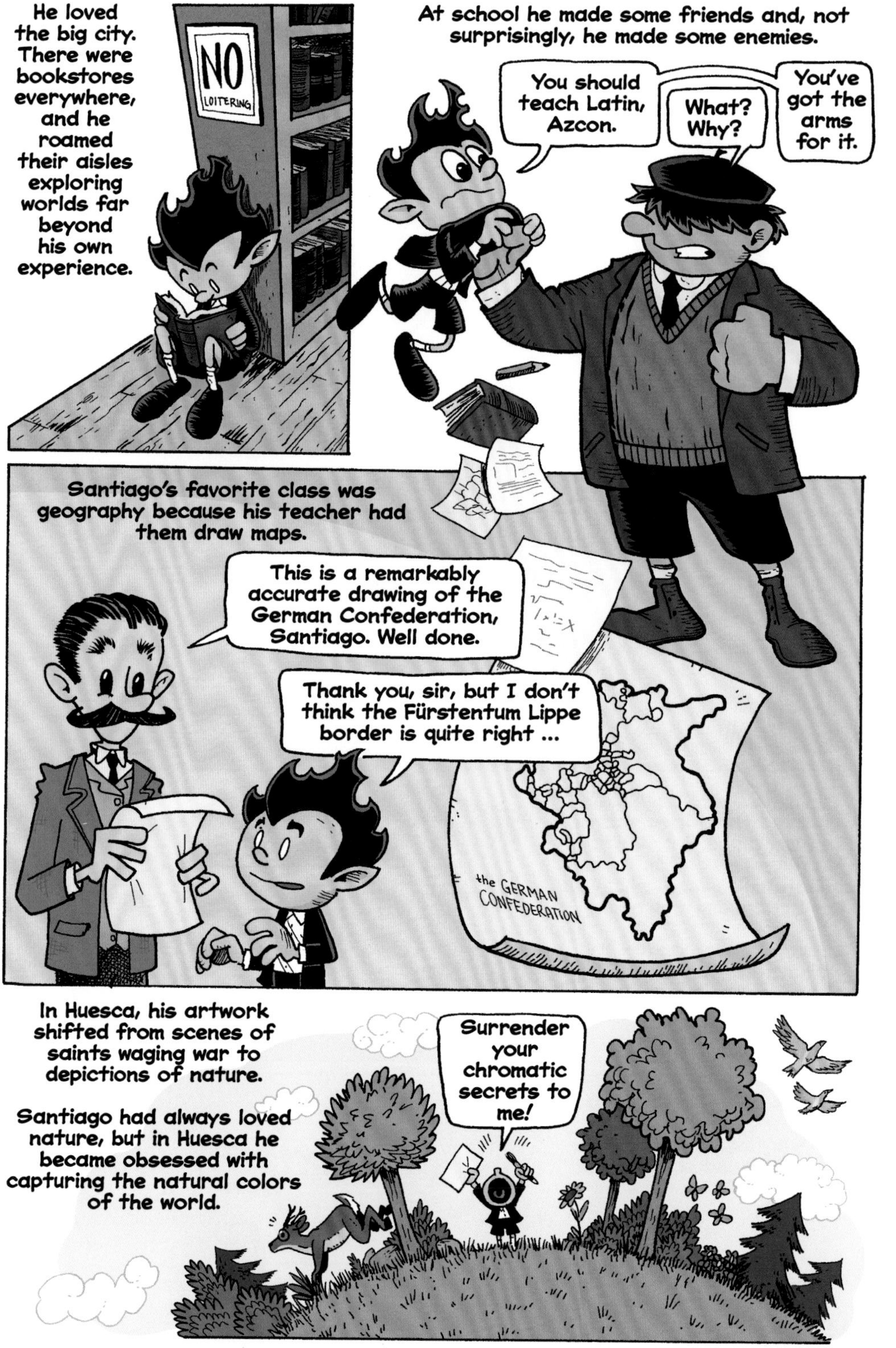
He loved the big city. There were bookstores everywhere, and he roamed their aisles exploring worlds far beyond his own experience.
NO LOITERING
At school he made some friends and, not surprisingly, he made some enemies.
You should teach Latin, Azcon.
What? Why?
You've got the arms for it.
Santiago's favorite class was geography because his teacher had them draw maps.
This is a remarkably accurate drawing of the German Confederation, Santiago. Well done.
Thank you, sir, but I don't think the Fürstentum Lippe border is quite right ...
the GERMAN CONFEDERATION
In Huesca, his artwork shifted from scenes of saints waging war to depictions of nature.
Santiago had always loved nature, but in Huesca he became obsessed with capturing the natural colors of the world.
Surrender your chromatic secrets to me!

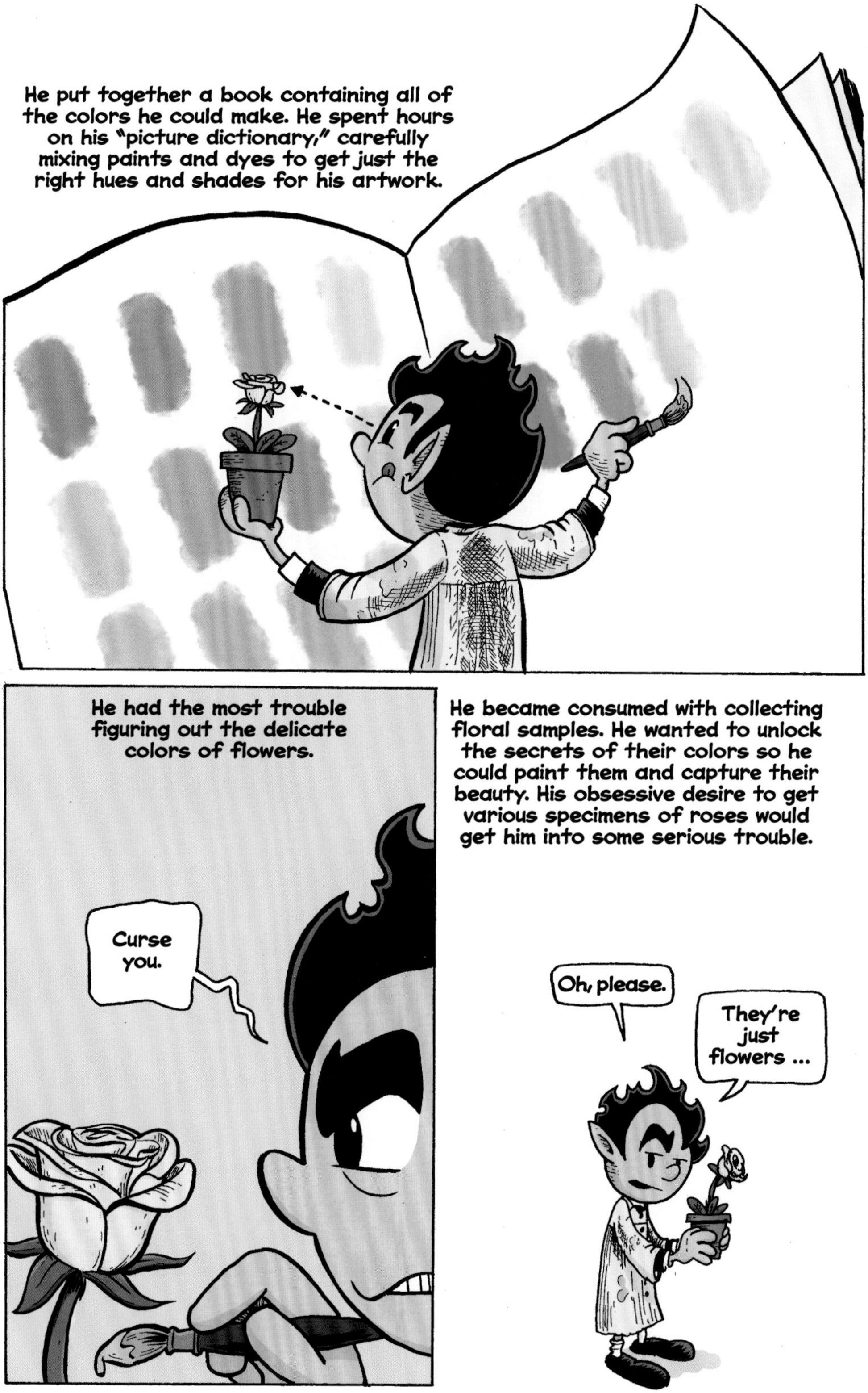
He put together a book containing all of the colors he could make. He spent hours on his "picture dictionary," carefully mixing paints and dyes to get just the right hues and shades for his artwork.
He had the most trouble figuring out the delicate colors of flowers.
Curse you.
He became consumed with collecting floral samples. He wanted to unlock the secrets of their colors so he could paint them and capture their beauty. His obsessive desire to get various specimens of roses would get him into some serious trouble.
Oh, please.
They're just flowers ...

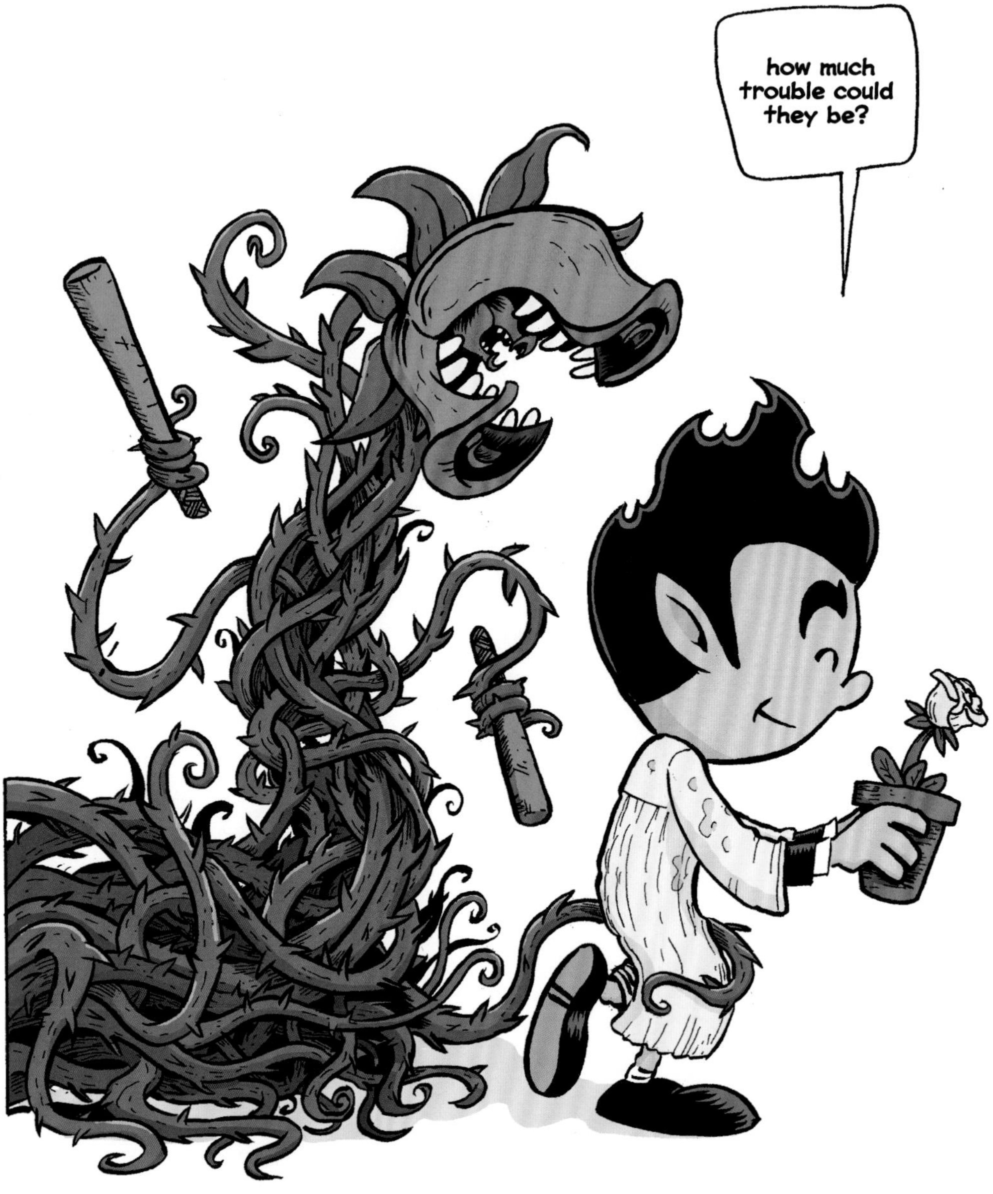
how much trouble could they be?

CHAPTER 8: THE ROSES OF DOOM

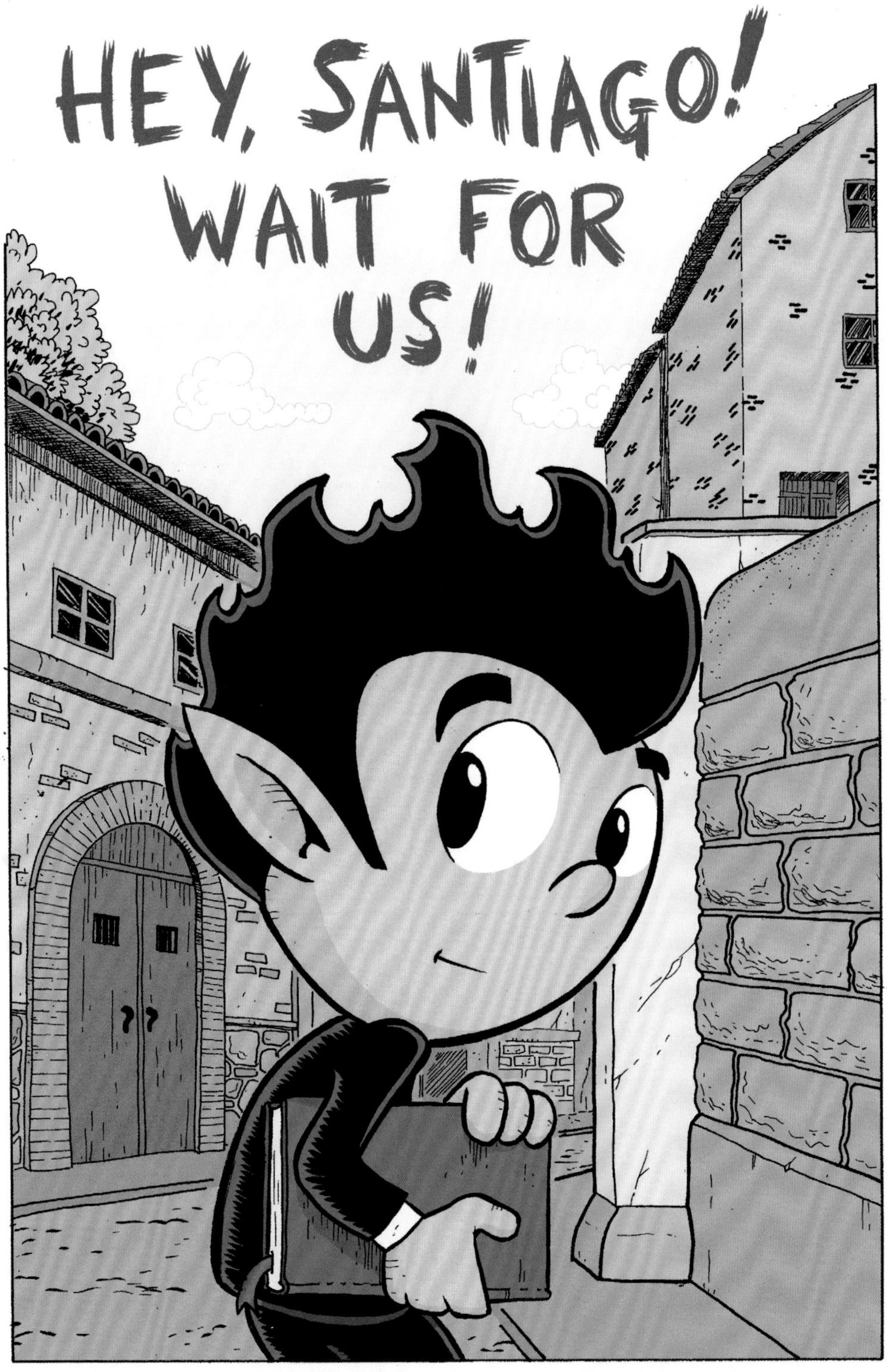
HEY, SANTIAGO! WAIT FOR US!

Hello, Jorge.

Hello, Rafael.

Is that your picture dictionary?

Why are you bringing that to school?

I'm going to color the maps I draw in geography.

Show-off.

I'm not a show-off.

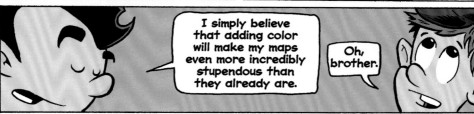

I simply believe that adding color will make my maps even more incredibly stupendous than they already are.

Oh, brother.

The colors in this book will help me transform my black-and-white maps into wondrous works of art!

HAH!

What do you know about art, goatflesh?

Wha—

What did you call me, Azcon?

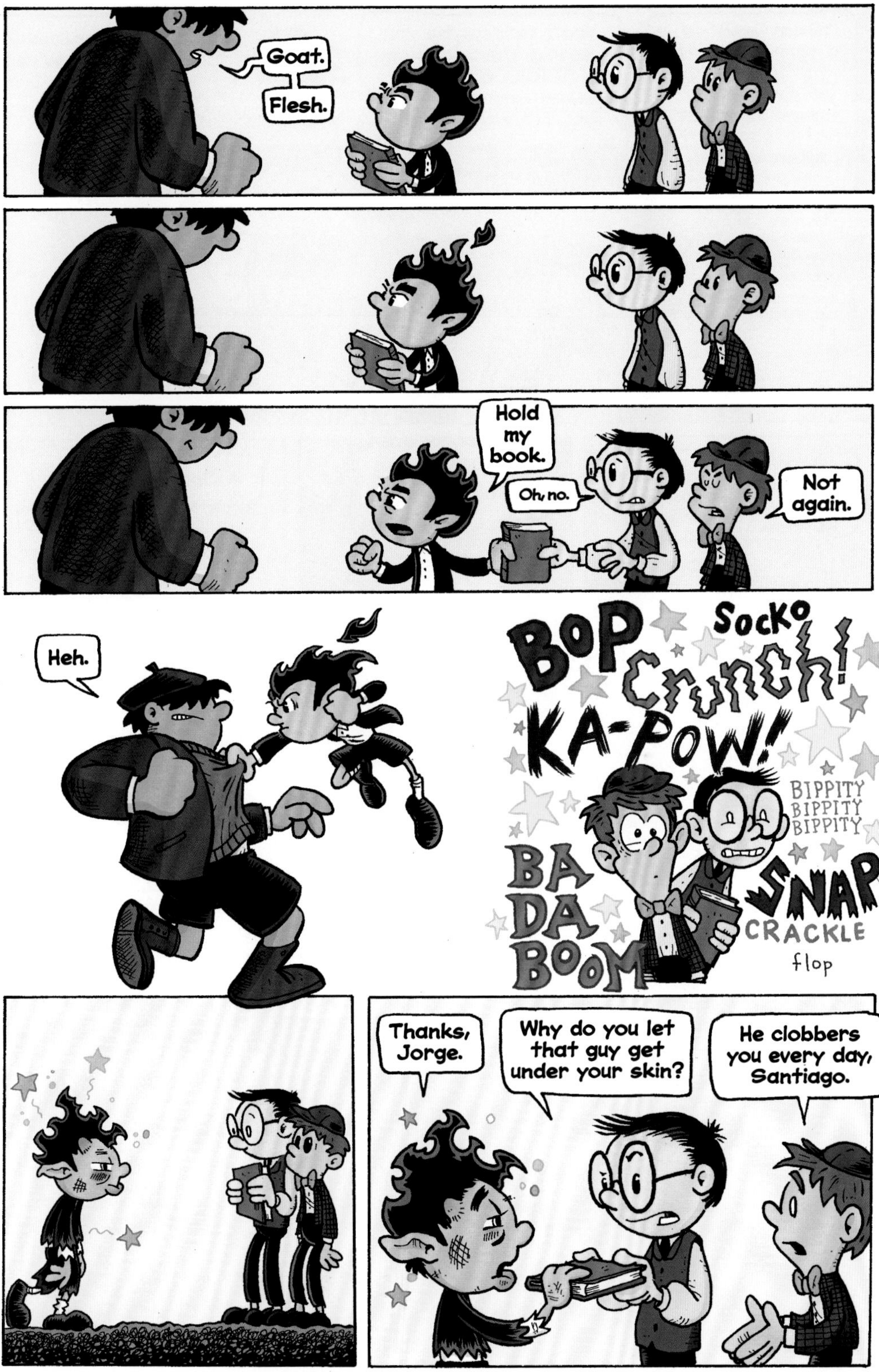

Goat.
Flesh.
Hold my book.
Oh, no.
Not again.
Heh.
BOP
Socko
Crunch!
KA-POW!
BIPPITY BIPPITY BIPPITY
BA DA BOOM
SNAP
CRACKLE
flop
Thanks, Jorge.
Why do you let that guy get under your skin?
He clobbers you every day, Santiago.

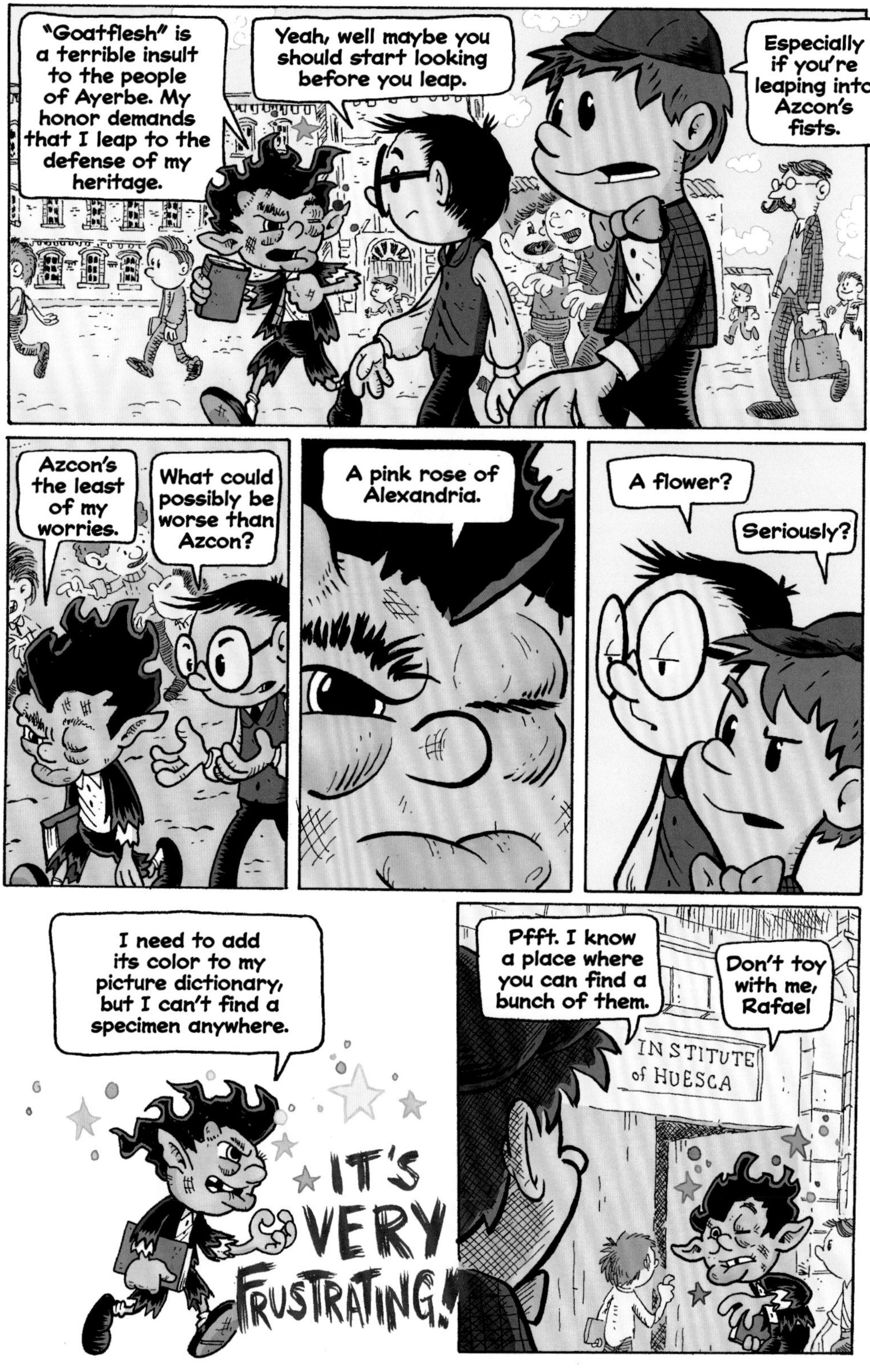
"Goatflesh" is a terrible insult to the people of Ayerbe. My honor demands that I leap to the defense of my heritage.
Yeah, well maybe you should start looking before you leap.
Especially if you're leaping into Azcon's fists.
Azcon's the least of my worries.
What could possibly be worse than Azcon?
A pink rose of Alexandria.
A flower?
Seriously?
I need to add its color to my picture dictionary, but I can't find a specimen anywhere.
IT'S VERY FRUSTRATING!
Pfft. I know a place where you can find a bunch of them.
Don't toy with me, Rafael
INSTITUTE of HUESCA

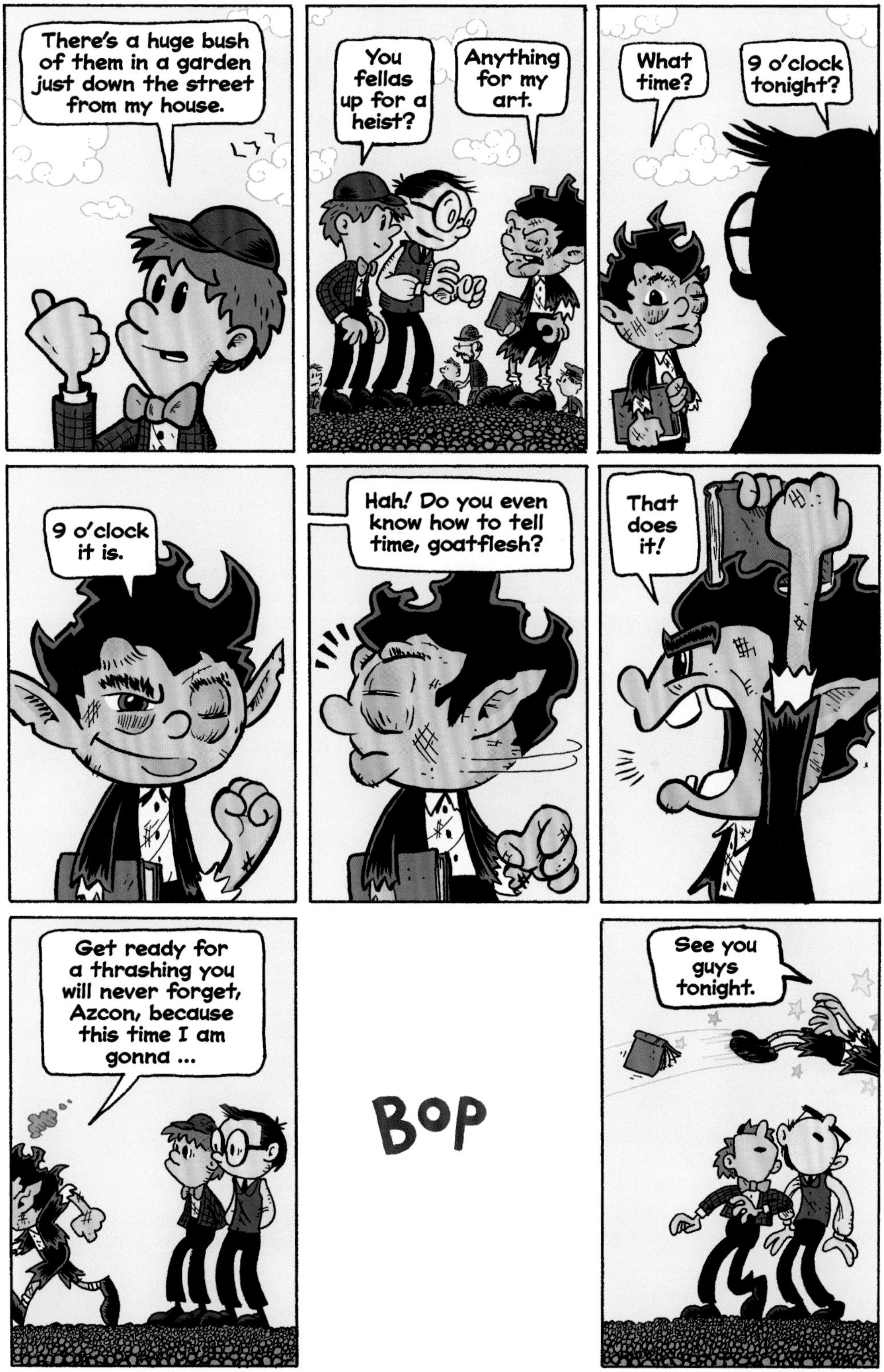

There's a huge bush of them in a garden just down the street from my house.
You fellas up for a heist?
Anything for my art.
What time?
9 o'clock tonight?
9 o'clock it is.
Hah! Do you even know how to tell time, goatflesh?
That does it!
Get ready for a thrashing you will never forget, Azcon, because this time I am gonna ...
BOP
See you guys tonight.

LATER THAT NIGHT

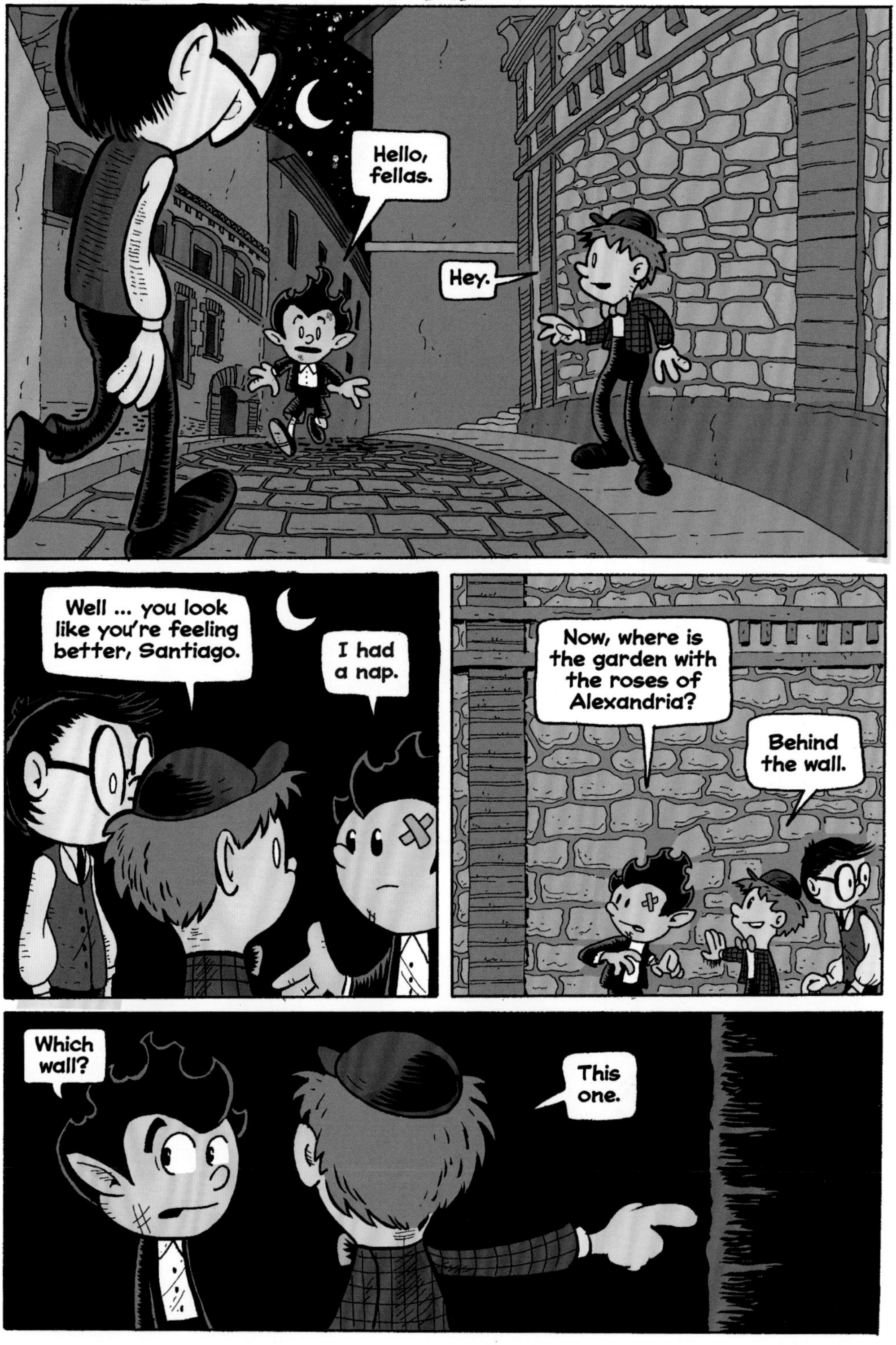

Hello, fellas.
Hey.
Well ... you look like you're feeling better, Santiago.
I had a nap.
Now, where is the garden with the roses of Alexandria?
Behind the wall.
Which wall?
This one.

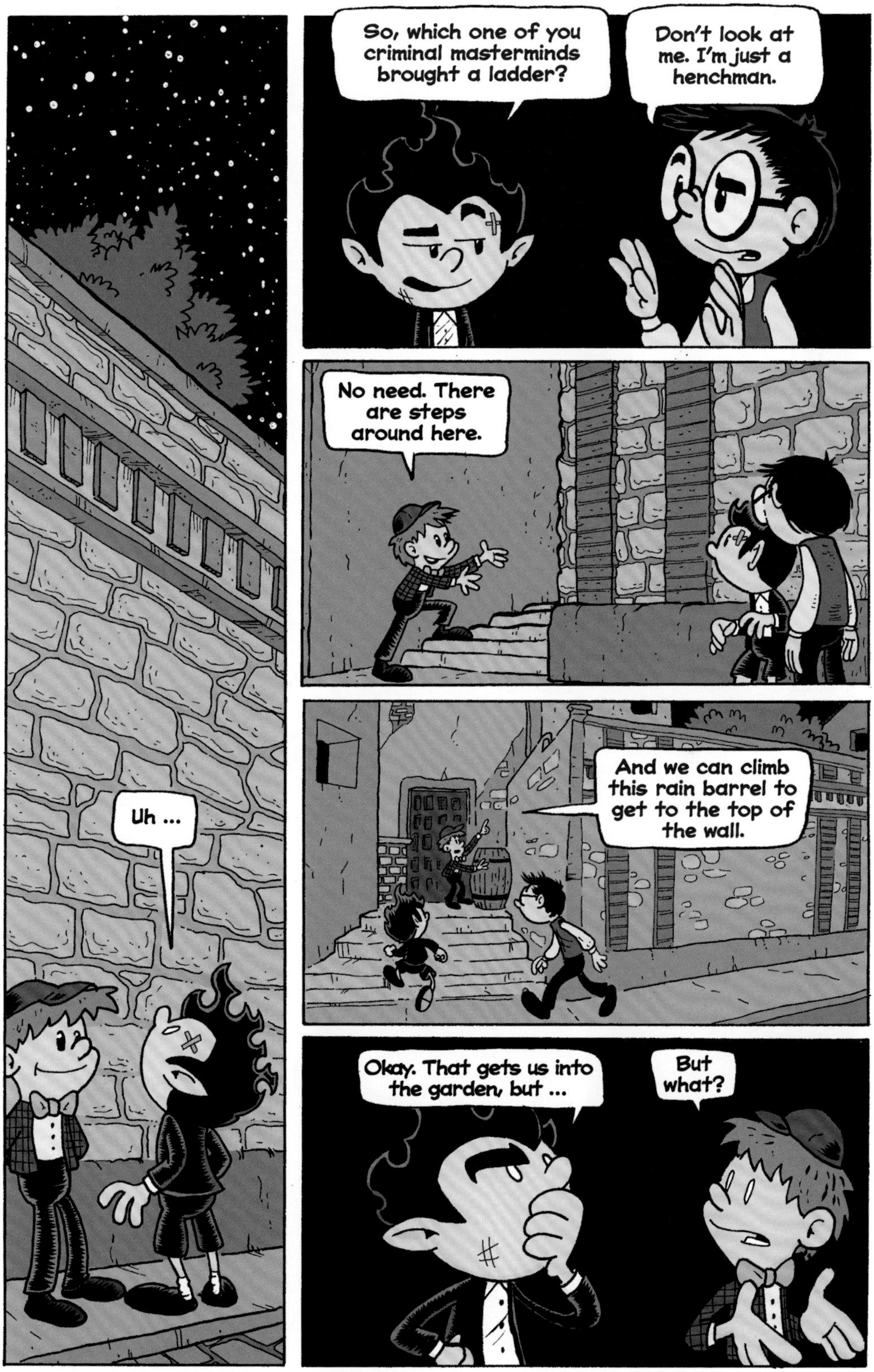

Uh ...
So, which one of you criminal masterminds brought a ladder?
Don't look at me. I'm just a henchman.
No need. There are steps around here.
And we can climb this rain barrel to get to the top of the wall.
Okay. That gets us into the garden, but ...
But what?

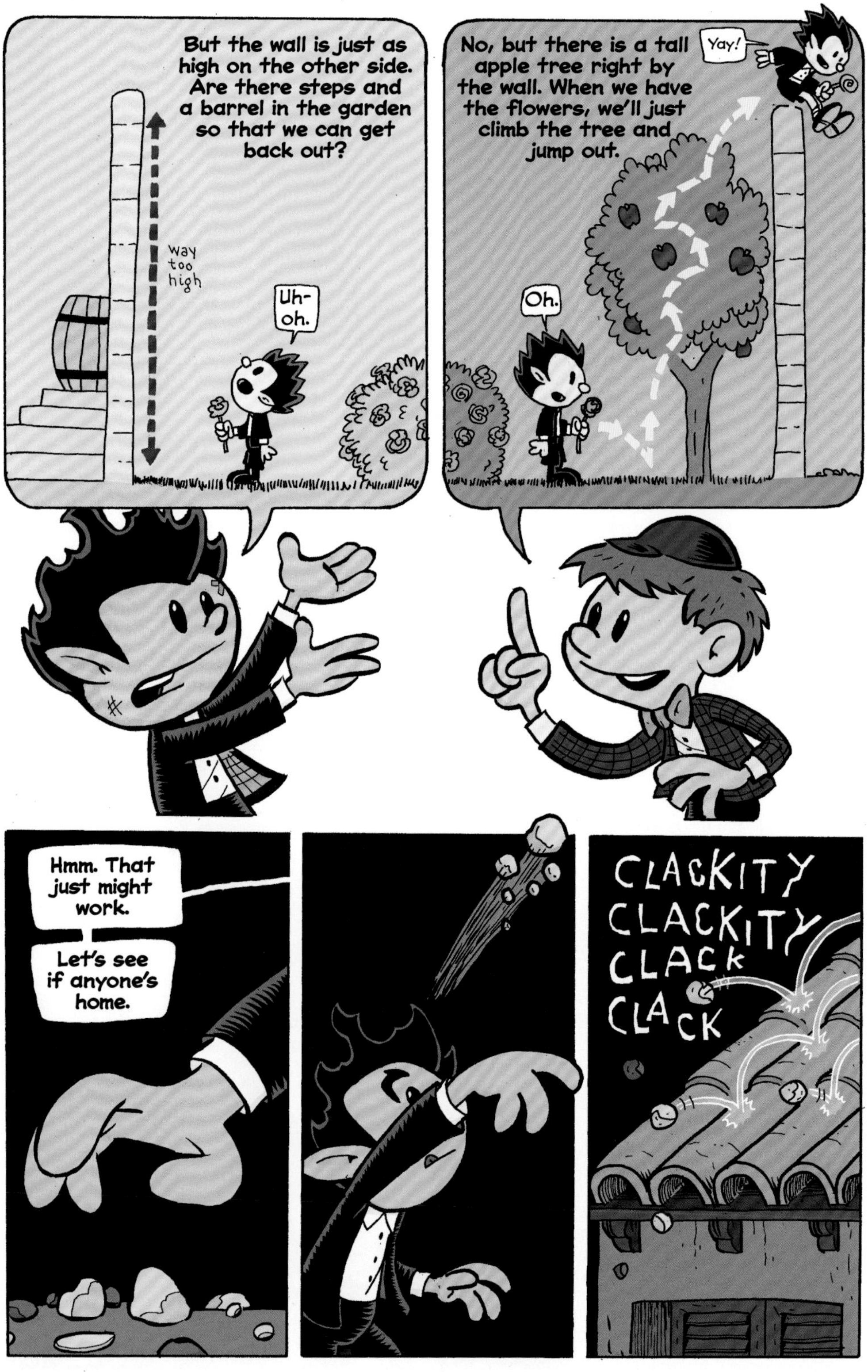
But the wall is just as high on the other side. Are there steps and a barrel in the garden so that we can get back out?
way too high
Uh-oh.
No, but there is a tall apple tree right by the wall. When we have the flowers, we'll just climb the tree and jump out.
Yay!
Oh.
Hmm. That just might work.
Let's see if anyone's home.
CLACKITY
CLACKITY
CLACK
CLACK

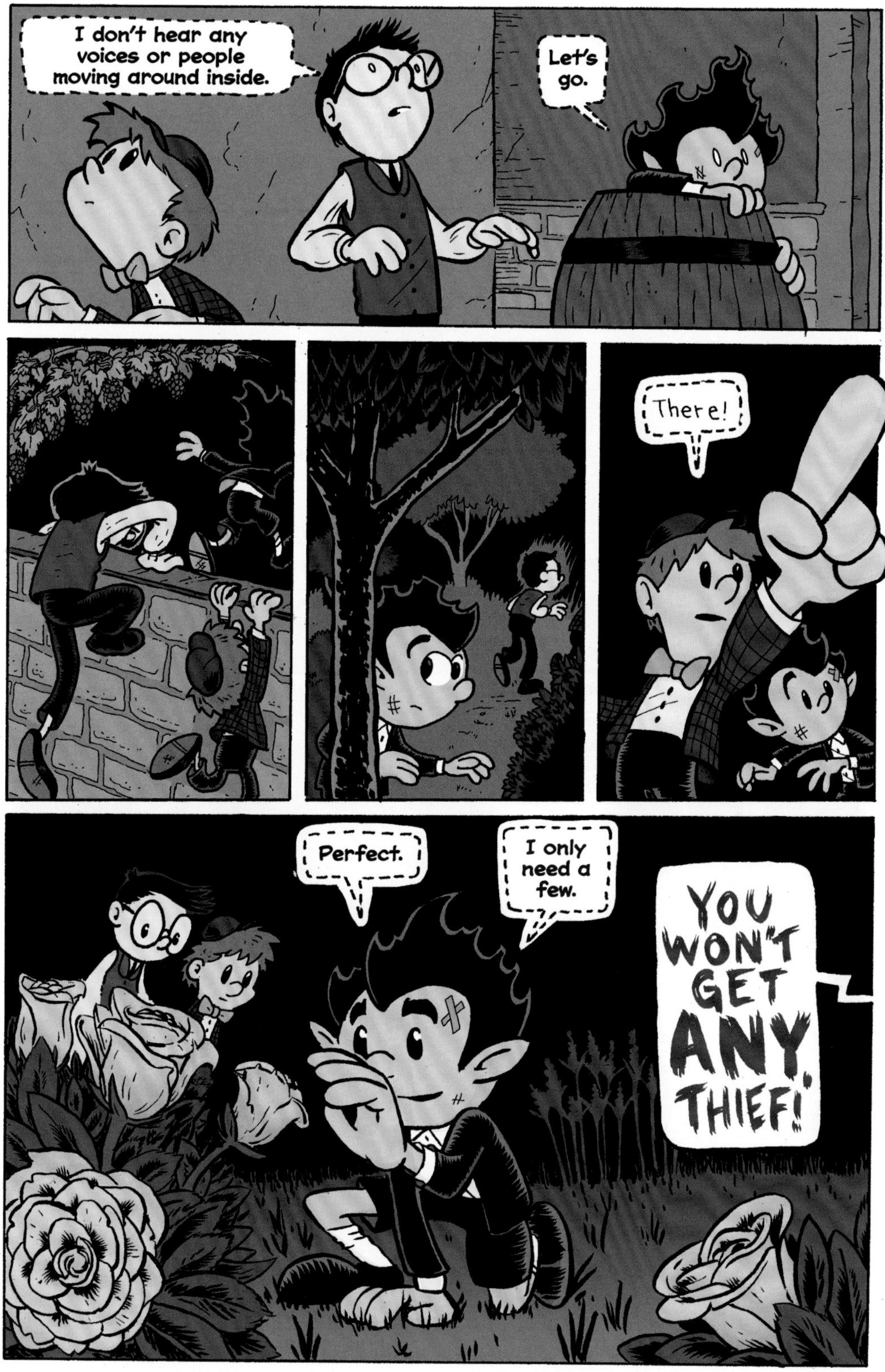
I don't hear any voices or people moving around inside.
Let's go.
There!
Perfect.
I only need a few.
YOU WON'T GET ANY, THIEF!

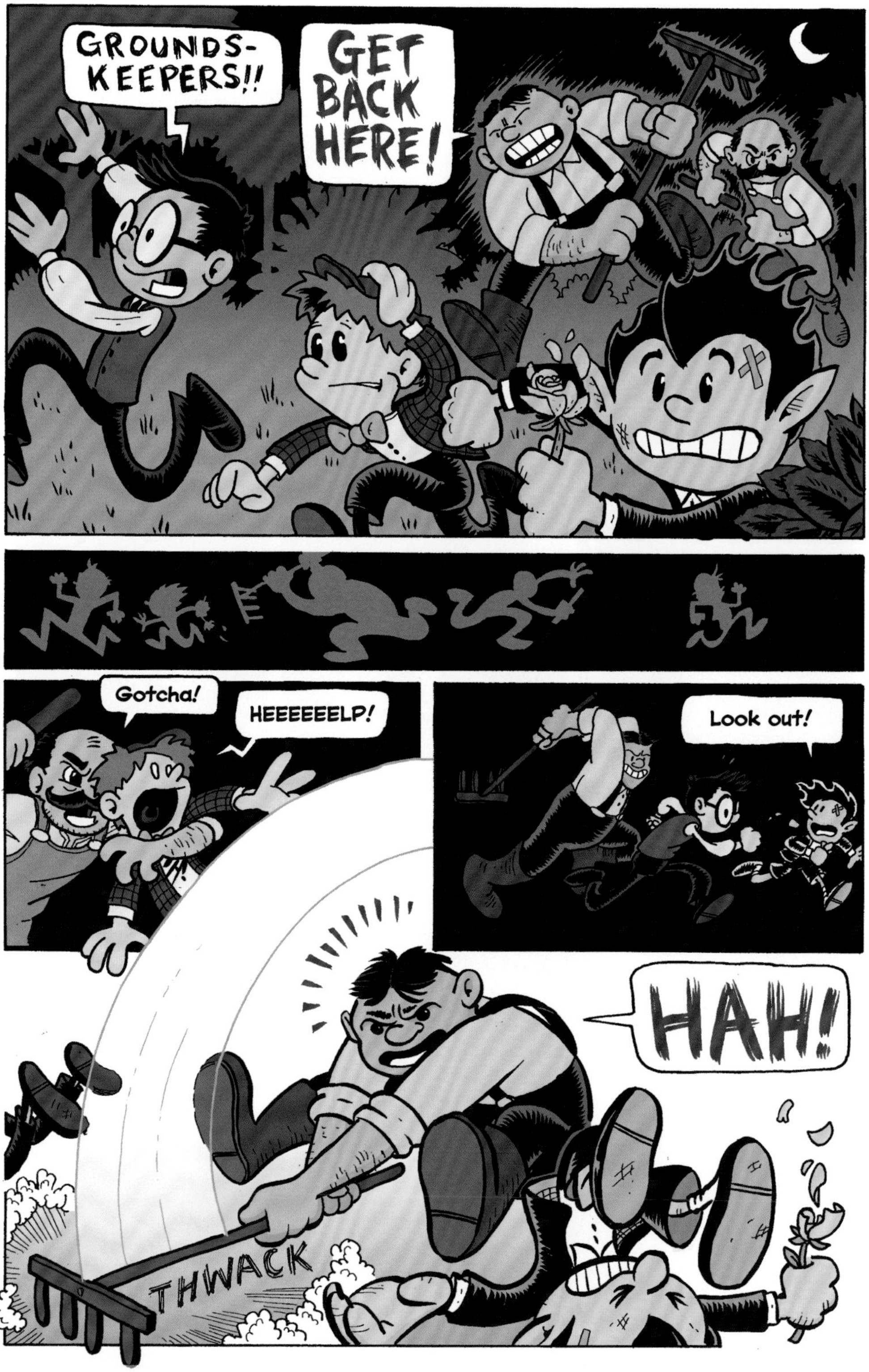
GROUNDS-KEEPERS!!
GET BACK HERE!
Gotcha!
HEEEEEEELP!
Look out!
HAH!
THWACK

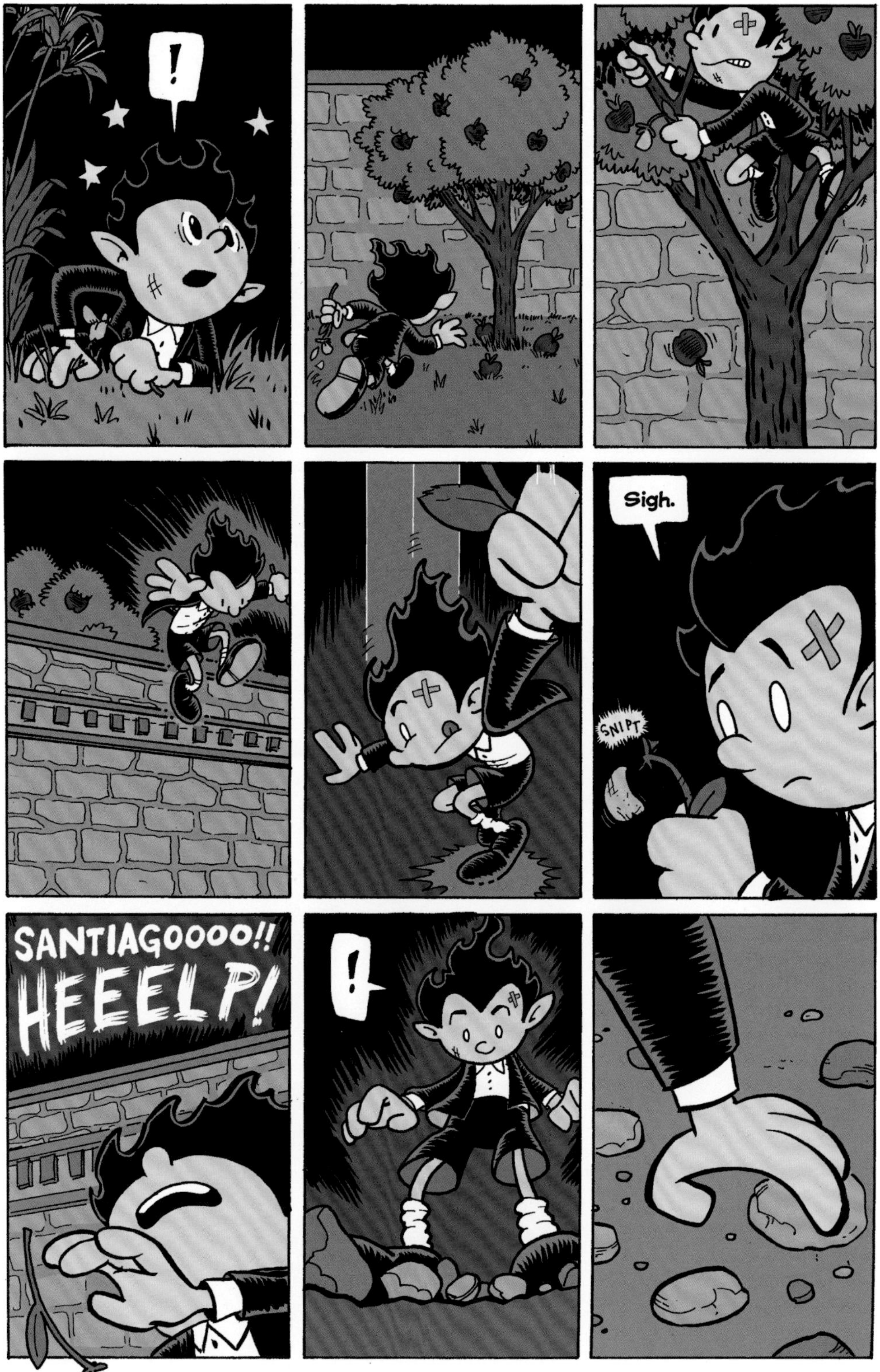
!
Sigh.
SNIPT
SANTIAGOOOO!!
HEEELP!
!

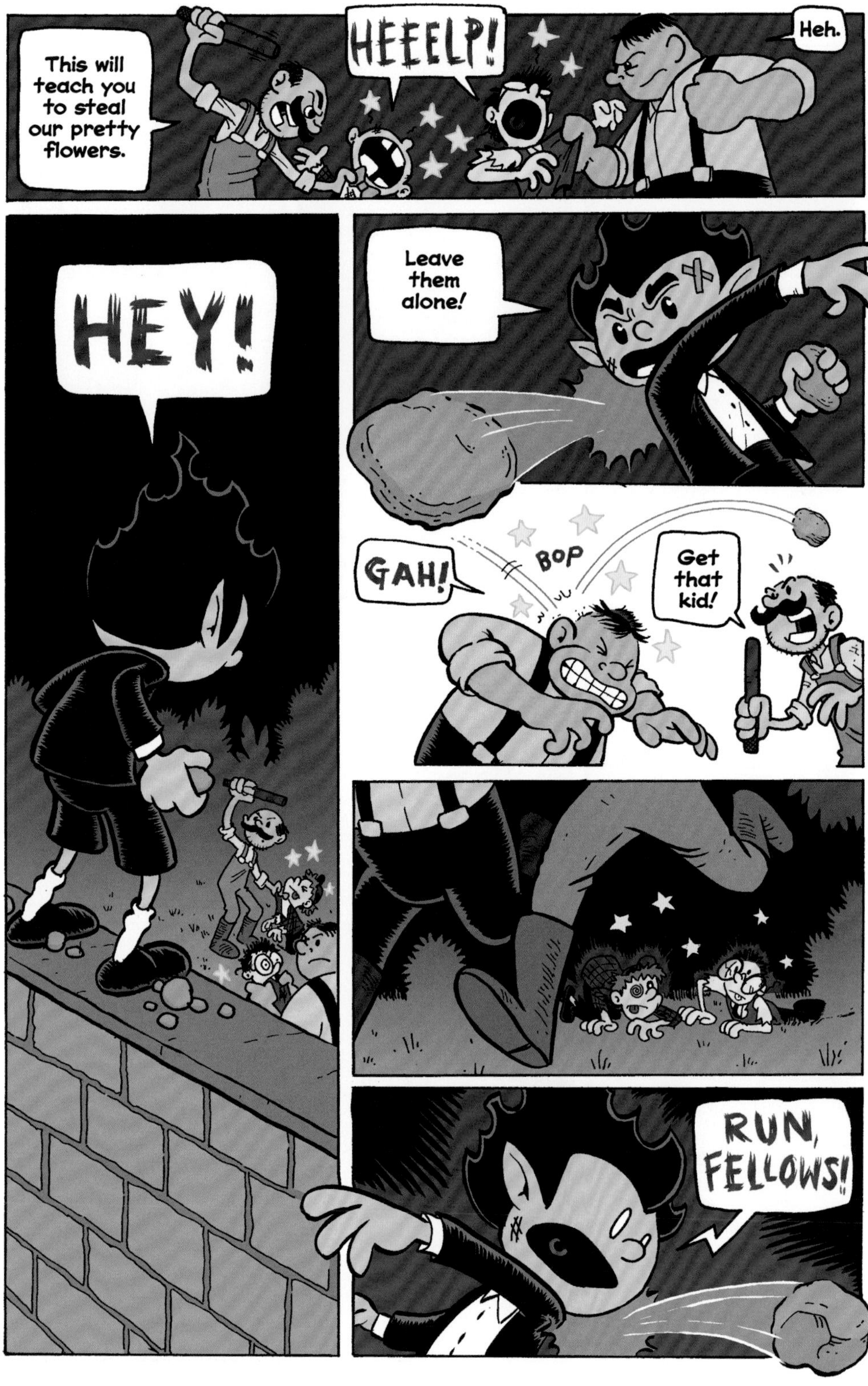
This will teach you to steal our pretty flowers.
HEEELP!
Heh.
HEY!
Leave them alone!
GAH!
BOP
Get that kid!
RUN, FELLOWS!

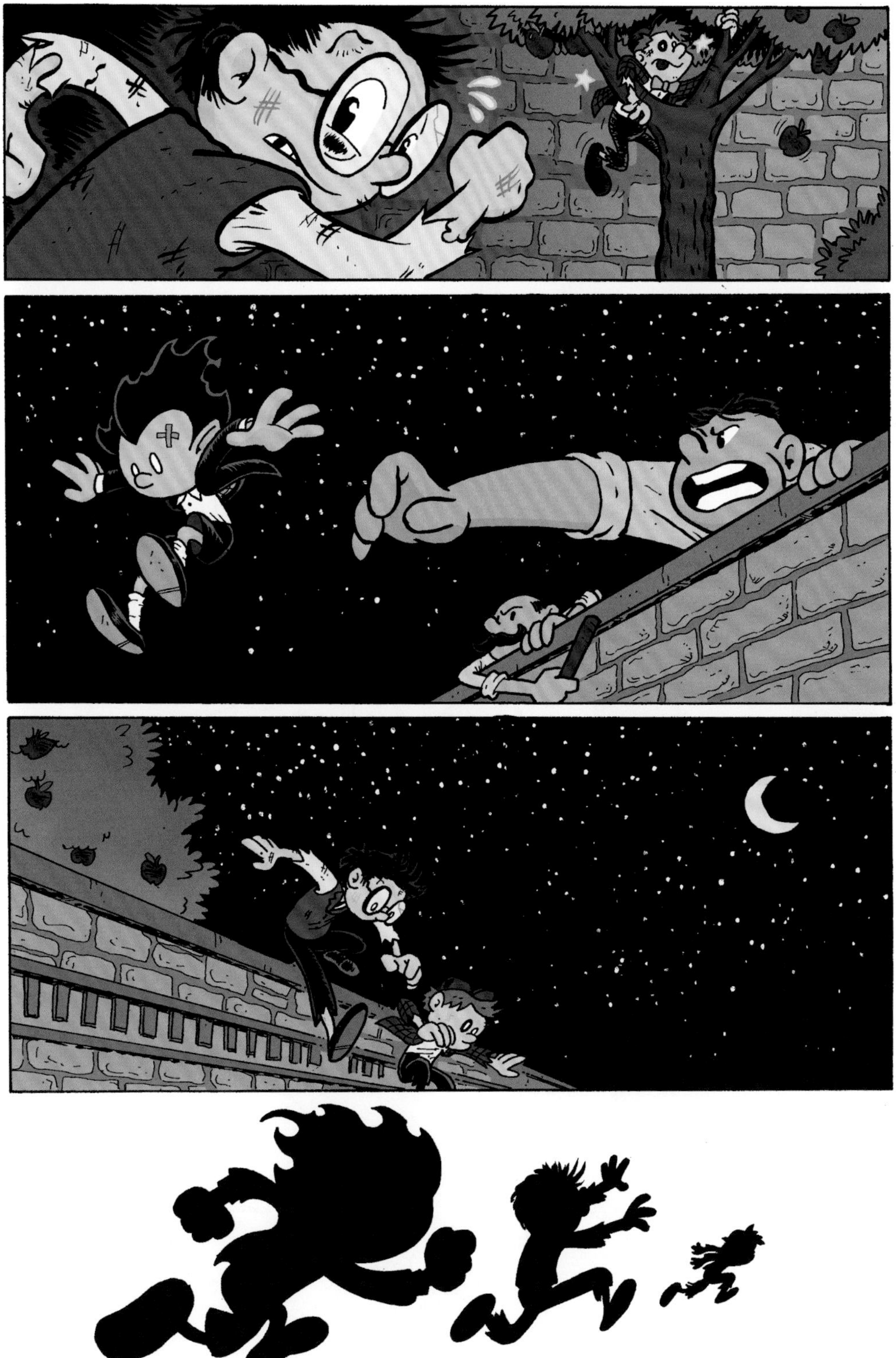

THE NEXT MORNING

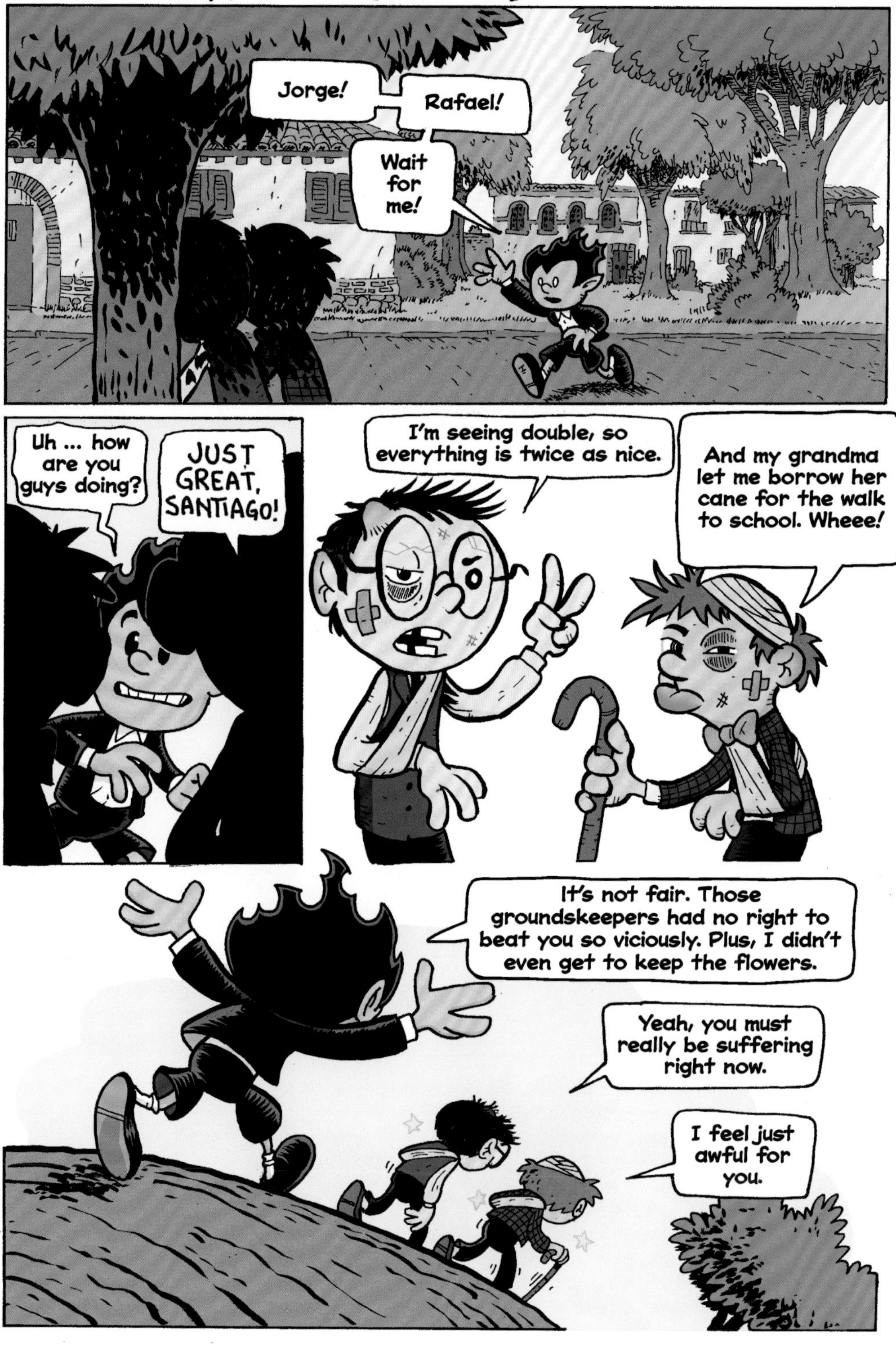

Jorge!
Rafael!
Wait for me!
Uh ... how are you guys doing?
JUST GREAT, SANTIAGO!
I'm seeing double, so everything is twice as nice.
And my grandma let me borrow her cane for the walk to school. Wheee!
It's not fair. Those groundskeepers had no right to beat you so viciously. Plus, I didn't even get to keep the flowers.
Yeah, you must really be suffering right now.
I feel just awful for you.

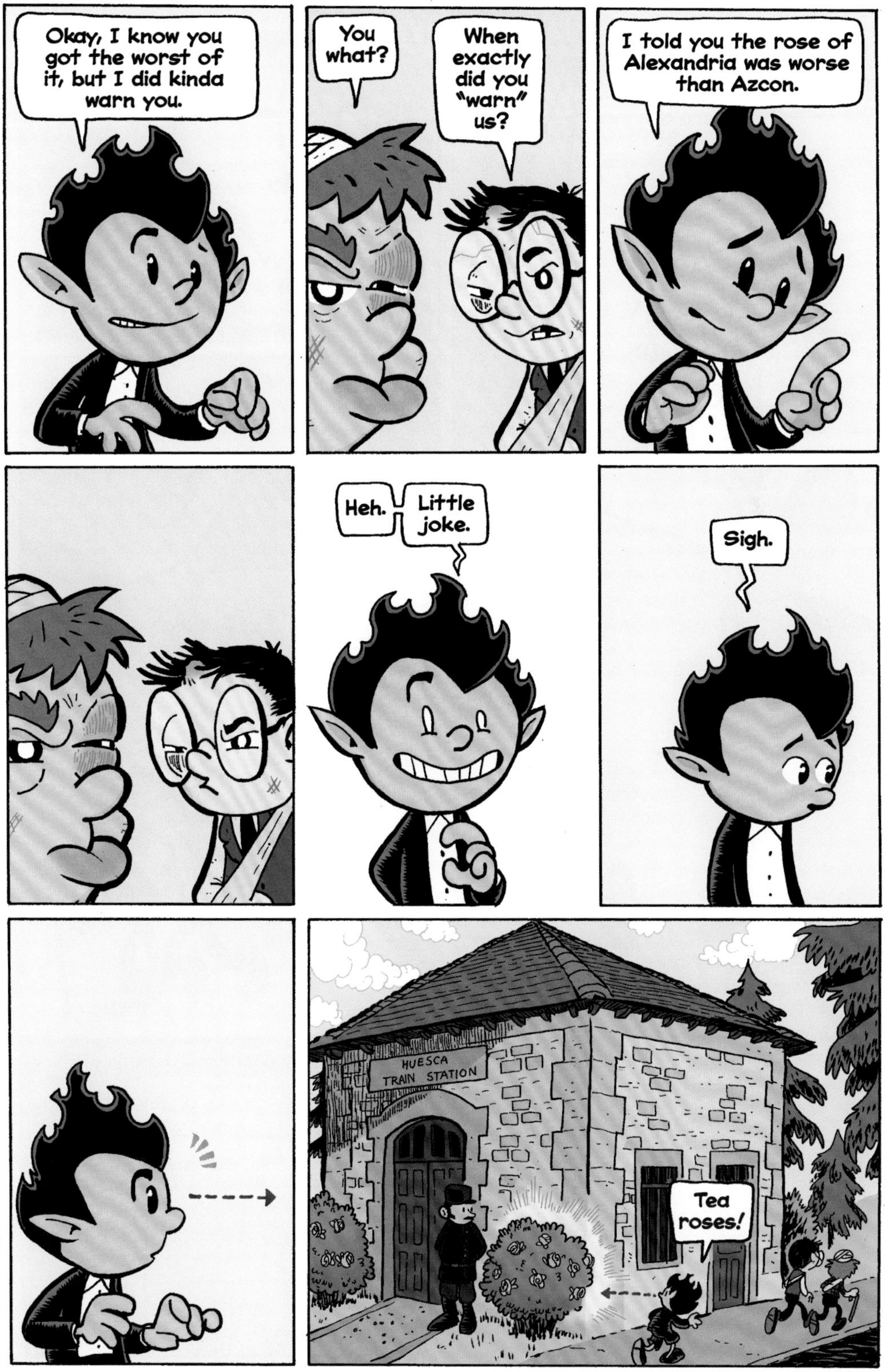
Okay, I know you got the worst of it, but I did kinda warn you.
You what?
When exactly did you "warn" us?
I told you the rose of Alexandria was worse than Azcon.
Heh.
Little joke.
Sigh.
HUESCA TRAIN STATION
Tea roses!

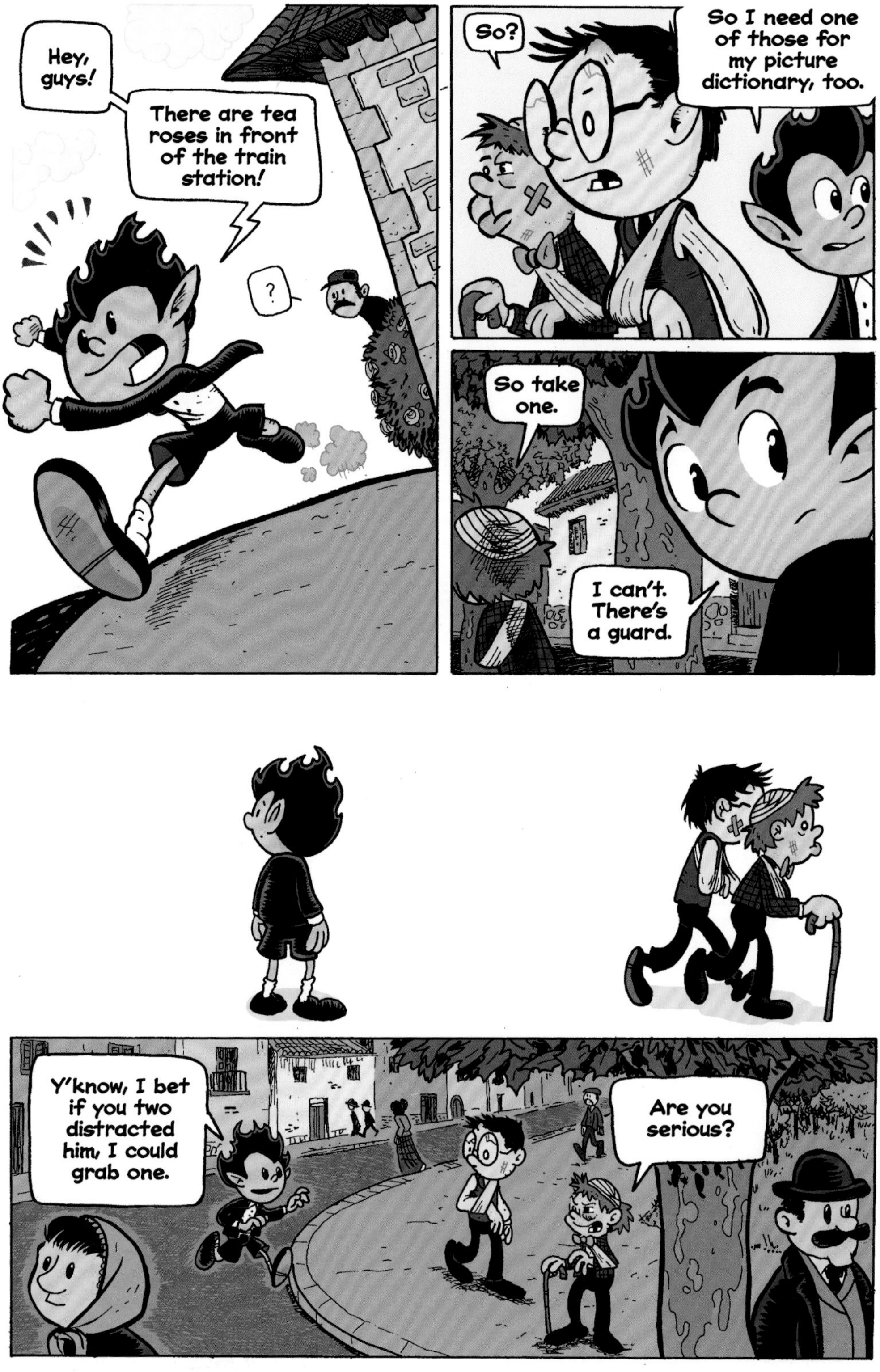
Hey, guys!
There are tea roses in front of the train station!
?
So?
So I need one of those for my picture dictionary, too.
So take one.
I can't. There's a guard.
Y'know, I bet if you two distracted him, I could grab one.
Are you serious?

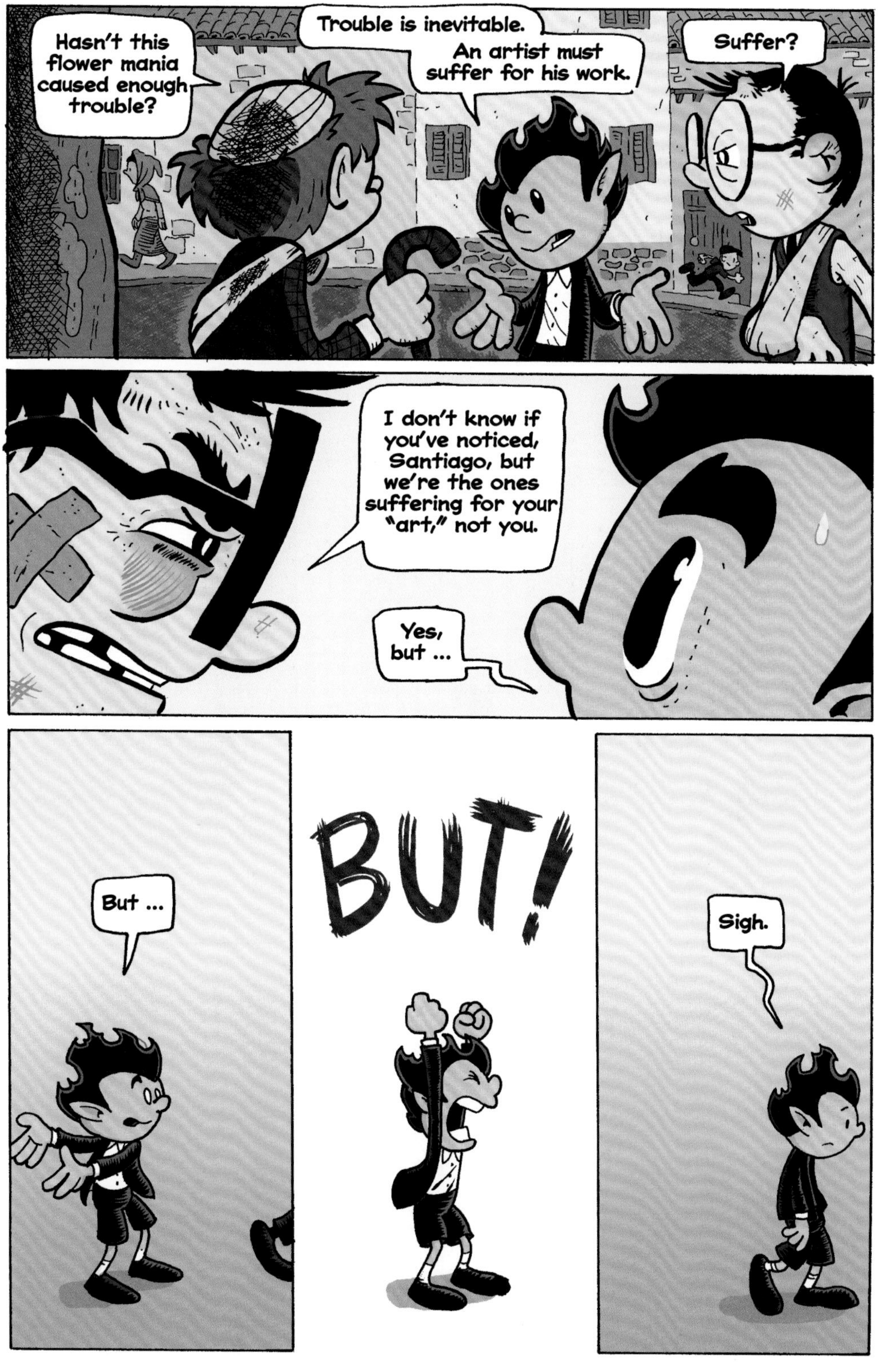
Hasn't this flower mania caused enough trouble?
Trouble is inevitable.
An artist must suffer for his work.
Suffer?
I don't know if you've noticed, Santiago, but we're the ones suffering for your "art," not you.
Yes, but ...
But ...
BUT!
Sigh.

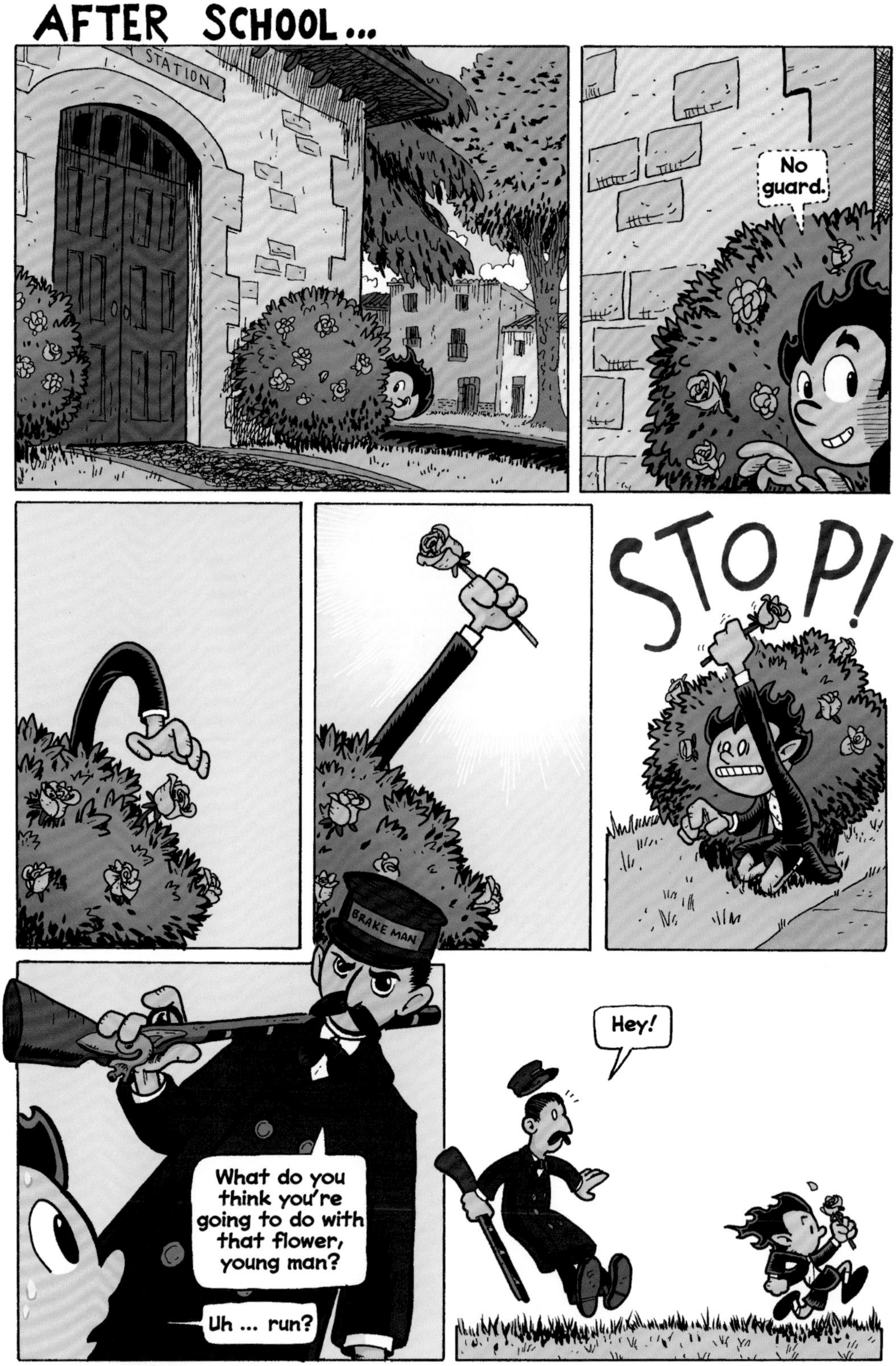
AFTER SCHOOL...
STATION
No guard.
STOP!
BRAKE MAN
What do you think you're going to do with that flower, young man?
Uh ... run?
Hey!

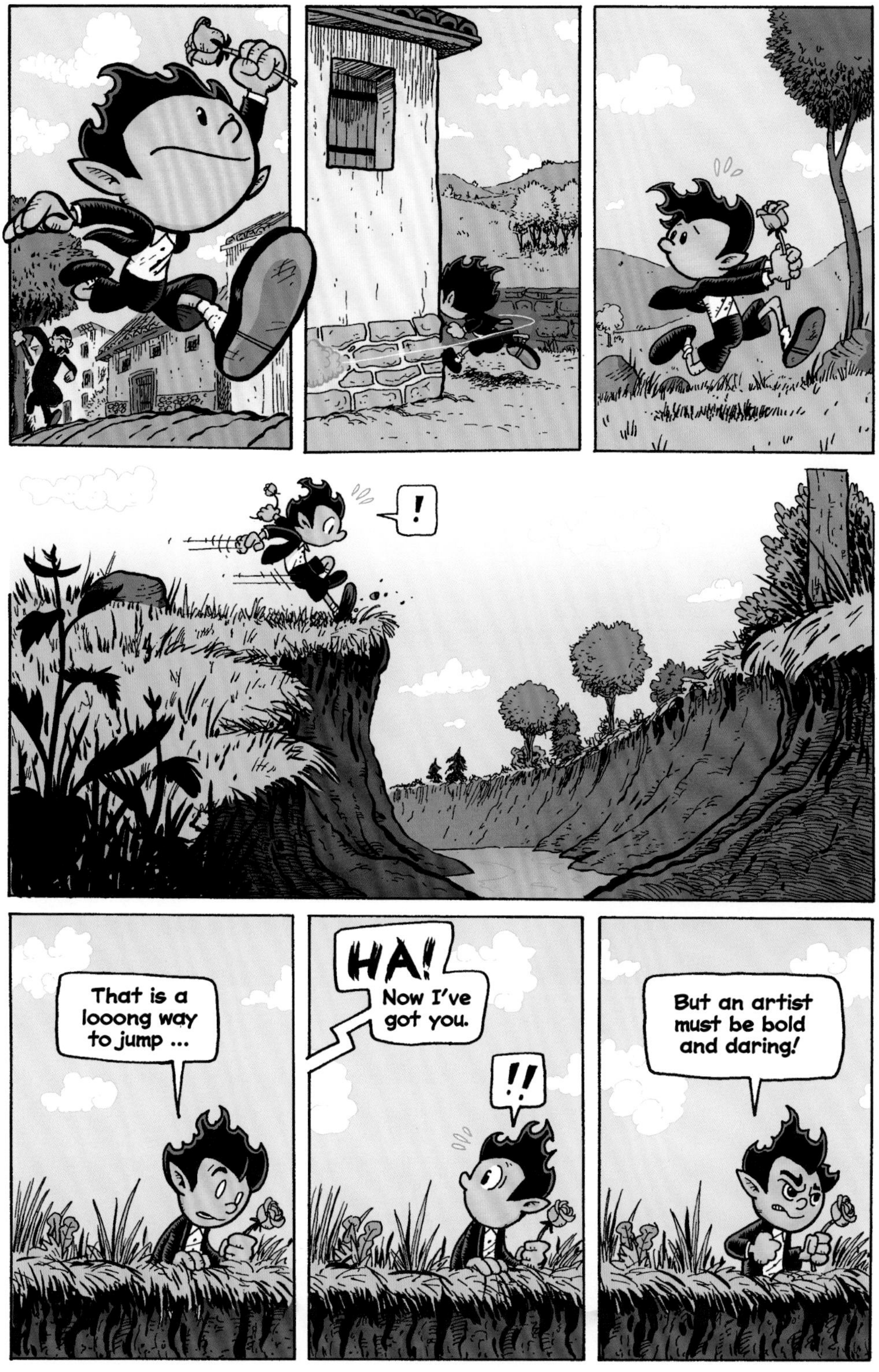
!
That is a looong way to jump ...
HA!
Now I've got you.
!!
But an artist must be bold and daring!

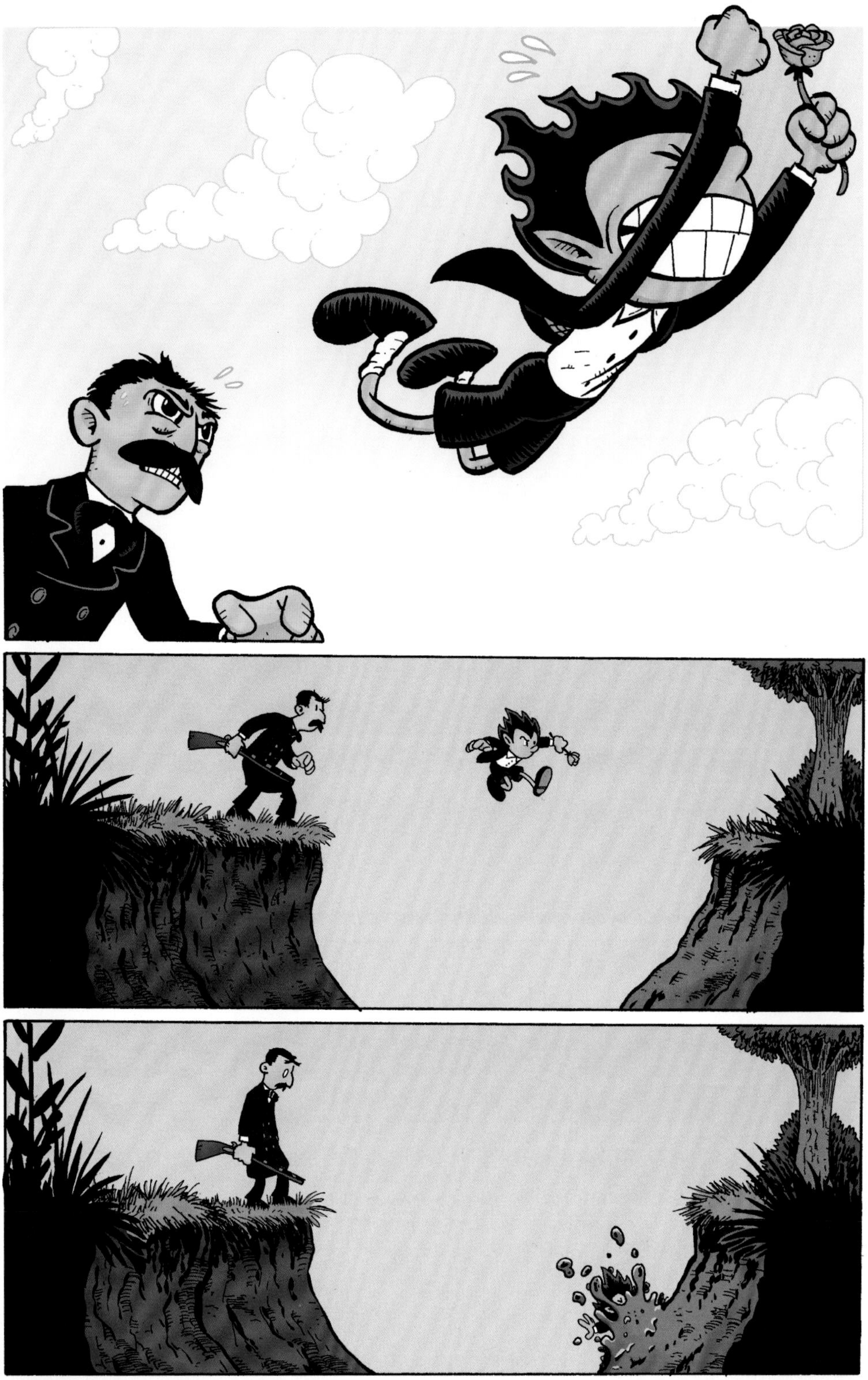

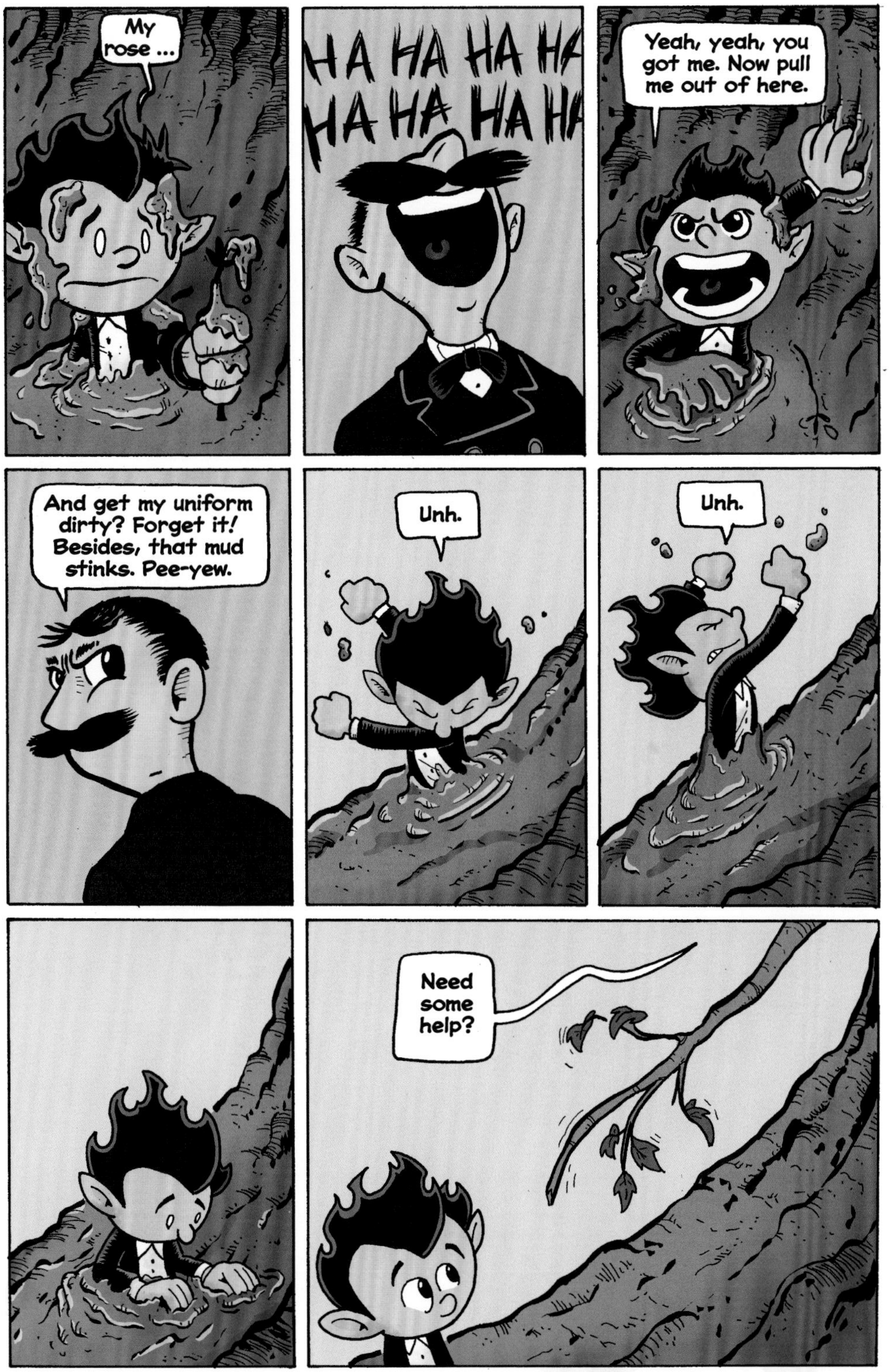
My rose ...
HA HA HA HA HA HA HA HA
Yeah, yeah, you got me. Now pull me out of here.
And get my uniform dirty? Forget it! Besides, that mud stinks. Pee-yew.
Unh.
Unh.
Need some help?

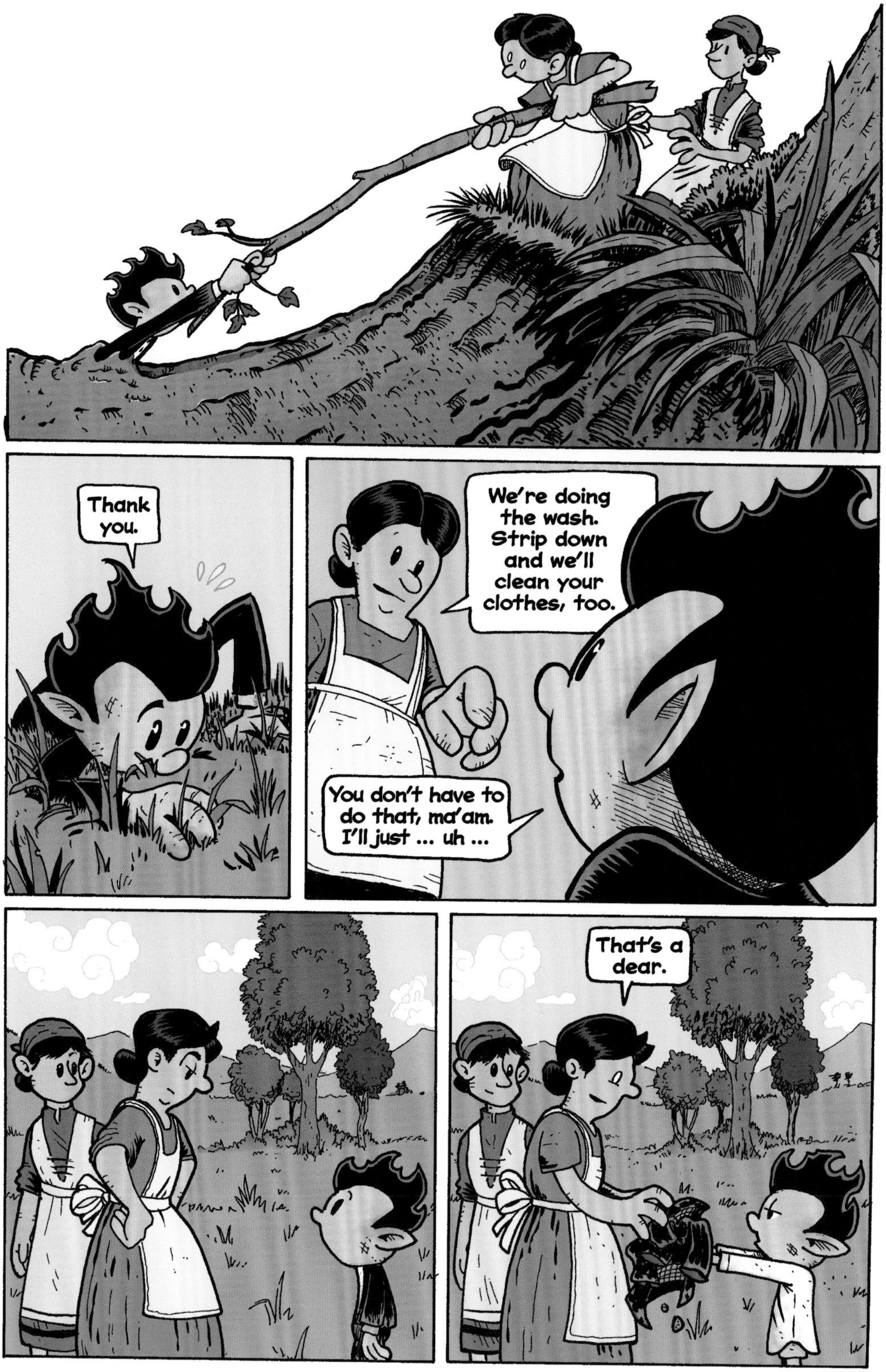
Thank you.
We're doing the wash. Strip down and we'll clean your clothes, too.
You don't have to do that, ma'am. I'll just ... uh ...
That's a dear.

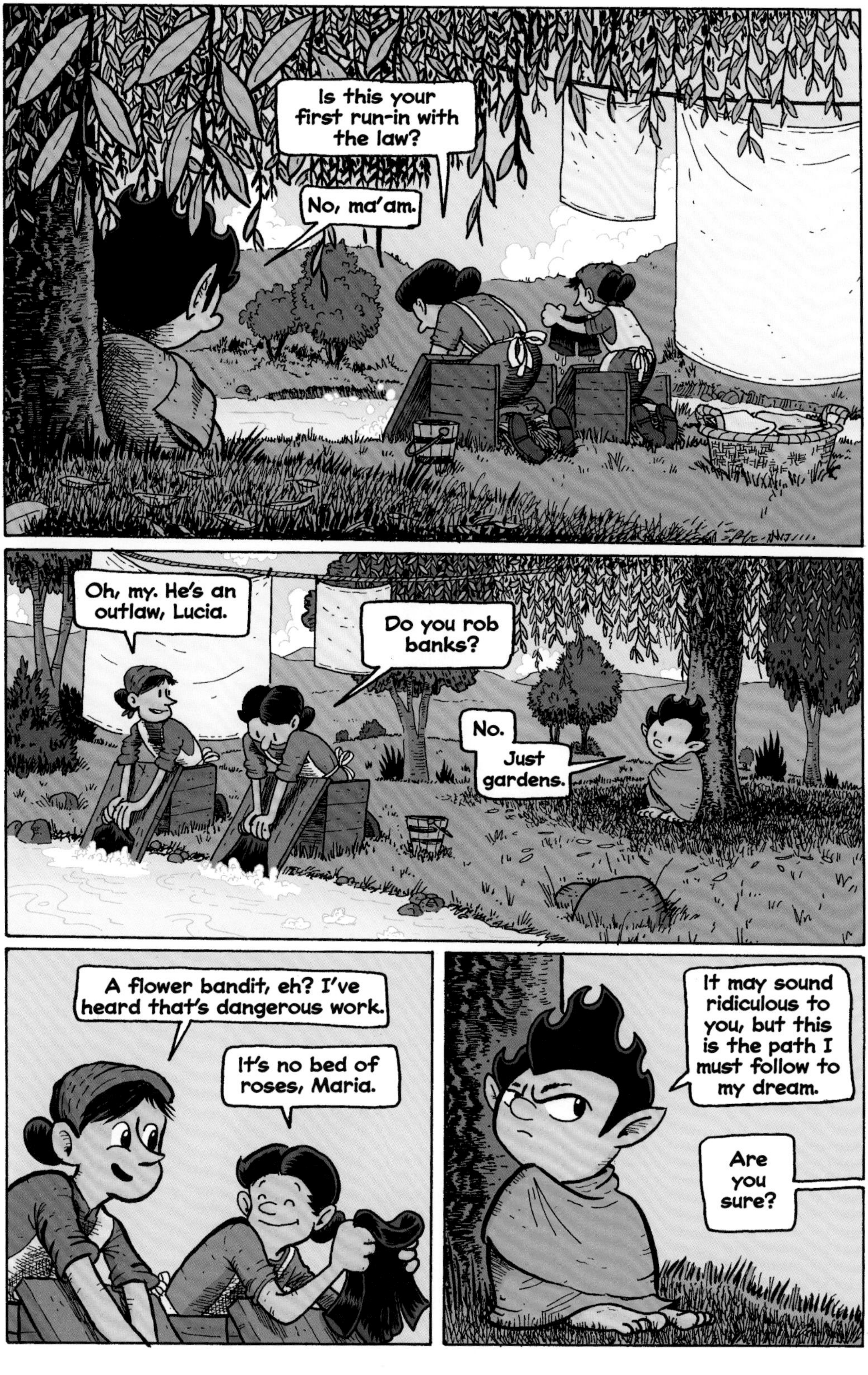
Is this your first run-in with the law?
No, ma'am.
Oh, my. He's an outlaw, Lucia.
Do you rob banks?
No.
Just gardens.
A flower bandit, eh? I've heard that's dangerous work.
It's no bed of roses, Maria.
It may sound ridiculous to you, but this is the path I must follow to my dream.
Are you sure?

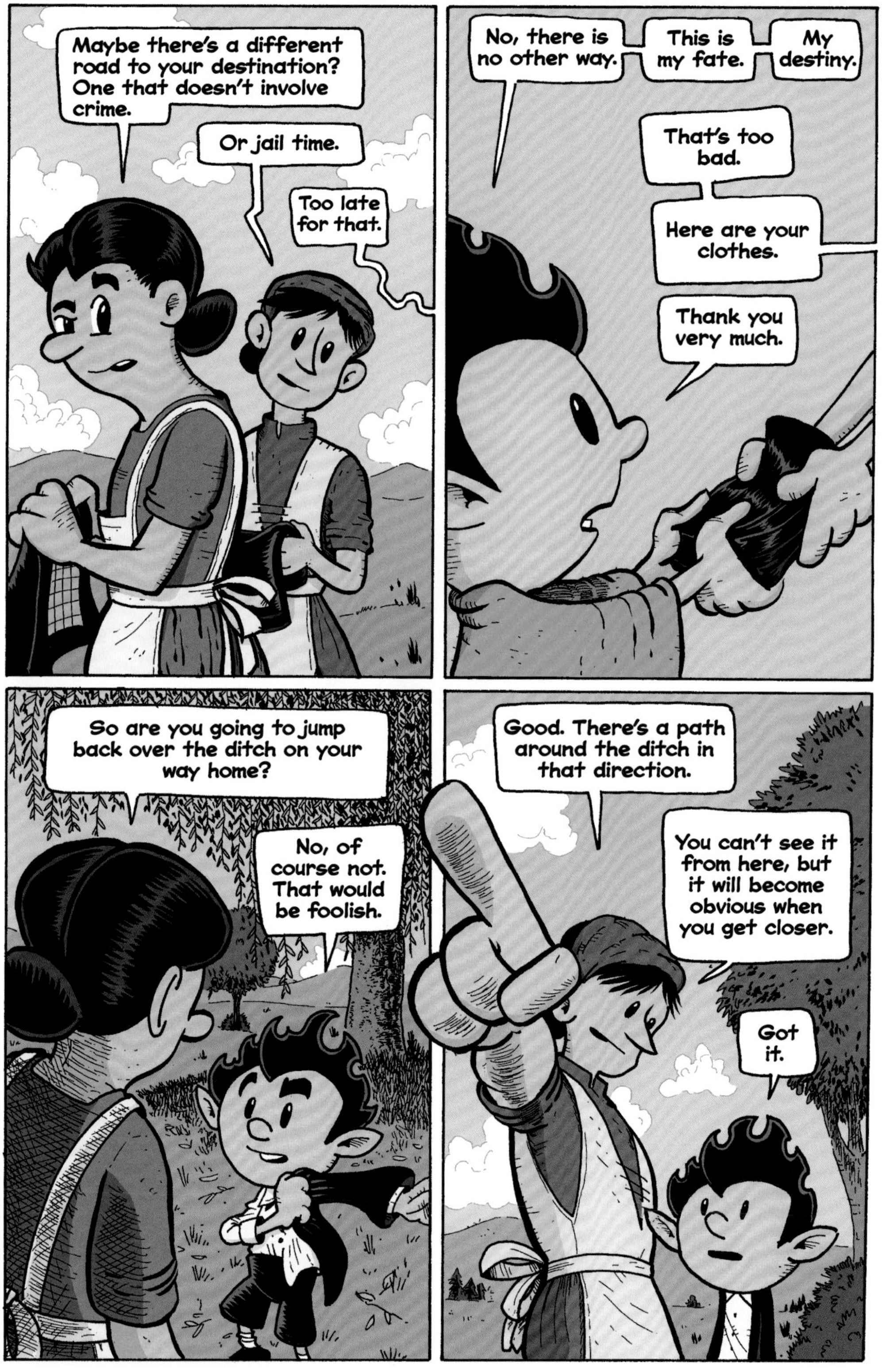

Maybe there's a different road to your destination? One that doesn't involve crime.
Or jail time.
Too late for that.
No, there is no other way.
This is my fate.
My destiny.
That's too bad.
Here are your clothes.
Thank you very much.
So are you going to jump back over the ditch on your way home?
No, of course not. That would be foolish.
Good. There's a path around the ditch in that direction.
You can't see it from here, but it will become obvious when you get closer.
Got it.

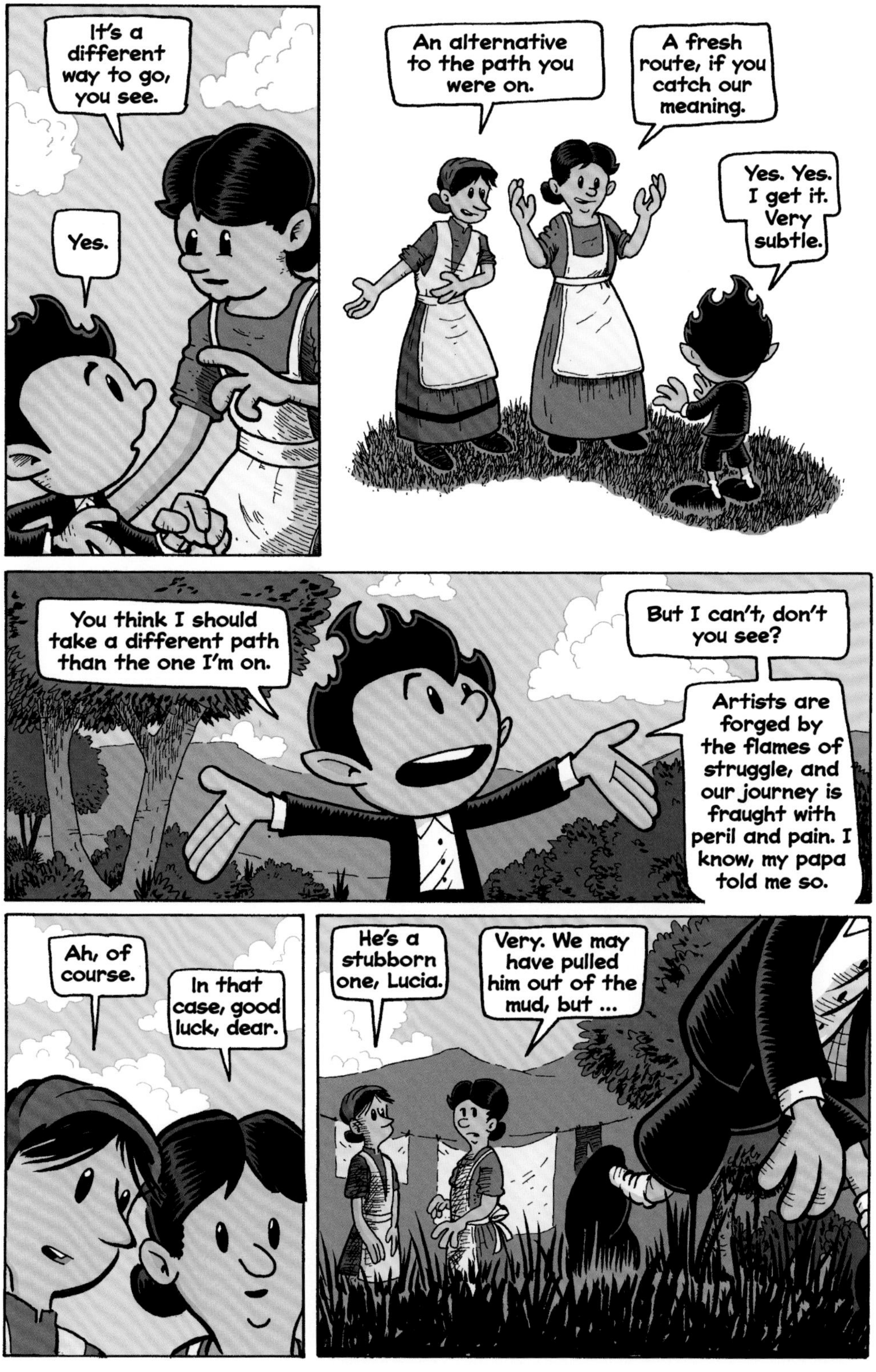
It's a different way to go, you see.
Yes.
An alternative to the path you were on.
A fresh route, if you catch our meaning.
Yes. Yes. I get it. Very subtle.
You think I should take a different path than the one I'm on.
But I can't, don't you see?
Artists are forged by the flames of struggle, and our journey is fraught with peril and pain. I know, my papa told me so.
Ah, of course.
In that case, good luck, dear.
He's a stubborn one, Lucia.
Very. We may have pulled him out of the mud, but ...

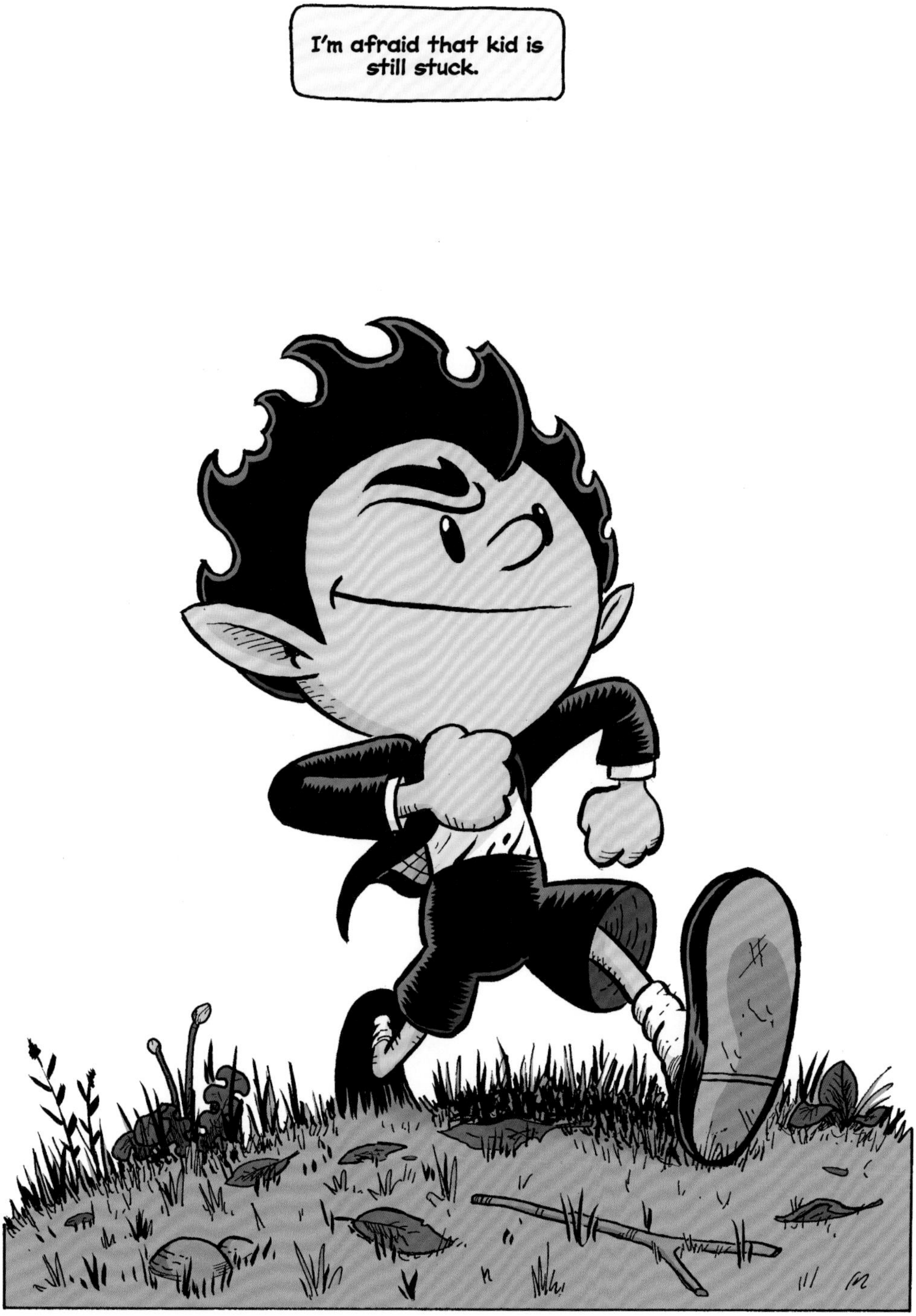
I'm afraid that kid is still stuck.

CHAPTER 9: IT'S COBBLIN' TIME!

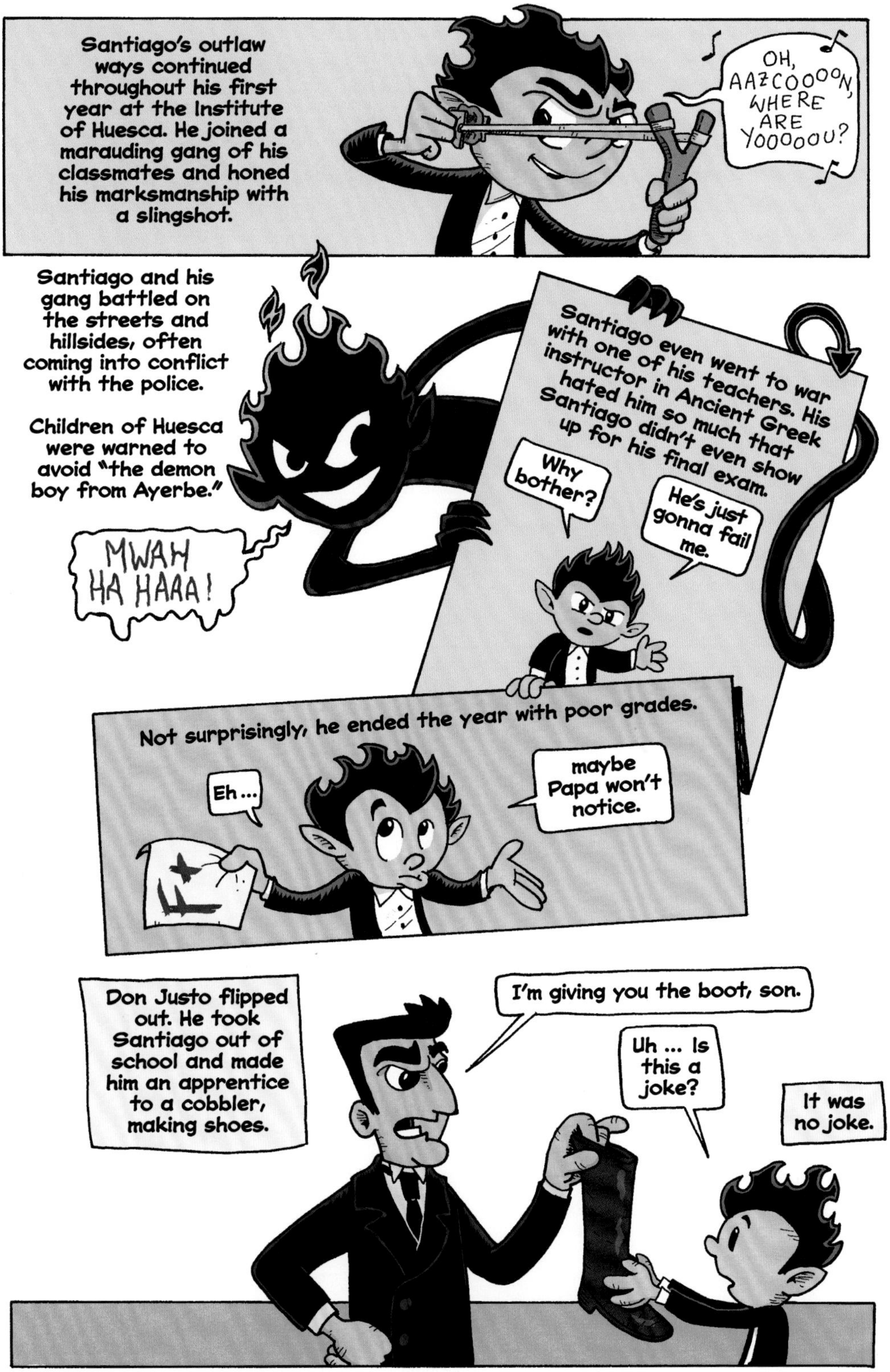

Santiago's outlaw ways continued throughout his first year at the Institute of Huesca. He joined a marauding gang of his classmates and honed his marksmanship with a slingshot.
OH, AAZCOOOON, WHERE ARE YOOOOOU?
Santiago and his gang battled on the streets and hillsides, often coming into conflict with the police.
Children of Huesca were warned to avoid "the demon boy from Ayerbe."
MWAH HA HAAA!
Santiago even went to war with one of his teachers. His instructor in Ancient Greek hated him so much that Santiago didn't even show up for his final exam.
Why bother?
He's just gonna fail me.
Not surprisingly, he ended the year with poor grades.
Eh ...
maybe Papa won't notice.
Don Justo flipped out. He took Santiago out of school and made him an apprentice to a cobbler, making shoes.
I'm giving you the boot, son.
Uh ... Is this a joke?
It was no joke.

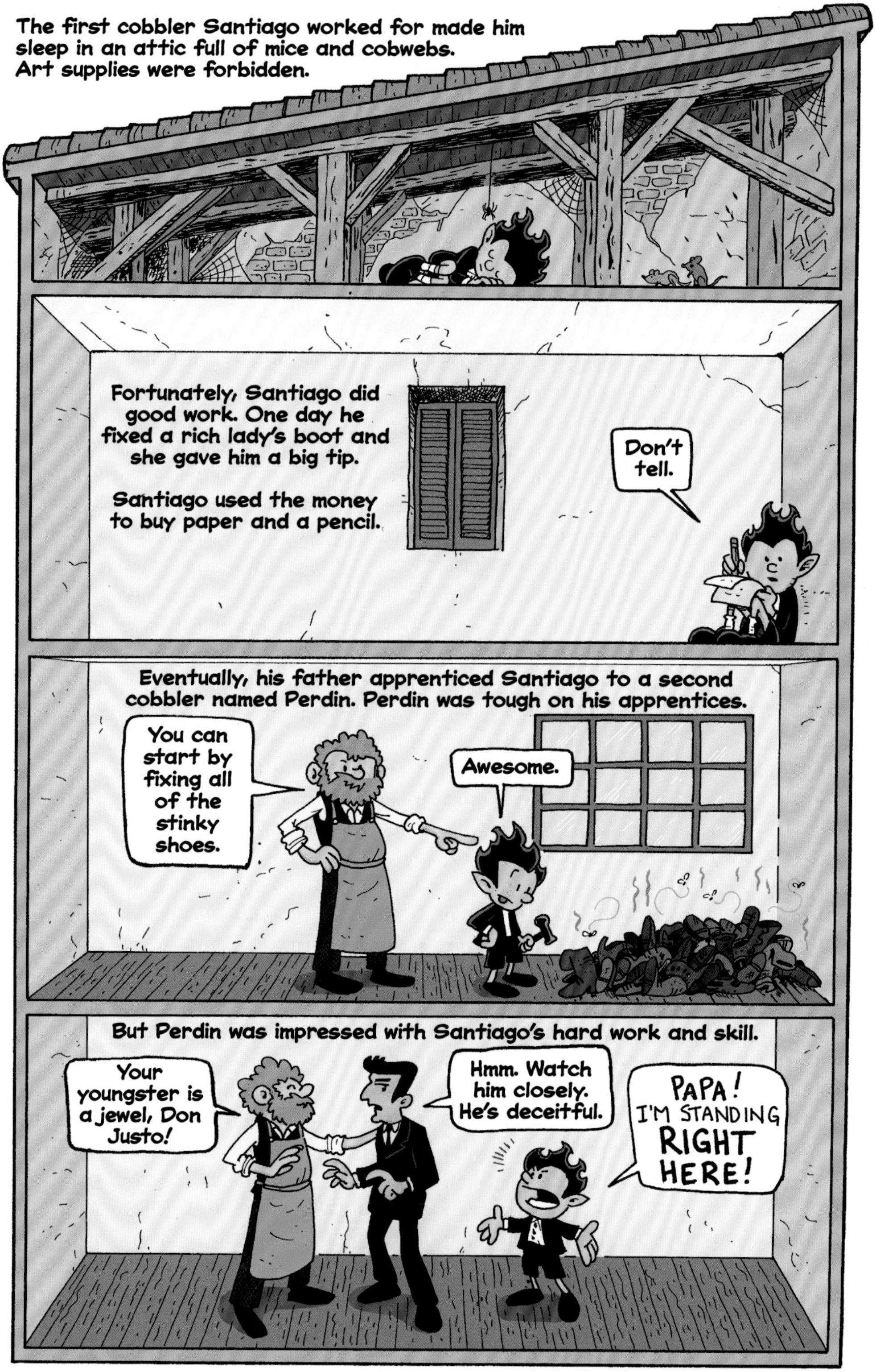
The first cobbler Santiago worked for made him sleep in an attic full of mice and cobwebs. Art supplies were forbidden.
Fortunately, Santiago did good work. One day he fixed a rich lady's boot and she gave him a big tip.
Santiago used the money to buy paper and a pencil.
Don't tell.
Eventually, his father apprenticed Santiago to a second cobbler named Perdin. Perdin was tough on his apprentices.
You can start by fixing all of the stinky shoes.
Awesome.
But Perdin was impressed with Santiago's hard work and skill.
Your youngster is a jewel, Don Justo!
Hmm. Watch him closely. He's deceitful.
PAPA! I'M STANDING RIGHT HERE!

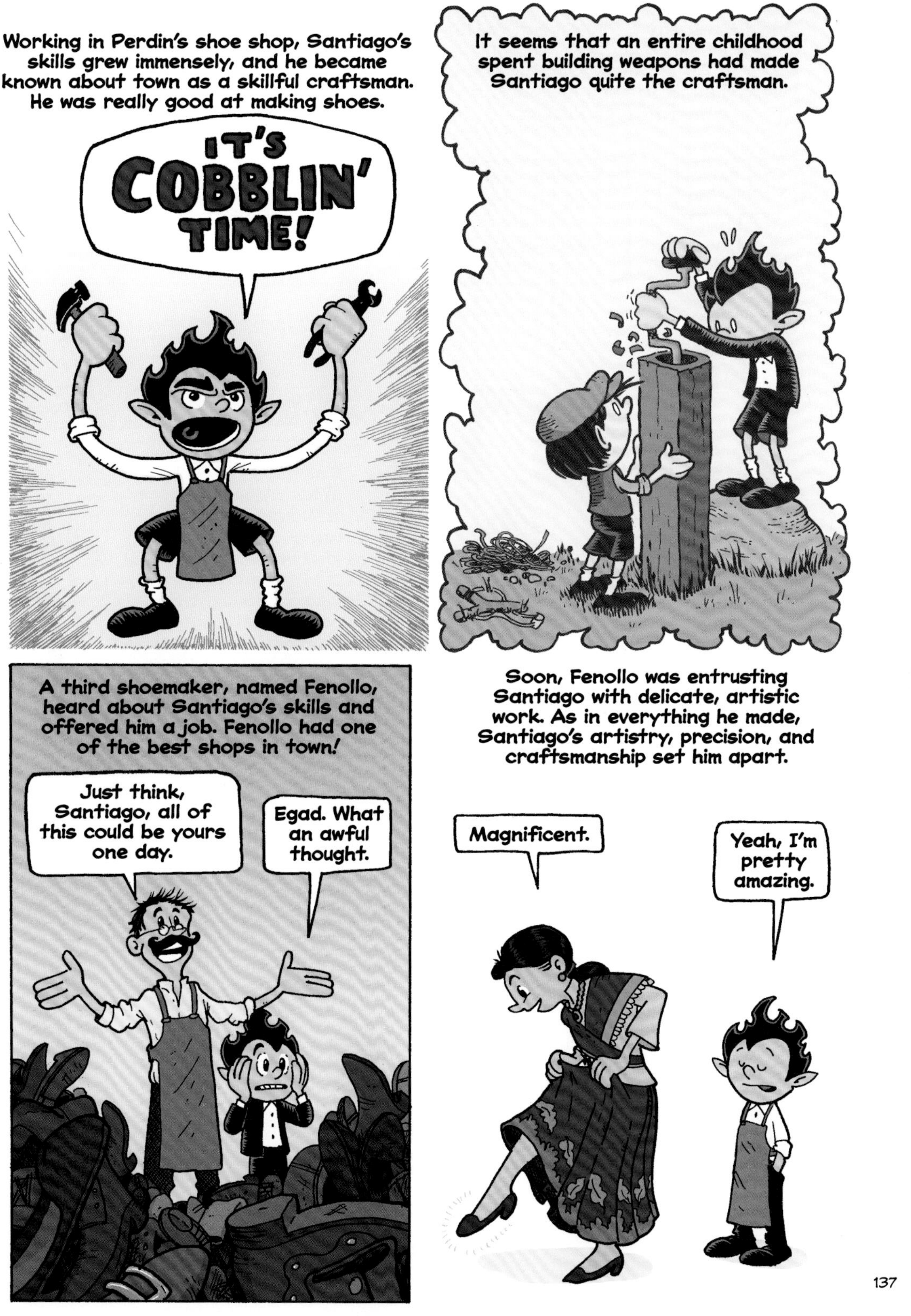

Working in Perdin's shoe shop, Santiago's skills grew immensely, and he became known about town as a skillful craftsman. He was really good at making shoes.
IT'S COBBLIN' TIME!
It seems that an entire childhood spent building weapons had made Santiago quite the craftsman.
A third shoemaker, named Fenollo, heard about Santiago's skills and offered him a job. Fenollo had one of the best shops in town!
Just think, Santiago, all of this could be yours one day.
Egad. What an awful thought.
Soon, Fenollo was entrusting Santiago with delicate, artistic work. As in everything he made, Santiago's artistry, precision, and craftsmanship set him apart.
Magnificent.
Yeah, I'm pretty amazing.

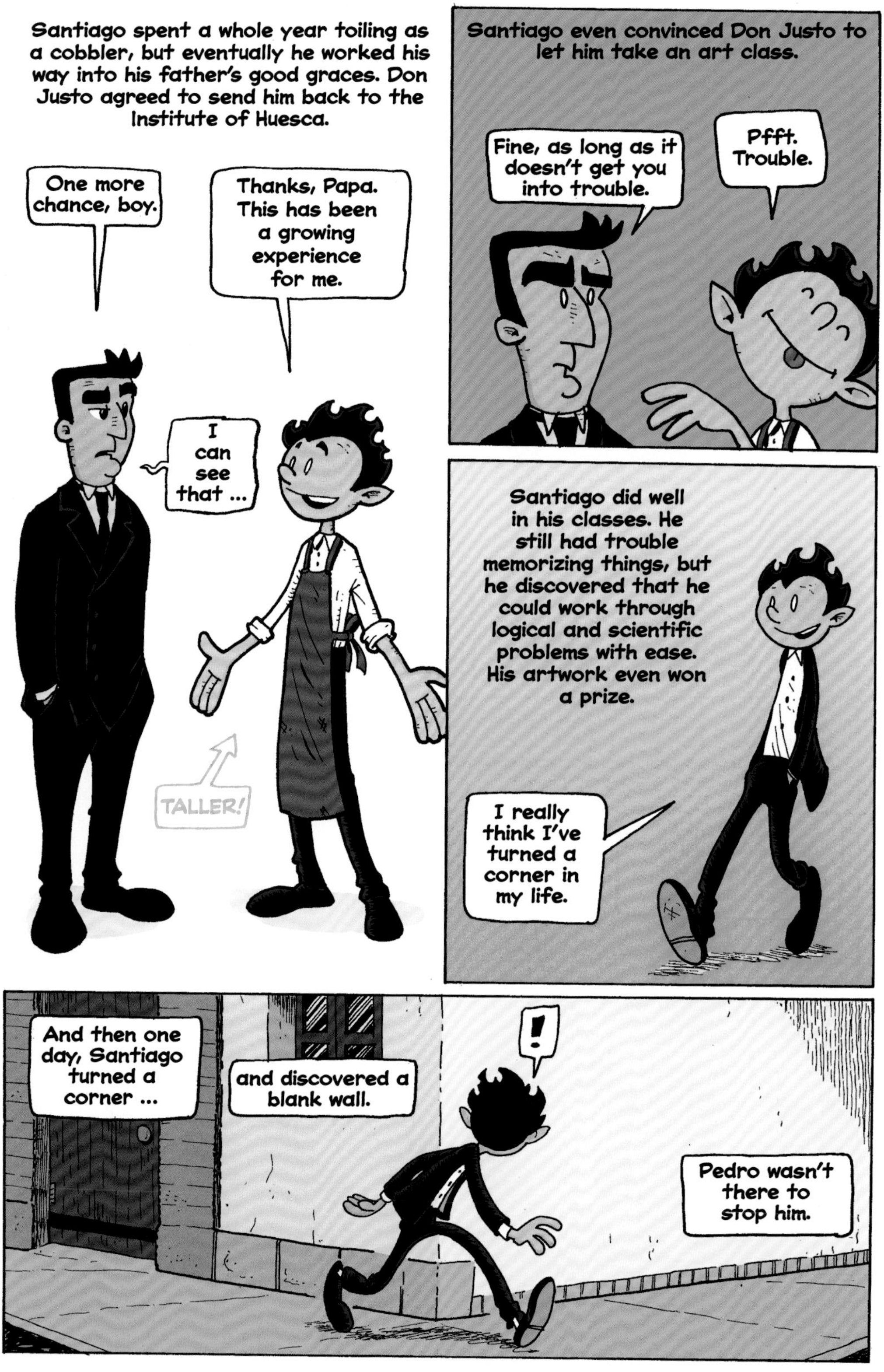
Santiago spent a whole year toiling as a cobbler, but eventually he worked his way into his father's good graces. Don Justo agreed to send him back to the Institute of Huesca.
One more chance, boy.
Thanks, Papa. This has been a growing experience for me.
I can see that ...
TALLER!
Santiago even convinced Don Justo to let him take an art class.
Fine, as long as it doesn't get you into trouble.
Pfft. Trouble.
Santiago did well in his classes. He still had trouble memorizing things, but he discovered that he could work through logical and scientific problems with ease. His artwork even won a prize.
I really think I've turned a corner in my life.
And then one day, Santiago turned a corner ...
and discovered a blank wall.
!
Pedro wasn't there to stop him.

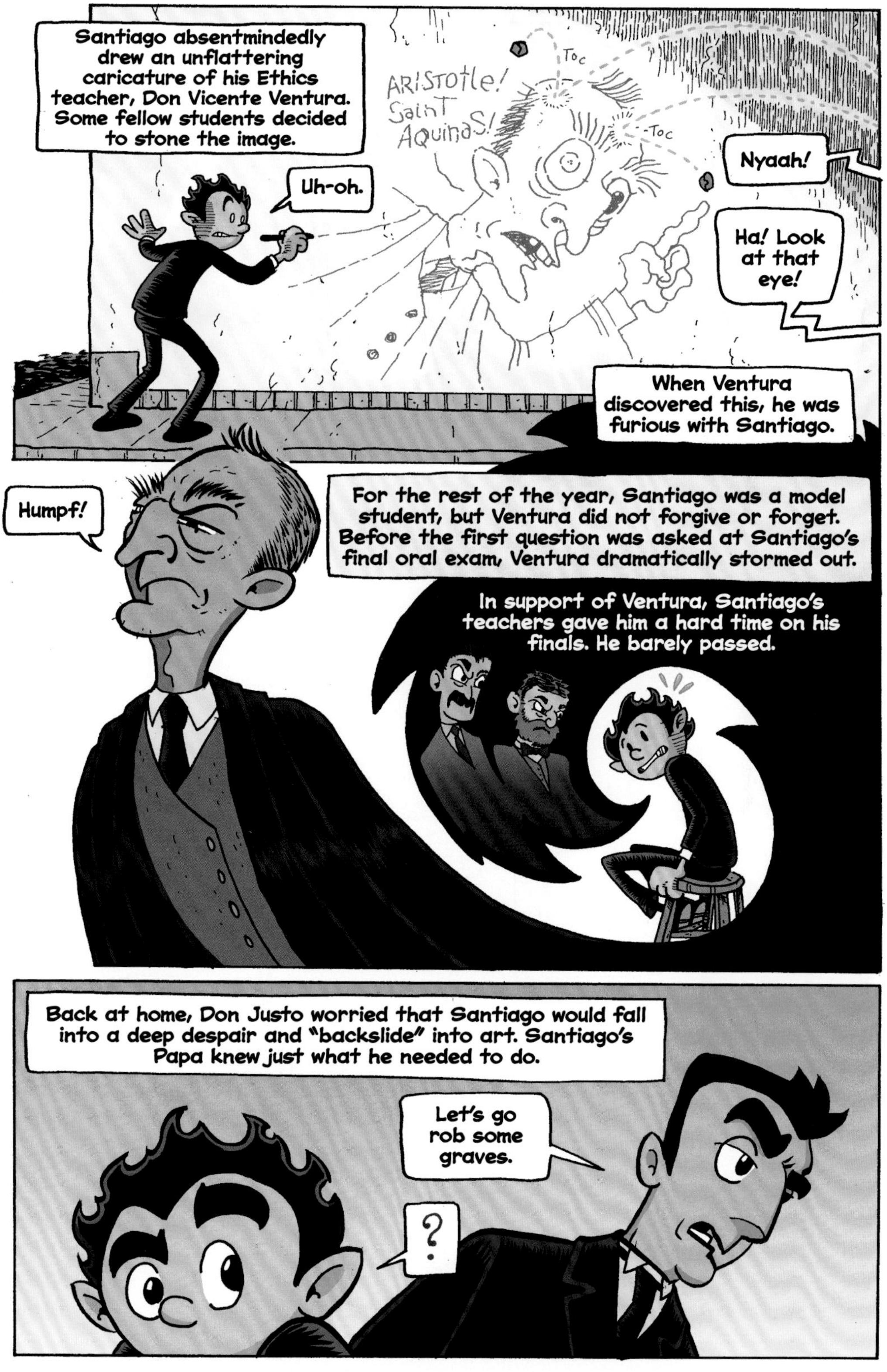
Santiago absentmindedly drew an unflattering caricature of his Ethics teacher, Don Vicente Ventura. Some fellow students decided to stone the image.
ARISTOTLE! Saint AQUINAS!
Toc
Toc
Uh-oh.
Nyaah!
Ha! Look at that eye!
When Ventura discovered this, he was furious with Santiago.
Humpf!
For the rest of the year, Santiago was a model student, but Ventura did not forgive or forget. Before the first question was asked at Santiago's final oral exam, Ventura dramatically stormed out.
In support of Ventura, Santiago's teachers gave him a hard time on his finals. He barely passed.
Back at home, Don Justo worried that Santiago would fall into a deep despair and "backslide" into art. Santiago's Papa knew just what he needed to do.
Let's go rob some graves.
?

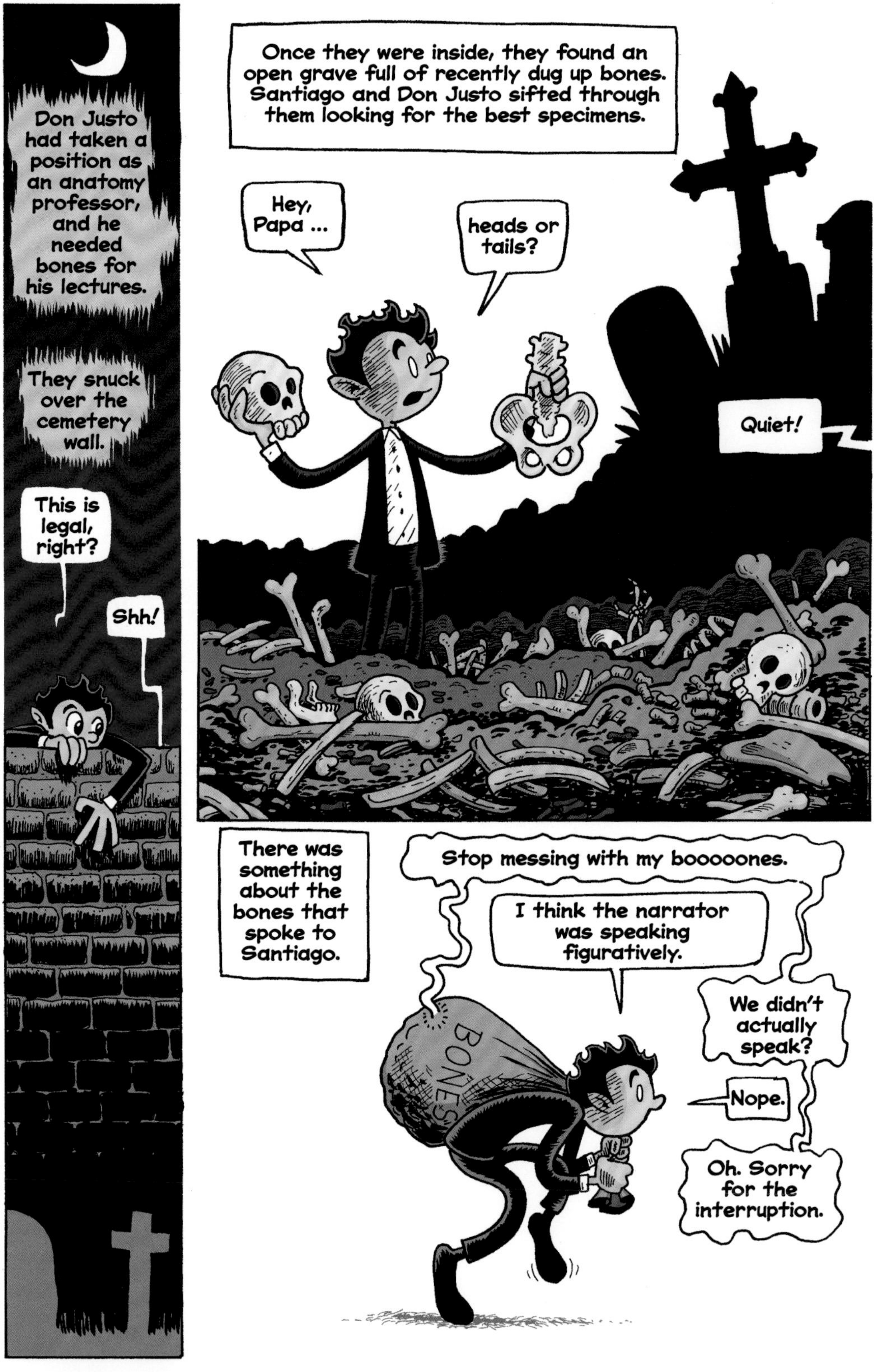

Don Justo had taken a position as an anatomy professor, and he needed bones for his lectures.
They snuck over the cemetery wall.
This is legal, right?
Shh!
Once they were inside, they found an open grave full of recently dug up bones. Santiago and Don Justo sifted through them looking for the best specimens.
Hey, Papa ...
heads or tails?
Quiet!
There was something about the bones that spoke to Santiago.
Stop messing with my booooones.
I think the narrator was speaking figuratively.
We didn't actually speak?
Nope.
Oh. Sorry for the interruption.
BONES

Each bone was an intricate piece of a delicate mechanism that Santiago loved taking apart and putting back together.

The bones were also naturally sculpted wonders that he loved to draw and paint.

That summer, Don Justo became Santiago's teacher again. An old barn was their classroom.

Definitely a step up from a cave.

Focus, boy.

It turned out that Santiago had a genius for anatomy.

Anatomy is the study of the bits and pieces of an organism's body. That includes everything from brains and hearts to tiny nerves and blood vessels. Santiago marveled at how all of the parts fit together. Since Don Justo was a professor of human anatomy at a medical school, he had access to corpses that were donated to science. Santiago and Don Justo would dissect them together ...

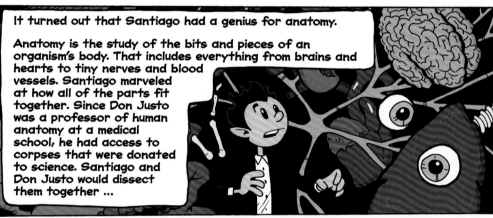

and Santiago painted beautiful diagrams of the organs they saw.

WHAT'S THIS?

DON JUSTO WAS IMPRESSED!

Wow, this leg bone! These lungs! Your paintings are great!

Are you messing with me?

141

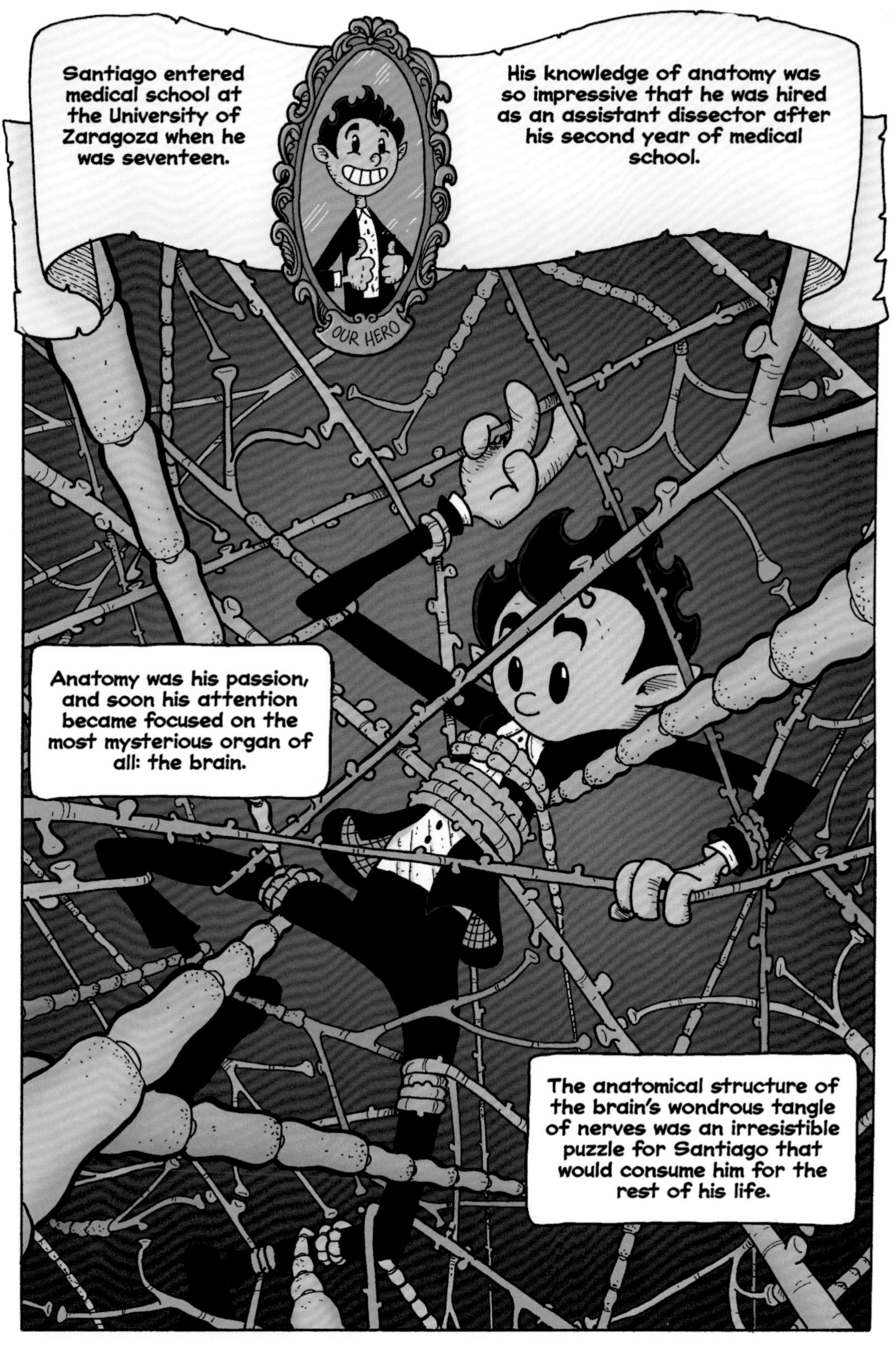
Santiago entered medical school at the University of Zaragoza when he was seventeen.
OUR HERO
His knowledge of anatomy was so impressive that he was hired as an assistant dissector after his second year of medical school.
Anatomy was his passion, and soon his attention became focused on the most mysterious organ of all: the brain.
The anatomical structure of the brain's wondrous tangle of nerves was an irresistible puzzle for Santiago that would consume him for the rest of his life.

CHAPTER 10: THINKING SMALL

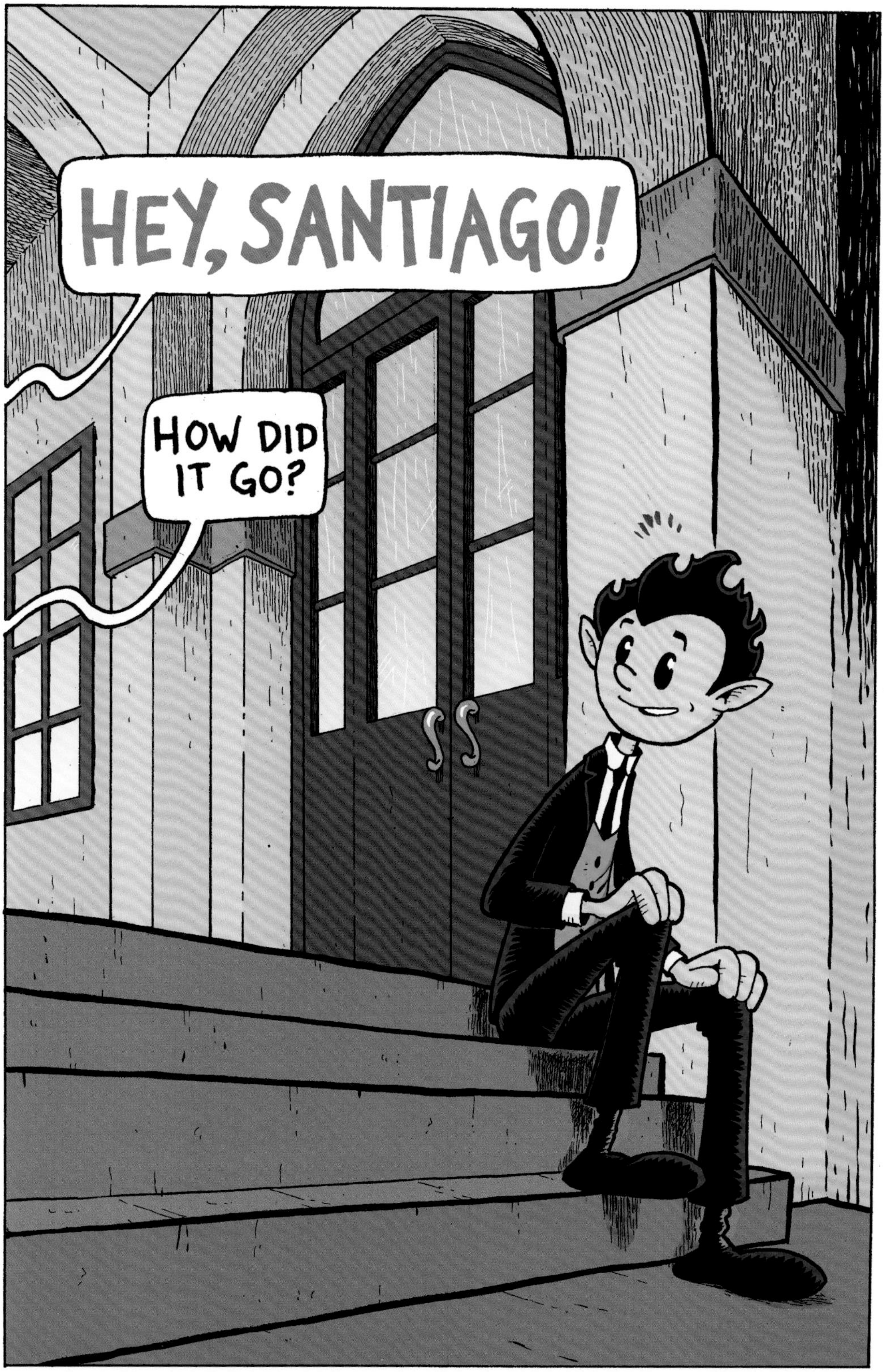
HEY, SANTIAGO!
HOW DID IT GO?

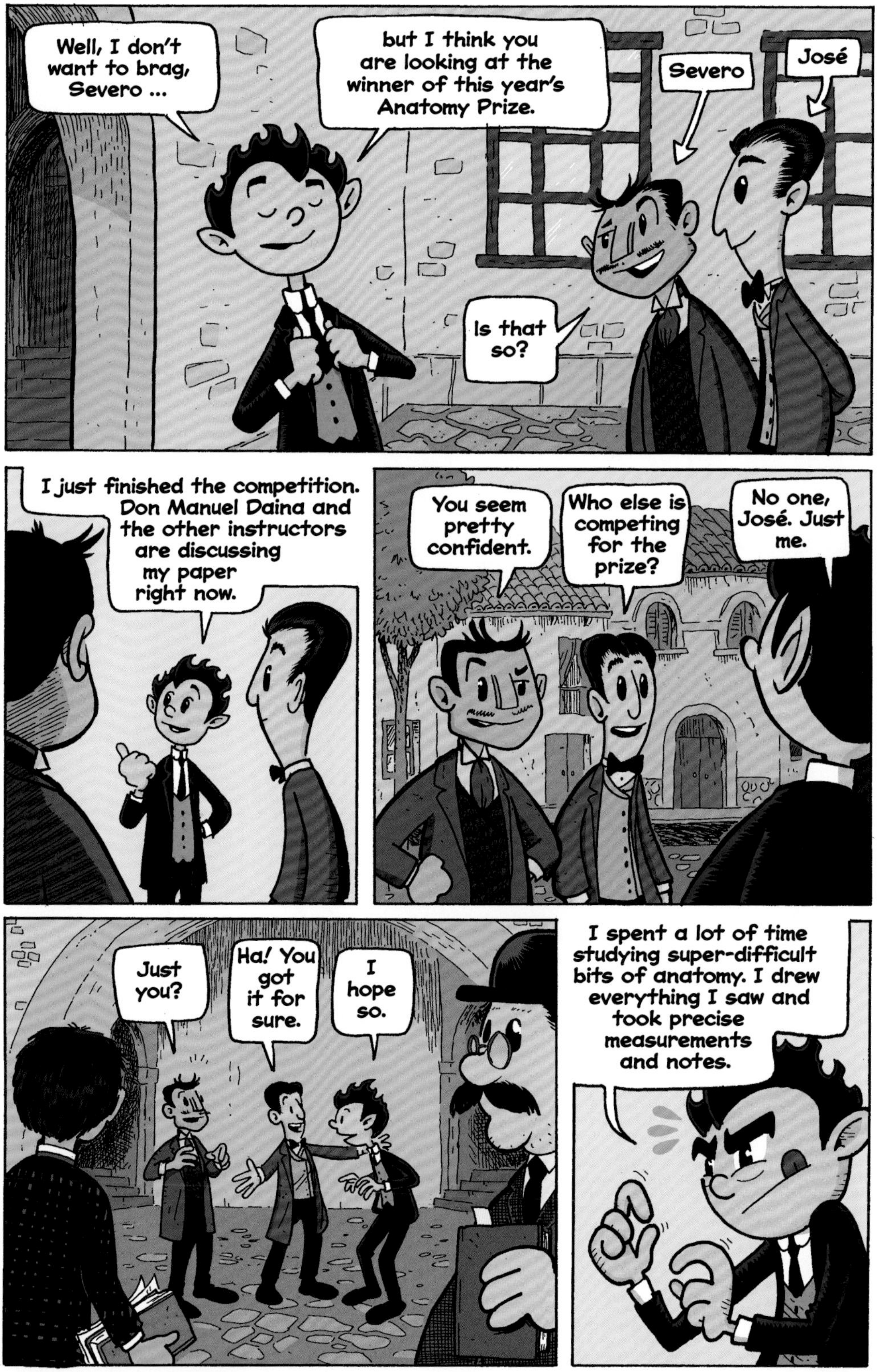
Well, I don't want to brag, Severo ...
but I think you are looking at the winner of this year's Anatomy Prize.
Severo
José
Is that so?
I just finished the competition. Don Manuel Daina and the other instructors are discussing my paper right now.
You seem pretty confident.
Who else is competing for the prize?
No one, José. Just me.
Just you?
Ha! You got it for sure.
I hope so.
I spent a lot of time studying super-difficult bits of anatomy. I drew everything I saw and took precise measurements and notes.

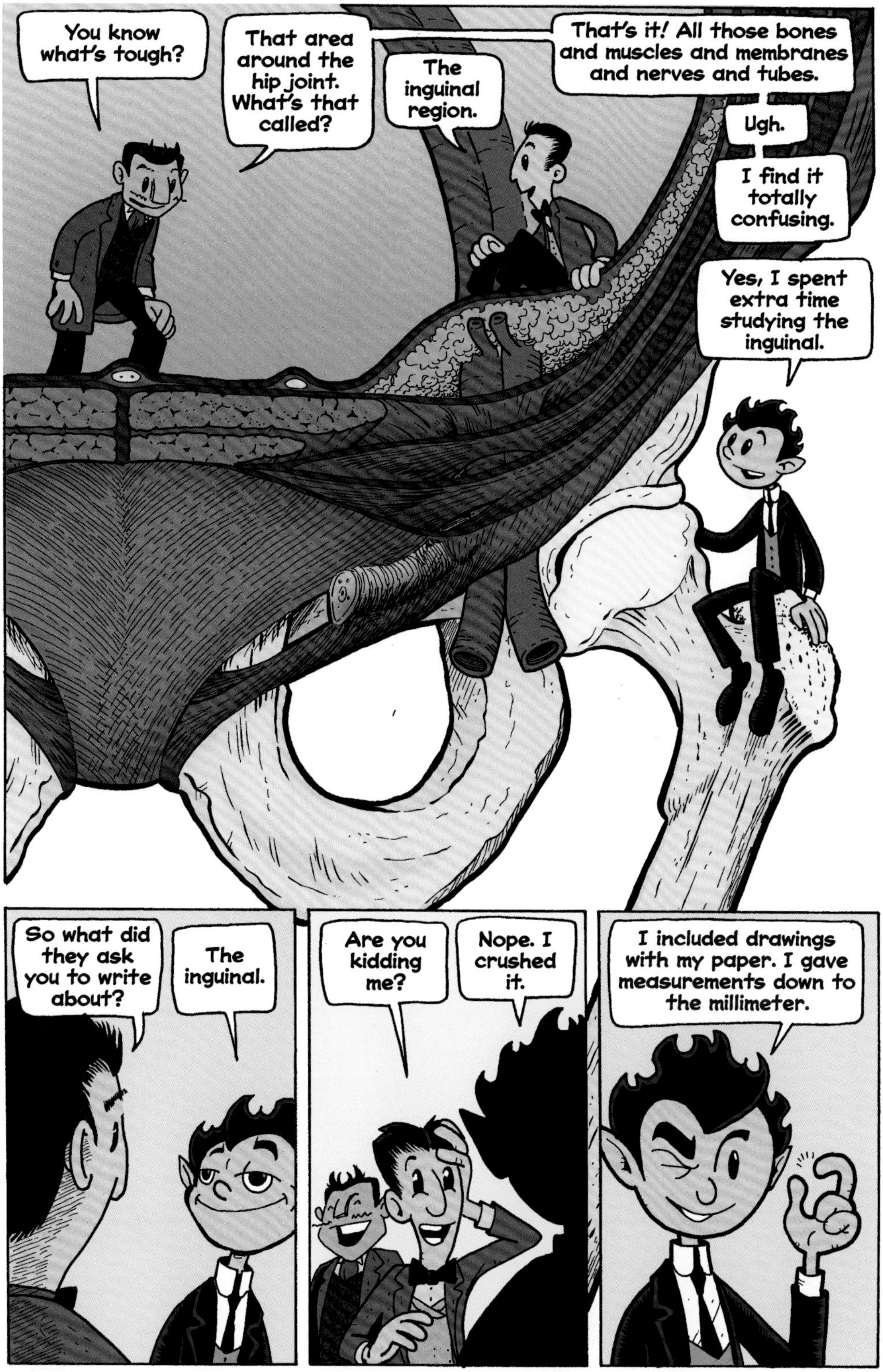
You know what's tough?
That area around the hip joint. What's that called?
The inguinal region.
That's it! All those bones and muscles and membranes and nerves and tubes.
Ugh.
I find it totally confusing.
Yes, I spent extra time studying the inguinal.
So what did they ask you to write about?
The inguinal.
Are you kidding me?
Nope. I crushed it.
I included drawings with my paper. I gave measurements down to the millimeter.

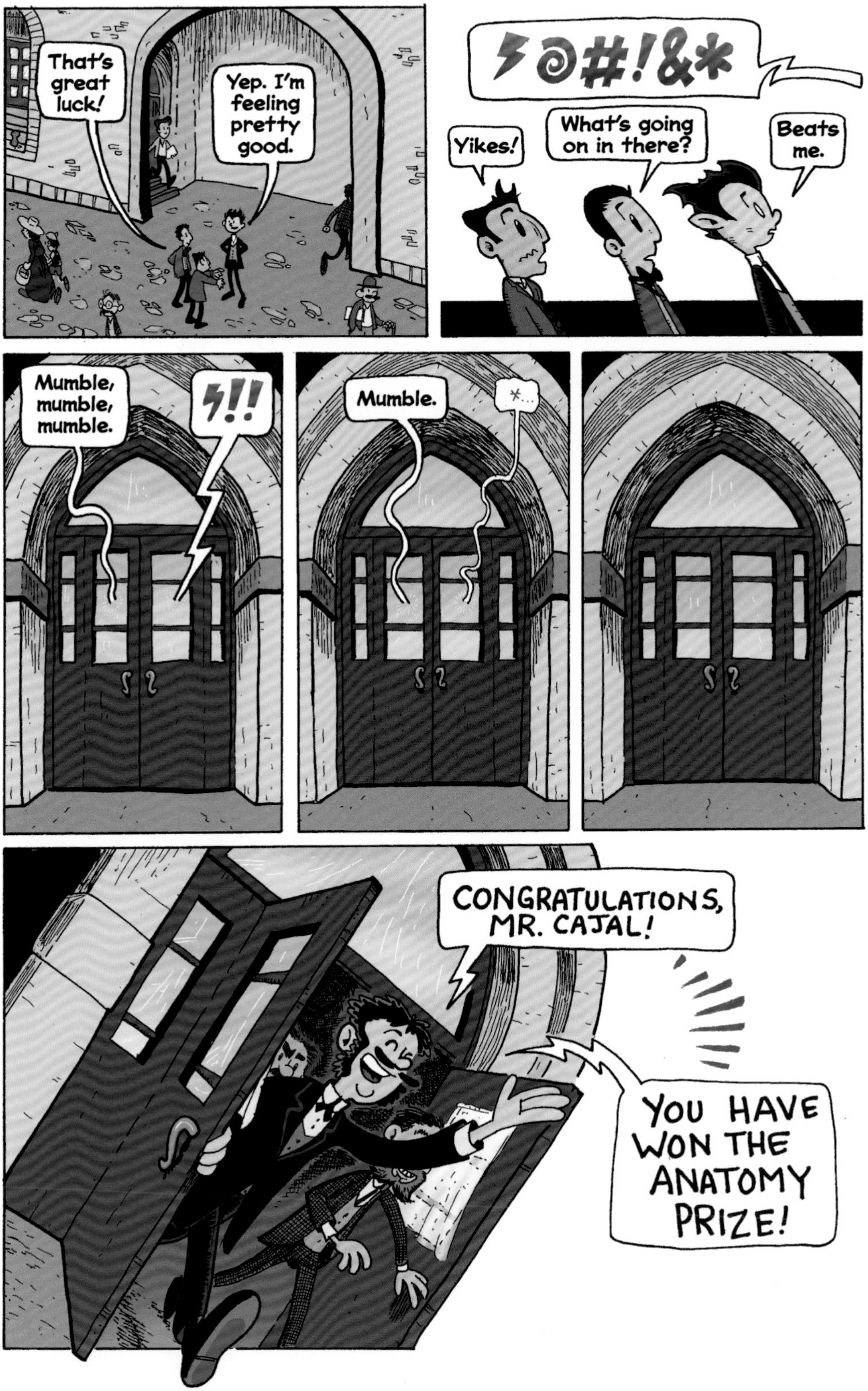
That's great luck!
Yep. I'm feeling pretty good.
ϟ@#!&*
Yikes!
What's going on in there?
Beats me.
Mumble, mumble, mumble.
ϟ!!
Mumble.
*...
CONGRATULATIONS, MR. CAJAL!
YOU HAVE WON THE ANATOMY PRIZE!

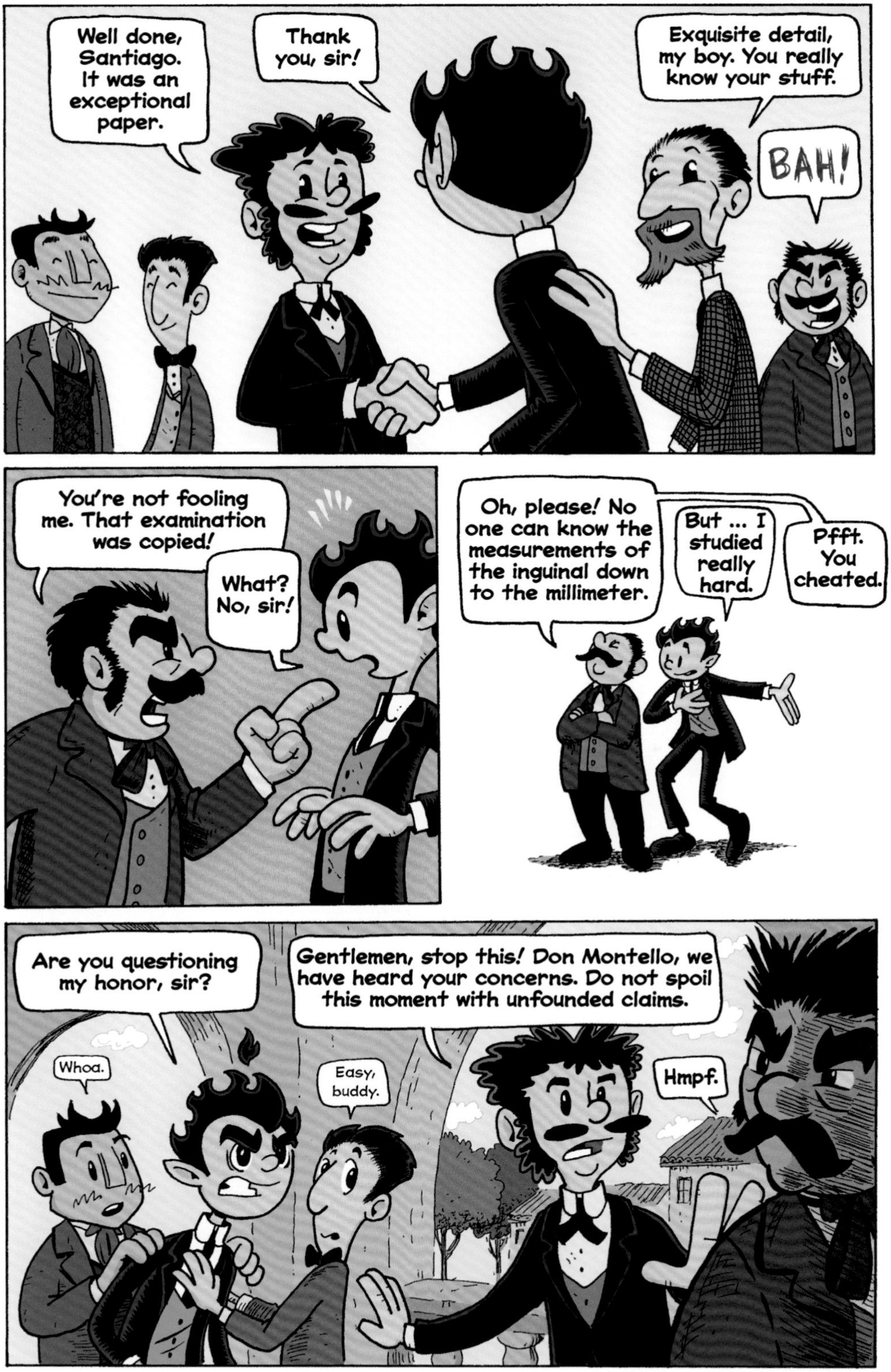

Well done, Santiago. It was an exceptional paper.
Thank you, sir!
Exquisite detail, my boy. You really know your stuff.
BAH!
You're not fooling me. That examination was copied!
What? No, sir!
Oh, please! No one can know the measurements of the inguinal down to the millimeter.
But ... I studied really hard.
Pfft. You cheated.
Are you questioning my honor, sir?
Whoa.
Easy, buddy.
Gentlemen, stop this! Don Montello, we have heard your concerns. Do not spoil this moment with unfounded claims.
Hmpf.

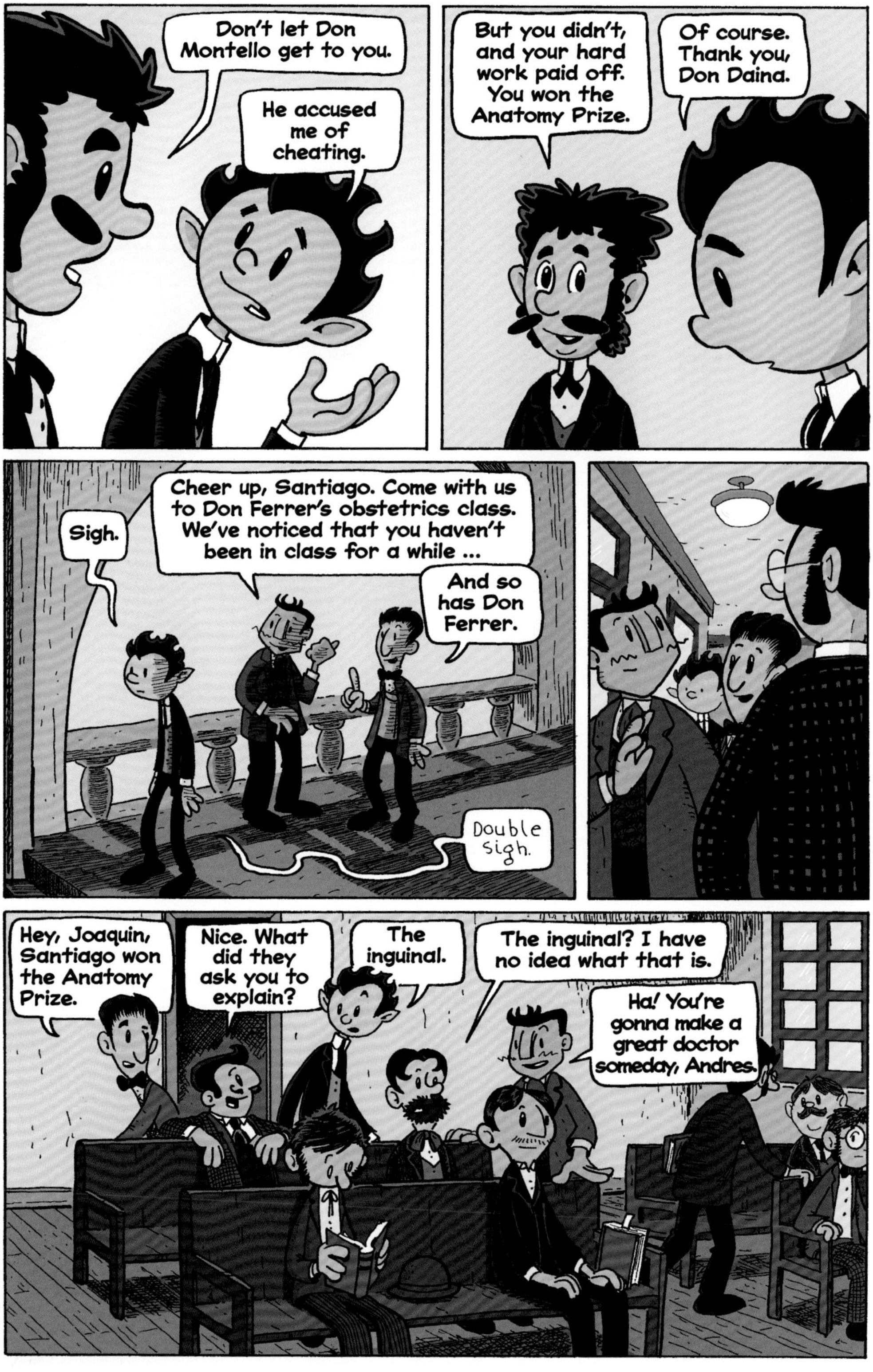
Don't let Don Montello get to you.
He accused me of cheating.
But you didn't, and your hard work paid off. You won the Anatomy Prize.
Of course. Thank you, Don Daina.
Sigh.
Cheer up, Santiago. Come with us to Don Ferrer's obstetrics class. We've noticed that you haven't been in class for a while ...
And so has Don Ferrer.
Double sigh.
Hey, Joaquin, Santiago won the Anatomy Prize.
Nice. What did they ask you to explain?
The inguinal.
The inguinal? I have no idea what that is.
Ha! You're gonna make a great doctor someday, Andres.

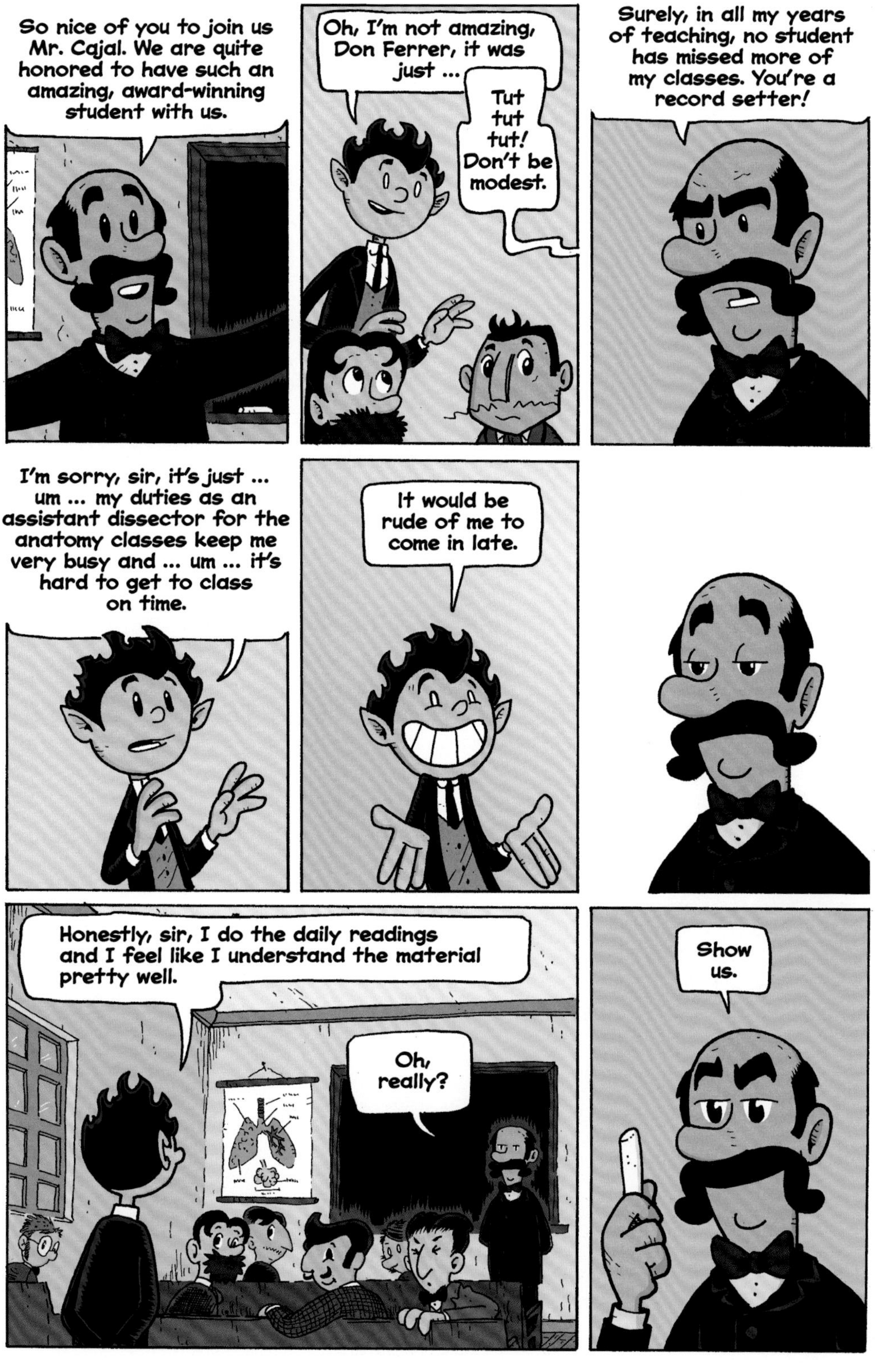
So nice of you to join us Mr. Cajal. We are quite honored to have such an amazing, award-winning student with us.
Oh, I'm not amazing, Don Ferrer, it was just ...
Tut tut tut! Don't be modest.
Surely, in all my years of teaching, no student has missed more of my classes. You're a record setter!
I'm sorry, sir, it's just ... um ... my duties as an assistant dissector for the anatomy classes keep me very busy and ... um ... it's hard to get to class on time.
It would be rude of me to come in late.
Honestly, sir, I do the daily readings and I feel like I understand the material pretty well.
Oh, really?
Show us.

I have spent several classes lecturing on the fetal membranes.

It's a very difficult topic, and few students master it.

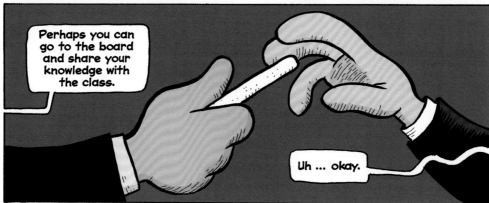

Perhaps you can go to the board and share your knowledge with the class.

Uh ... okay.

This blackboard is very big and ... uh ... very blank, Don Ferrer.

Fetal membranes, Santiago.

Fetal membranes ...

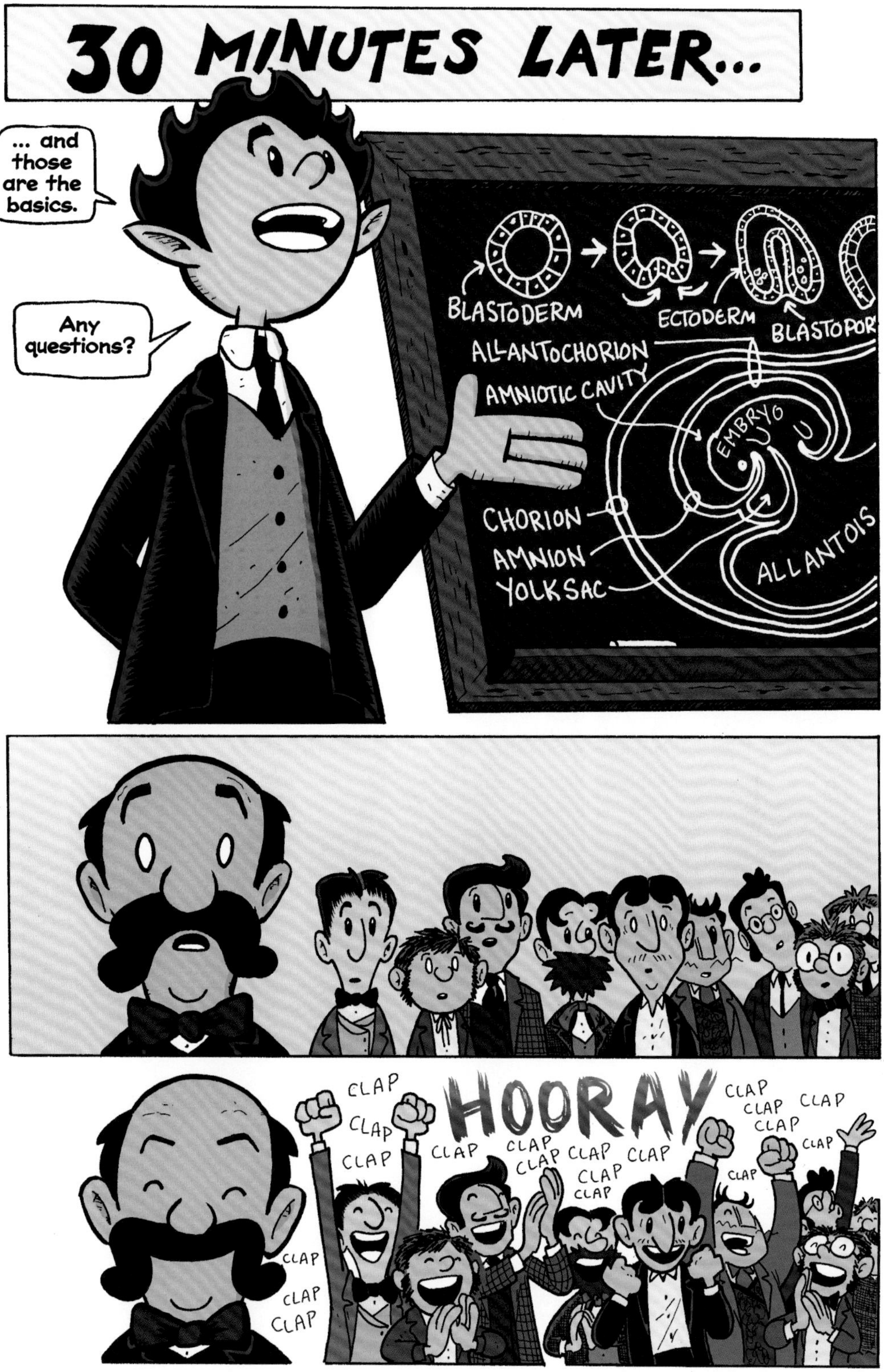
30 MINUTES LATER...
... and those are the basics.
Any questions?
BLASTODERM
ECTODERM
BLASTOPORE
ALLANTOCHORION
AMNIOTIC CAVITY
EMBRYO
CHORION
AMNION
YOLK SAC
ALLANTOIS
HOORAY
CLAP CLAP CLAP CLAP CLAP CLAP CLAP CLAP CLAP CLAP CLAP CLAP CLAP CLAP CLAP CLAP CLAP CLAP CLAP

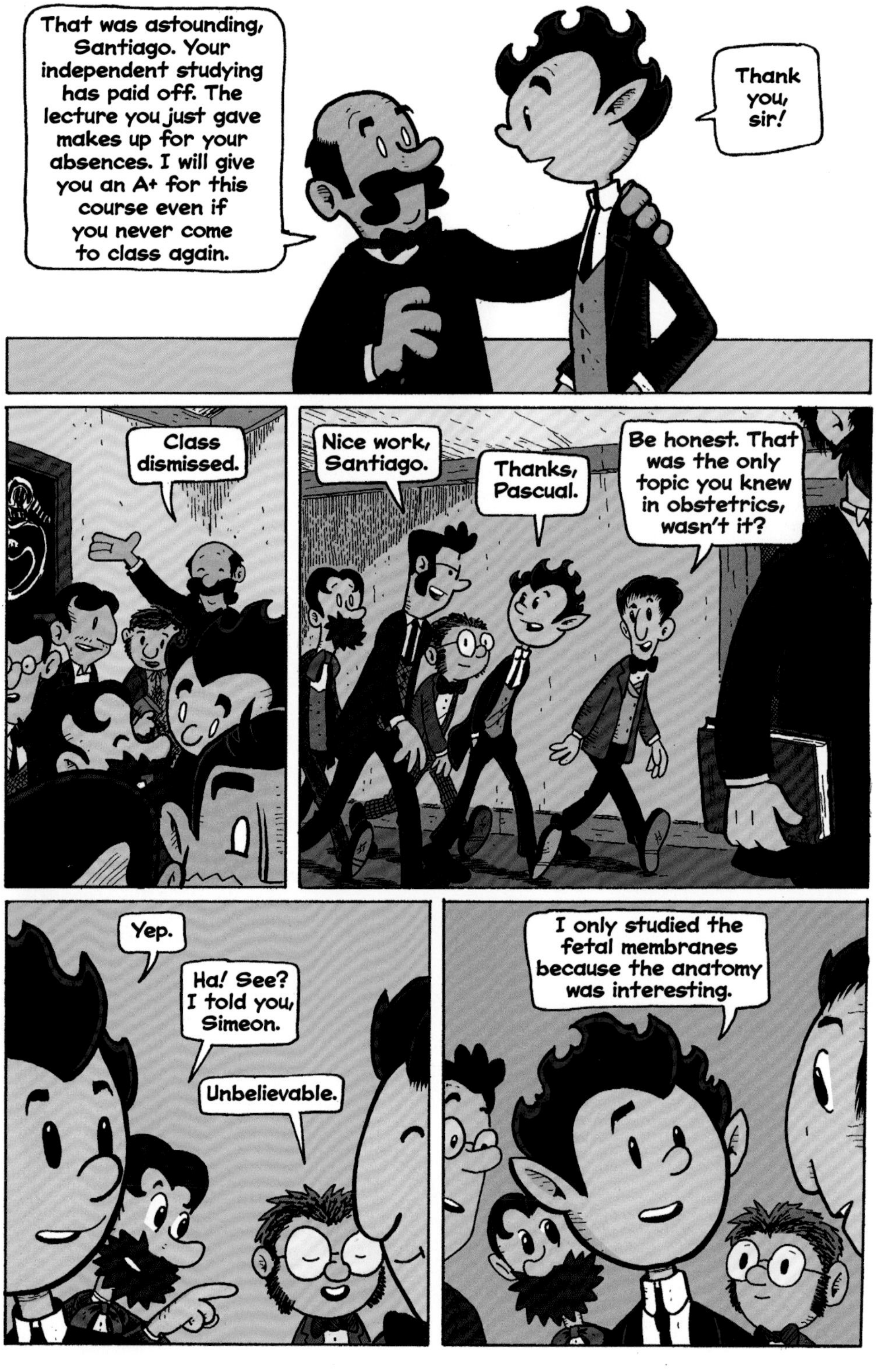
That was astounding, Santiago. Your independent studying has paid off. The lecture you just gave makes up for your absences. I will give you an A+ for this course even if you never come to class again.
Thank you, sir!
Class dismissed.
Nice work, Santiago.
Thanks, Pascual.
Be honest. That was the only topic you knew in obstetrics, wasn't it?
Yep.
Ha! See? I told you, Simeon.
Unbelievable.
I only studied the fetal membranes because the anatomy was interesting.

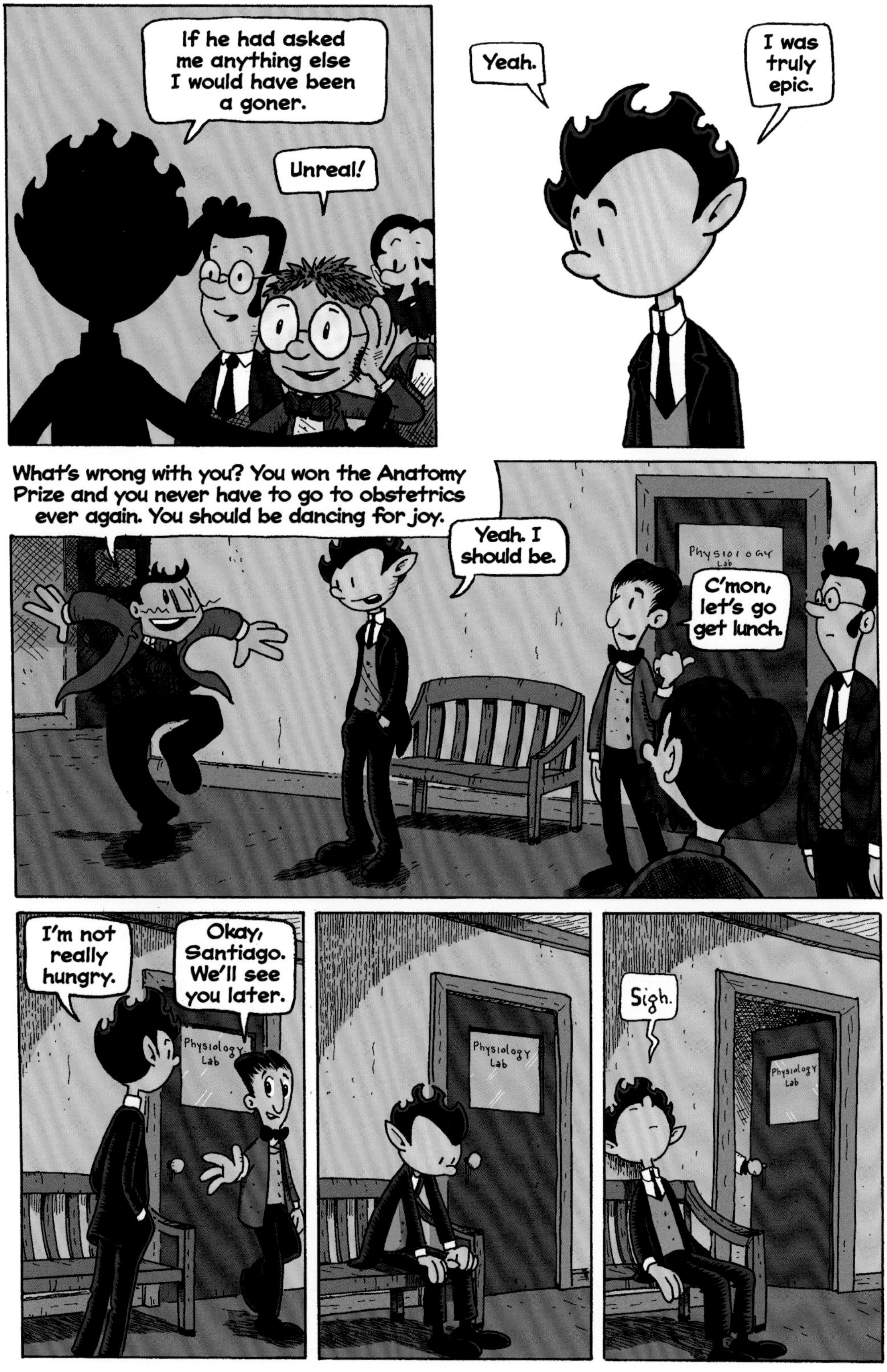
If he had asked me anything else I would have been a goner.
Unreal!
Yeah.
I was truly epic.
What's wrong with you? You won the Anatomy Prize and you never have to go to obstetrics ever again. You should be dancing for joy.
Yeah. I should be.
Physiology Lab
C'mon, let's go get lunch.
I'm not really hungry.
Okay, Santiago. We'll see you later.
Physiology Lab
Physiology Lab
Sigh.
Physiology Lab

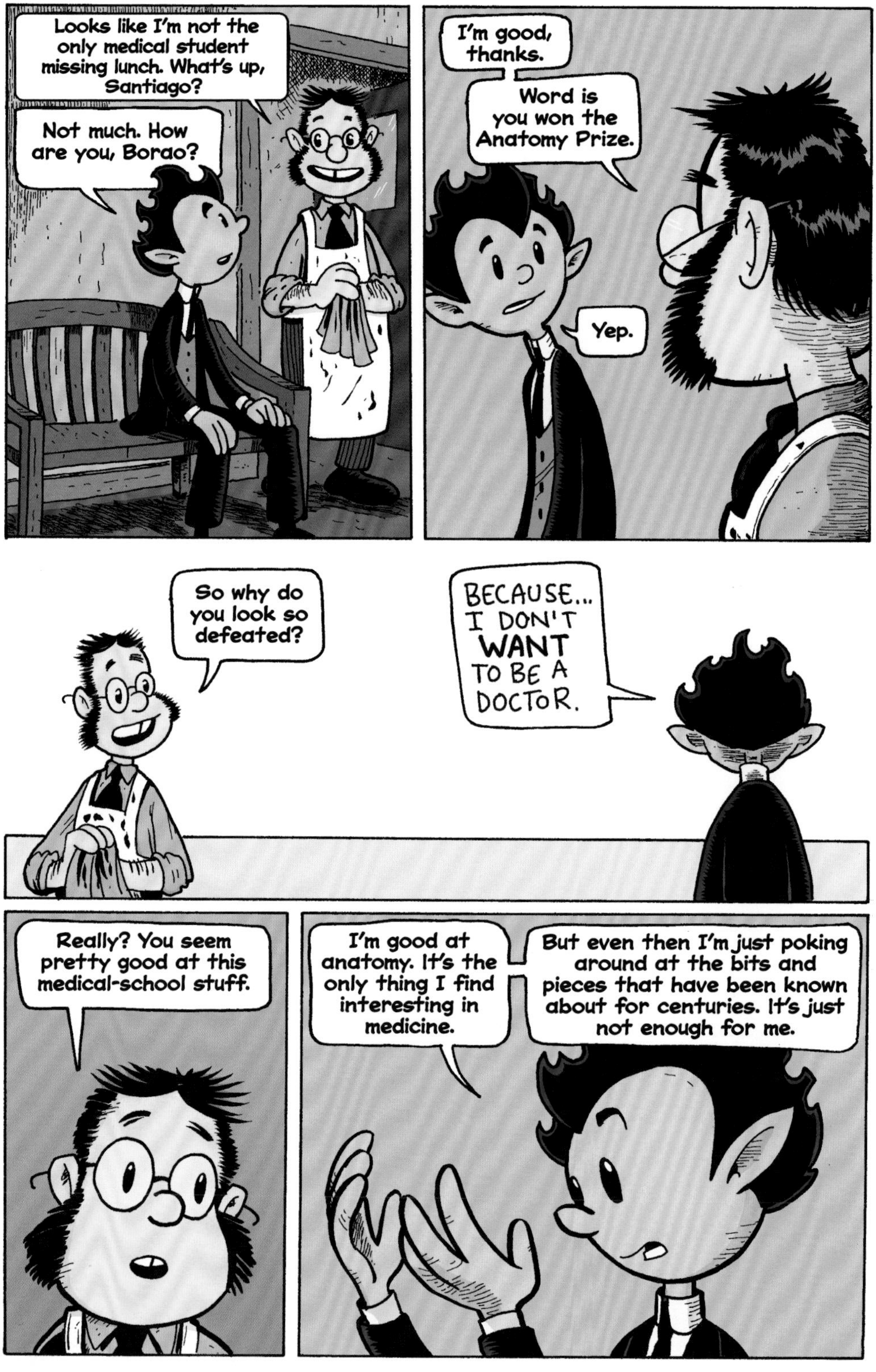

Looks like I'm not the only medical student missing lunch. What's up, Santiago?
Not much. How are you, Borao?
I'm good, thanks.
Word is you won the Anatomy Prize.
Yep.
So why do you look so defeated?
BECAUSE... I DON'T WANT TO BE A DOCTOR.
Really? You seem pretty good at this medical-school stuff.
I'm good at anatomy. It's the only thing I find interesting in medicine.
But even then I'm just poking around at the bits and pieces that have been known about for centuries. It's just not enough for me.

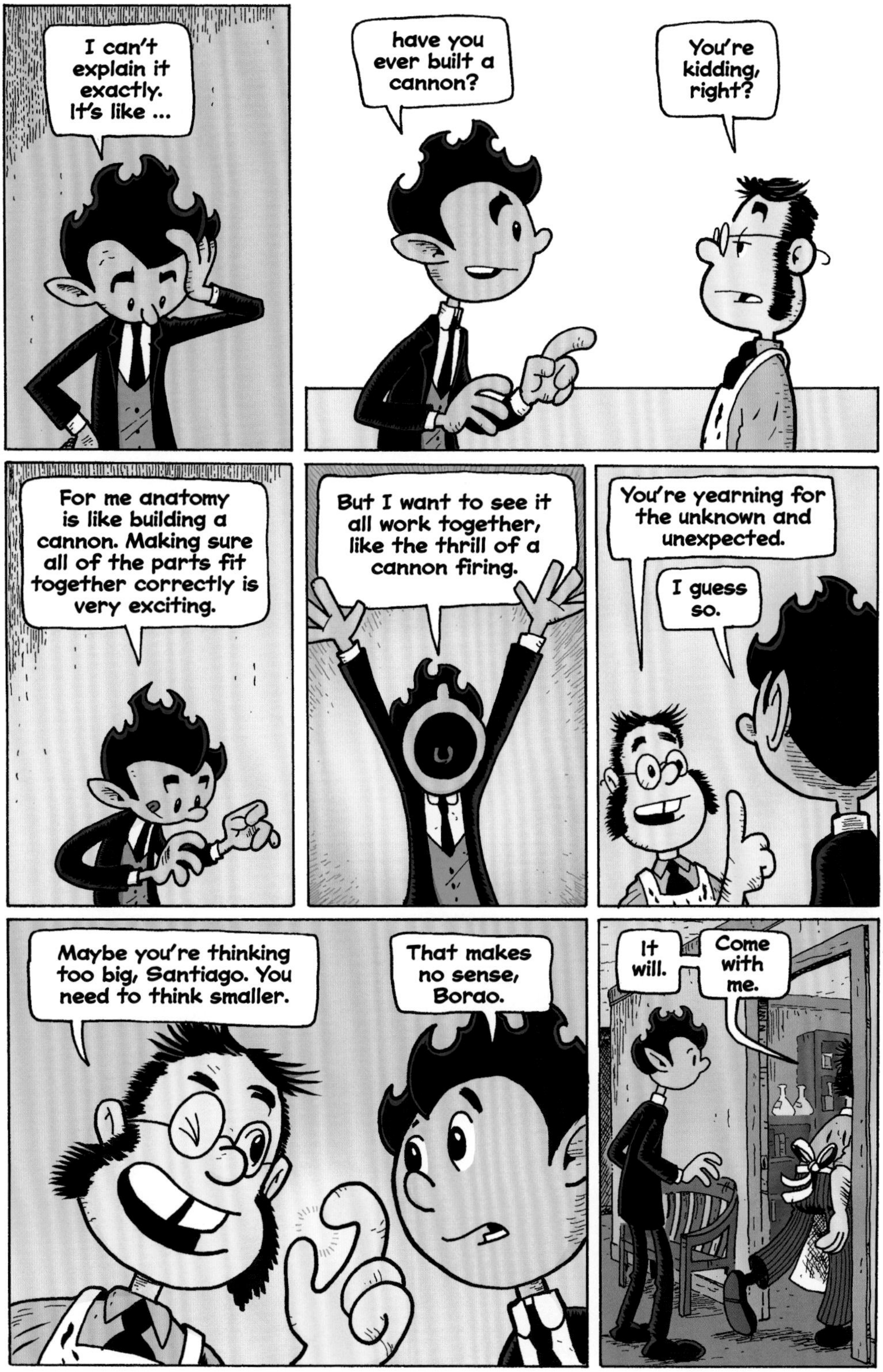
I can't explain it exactly. It's like ...
have you ever built a cannon?
You're kidding, right?
For me anatomy is like building a cannon. Making sure all of the parts fit together correctly is very exciting.
But I want to see it all work together, like the thrill of a cannon firing.
You're yearning for the unknown and unexpected.
I guess so.
Maybe you're thinking too big, Santiago. You need to think smaller.
That makes no sense, Borao.
It will.
Come with me.

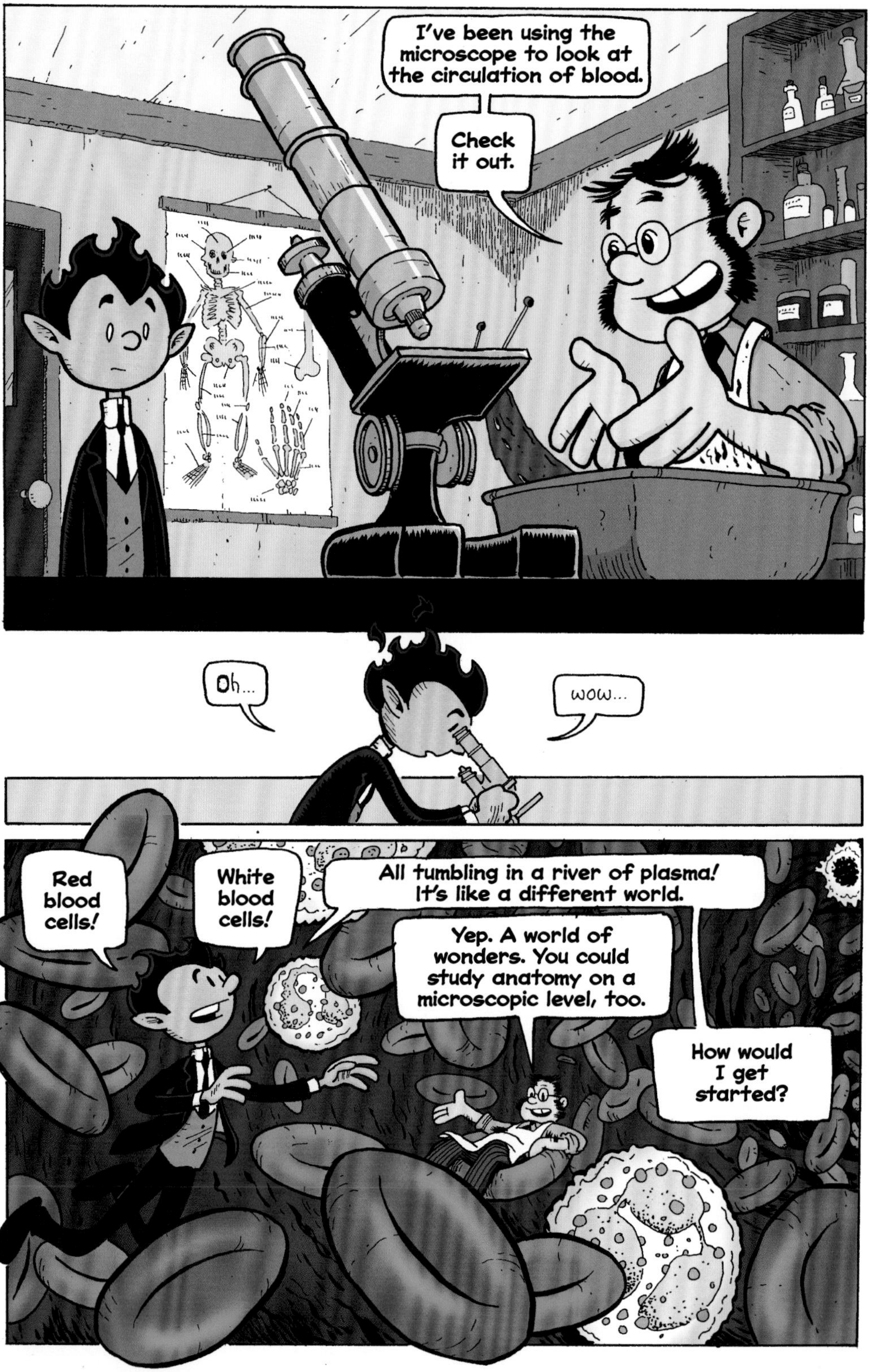

I've been using the microscope to look at the circulation of blood.
Check it out.
Oh...
wow...
Red blood cells!
White blood cells!
All tumbling in a river of plasma! It's like a different world.
Yep. A world of wonders. You could study anatomy on a microscopic level, too.
How would I get started?

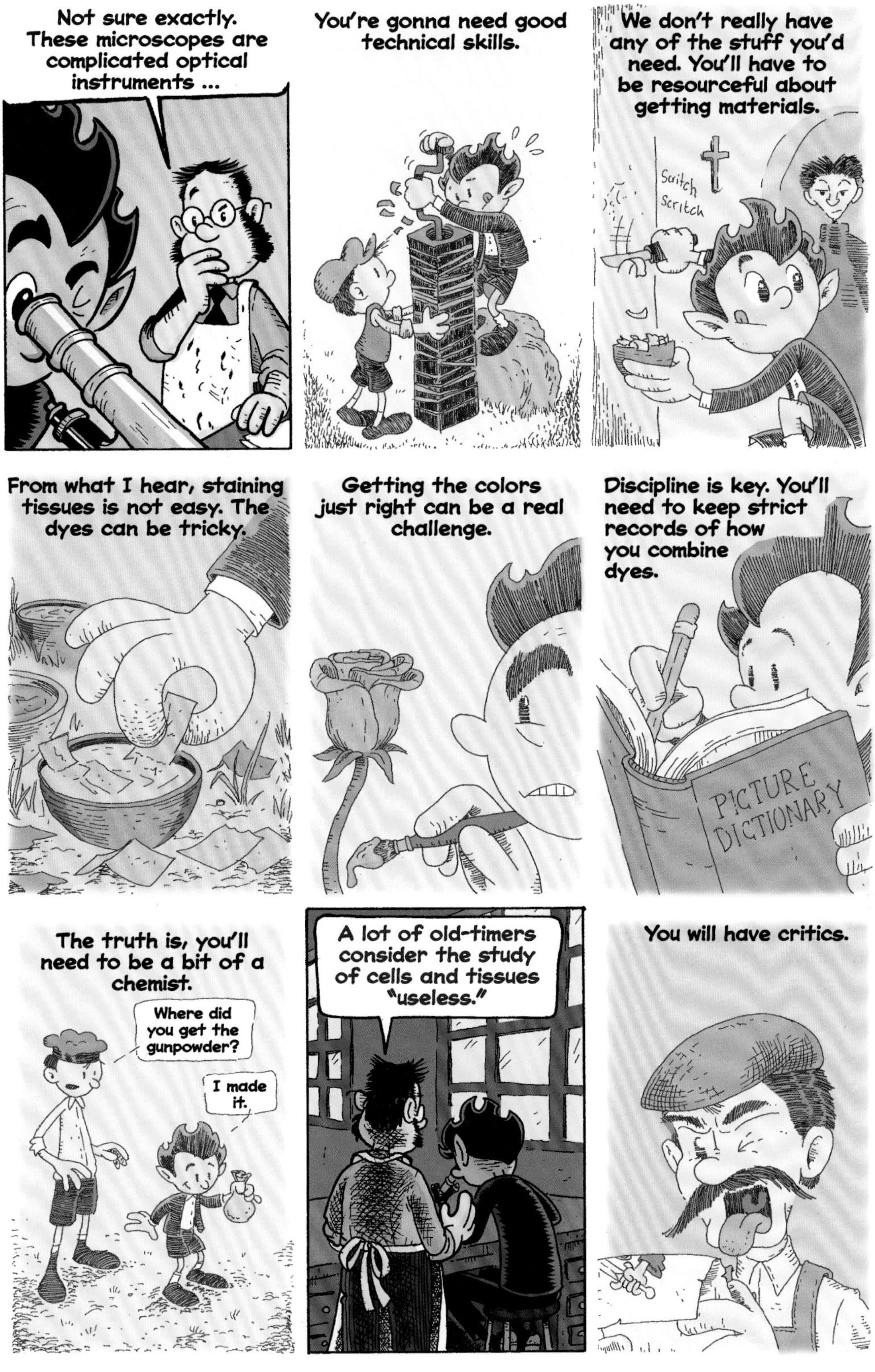
Not sure exactly. These microscopes are complicated optical instruments ...
You're gonna need good technical skills.
We don't really have any of the stuff you'd need. You'll have to be resourceful about getting materials.
Scritch
Scritch
From what I hear, staining tissues is not easy. The dyes can be tricky.
Getting the colors just right can be a real challenge.
Discipline is key. You'll need to keep strict records of how you combine dyes.
PICTURE DICTIONARY
The truth is, you'll need to be a bit of a chemist.
Where did you get the gunpowder?
I made it.
A lot of old-timers consider the study of cells and tissues "useless."
You will have critics.

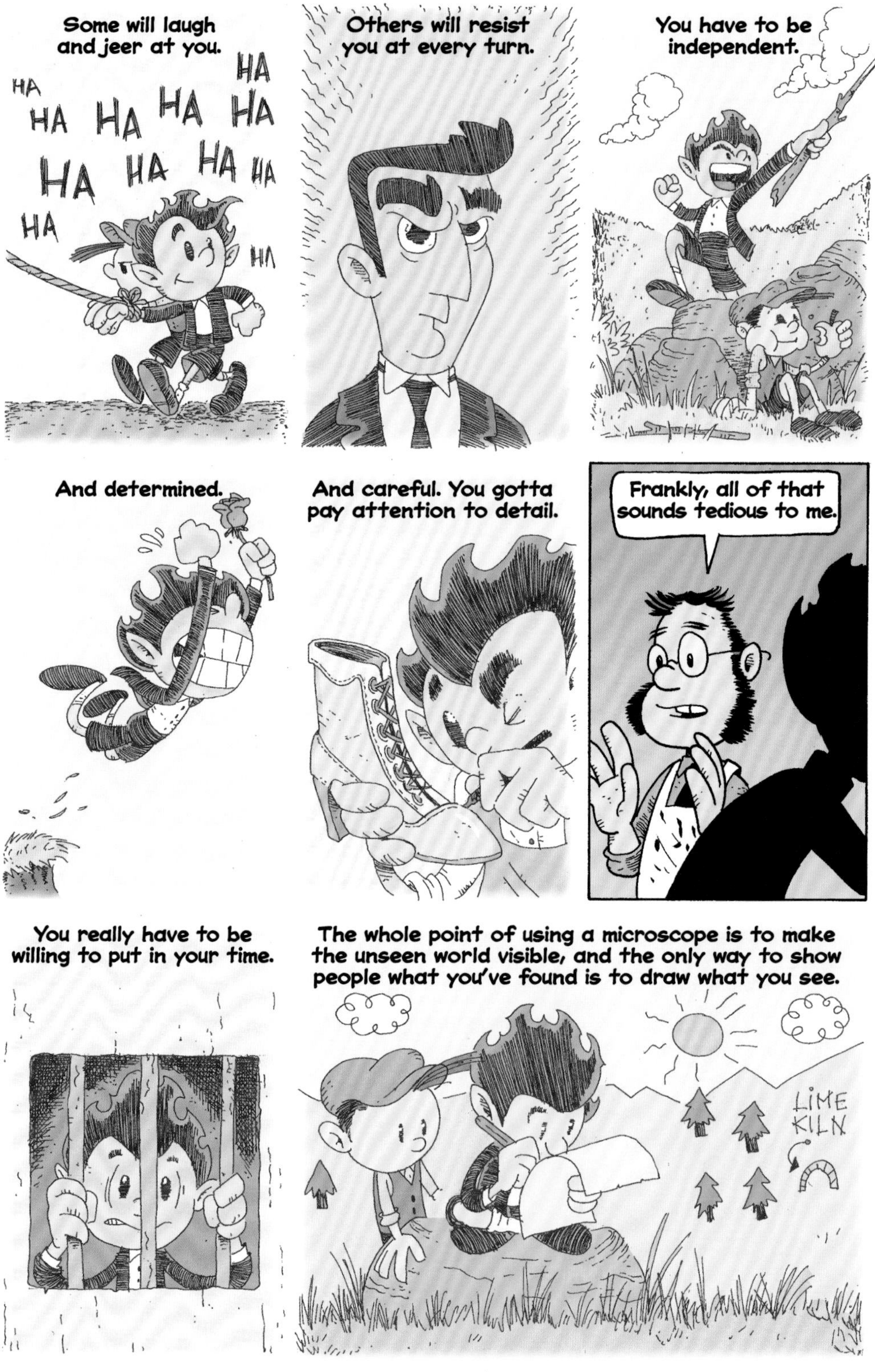
Some will laugh and jeer at you.
HA HA HA HA HA HA HA HA HA HA HA HA
Others will resist you at every turn.
You have to be independent.
And determined.
And careful. You gotta pay attention to detail.
Frankly, all of that sounds tedious to me.
You really have to be willing to put in your time.
The whole point of using a microscope is to make the unseen world visible, and the only way to show people what you've found is to draw what you see.
LIME KILN

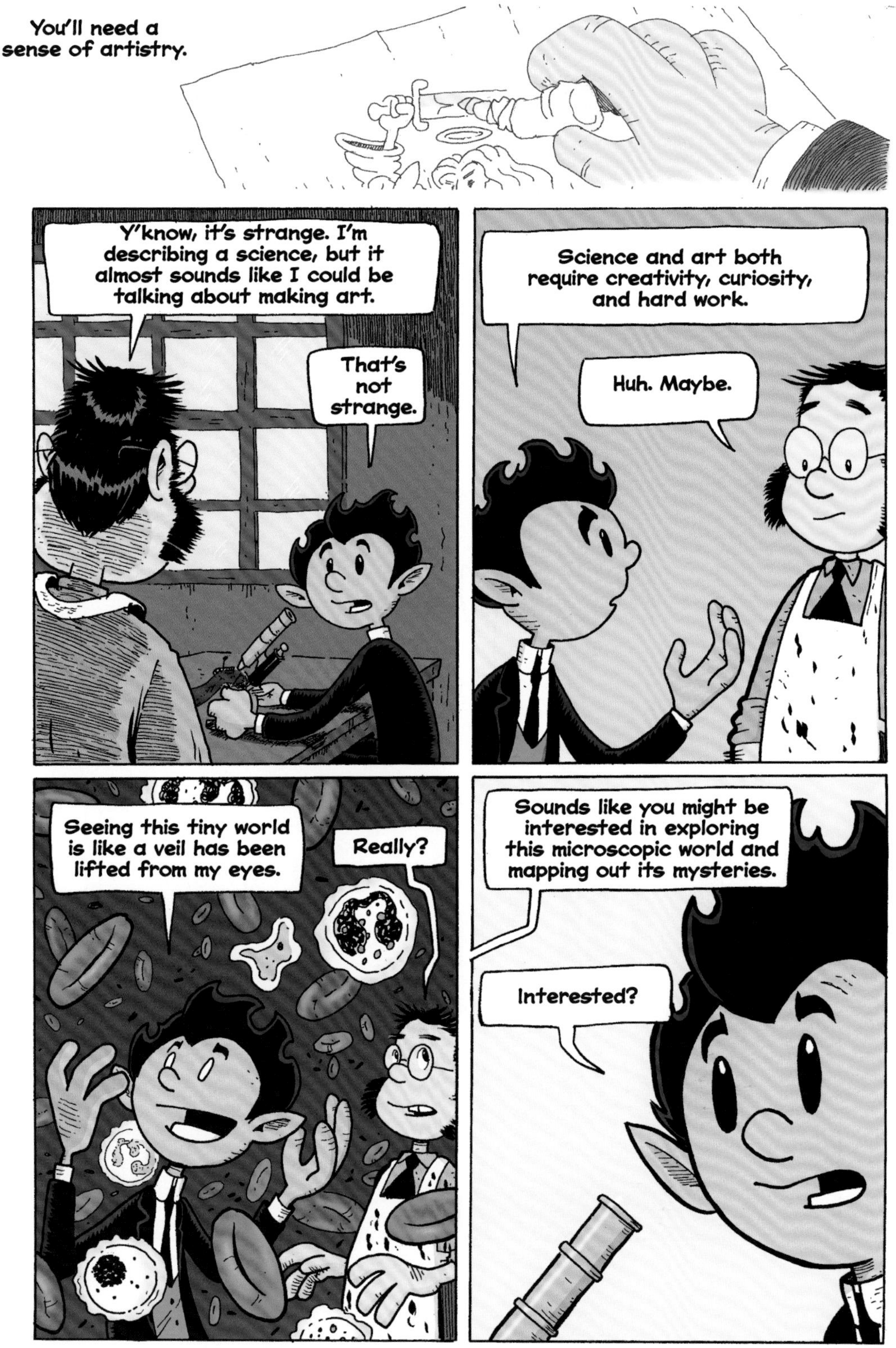
You'll need a sense of artistry.
Y'know, it's strange. I'm describing a science, but it almost sounds like I could be talking about making art.
That's not strange.
Science and art both require creativity, curiosity, and hard work.
Huh. Maybe.
Seeing this tiny world is like a veil has been lifted from my eyes.
Really?
Sounds like you might be interested in exploring this microscopic world and mapping out its mysteries.
Interested?

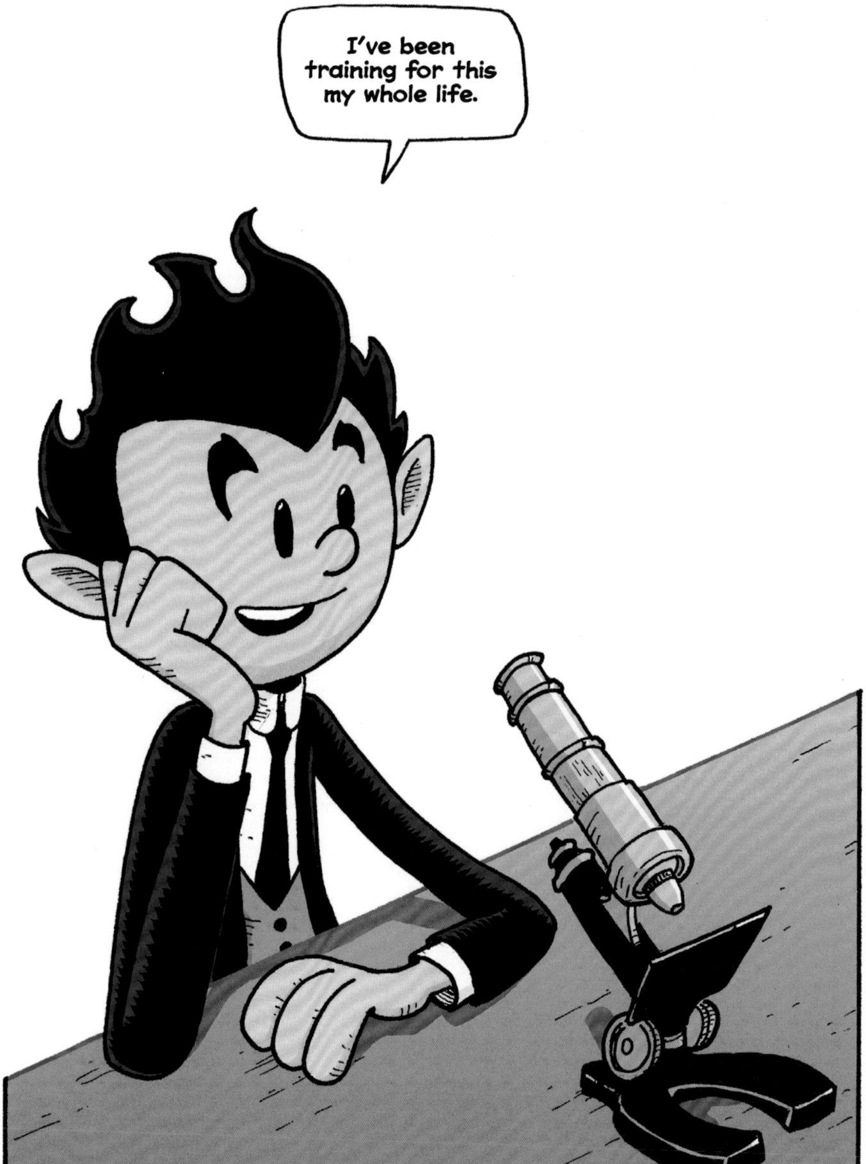
I've been training for this my whole life.

CHAPTER 11: A BOY AND HIS MICROSCOPE

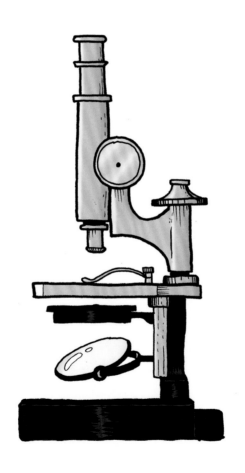

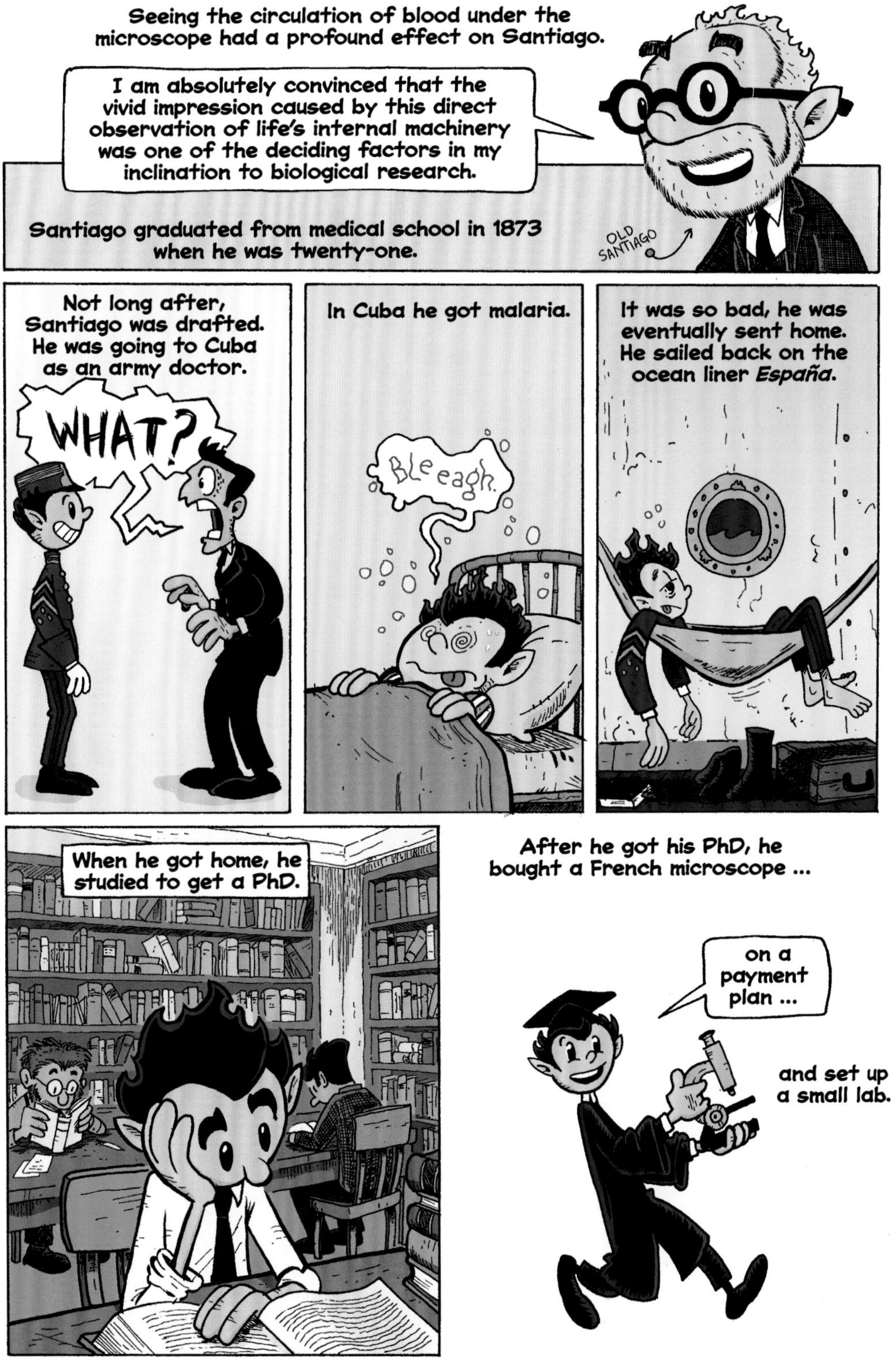
Seeing the circulation of blood under the microscope had a profound effect on Santiago.
I am absolutely convinced that the vivid impression caused by this direct observation of life's internal machinery was one of the deciding factors in my inclination to biological research.
Santiago graduated from medical school in 1873 when he was twenty-one.
OLD SANTIAGO
Not long after, Santiago was drafted. He was going to Cuba as an army doctor.
WHAT?
In Cuba he got malaria.
Bleeagh.
It was so bad, he was eventually sent home. He sailed back on the ocean liner *España*.
When he got home, he studied to get a PhD.
After he got his PhD, he bought a French microscope ...
on a payment plan ...
and set up a small lab.

Santiago wanted to get a job as a professor at a university and study the microscopic structures of living organisms. When a professor position opened at the University of Zaragoza, Don Justo pushed Santiago to compete for it. Santiago didn't feel ready, but he did as his father asked.

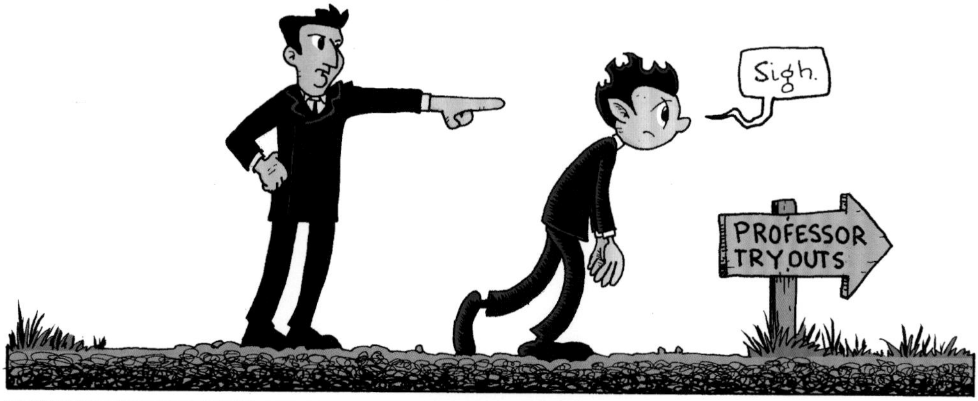
Sigh.
PROFESSOR TRY OUTS

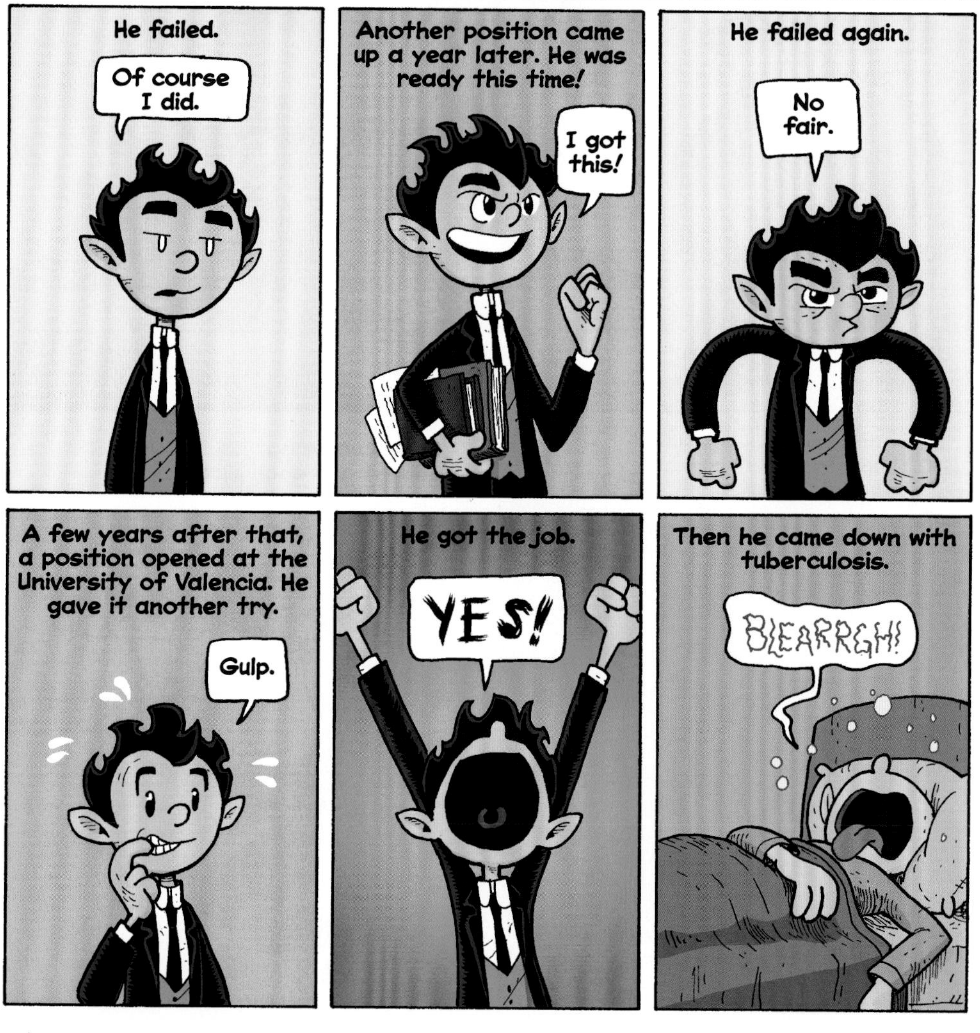
He failed.
Of course I did.
Another position came up a year later. He was ready this time!
I got this!
He failed again.
No fair.
A few years after that, a position opened at the University of Valencia. He gave it another try.
Gulp.
He got the job.
YES!
Then he came down with tuberculosis.
BLEARRGH!

He thought he was going to die.

Ugh.

But he didn't!

YES!

Not long after he recovered, he met Silveria Fañanás García.

They soon married and started a family. They would eventually have seven children.

Fe
Santiago
Paula
Pilar
Luis
Jorge
Enriqueta

He grew a beard.

As a young professor, he helped save a bunch of people in Valencia from a deadly cholera outbreak.

The people of Valencia were so grateful that they bought him a super-fancy Zeiss microscope.

Over the next several years, Santiago used his microscope to study everything from insect muscles to eyeball lenses. He used stains and dyes to "paint" the microscopic structures and make them easier to see. And, of course, he drew everything that he saw.

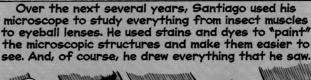

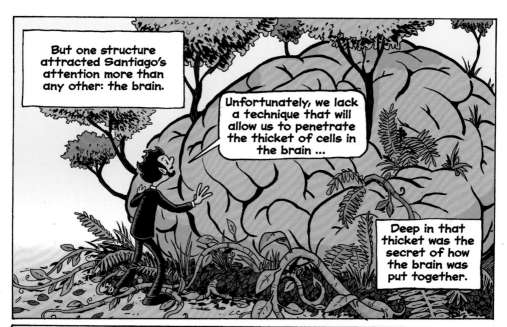

But one structure attracted Santiago's attention more than any other: the brain.

Unfortunately, we lack a technique that will allow us to penetrate the thicket of cells in the brain ...

Deep in that thicket was the secret of how the brain was put together.

Modern scientists know that the brain is part of a complex network called the nervous system. The nerve cells of the nervous system branch throughout our bodies and do three main things.

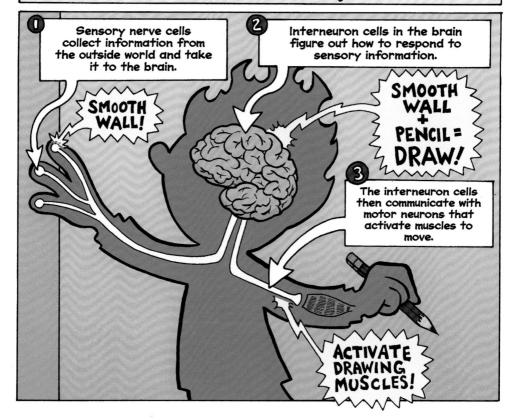

1 Sensory nerve cells collect information from the outside world and take it to the brain.

2 Interneuron cells in the brain figure out how to respond to sensory information.

SMOOTH WALL!

SMOOTH WALL + PENCIL = DRAW!

3 The interneuron cells then communicate with motor neurons that activate muscles to move.

ACTIVATE DRAWING MUSCLES!

But in Santiago's time, scientists didn't know how the nervous system was put together.

Some thought the nerve cells of the brain were all interconnected like a big net.

Others thought they were separate cells that could somehow talk to each other.

Scientists were trying to explore the brain and nervous system with the microscope, but having limited success.

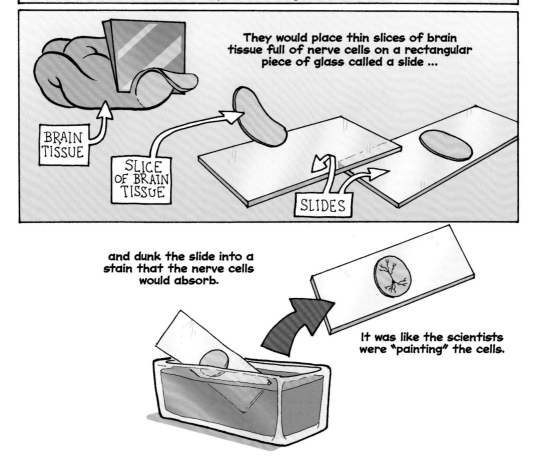

They would place thin slices of brain tissue full of nerve cells on a rectangular piece of glass called a slide ...

BRAIN TISSUE

SLICE OF BRAIN TISSUE

SLIDES

and dunk the slide into a stain that the nerve cells would absorb.

It was like the scientists were "painting" the cells.

RED BLOOD CELLS

BONE CELL

STOMACH GOBLET CELL

NERVE CELL

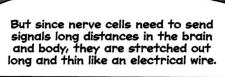

Most cells in the body are round or squarish and are relatively easy to stain.

But since nerve cells need to send signals long distances in the brain and body, they are stretched out long and thin like an electrical wire.

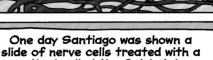

Their delicate fibers are all tangled together and very hard to see under the microscope.

One day Santiago was shown a slide of nerve cells treated with a method called the Golgi stain.

It rocked his world.

Wow! The image is so much better. This is the technique I've been waiting for!

The Golgi stain caused a chemical reaction in one out of every twenty nerve cells on a slide. These cells became darkly stained, while the other nerve cells on the slide remained unstained and invisible.

Using this technique, scientists could easily see a few sharply outlined nerve cells among the brain's tangled thicket!

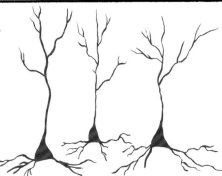

Still, the technique needed improvement to see all of the little branches on a very long nerve cell.

So, like an artist trying to get his colors just right, Santiago worked long, tedious hours experimenting with new ways to use the Golgi stain on brain cells.

He eventually improved the technique so that he could see enough of the cells to understand whether or not the nerve cells of the brain were connected like a big net or made of individual cells that work together.

He drew illustrations of what he saw.

The results were clear.

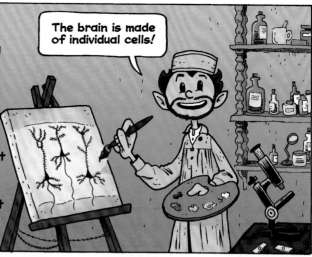

The brain is made of individual cells!

Santiago published his revolutionary results.

Ta-daaaaa!

No one paid any attention.

So he went to science conventions in other countries to show off his microscopic works of art.

No one paid any attention.

Then, one day, a famous Swiss scientist noticed his work. He was impressed.

Mein Gott!

Dr. Rudolf Albert von Kölliker

After that, everyone paid attention to Santiago.

His beautiful slides of the delicate branching nerve cells were a big deal. A brain built of little cells talking to each other could grow and change.
Listen up! This is important!
It could build new connections when we learn something ...
SPROUT
Really important!
Got it!
or cut connections we aren't using.
I got nothing to say.
SHRIVEL
Me neither.
Santiago described it just like an artist would.
Imagine that anyone could, if they so desired, be the sculptor of their own brain.
In other words, when you learn something new, you change the connections in your brain, and that "sculpts" it into a different shape.
SANTIAGO'S BRAIN
CLAY

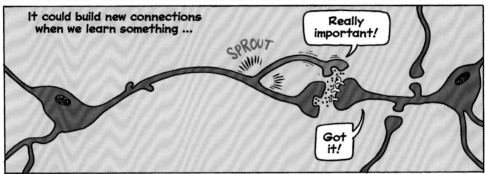

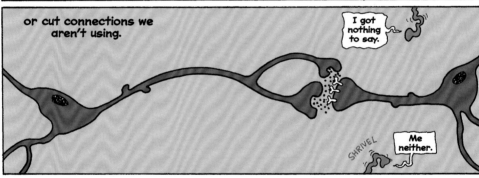

Santiago's research explained how the nerves in the brain are organized.

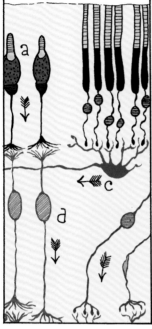

He described how those nerves grow and develop into mature neurons.

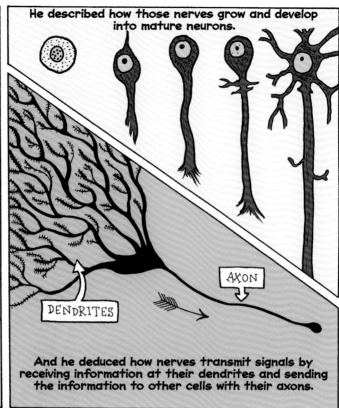

DENDRITES

AXON

And he deduced how nerves transmit signals by receiving information at their dendrites and sending the information to other cells with their axons.

Santiago's new ideas made scientists all over the world sculpt their brains into a new shape.

In 1894, he was invited to give the Croonian Lecture at the Royal Society in England. It was a huge honor, and the trip would last several weeks.

Santiago wanted to go, but there was one problem ...

173

His youngest
daughter, Pilar,
was very, very sick.

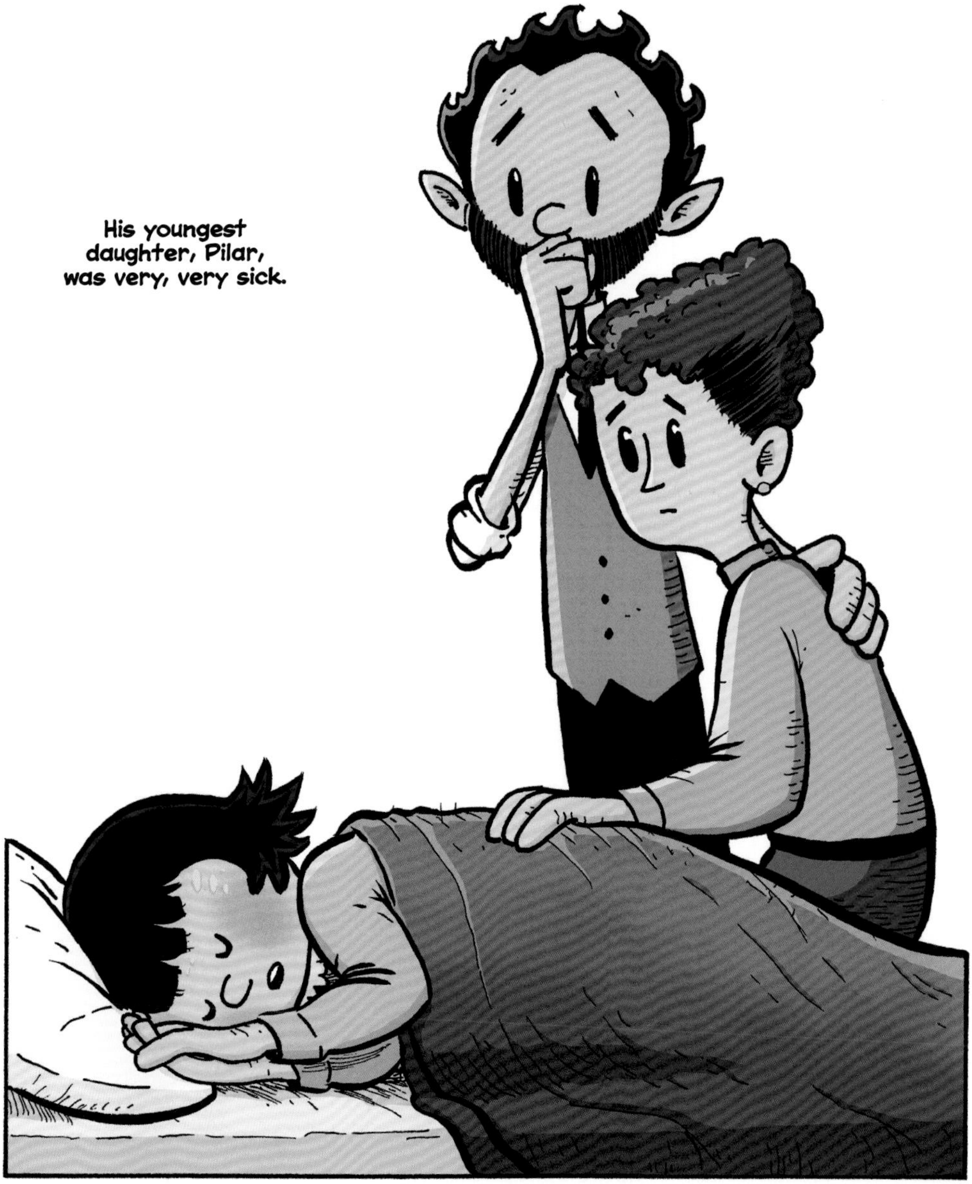

CHAPTER 12: THE INVISIBLE MYSTERY FOREST

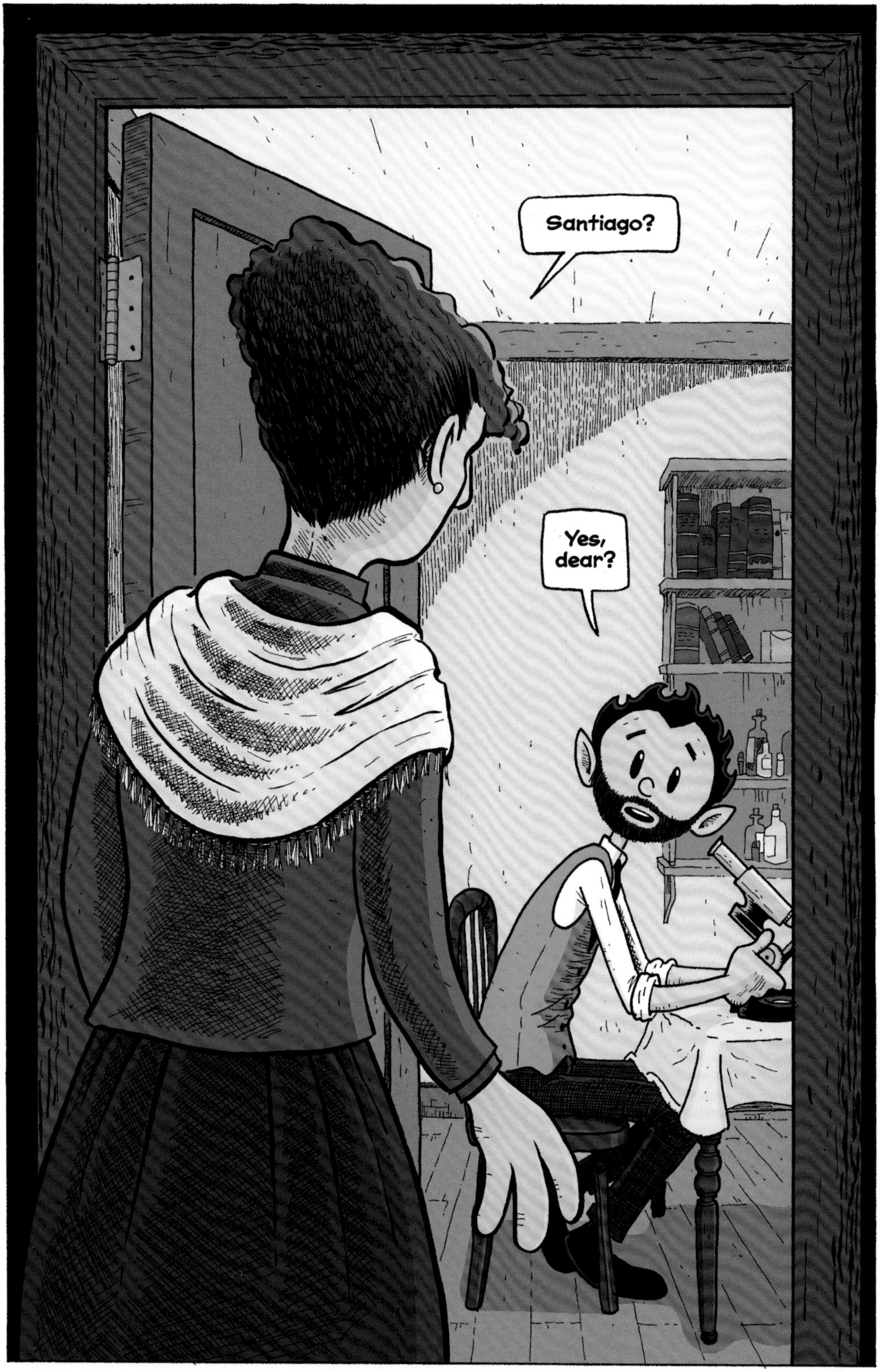
Santiago?
Yes, dear?

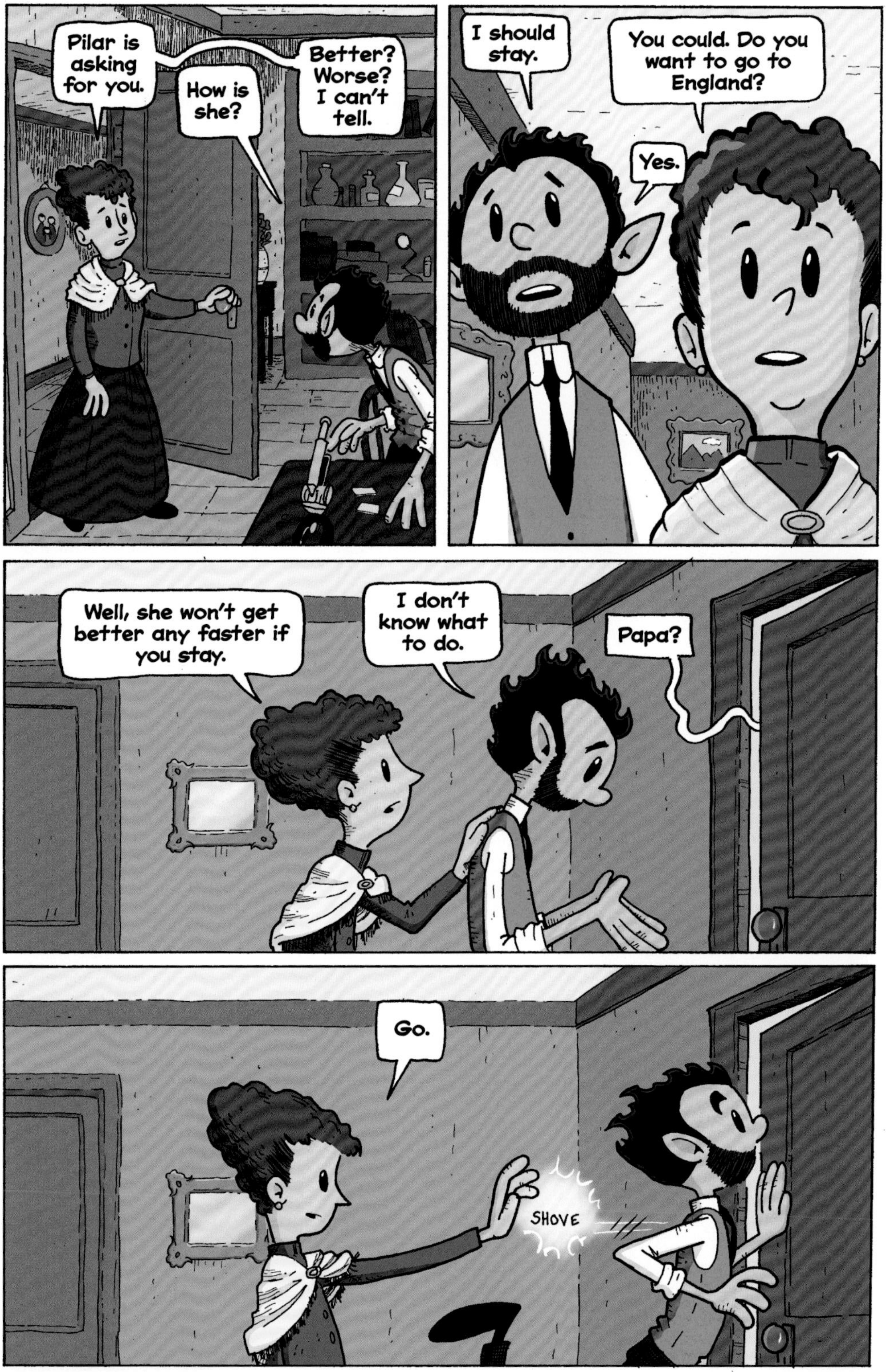
Pilar is asking for you.
How is she?
Better? Worse? I can't tell.
I should stay.
You could. Do you want to go to England?
Yes.
Well, she won't get better any faster if you stay.
I don't know what to do.
Papa?
Go.
SHOVE

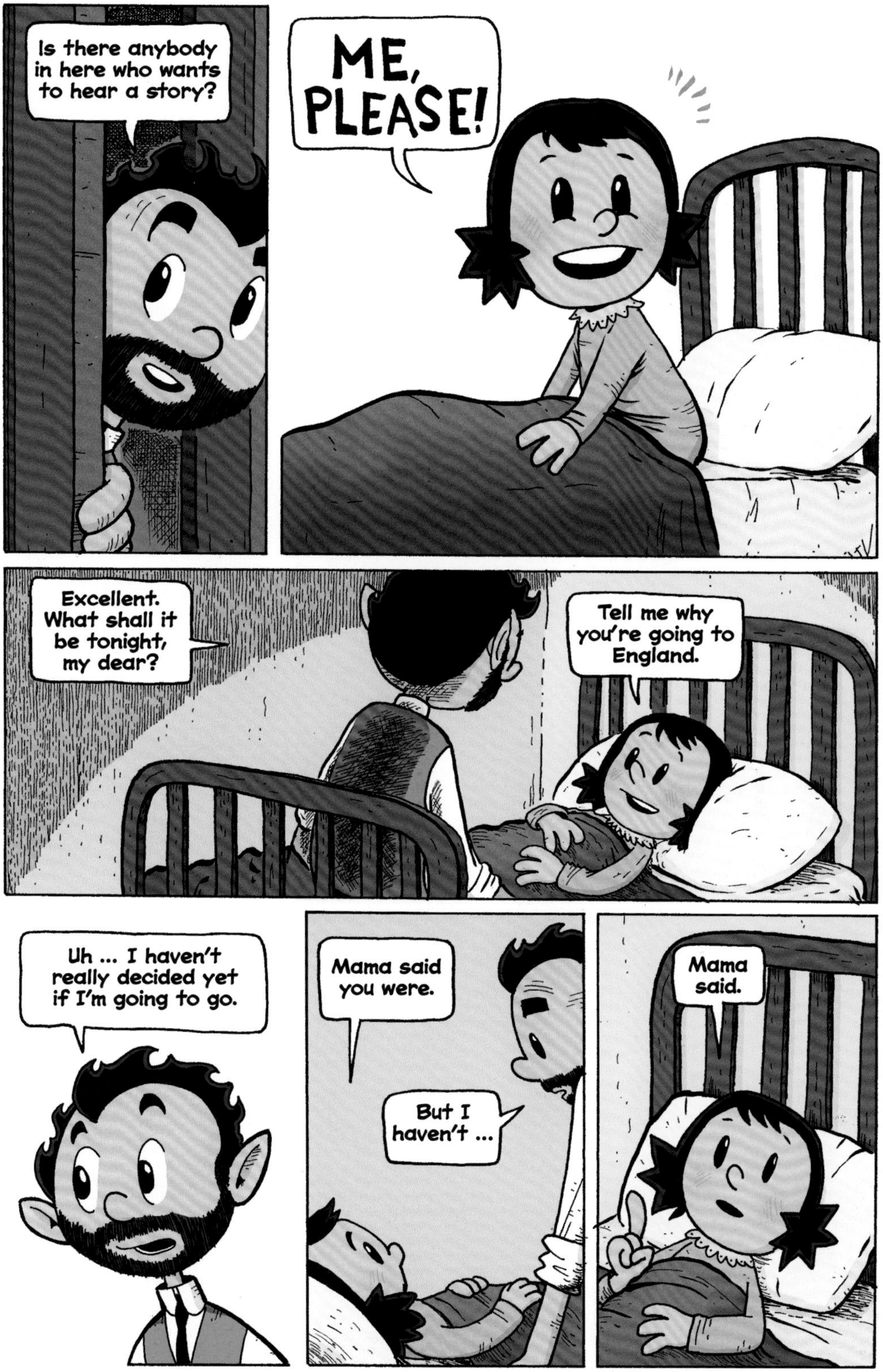
Is there anybody in here who wants to hear a story?
ME, PLEASE!
Excellent. What shall it be tonight, my dear?
Tell me why you're going to England.
Uh ... I haven't really decided yet if I'm going to go.
Mama said you were.
But I haven't ...
Mama said.

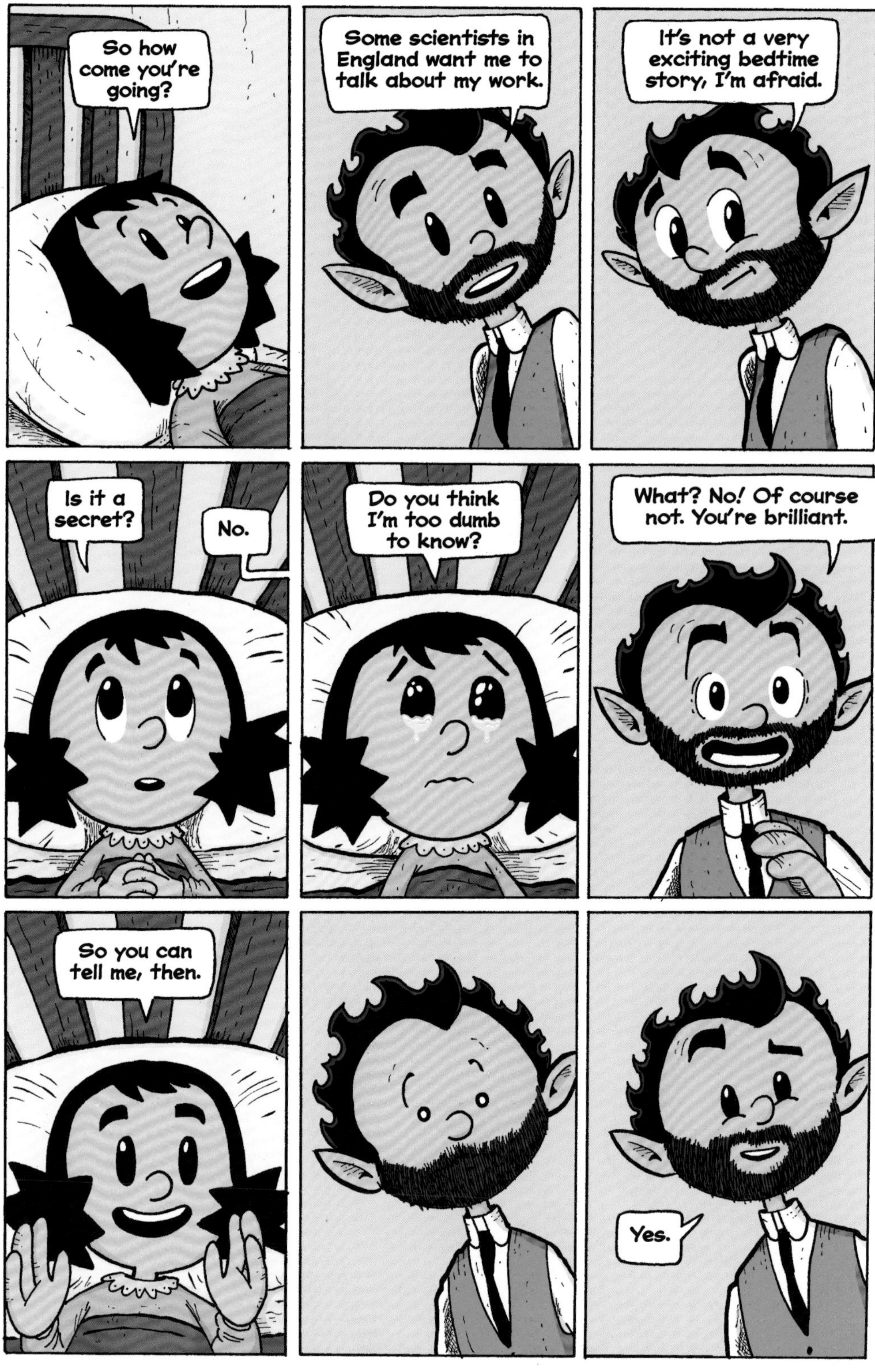
So how come you're going?
Some scientists in England want me to talk about my work.
It's not a very exciting bedtime story, I'm afraid.
Is it a secret?
No.
Do you think I'm too dumb to know?
What? No! Of course not. You're brilliant.
So you can tell me, then.
Yes.

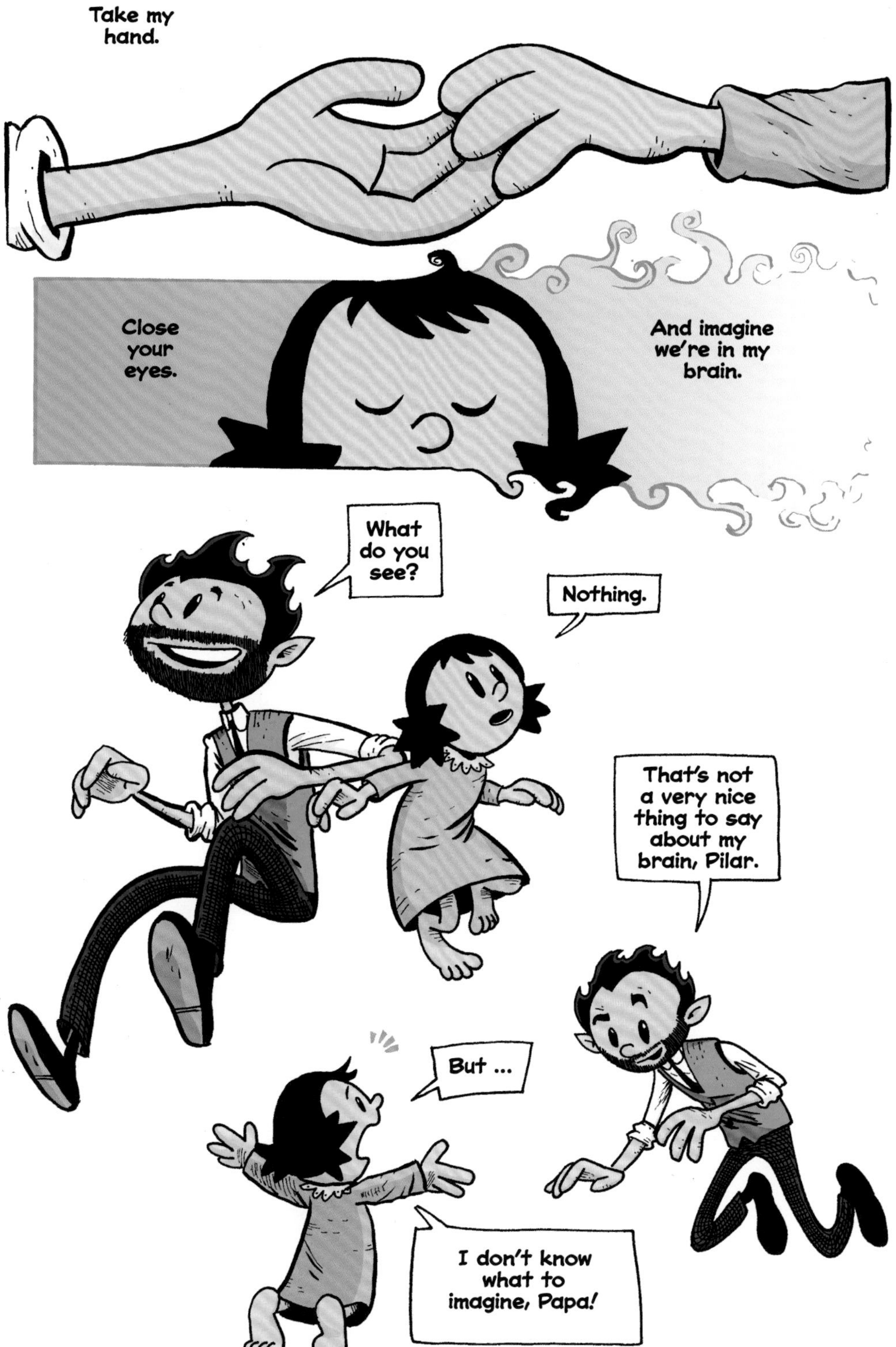
Take my hand.
Close your eyes.
And imagine we're in my brain.
What do you see?
Nothing.
That's not a very nice thing to say about my brain, Pilar.
But ...
I don't know what to imagine, Papa!

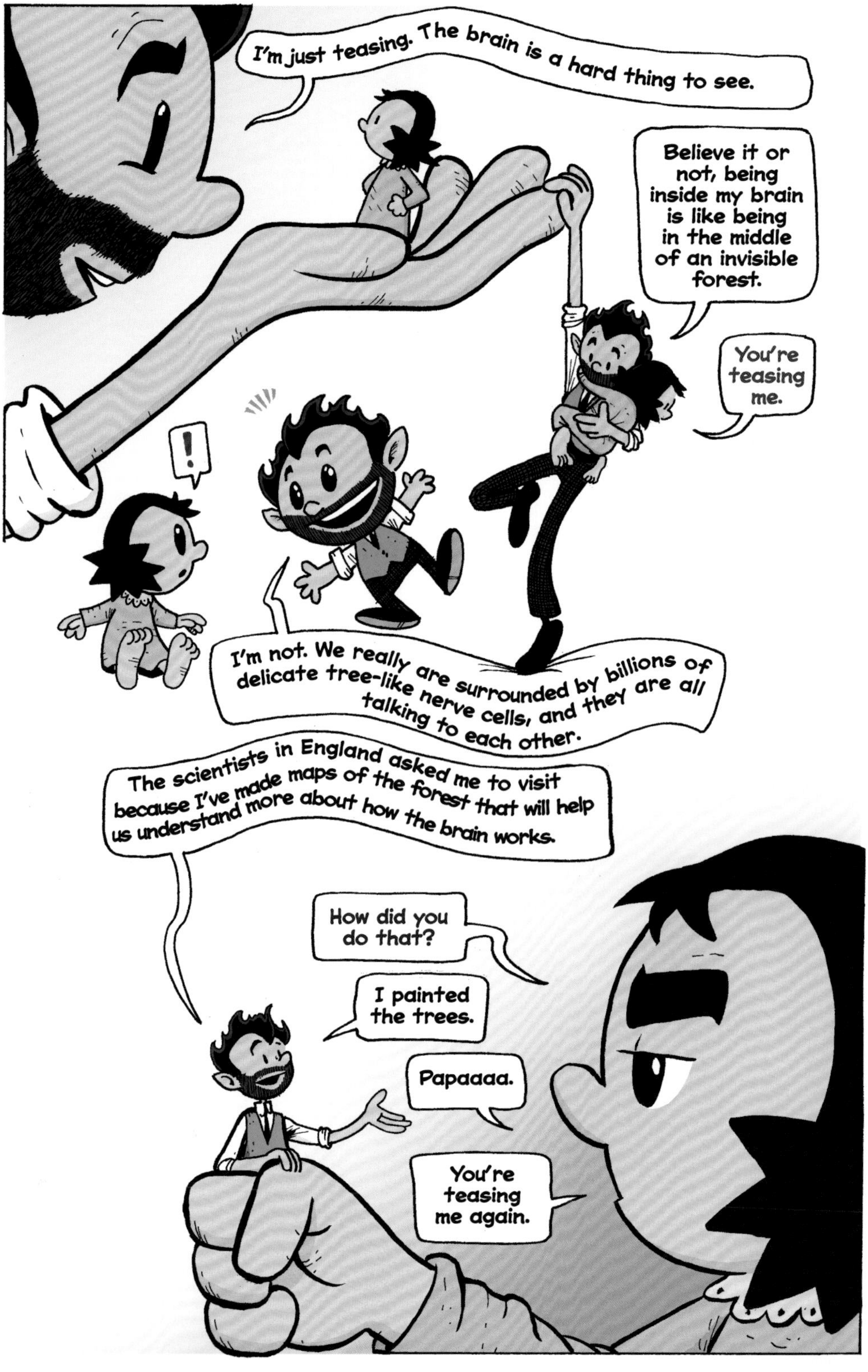

I'm just teasing. The brain is a hard thing to see.
Believe it or not, being inside my brain is like being in the middle of an invisible forest.
You're teasing me.
!
I'm not. We really are surrounded by billions of delicate tree-like nerve cells, and they are all talking to each other.
The scientists in England asked me to visit because I've made maps of the forest that will help us understand more about how the brain works.
How did you do that?
I painted the trees.
Papaaaa.
You're teasing me again.

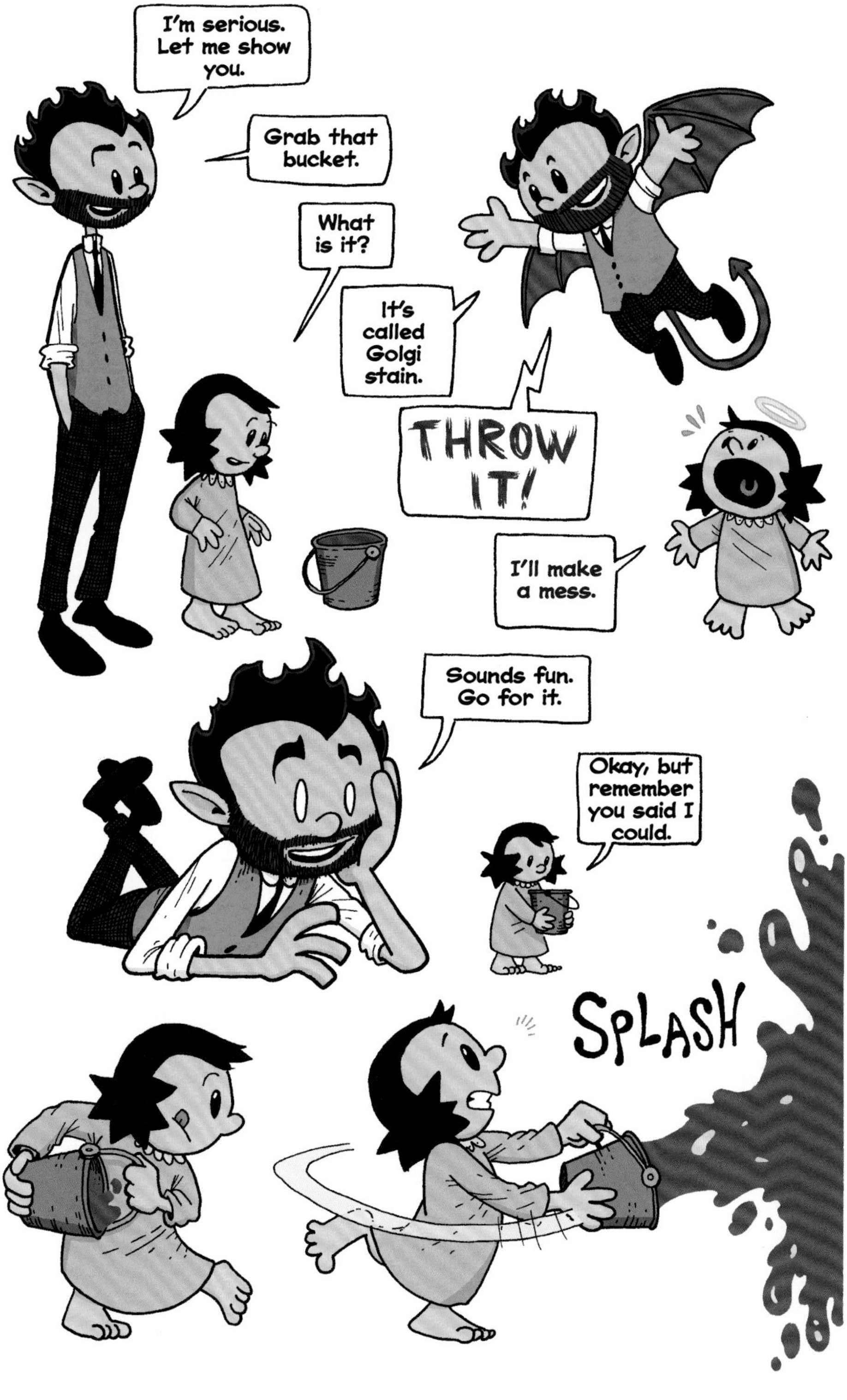
I'm serious. Let me show you.
Grab that bucket.
What is it?
It's called Golgi stain.
THROW IT!
I'll make a mess.
Sounds fun. Go for it.
Okay, but remember you said I could.
SPLASH

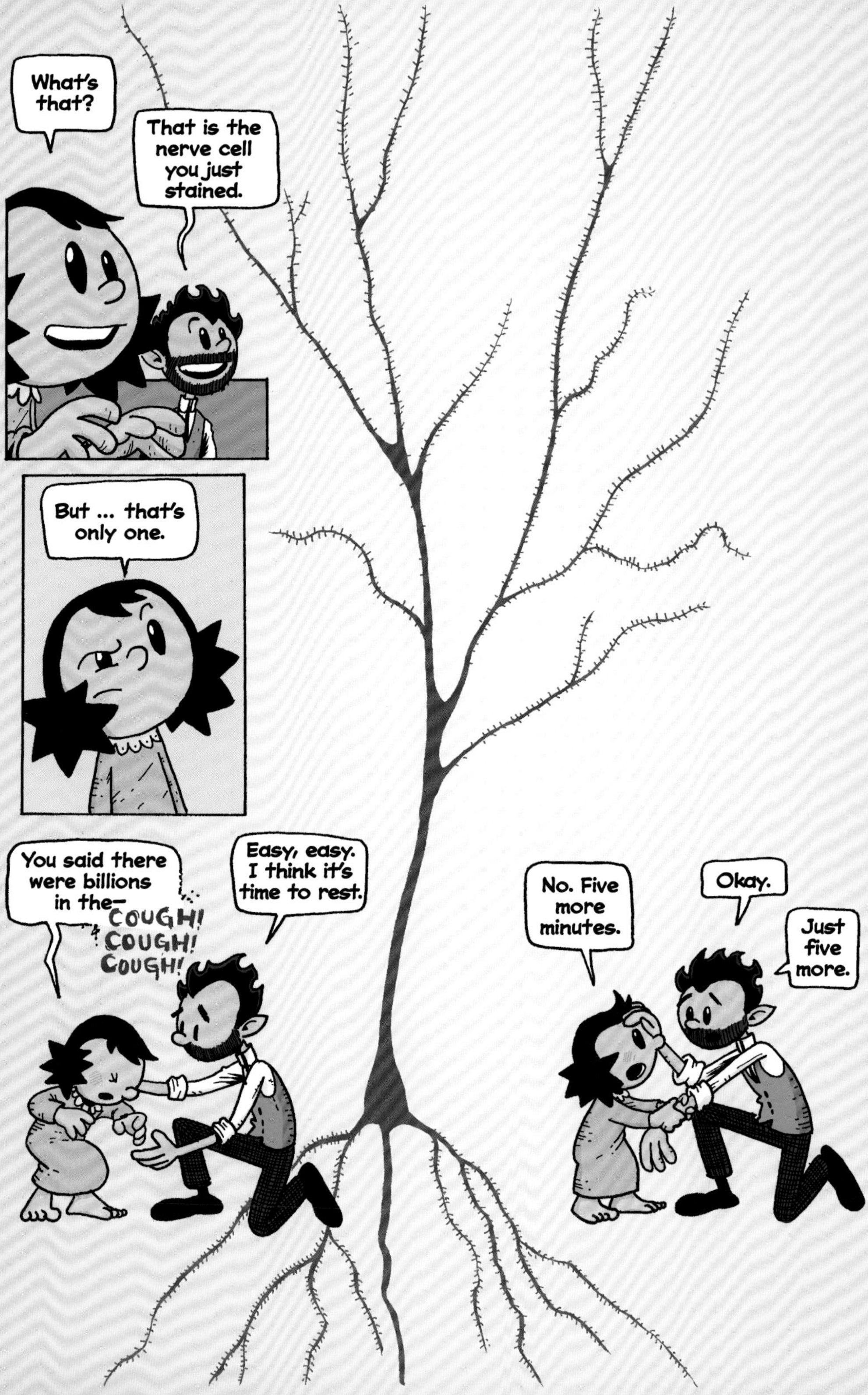
What's that?
That is the nerve cell you just stained.
But ... that's only one.
You said there were billions in the—
COUGH! COUGH! COUGH!
Easy, easy. I think it's time to rest.
No. Five more minutes.
Okay.
Just five more.

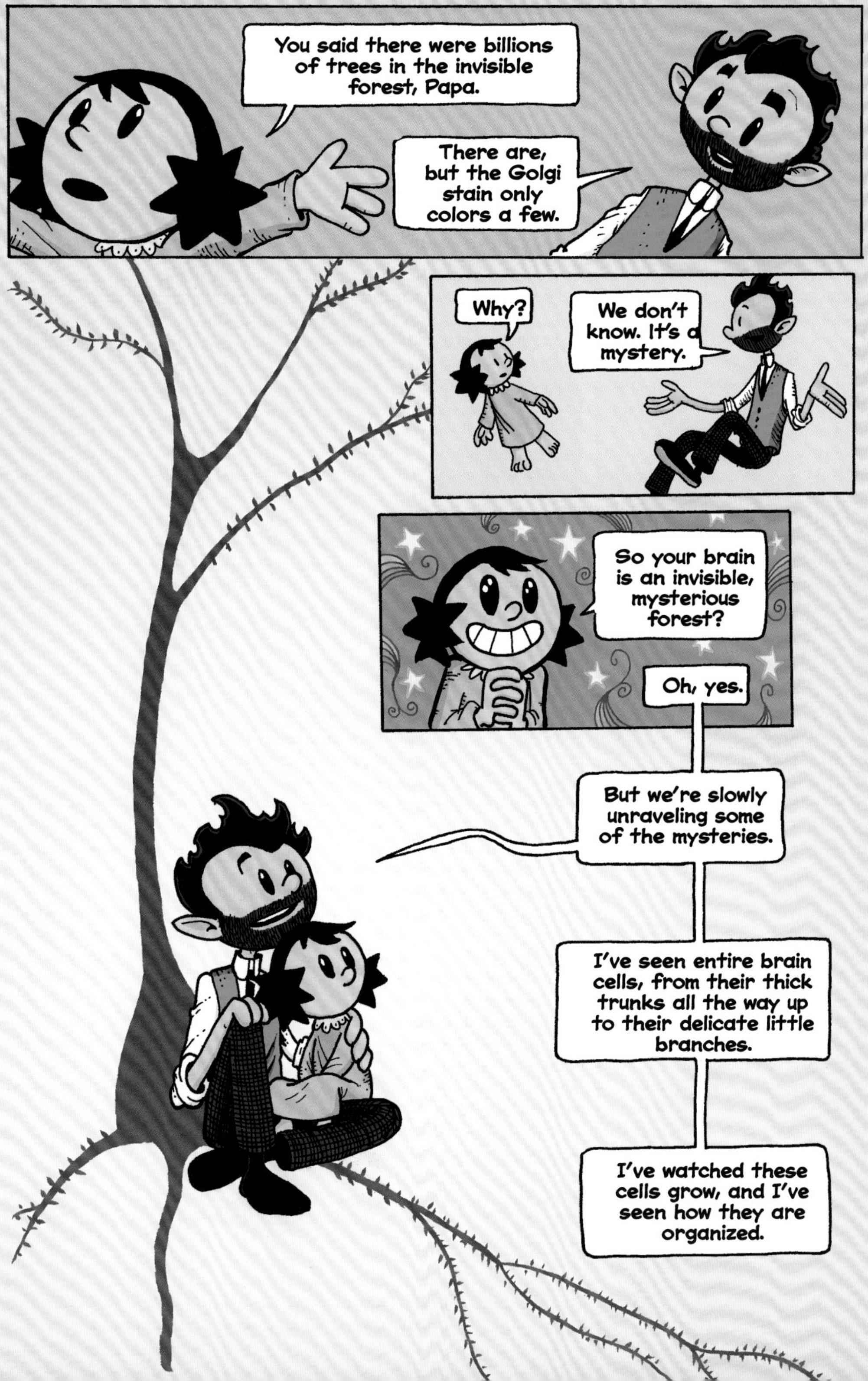
You said there were billions of trees in the invisible forest, Papa.
There are, but the Golgi stain only colors a few.
Why?
We don't know. It's a mystery.
So your brain is an invisible, mysterious forest?
Oh, yes.
But we're slowly unraveling some of the mysteries.
I've seen entire brain cells, from their thick trunks all the way up to their delicate little branches.
I've watched these cells grow, and I've seen how they are organized.

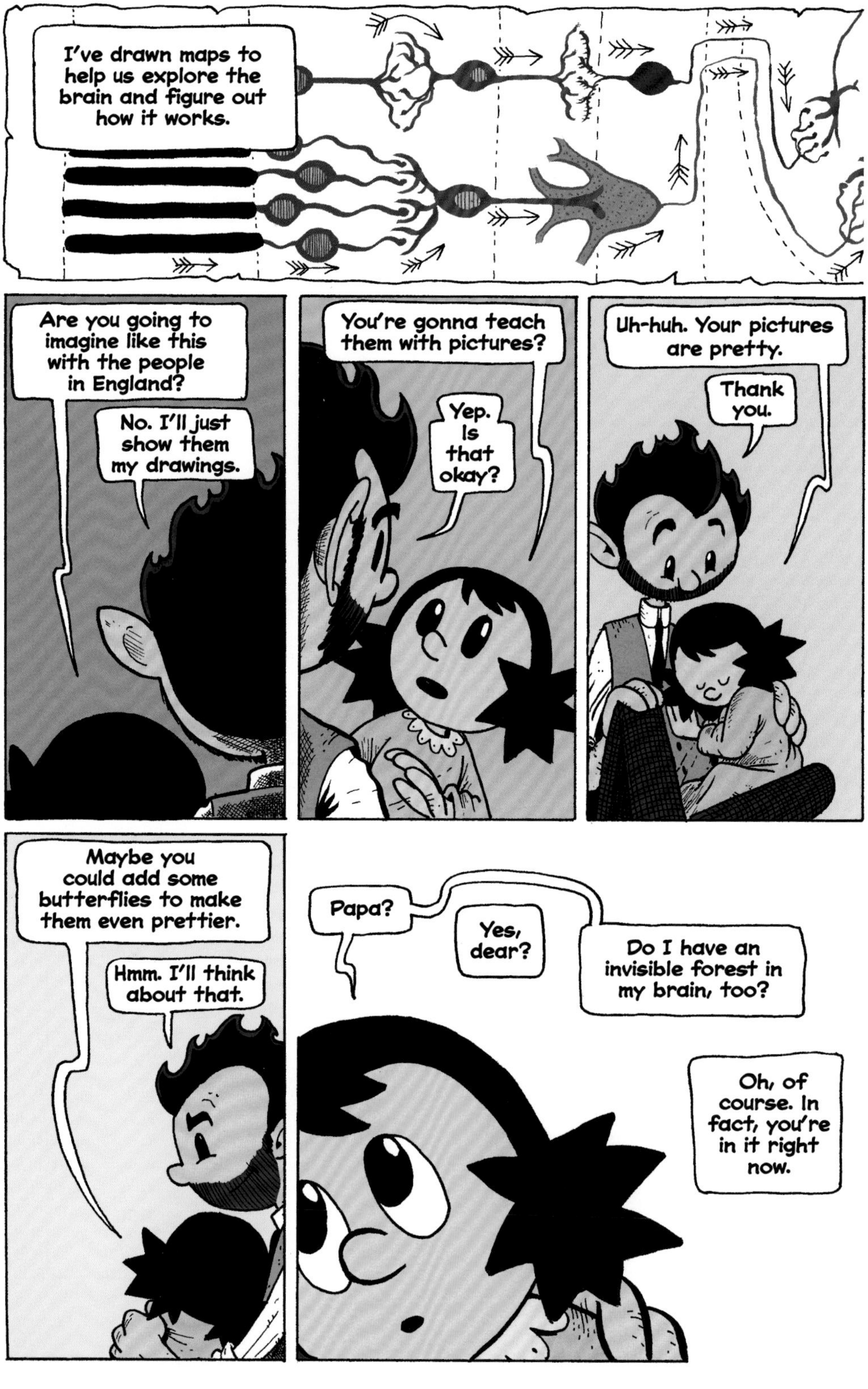
I've drawn maps to help us explore the brain and figure out how it works.
Are you going to imagine like this with the people in England?
No. I'll just show them my drawings.
You're gonna teach them with pictures?
Yep. Is that okay?
Uh-huh. Your pictures are pretty.
Thank you.
Maybe you could add some butterflies to make them even prettier.
Hmm. I'll think about that.
Papa?
Yes, dear?
Do I have an invisible forest in my brain, too?
Oh, of course. In fact, you're in it right now.

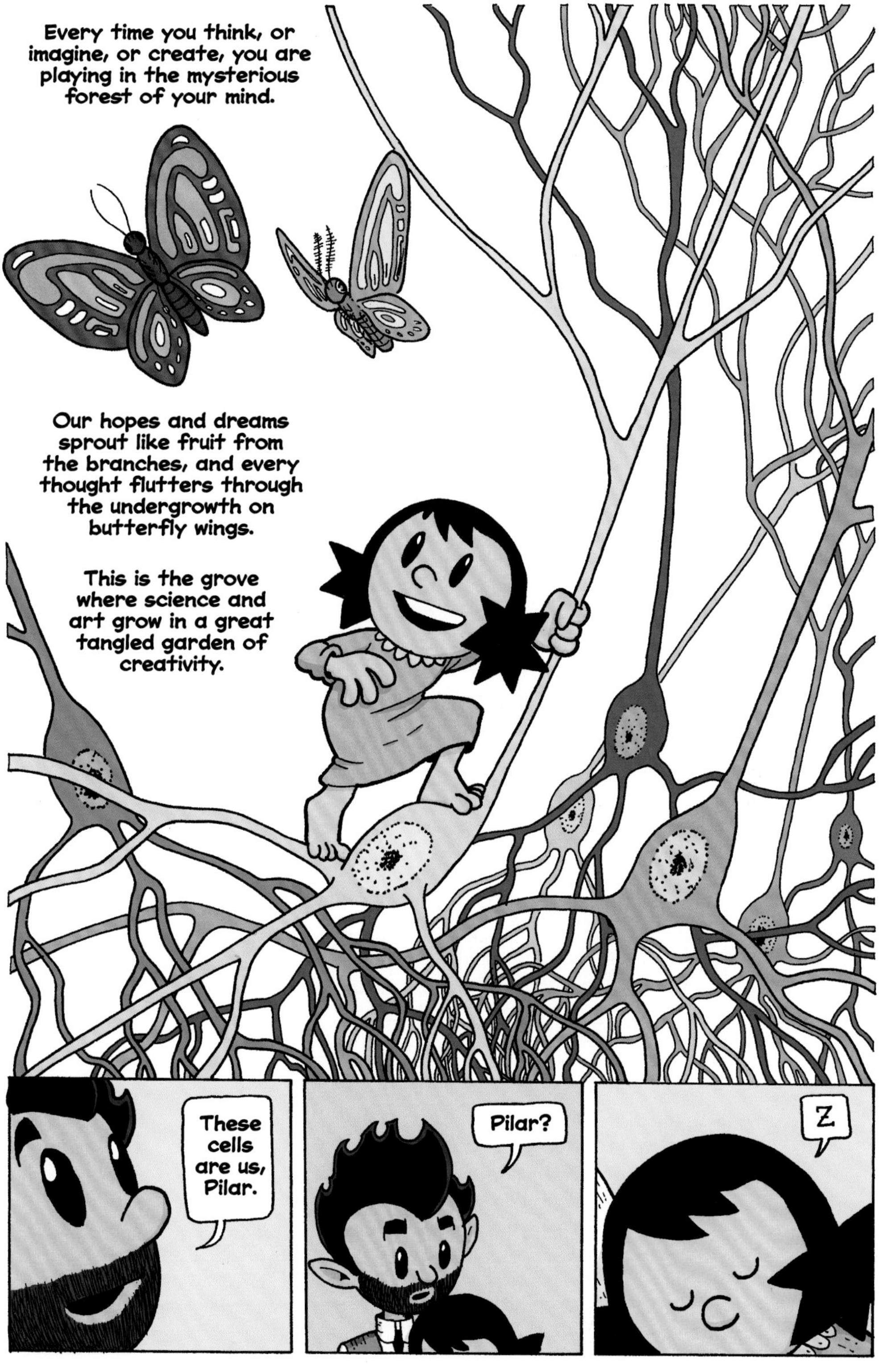

Every time you think, or imagine, or create, you are playing in the mysterious forest of your mind.
Our hopes and dreams sprout like fruit from the branches, and every thought flutters through the undergrowth on butterfly wings.
This is the grove where science and art grow in a great tangled garden of creativity.
These cells are us, Pilar.
Pilar?
Z

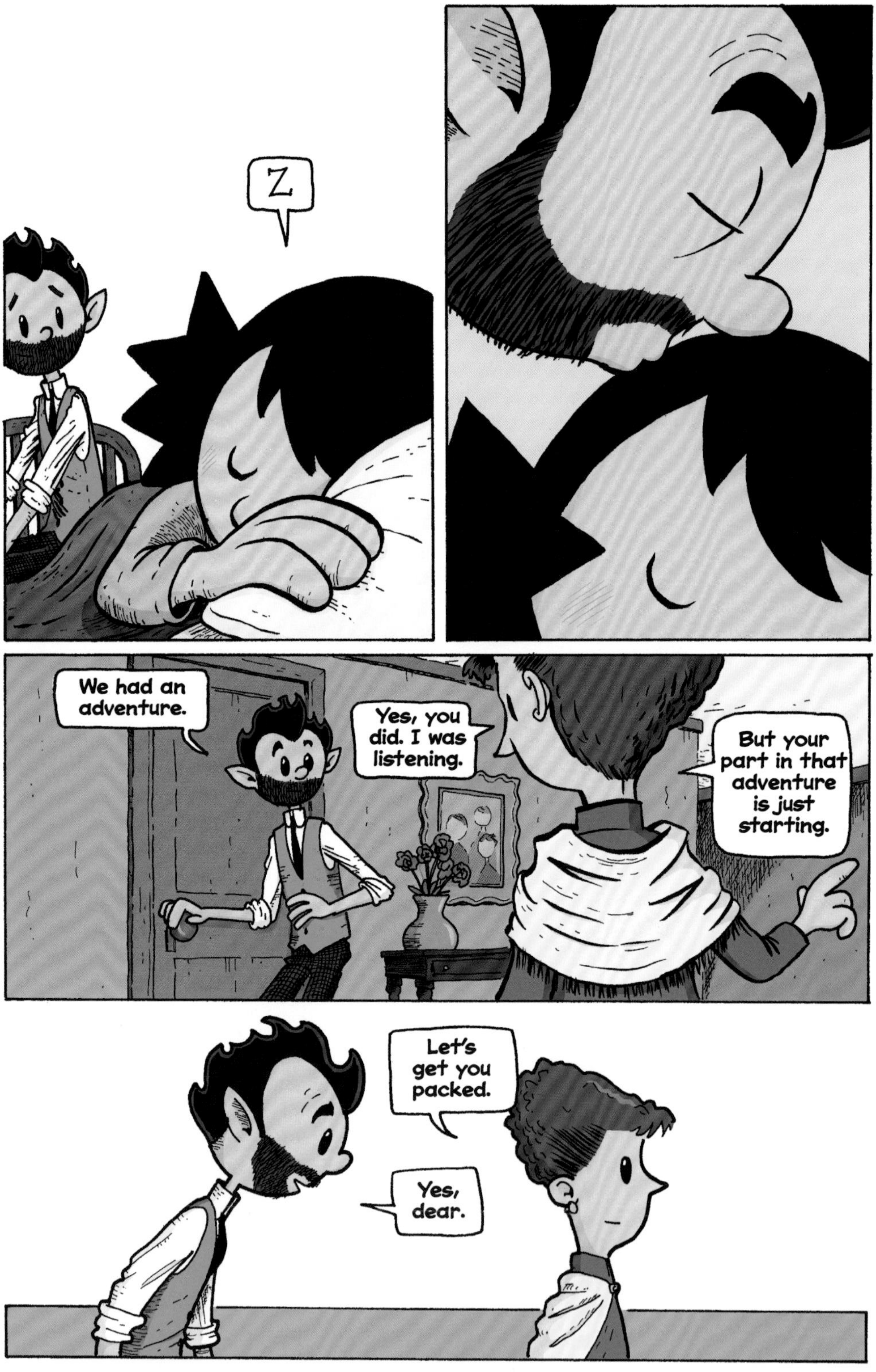
Z
We had an adventure.
Yes, you did. I was listening.
But your part in that adventure is just starting.
Let's get you packed.
Yes, dear.

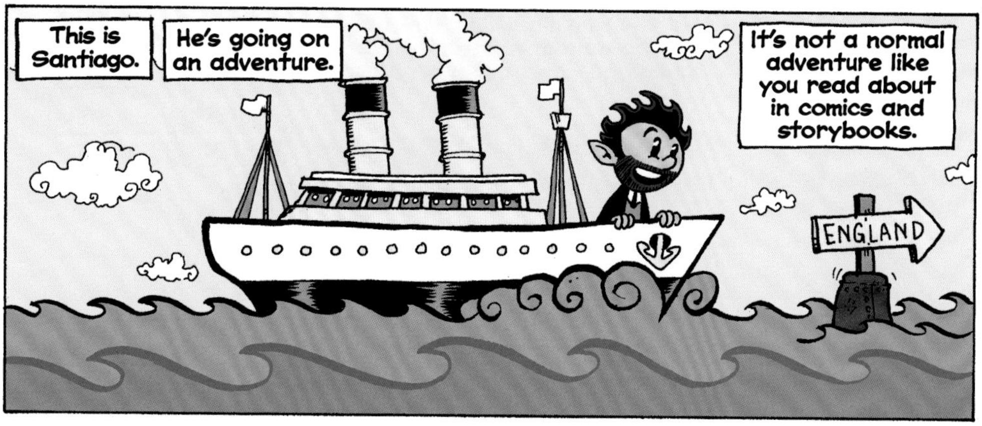
This is Santiago.
He's going on an adventure.
It's not a normal adventure like you read about in comics and storybooks.
ENGLAND

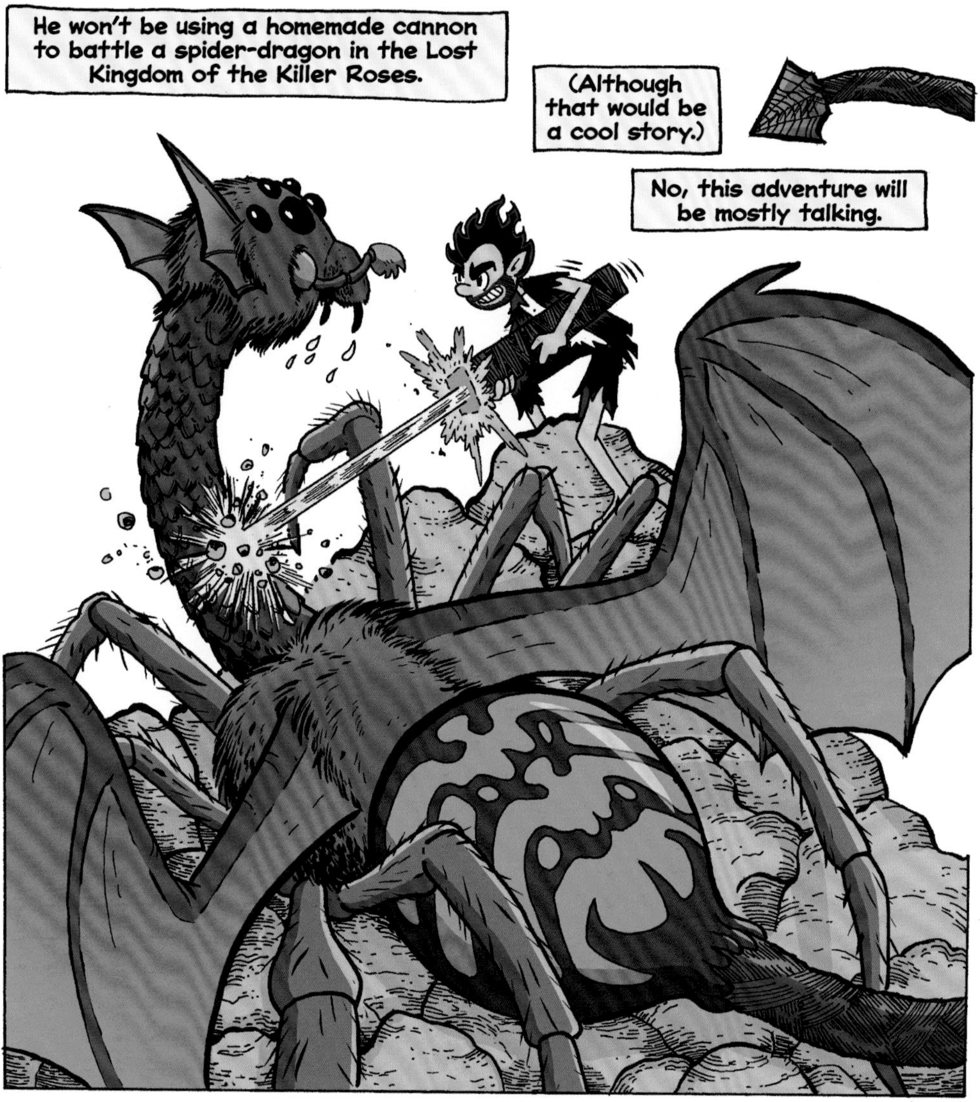
He won't be using a homemade cannon to battle a spider-dragon in the Lost Kingdom of the Killer Roses.
(Although that would be a cool story.)
No, this adventure will be mostly talking.

Santiago told the English scientists a story about a clever young artist who wandered into the dense thicket of the brain and came out a great scientist.

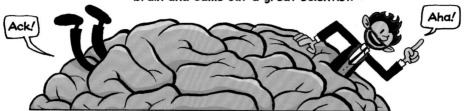

Ack!

Aha!

Santiago's beautiful drawings transformed the impenetrable forest of the brain and nervous system into a well-laid-out park.

It was a wondrous place.

After about a month, his adventure was over and Santiago returned to his beloved home ...

but his mind stayed and played in that beautiful park for the rest of his life.

WA-HOO!

EPILOGUE

**When Santiago returned from his big adventure in England,
Pilar was all better.**

**In 1906, he won the Nobel Prize
for his microscopic masterpieces.**

**His artistry would forever change the way we think
about the way we think.**

Santiago was fascinated by photography. This is a self-portrait of him in his lab, circa 1885.

c
d
a
b

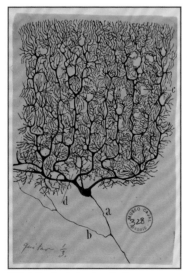

This is Santiago's drawing of a human Purkinje neuron. Purkinje cells are found in the cerebellum of the brain and help coordinate our physical movements.

a
b
c
d
z
e
f
f
f
f
g
h
i
j
r
r

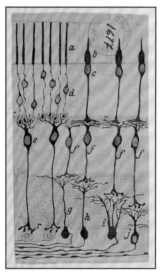

Santiago beautifully drew the cells in the retina of the eye. The rods (a) and cones (b) absorb light, and that light signal is processed by the cells in the layers below (c–j).

SANTIAGO RAMÓN Y CAJAL

(May 1, 1852–October 17, 1934)

"A good drawing, like a good microscope preparation, is a fragment of reality, scientific documents that indefinitely maintain their value and whose study will always be useful, whatever interpretation they might inspire."

—Santiago Ramón y Cajal, 1899, *Textbook of the Nervous System of Man and the Vertebrates* (Cajal 1899–1904, vol. 1, p. X) as cited in DeFelipe's *Cajal's Butterflies of the Soul*, 2010

SOURCE NOTES

CHAPTER 1: THE FIRST MISCHIEF

Pages 3–8: The horse-kick story is from Chapter I of a memoir that Santiago wrote:

"A certain piece of mischief perpetrated when I was about three or four years old might have put a tragic end to my life. It was in the town of Luna. I was playing on a threshing floor on the town common when I had the devilish idea of beating a horse. The animal, somewhat wild and vicious, gave me a terrible kick on the forehead, so that I fell senseless, bleeding profusely and in such a plight that they thought me dead. The wound was very serious; but I recovered, after making my parents pass days of great anxiety. This was my first mischief; we shall see later that it was not my last." (Santiago Ramón y Cajal, *Recollections of My Life*, p. 7)

Page 8: This page is a collage of four different images from Cajal's research into the nervous system. Each of these drawings was featured in a book called *The*

Beautiful Brain: The Drawings of Santiago Ramón y Cajal. I have described them below and provided the page reference in case you want to check my work.

The cells arching over the top of the image are based on "Cells in the retina of the eye," p. 89. The branching, freckled cells along the right-hand side of the image can be found in "Neurons in the superior cervical ganglion," p. 63. The big branching cell taking up the bottom and lower left side of the image is "A Purkinje cell from the human cerebellum," p. 48. The three big cells surrounded by smaller spidery cells on the left of the image are from "Gray matter astrocytes in the spinal column," p. 74.

CHAPTER 2: THE MAGIC WAND

I used Street View on Google Maps to navigate through Ayerbe. Many of the images you see are based on or inspired by screenshots I took as I digitally strolled around a city 3,865 miles from my home.

Page 11: Santiago's parents, Don Justo and Antonia, had four children. Santiago was the oldest and Pedro was the second child. Pedro would grow up to be a faculty member at the Zaragoza School of Medicine.

Page 12, panel 1: I really like the door I drew in this panel. I also like the woman I drew in the panel. Unfortunately, they're out of proportion. The door is either very small or she is the Giantess of Ayerbe. I figured I was going to have to redraw it, but on a lark I did a Google search to see if there were any legends about giants in Ayerbe. Imagine my surprise when I discovered that as a part of the Feast of Saint Leticia, the citizens of Ayerbe parade through town with giant, two-story-tall statues. In 2005 Ayerbe hosted the sixth meeting of the Giants of Aragon, with seventy-two giant statues in attendance! That was such a cool coincidence that I decided to leave her in. You can read a bit more here: https://en.wikipedia.org/wiki/Ayerbe.

Page 14, panel 1: "I suddenly descried a wall which was freshly plastered and perfectly white. In those heroic times of my graphic mania, a clean surface, smooth and unadorned, constituted an irresistible temptation to pictorial efforts, and attracted me as a light attracts a night-flying moth." (*Recollections*, p. 133)

Page 16, panel 2: Santiago doesn't provide many particulars about his family. I had to poke around the internet to find the names of his wife and kids because they aren't in his memoir. Fortunately, he does mention the names of some of his friends from Ayerbe, including Tolosana, Pena, Fenollo, Sanclemente, and Caputillo. I got the impression that these guys and a few others were the members of Santiago's "gang." They ran about town, acting out wars, breaking street lamps, throwing rocks at each other, and stealing fruit from orchards. It's no wonder they found their way onto the city of Ayerbe's "Index of Bad Companions."

Page 17: The slingshot appears to have been Santiago's weapon of choice. He not only used it with remarkable accuracy, but making them became a specialty of his.

"I was entrusted with the delicate commission of making the slings, which I constructed of hemp and pieces of goat-skin provided by my playmates. More than once it occurred that, lacking old leather, we had to make use of the material of our boots, the height of which, naturally, diminished progressively. Who could recount the indignation of our parents upon observing the retrograde evolution of our footwear." (*Recollections*, p. 33)

Page 20, panel 3: No mentions of spider-dragons are made anywhere in Santiago's writing. I just thought it would be a fun thing to draw (and it was).

Page 20, panel 5: "For him [Santiago's father] ignorance was the greatest of all misfortunes and teaching the most noble of duties. I remember well the enthusiasm which, in spite of my tender age, he put into teaching me French. The study of this language took place in an abandoned shepherd's cave . . . to which we were in the habit of retreating to concentrate on the work and avoid visits and interruptions." (*Recollections*, p. 15)

Page 21, panel 1: Santiago's father taught him a lot in that cave, but the French Santiago learned would become one of the main languages he used to communicate his results to the world. The French text depicted here is from Homer's *The Odyssey*. Here it is in English:

"Telemachus headed down to his father's storeroom, broad and vaulted, piled high with gold and bronze, chests packed with clothing, vats of redolent oil." (Homer, *The Odyssey*, chapter 2, lines 373–375)

In *The Odyssey*, Telemachus is the son of Ulysses. I used a quote from *The Odyssey* because of the following comment by Santiago:

"Whenever I see a copy of Telemachus, there rises in my memory the image of the cave referred to, the recesses and windings of which I still see after sixty-five years as if they were before me now." (*Recollections*, p. 15)

Since most people don't refer to *The Odyssey* as "a copy of Telemachus," I don't think he is referring to Homer's epic poem here. My best guess is that he is referring to a French book called *The Adventures of Telemachus* that was written by Fenelon, Archbishop of Cambria, in 1699. The book tells a tale of Telemachus and his tutor Mentor (Athena in disguise). Perhaps this is the novel Don Justo used to teach Santiago to read and speak French.

Page 22: Santiago and Pedro had good reason to run away. Don Justo's "discipline" was severe and abusive.

"The announcement of these paternal floggings, which . . . began with a whip and ended with a cudgel and tongs, inspired us with absolute terror." (*Recollections*, pp. 45–46)

Page 23: "My habitual reclusiveness did not spring from aversion to social intercourse . . . it sprang from the need to remove myself during my artistic efforts and my clandestine manufacture of instruments of music and of war from the severe vigilance of older people." (*Recollections*, pp. 35–37)

Page 24, panel 3: "I could not draw at home because my parents considered painting a sinful amusement." (*Recollections*, p. 36)

Page 25, panel 4: "Translating my dreams on to paper, with my pencil as a magic wand, I constructed a world according to my fancy, containing all those things which nourished my dreams." (*Recollections*, p. 38)

CHAPTER 3: IN THE WILDERNESS

In *Recollections*, Santiago relates how he and Pedro ran away. It is only one paragraph, but it provided all the specifics for this chapter in the story, including skipping school, running away, living in the wilds on fruit, and hiding out in an old lime kiln. Santiago ends the tale with the following evocative description of what happened when his father found them:

"He shook us violently, bound us arm to arm, and led us in that shameful attitude back into town, where we had to endure the jeers of the women and children in the streets." (*Recollections*, p. 44)

Page 29: Santiago's father was Justo Ramón (1822–1903). He was a strict and often abusive father. But Santiago admired his father for his extraordinary work ethic, skills as a surgeon, and ability to teach. Despite the battle he waged with his father over art and science, he would credit his father with much of his success.

"He was a man of vigorous mentality, in whom the finest qualities found their highest expression. With his blood he transmitted to me traits of character to which I owe everything that I am: a profound belief in the sovereign will; faith in work; the conviction that a persevering and deliberate effort is capable of moulding and organizing everything, from the muscle to the brain, making up the deficiencies of nature and even overcoming the mischances of character—the most difficult thing in life." (*Recollections*, p. 4)

Page 37, panels 2–4: "My father was a man of great energy, an extraordinarily hard worker, and full of noble ambition." (*Recollections*, p. 3)

The story of Santiago's father is a true rags-to-riches tale. When Justo Ramón Casasús was orphaned at the age of twelve, his older brother got the family farm and Justo was left with his ambition. He worked for years to become a doctor. His success in his endeavors was due in no small part to his resourcefulness. As a young doctor, he would walk through the wooded countryside as he made the rounds in his medical district. Seeing all of the wild game gave him a love for hunting. As Santiago points out in his memoir, the profits from his hunting and medical practice paid off.

"With the returns from these two, the partridges and patients, he was able, after two years in Petilla, to furnish a modest home and marry a girl from his home town with whom he had been in love for many years." (*Recollections*, p. 4)

Page 39, panel 7: "Upon his return from the outlying villages, my father would inquire into the misdeeds and excesses of his sons and, rising in anger, would favor us with a formidable thrashing, besides reproaching my poor mother (a thing that distressed us greatly) for what he called her carelessness and excessive softness towards us." (*Recollections*, p. 43)

Page 41: "In order to persuade me and lead me into what he considered the better way, he told me stories about people he had known, unsuccessful artists, painters of historical pictures with too much history and little money; of writers who thought themselves geniuses and ended as miserable reporters or as hungry clerks of town councils; of musicians who were resolved to emulate Beethoven and Mozart but who ended as defeated and greasy village organists. As a final argument and by way of consolation, he promised me that when I should be a doctor, that is to say at twenty-one years of age, when my economic position would be assured, I should be able to wander as much as I would through the chimerical regions of art; but meanwhile his duty was to provide me with an honest and peaceful manner of life capable of keeping me from want." (*Recollections*, p. 49)

CHAPTER 4: THE PAINTER

Page 45: The parish church of San Pedro, Ayerbe, Spain. Drawn from a photo found on Google Maps. It was here that Santiago acquired material for "[o]ne of the copies of the Apostle St. James drawn on paper and illuminated with certain colors which I was able to 'snitch' from the church." (*Recollections*, p. 40)

Page 46, panel 1: Interior details of the church were found at the following links:
http://dondeverorganos.blogspot.com/2018/07/iglesia-de-san-pedro-ayerbe-es.html
https://commons.wikimedia.org/wiki/File:AYERBE._PARROQUIA.jpg
http://f1845monclusrodrigo.blogspot.com/p/comarca-de-la-hoya-2_23.html

Page 47, panel 9: *Raspador* means "scraper" in Spanish. I took the name for Señor Raspador from Santiago's description of the plasterer as a "wall scraper."

Page 49: Santiago recruited others in his endeavors. He once compiled an impressive collection of bird eggs.

"In order to help my collection (upon which my father looked favourably) I offered the boys and farm labourers a cuaderna for each nest which they showed me." (*Recollections*, p. 17)

According to the translator of Cajal's memoir, a cuaderna was equal to one U.S. penny.

Page 50, panel 2: Peaches may not seem like a jackpot, but fruit figured prominently in the gang's escapades.

"To attack orchards, and at the time of the grape harvest to steal grapes, figs, and peaches; such were the favorite occupations of the youths who I soon had the unenviable honor of counting myself." (*Recollections*, pp. 29–30)

Page 51, panel 4: "Thus, there began between my parents and me a silent war of duty against desire." (*Recollections*, p. 41)

Page 52, panel 2: Santiago notes that "Pedro was a boy as docile and attentive as he was diligent and punctilious. He possessed, no doubt, artistic inclinations and a passion for war-like games; but these tastes were not strong enough to lead him out of the way in which he should go." (*Recollections*, pp. 106–107)

But Pedro would eventually surprise them all.

"[Pedro] . . . embarked upon an adventure of truly epic character. With a display of determination almost unbelievable in a boy of seventeen or eighteen, he discarded his student's gown and fled from home in company of a certain seductive adventurer. After embarking at Burdeos he eventually reached Uruguay where he passed through the most surprising experiences and dangerous episodes. Contrary to my father's predictions, his proper, impeccable, submissive and obedient son surpassed at one bound all the boasted wildness of his first born. I was left as if humbled by my failure to do anything so great." (*Recollections*, p. 204)

Pages 54–55: "I took pleasure in adorning my drawings with colours, which I obtained by scraping the paint from walls or by soaking the bright red and dark blue bindings of the little books of cigarette paper, which at the time were painted with soluable colours. I remember that I attained great skill in extracting the dye from coloured papers, which I employed also in place of brushes damped and rolled up in the shape of a stump; an occupation which was forced upon me by the lack of a box of paints and of money to buy them." (*Recollections*, p. 36)

Page 56: The portrait of St. James drawn here is a bit tamer than the one Santiago describes in his memoir.

"I delighted in representing him as I had seen him in prints, or else galloping intrepidly over a large surface . . . his blood-stained sword in his right hand and his shield in his left. With what pious care I coloured the helmet with a little gamboge and passed a band of blue along the sword, and lingered over the black beards, which I made long and wavy as I supposed that those of the Apostles must be!" (*Recollections*, p. 40)

Page 57, panel 2: Eventually, Santiago's beautiful drawings of the brain would be featured in museums. As of this writing, an art exhibit called *The Beautiful Brain: The Drawings of Santiago Ramón y Cajal* is touring the United States. A companion book of the same name is also available and is listed in the bibliography.

Page 58, panel 2: Santiago's mother was Antonia Cajal Puente (1819–1898), and as far as I can tell from his writing, Santiago revered her. She doesn't appear often in his memoir, but what I have read left me with the impression of a woman who offered a bit of a respite from his father's domineering, severe parenting. Here she is in Santiago's own words:

"My mother, according to those who knew her in her youth, was a beautiful and robust highland woman . . .

"Of the beauty of my mother and her excellent qualities, not a single trace was transmitted to any of the four brothers and sisters who were, both physically and morally, almost exact reproductions of our father." (*Recollections*, p. 4)

She also seems to have played a primary role in resourcefully managing the day-to-day life of the household. This was done because of "an incurable fear of poverty":

"My poor mother, who was already very economical and a good manager by nature, made incredible sacrifices to obviate any superfluous expenditure and to conform with the system of exaggerated foresight. It was necessary to economize at all costs." (*Recollections*, p. 37)

Pages 61–63: Santiago tells the plasterer story in his memoir. He recounts a significant amount of what was said. I have used a portion of the plasterer's comments and updated the language a bit for a modern reader. Below is the original exchange as recalled by Santiago. As you can see, according to him, the original review was far more scathing and mean-spirited. The plasterer speaks first:

"'What a daub! Neither is this an Apostle, nor has the figure proportions, nor are the draperies right—nor will this child ever be an artist.' I remained stricken dumb by the categorical verdict. My father dared to reply, 'But does the boy really show no aptitude for art?' 'None, my friend,' replied the scraper inexorably, and turning to me, he added, 'Come here, Mr. Painter of mannikins, and look at the large hands of your apostle. They are like glove maker's samples! Look at the shortness of the body, where the eight heads' length prescribed by the canons have diminished to a bare seven, and, finally, look at the horse, which appears to have been taken from a merry-go-round.'" (*Recollections*, p. 40–41)

Note: The above comment about draperies does not refer to curtains hanging on a window. I checked with my colleague in the art department, Dr. Jennifer Streb, and she said that this was probably referring to the folds and draping of clothing.

Page 63, panels 2–3: There is no evidence that Don Justo paid the plasterer for his comments. I have added this in part for dramatic effect, but also because the entire scenario seems a bit fishy to me. Don Justo was a very practical man, but he was also well educated. It is hard to imagine that he thought the plasterer would give a legitimate assessment of Santiago's artistic ability. It feels to me like a setup to divert Santiago from an artistic career and set him on the "right" path to becoming a doctor. In the wake of the evaluation, Santiago notes that "the opinion of the dauber of walls was received in my family like the pronouncement of an Academy of Fine Arts." (*Recollections*, p. 41)

Page 64: "Farewell to ambitious dreams of glory, illusions of future generations. I must exchange the magic palette of the painter for the nasty and prosaic bag of surgical instruments. The enchanted brush, the creator of life, must be given up for the cruel scalpel, which wards off death; the maulstick of the painter, like the scepter of a king, for the knotted walking-stick of a village doctor." (*Recollections*, p. 42)

Page 65, panels 2 and 4: On the same site on which I found the original door to the house, I also found a picture of Santiago's childhood staircase. Panels 2 and 4 are taken directly from a black-and-white photo made before the renovation of the house into the Centro de Interpretación Ramón y Cajal.

Page 65, panel 5: I couldn't find a picture of Santiago's Ayerbe bedroom, but I did find a picture of a bedroom in the house where he was born, in Petilla de Aragón. I have used that picture for reference here.
http://www.casaubieto.com/blog/s-ramon-y-cajal-3-altoaragones-criado-en -ayerbe-i/

Page 66, panel 1: This comment is based upon a quote from a short essay written about Santiago by Dr. R. Salillas, one of his classmates and colleagues. Salillas wrote of Santiago that "[h]e had no masters, nor did he want any." The essay is reproduced in a footnote in chapter XVIII of Santiago's memoir. (*Recollections*, pp. 159–161)

Pages 65–68: Again, this conversation is a fiction created for the story. It may seem out of character for his mother, since we have already established that Santiago's mom and dad considered art a waste of time. However, Santiago writes most about his father's opposition to a life as an artist, and there is a precedent for Antonia secretly subverting Justo's wishes. Consider the following anecdote:

"In my home books of recreation were not permitted. It is true that my father possessed a few works of fiction, but he concealed them from our wild curiosity, as if they were deadly poison. In his opinion, young people should not distract their imaginations with frivolous reading during the formative period. In spite of the prohibition, my mother, unknown to the head of the house, allowed us to read some cheap romantic novels which she had kept in the bottom of a trunk since before she was married. . . . It is superfluous to say that my brothers and sisters as well as I read them with immediate enthusiasm, evading the jealous vigilance of the head of the family." (*Recollections*, p. 100)

CHAPTER 5: THE KING OF ROOSTERS

Santiago dedicates three chapters of his memoir to his first year at the Piarist school in Jaca. It sounds like a terrifying experience. Our story only scratches the surface of some of the drama.

Page 71, panel 1: "I thought of the sobs of my mother at parting from her son." (*Recollections*, p. 50)

Page 71, panel 4: "The director . . . introduced us to Father Jacinto . . . who was at that time the terrible horse breaker of the community, and whom, according to report, no rebel had yet been able to resist. In truth I was somewhat alarmed, though only a little, at the sight of the gigantic stature, the broad shoulders, and massive fists of the dominie, who seemed to have been built expressly to overcome untamed colts. I restricted myself to saying under my breath, 'Well, we shall see.'" (*Recollections*, pp. 51–52)

Page 71, panel 6: It seems impossible to believe that these weapons of torture were used on kids, but they are no exaggeration. Santiago lists the punishments on page 56 of his memoir.

Page 72, panels 3–6: Starving, prison, and Santiago's daring escapes are described in chapter XI of his memoir.

Page 73, panel 1: If I am translating correctly, *rey de gallos* means "King of Roosters." There was no picture of the costume but I did my best based on Santiago's description:

"I was decked out with a grotesque robe and crowned with an enormous mitre decorated with many-coloured feathers." (*Recollections*, p. 66)

CHAPTER 6: THE CALAMITY CANNON

Pages 77–78: "When I returned to Ayerbe for the ensuing vacation, my poor mother hardly knew me, so much had I been reduced by the reign of terror and dietetic restriction . . . dried up, wiry, with angular face and sunken eyes, shanks long and knotted, nose and chin sharp and pointed, I seemed to be in the last stage of consumption. Thanks to the solicitous care of my mother, the open-air life, and nutritious food, I soon recovered my strength." (*Recollections*, p. 69)

Page 77, panel 2: Pabla Ramón y Cajal (1857–circa 1944) was the third child born to Antonia Cajal and Justo Ramón. She would have been six or seven when Santiago returned from his first year of school at Jaca.

Page 81: Despite his reputation as a troublemaker, Santiago was also an adept artisan. He made musical instruments for festive occasions in Ayerbe, as well as slingshots, helmets, bows, and arrows that "not only had great range, but flew without swerving or turning from their course." (*Recollections*, p. 33)

Pages 81–97: The cannon story is featured on pages 69–73 of *Recollections*. It includes the details of how the armament was made, as well as a full breakdown of the aftermath, including his imprisonment.

Page 85: Santiago was a clever chemist and describes in his memoir how he made gunpowder:

"The mysterious energy concealed in the gunpowder caused me an indefinable surprise. Every discharge of a skyrocket, every report of a firearm was for me a stupendous miracle. Lacking money to buy gunpowder, I sought to find out how to make it and finally by experiments I succeeded in the attempt. I used to procure the sulphur in the shop, the saltpeter in the cellar of the house, the charcoal in charred soft wood. Having prepared the mixture, I sifted it with the greatest care and dried it in the sun; except once when, becoming impatient of the excessive humidity of the atmosphere, I placed the earthen pot with the ingredients in a water bath and the devil decreed that a spark should catch in the powder, which was not yet quite dry, and produce a great flame. Fortunately all these operations of alchemy were carried out on the roof of the house to avoid indiscretions. If they had been performed inside, heaven knows what might have happened!" (*Recollections*, p. 75)

Page 91, panel 2: Santiago's Ayerbe home is currently a museum called the Centro de Interpretación Ramón y Cajal. The door depicted here is based on the current door to the museum and not the one that was actually on his house when he was a boy. I found a picture of the original door and tried to make the change, but it never looked right. I gave up and went with the more traditional door. A picture of the original door can be found at the link below: http://www.casaubieto.com/blog/s-ramon-y-cajal-13-una-puerta-con-historia/#prettyPhoto.

Page 92: Santiago's bad reputation probably cost him greater punishment than his colleagues in crime.

"Whether deserved or not, my fame as a mischievous rascal grew from day to day, with a good deal of sorrow to my parents, who were seized with righteous indignation whenever they received complaints from injured neighbors." (*Recollections*, p. 34)

Blowing up the neighbor's gate was bad, but the consequences might have been less if Santiago hadn't already had a reputation for making trouble. When the neighbor complained to the mayor, "[t]he petty official, who had already complaints of other damage which I had done, took advantage of the occasion presented to teach me an unforgettable lesson and, coming to my house with the constable, consigned me to the local jail." (*Recollections*, p. 71)

It is no surprise, then, that Don Justo was not pleased with Santiago and looked favorably on his incarceration.

"This took place with the sanction of my father, who considered that my imprisonment would be a good and efficacious treatment for my correction." (*Recollections*, p. 71)

Page 92, panel 3: Santiago may look like he was alone in his cell, but he had company.

"This effervescence of hungry life filled my mind with dread; for there the *Aspergillus niger* spread its dusky carpets and the jumping flea, the night walking bedbug, the vile louse, and even the insignificant cockroach—the plague of kitchens and bakeshops—walked about freely or made themselves at home. All these table companions, which had been waiting for months for the ever postponed feast, seemed to tremble with delight at scenting the new prey." (*Recollections*, p. 72)

Aspergillus niger is a black mold that primarily infects fruits and vegetables. It can also cause a lung disease known as aspergillosis.

Page 93, panel 2: "As I heard the creaking of the bolt which locked me away for I knew not how long and the indistinct sound of the receding footsteps of my jailer, I lost my serenity." Don Justo "even went so far as to order that I should be deprived of food throughout the duration of my confinement." (*Recollections*, p. 71)

Page 94: Here is another incident that suggests Antonia was willing to undermine Justo's severe discipline:

"Three or four days passed this way. The matter of starvation, however, was only a threat, not because my father repented of the hard sentence which he had delivered, but because of the commiseration of a certain kind lady of our acquaintance, Doña Bernardina de Normante, who, with the connivance of my mother, doubtless, broke the severe order, sending me from the day following my imprisonment excellent viands [a *viand* is an item of food] and delicious fruits . . . the chops, pies, biscuits, and cakes were to me like a taste of heaven." (*Recollections*, p. 72)

Pages 95–96: The exchange with the guard is entirely fictional, but springs from a quote in which Santiago says the constable planned to "teach me an unforgettable lesson." (*Recollections*, p. 71)

CHAPTER 7: COLOR QUEST

Building a cannon is a very, very bad idea. If you are ever tempted to do so, please remember this one piece of advice: don't do it.

CHAPTER 8: THE ROSES OF DOOM

Page 108: Santiago doesn't mention the names of his rose heist companions, so I needed to come up with some authentic names for the period. I poked around several different archives and name lists. As I was perusing one, I came across the name "Jorge" and I thought, "Hey, just like my pal Jorge Aquirre, stellar author of the graphic novels *Giants Beware!*, *Dragons Beware!*, and *Monsters Beware!*" This thought was immediately followed by another thought: "Jorge's artistic partner on the Chronicles of Claudette series is the incomparable Rafael Rosado." Turns out both names were on the list I was looking at. So, Santiago's buddies in the story are friends of mine in real life. Well, I hope they're still my friends after Santiago led them into that very dangerous garden.

Page 108: Azcon is one of a handful of names Santiago mentions in the stories of his youth. It is clear that Azcon was a bully and an antagonist of Santiago. As an out-of-towner at the Institute of Huesca, Santiago was the target of several bullies. They picked on him for his clothes (apparently his overcoat was unfashionably long) and called him "goatflesh" (a derogatory term for people from Ayerbe). Santiago rose to the bait, charging in to defend his honor and routinely getting thrashed.

Page 112: The rose bandits met at 9 p.m. This specific time is mentioned in Santiago's memoir, and it leaps out as a very unusual detail to include. I suppose when you suffer such a distinct trauma, the time sticks in your head. According to his memoir, there were three friends that joined him, but I decided to stick with Jorge and Rafael for simplicity's sake. Most of the details of this story are taken directly from his accounting, from the rocks on the roof to the apple tree they used to escape. (*Recollections*, pp. 94–96.)

Pages 124–132: The incident with the brakeman and the laundry ladies is recounted at the end of chapter XII in Santiago's memoir. I've added the dialogue, but most of the events are as he described.

CHAPTER 9: IT'S COBBLIN' TIME!

Page 135: One of the kids who was warned by her father to avoid the Demon of Ayerbe was Silveria Fañanás García, the little girl who would grow up to marry Santiago.

Page 137, panel 1: This panel is a visual homage to a drawing by the great Jack Kirby. I used to have a T-shirt with a Kirby illustration of the Fantastic Four's Thing standing in this pose and shouting his catch phrase, "It's clobberin' time!" It was my favorite shirt ever. Not sure why. Maybe it made me feel tough. In any event, I had been imagining this panel since I started writing the book, and it was super-fun to draw. I even tried to approximate the font used on the T-shirt.

Page 141, panel 6: Don Justo actually liked Santiago's anatomical paintings so much that he wanted to collect them and publish them in a book. Unfortunately, color printing technology at the time wasn't good enough to reproduce Santiago's paintings adequately.

"Gradually my anatomical water-colours grew into a very large portfolio, of which my father was quite proud. His enthusiasm went so far as seriously to plan the publication of an atlas of anatomy. Unfortunately, the backward state of the art of graphic reproduction in Zaragoza prevented the realization of the project." (*Recollections*, p. 170)

CHAPTER 10: THINKING SMALL

This chapter contains three stories from Santiago's life as a student. The first two stories come from chapter XX of his memoir, and the third comes from his book *Advice for a Young Investigator*, which was my first introduction to Santiago Ramón y Cajal. I was assigned to read it by Dr. Sunny Boyd, one of the faculty on my dissertation committee. It had a big effect on me.

Here are excerpts from the stories as Santiago told them. The first involves the Anatomy Prize. As you will see, he's a great storyteller.

"The examination arrived and I went up alone. I was assigned the inguinal ring and wrote about it at great length, ornamenting my description with a variety of diagrams and carrying my care of details so far as to indicate the dimensions in millimeters. While my paper was being read, I awaited proudly and confidently the verdict of the tribunal. From the anteroom I heard the judges disputing hotly. 'What can be happening?' I asked myself in great alarm. Finally, I learned that the jury had awarded me the prize. When they came out, Daina and his colleague embraced me and congratulated me, but Don Nicolas Montello (professor of surgical pathology) accosted me and said with a sour expression, 'Understand that you are not fooling me. That is copied!' In vain I tried respectfully to disabuse him of his error. In the opinion of the worthy Montello, it was impossible that a student should remember in millimeters the diameter of the inguinal canal. Fortunately, my master, Daina, who knew me well, defended me warmly. With his sensitive prudence, moreover, he forestalled the outburst of my anger, a passion to which at that time I was extraordinarily prone." (*Recollections*, pp. 172–173)

My favorite part of the fetal membrane story is that Santiago actually said "I was truly epic" in his memoir. I love it because the declaration sounds so modern and full of the same bravado we might expect from someone saying it today.

"Of Ferrer, our instructor in obstetrics, I have an amusing reminiscence. He reproved me one day—and with justice—for my irregular attendance at his class, rejecting indignantly the excuse which I offered, namely that my work in the dissecting room deprived me of the pleasure of listening to him assiduously. 'Nevertheless,' I added foolishly and vain-gloriously, 'I study the lessons assigned every day and believe that I am reasonably up in the subject.' 'That we shall see right now,' replied the teacher with annoyance, and, thinking to put me into difficulty, he asked me about the origin of the fetal membranes, a subject which he had developed with great enthusiasm. Seizing opportunity by the forelock, I solemnly approached the blackboard and, without becoming in the least excited, proceeded to spend more than half an hour drawing colored diagrams to show the stages of the development of the blastoderm, the umbilical vesicle, the allantois, etc., explaining at the same time what the figures represented. I was truly epic! The worthy Ferrer followed me with rapture. He had thought to humble me and had actually brought me resounding glory. The whole class applauded their fellow student. My assurance and coolness in discoursing upon embryological subjects, which most of the students of obstetrics usually learn pretty badly, gave him such a high opinion of my studiousness that, after accepting my earlier excuses, he declared that I could count on passing the examinations with a record of 'excellent' even if I did not attend the class any more. 'The lecture which you have just given us deserved this standing and makes up for your negligence.' I took advantage of his permission to the limit. Only from time to time did I appear at the class, as if I were conferring a favour. The reader will have guessed that my brilliant triumph was the result of luck." (*Recollections*, pp. 178–179)

Finally, a fellow student working as a physiology assistant was the first to show Santiago the wonders of the microscopic world:

"One of my friends, Mr. Borao (a physiology assistant), was kind enough to demonstrate the circulation in the frog's mesentery to me. During the sublime spectacle, I felt as though I were witnessing a revelation. Enraptured and tremendously moved on seeing the red and white blood cells move about like pebbles caught up in the force of a torrent; on seeing how the elastic properties of red corpuscles allowed them suddenly to regain their shape like a spring after laboriously passing through the finest capillaries . . . I am absolutely convinced that the vivid impression caused by this direct observation of life's internal machinery was one of the deciding factors in my inclination to biological research." (*Advice for a Young Investigator*, pp. 63–64)

CHAPTER 11: A BOY AND HIS MICROSCOPE

Page 170, panels 3-4: A neuroscientist named Dr. Luis Simarro Lacabra introduced Santiago to the Golgi stain. Simarro Lacabra knew how to makes the slides and had modified the original Golgi stain slightly. When he saw the slides, Santiago immediately realized how important this technique was. He set about to modify it even more so that he could explore the nervous system. (Rapport, *Nerve Endings*, pp. 94–95).

Page 171, panel 6: In art and science, so much can hinge on who notices your work and how it is presented to the world. Santiago's work caught the eyes of several prominent biologists at the time, the most influential of whom was Dr. Rudolf Albert von Kölliker. Kölliker was amazed by Santiago's work and wanted the whole world to know about it.

"Among those who showed most interest in my demonstration I should mention His, Schwalbe, Retzius, Waldeyer, and especially Kolliker. As was to be expected, these savants, then world celebrities, began their examination with more scepticism than curiosity. . . . Finally, the prejudice against the humble Spanish anatomist vanished and warm and sincere congratulations burst forth. . . . The most interested of my hearers was A. Kolliker, the venerable patriarch of German histology. At the end of the session he took me in a splendid carriage to the luxurious hotel where he was staying; entertained me at dinner; presented me afterwards to the most important histologists and embryologists of Germany, and, finally, made every effort to render my sojourn in the Prussian capital agreeable. 'The results that you have obtained are so beautiful,' he said to me, 'that I intend to undertake a series of confirmatory studies immediately, adopting your technique. I have discovered you, and I wish to make my discovery known in Germany.'" (*Recollections*, pp. 356–357)

My drawings based on Santiago's drawings:

Page 173, panel 1: "Structure of the retina indicating the flow of information" (*The Beautiful Brain*, p. 95)

Page 173, panel 2: "Stages of neuron development" (*The Beautiful Brain*, p. 159)

Page 173, panel 3: This drawing is based on Santiago's drawings of a Purkinje neuron. These neurons are found in the cerebellum.

CHAPTER 12: THE INVISIBLE MYSTERY FOREST

Although Santiago mentions in his memoir that one of his daughters fell sick before he left for the Croonian Lecture, he doesn't say which one.

"One of my daughters took seriously ill at the same time. My paternal instinct was disturbed and protested against leaving the patient, despite the encouraging prognoses made to tranquilize me by Dr. Hernando, the family physician and a generous friend of my family." (*Recollections*, p. 418)

So which daughter was ill? I had to guess. Santiago received the invitation to speak in England in 1894. At that time, his daughter Fe would have been fourteen, Paula would have been ten, Enriqueta would have been seven, and Pilar was four or five. I chose Pilar because when my kids were four they were full of questions and wonder. They loved hearing stories and I loved telling them.

Page 179, panel 1: Santiago also loved to tell stories. One of the things I admired most about Santiago was that he wasn't just a scientist and an artist. He was also a storyteller and science communicator. He even wrote a handful of fictional short stories to explain various aspects of science. Several of these have been collected in a volume called *Vacation Stories*. Many of the stories feel dated now, but I admire that he was using stories to share the joys of science with the world.

Page 186, panel 1: Drawing of the retina, top of page, *The Beautiful Brain*, p. 85

Page 187, panel 1: The butterflies in this image are no coincidence. I am paraphrasing (visually and in the text) what Santiago put much more elegantly in his memoir:

"My attention was drawn to the flower garden of the grey matter, which contained cells with delicate and elegant forms, the mysterious butterflies of the soul, the beating of whose wings may someday . . . clarify the secret of mental life." (*Recollections*, p. 363)

Page 190, panel 2: The image of the nervous system as a well-laid-out park comes from a toast by Michael Foster, Santiago's host for the Croonian Lecture.

"At the time for champagne, there were enthusiastic toasts to English and Spanish science and declarations of cordial intellectual fraternity between the two nations. I still remember part of the eloquent discourse of Mr. Foster, a witty and original speaker. . . . He said, among other things flattering to Spain and to me, that, thanks to my work, the impenetrable forest of the nervous system had been converted into a well laid out and delightful park." (*Recollections*, p. 421)

BIBLIOGRAPHY

All of these books provided references for this story. In some cases they had interesting details, and in others they provided valuable images. However, the vast majority of this story is drawn from Santiago's own words in his memoir, *Recollections of My Life.*

Cannon, Dorothy F. *Explorer of the Human Brain: The Life of Santiago Ramón y Cajal (1852–1934)*. New York: Henry Schuman, 1949.

DeFelipe, Javier. *Cajal's Butterflies of the Soul: Science and Art*. New York: Oxford University Press, 2010.

Finger, Stanley. *Minds Behind the Brain: A History of the Pioneers and Their Discoveries*. New York: Oxford University Press, 2000.

Homer. *The Odyssey*. Translated by Robert Fagles. New York: Viking Penguin, 1996.

Newman, Eric A., Alfonso Araque, and Janet M. Dubinsky, eds. *The Beautiful Brain: The Drawings of Santiago Ramón y Cajal*. With essays by Larry W. Swanson, Lyndel King, and Eric Himmel. New York: Abrams, 2017.

Ramón y Cajal, Santiago. *Advice for a Young Investigator*. Translated by Neely Swanson and Larry W. Swanson. Cambridge, MA: MIT Press, 1999.

———. *New Ideas on the Structure of the Nervous System in Man and Vertebrates*. Translated by Neely Swanson and Larry W. Swanson. Cambridge, MA: MIT Press. 1990.

———. *Recollections of My Life*. Translated by E. Horne Craigie and Juan Cano. Cambridge, MA: MIT Press, 1996.

———. *Texture of the Nervous System of Man and the Vertebrates*. Edited and translated by Pedro Pasik and Tauba Pasik. 3 vols. Springer-Verlag, Vienna. 1999–2002.

———. *Vacation Stories: Five Science Fiction Tales*. Translated by Laura Otis. Urbana: University of Illinois Press, 2001.

Rapport, Richard. *Nerve Endings: The Discovery of the Synapse*. New York: Norton, 2005.

Williams, Harley. *Don Quixote of the Microscope: An Interpretation of the Spanish Savant Santiago Ramón y Cajal (1852–1934)*. London: Jonathan Cape, 1954.

WEBSITES

http://dondeverorganos.blogspot.com/2018/07/iglesia-de-san-pedro-ayerbe-es.html

https://commons.wikimedia.org/wiki/File:AYERBE._PARROQUIA.jpg

http://f1845monclusrodrigo.blogspot.com/p/comarca-de-la-hoya-2_23.html

ACKNOWLEDGMENTS

I am deeply grateful for the help of the following people. Without their inspiration, feedback, support, talent, hard work, and willingness to point me in the right direction, this book would not have been possible. Lisa Hosler, Max Hosler, Jack Hosler, Judy Hansen, Margaret Ferguson, Hilary Sycamore, Karina Edwards, Sunny Boyd, Harry Itagaki, Laura White, Cathy Stenson, John Kerschbaum, Frances Corona, Norah Kerschbaum, Balint Kacsoh, Eric Newman, Larry Swanson, Ben Ehrlich, Juan De Carlos, Ricardo Martínez Murillo, María José Acuyo Ruiz, and the Cajal Institute.